GROWING OLD IN THE MIDDLE AGES

GROWING OLD IN THE MIDDLE AGES

'Winter clothes us in shadow and pain'

Shulamith Shahar

Translated from the Hebrew by
Yael Lotan

London and New York

First published in Hebrew by Dvir Publishing House,
Tel-Aviv, in 1995.
English edition first published 1997
by Routledge
11 New Fetter Lane, London EC4P 4EE

Simultaneously published in the USA and Canada
by Routledge
29 West 35th Street, New York, NY 10001

Phototypeset in Garamond by Intype London Ltd

Printed and bound in Great Britain by
Mackays of Chatham PLC, Chatham, Kent

British Library Cataloguing in Publication Data
A catalogue record for this book is available from the British Library

Library of Congress Cataloging in Publication Data
Shahar, Shulamith.
[Horef ha-'oṭeh otanu. English]
Growing old in the Middle Ages: "winter clothes us in shadow and
pain"/Shulamith Shahar.
Translated from the Hebrew.
Includes bibliographical references and index.
1. Aged–Europe–History.   2. Aging–Social aspects–Europe–
History.   3. Social history–Medieval, 500–1500.   I. Title.
HQ1064.E8S5313   1996   96–4587
305.26'094–dc20   CIP

ISBN 0–415–14126–5

To my sister and brother-in-law, Naomi and
Meir Zorea, with love

The truth is that the winter season treats us very differently from the trees, for winter lightens the trees, unclothing and stripping them of leaves, but to us old men winter brings burdens and clothes us in shadow and pain.

Leon Battista Alberti, *The Book of the Family*

If heaven had feelings, it too would grow old.
Li He (791–817 AD), 'Song of the Bronze Immortal Taking Leave of
Han'

The real difference between God and human beings, he thought, was
that God cannot stand continuance. No sooner has He created a
season or a year, or a time of the day, than He wishes for something
quite different, and sweeps it all away. No sooner was one a young
man, and happy at that, than the nature of things would rush one
into marriage, martyrdom or old age.

Isak Dinesen, *The Monkey*

Old men were ever fated
The flight of childhood
Hopeless to bewail.

Adalberon of Laon (*c.* 1030), 'Poem to King Robert'

Old age is final;
Youth is God's gift.

Eustache Deschamps (14th century), 'Ballad on Old Age'

You longed to pass through its gate, you desired to reach it, you
feared you might not attain it, but once arrived – you began to moan.
Everyone wants to reach old age, but none wants to be old.
Bernardino of Siena (Early 15th century), 'Sermon on the Trials and
Tribulations of Man's Life, Particularly on Old Age'

'Whoever does not wish to die young, must needs grow old.' This is
one of those worn platitudes which combine absurdity with com-
monsense.

Jean Améry (1968), *On Growing Old*

CONTENTS

INTRODUCTION
On the History of Old Age in Medieval Europe

In the Middle Ages old people were regarded both as part of the symbolic order of the world and society, and as an actual component of society. Various representations and discourses expanded on the binary contrast old/young man, old/young woman. In the division of the cycle of life into stages – divisions which were more symbolic than biological or social – old age represented a distinct and final stage. The law – which, among other things, reflects the society's self-image – made special concessions to the old. In scientific and medical texts, and also in the moral literature, there were descriptions and analyses of the physical and mental characteristics of the aged, as well as guidelines on how to preserve their health and delay bodily decline. And in the moral literature there were guidelines concerning the appropriate way of life for the old. Moral literature, tales and popular sayings defined the proper conduct of offspring towards their old parents.

During the High and Late Middle Ages, though children participated to a greater extent in the society of adults than they did in later periods, there existed institutions designed exclusively for children and youths. For the children there were schools, and though adults too attended the universities, the bulk of the students were boys and youths. In fifteenth-century Florence there was a fraternity for boys of ten to 19 years of age, another one for 19–year-olds and up, as well as adult fraternities. In some English towns, too, there were already in the fourteenth century religious guilds for boys and youths alone, and devotional cults made up of children, both boys and girls.[1] There is no mention of special organizations for the aged as sub-groups (like today's veteran organizations, or the clubs for the pensioners of particular institutions), nor of general organizations for the aged (like today's senior citizens' clubs and pensioners' political parties). But categorization according to age or stage of life was common in the Middle Ages. From the twelfth century on people were categorized as belonging to the Church or the laity; by their occupations or social class; by gender; by marital status, as well as by the age group to which they belonged. Manuals for confessors and the guidelines of the church councils instructed the confessor to verify who the confessing person was: a layman

1

or a member of the Church (and if the latter, a monk or a cleric); a free man or a serf; rich or poor; healthy or sick; married or single; sensible or a fool; and in addition, a child, an adolescent, an adult or an aged person.[2] In the rule that Francis of Assisi wrote for his order in 1211, in which he called for faith, prayer and penitence, he distinguished between churchmen and the laity; men and women; maidens and married women; rich and poor; peasants; rural and urban labourers; kings and princes; masters and servants; the healthy and the sick; as well as between infants, adolescents, youths and the old (*infantes, adolescentes, iuvenes et senes*).[3] As we shall see in the following chapter, secular legislation imposed different duties upon different age groups, or exempted particular age groups from certain duties.

It is known that age serves as a basic organizing principle in only a small number of societies. (In some of these, the dominance of this principle has led to the old and the young living in separate communities).[4] However, grading people by age and distinguishing between the different generations seems to be a universal form of social categorization, though the status of the old-age group is not the same in all societies. Anthropologists have tried to examine the mechanisms governing the interaction between the physical, socio-economic and cultural factors which determine the status of the aged in different societies, as well as the connection between age as an organizing principle and other organizing principles, such as kinship and socio-economic standing.[5]

During the High and Late Middle Ages the age group of the old belonged to the margin, and old women were doubly marginalized: as women and as old people. Whenever an event was described in which everyone took part (or that the author wished to depict as such), the adult males are described as being at the centre of the action, while the margins include the children and/or women and the aged. A thirteenth-century chronicler, describing the movement of the Flagellants in Italy, wrote that noblemen and low-born men, the young and the old, and even five-year-old children, scourged themselves.[6] It is unlikely that five-year-old children actually flogged themselves, and doubtful that old people did so. They are listed among the Flagellants to emphasize the universality of the phenomenon. Clearly, the mention of the nobles and the low-born refers to adult men. The children and the aged are the complementary margins. On occasion the old in the margins are mentioned without reference to the centre of power. The chronicler Matthew Paris, who described the preparations for the 1241 Crusade, wrote that women, old men, the sick and disabled and even children took up the cross. They took it up knowing that they would not set out on the journey, but so that later they might seek a dispensation to send someone else on the journey and thus they too would win the remission of sins which had been promised to the Crusaders.[7] In this case, the common denominator of the children, women,

2

the disabled and the old was their physical frailty, which barred them from fighting. When Thomas Aquinas dealt with the question as to who may be given the sacrament of confirmation, he distinguished between the earthly and the heavenly plane: in the latter everyone may do battle for the Lord, even children, women, slaves and the old.[8] In earthly struggles, however, a suitable age, physical strength and status are required, and therefore children, old people, women and slaves were excluded from taking part in them. The categories which Aquinas assigns to the margins are based on age – children and the old; gender – women; and status – slaves. Sometimes the chief factor of marginality was the social status, and the old were listed within the low social stratum, alongside cripples and strangers. In the lives of the saints (seventh to tenth centuries), writers sometimes distinguished between two standards of conduct among the mourners for the dead saint. Whereas the ecclesiastics mourned in a restrained manner, some of the laity grieved noisily: they wailed aloud, beat their breasts and threw themselves on the saint's corpse. According to the writers, those who followed this popular tradition were not the laymen as such, but shepherds, poor folk, strangers and old people.[9]

A learned jurist in the thirteenth century stated that legal aid should be given to those who do not know how to present their cases as plaintiffs, or how to defend themselves when accused, namely, children, women and the old.[10] In this category the common denominator is not the physical but the mental feebleness of the marginalized ones. Maimonides, commenting on the Talmudic text, placed the aged among those who are incapable of mercy: 'Neither a very old man nor a eunuch may serve in the Sanhedrin, because of their cruelty, nor any man who has no sons to make him merciful.'[11] The eunuch was marginalized in every society, and so was the childless man in Jewish society, with its precept 'be fruitful and multiply'. According to Maimonides, they shared with the aged an absence of mercy. The perception of the old as a marginal group, to be numbered with the other marginalized categories we have mentioned, did not result from their being a small percentage of the population. Medieval society, like all traditional societies, had a high birthrate, and despite the high infant mortality, children constituted a large part of the population, as of course did the women. Indeed, the number of women was not as a rule much less than the number of men, and in certain times and places even exceeded it. But despite their great numbers they, like the children, were not part of the centre of power. As for the peasants, they constituted the great majority of the population of Western Europe. If the aged were counted among the weak members of society along with the children (on grounds of age), women (because of their sex), and peasants and shepherds (because they belonged to the lowest social stratum), it was because they were considered to be physically or mentally feeble, or both, and did not belong to the centre of power.

Needless to say, a person's status in the Middle Ages, as in all human societies, was not determined by age alone. Old people of different social strata differed not only in their standard of living; their position in society was determined by their economic condition, their social affiliations and their personalities. Belonging as they did to various socio-economic strata, there could also be conflicts of interests among them. The same may be said of women (though the law placed some restrictions on all women). However, in the above statements these various distinctions are ignored. The old are depicted as a single group, united by certain common qualities as well as by their marginality and weakness. Likewise in the sermons addressed to the aged, as in most sermons addressed to women and children, they were treated as a single group.

The contrast young man/old man, young woman/old woman is one of the binary contrasts by which human thought seeks to make symbolic order in life and the world. The contrast is frequently referred to in medieval texts, as we shall see in the second chapter. At this point I shall confine myself to one such binary contrast in one particular symbolic ritual. The ordinance of the Guild of St Helena (the mother of Emperor Constantine) in Beverley, England, in the latter half of the fourteenth century, prescribed the order of the procession on the patron saint's day:

> They will choose a good-looking youth, the fairest they can find, and clothe him in the garments of a queen like the sainted Helena, and before him shall walk an old man bearing a cross, and another old man bearing a censer, recalling the finding of the Holy Cross (by Queen Helena).[12]

The old man, the young man's opposite, was sometimes described as being childlike. As we shall see in the following chapters, the image of the old man in Medieval culture was an ambivalent one, just as the image of the child was not free from ambiguity. Old age was represented, on the one hand, as the stage of life in which the person goes into a physical and mental decline, develops negative qualities, suffers and is full of anxiety; and on the other hand, as the stage at which one attains wisdom, serene freedom from lusts, and the ability to counsel others and look after the salvation of one's own soul. Various discourses listed the 'positive' and the 'negative' qualities of the old person. In a medical context, the analogy between the old person and the child was based on the theory of humours, but the analogy was not confined to these texts. According to the theory of humours, the humours of the elderly, and especially the very old, underwent changes of psychosomatic significance, giving rise to childish qualities.[13] The old man does not go back to being innocent, goodnatured, free from spite and rage like a child, but rather develops the child's 'negative' qualities: limited wit, poor discrimination, bodily weakness and loss of control. Some of the comparisons referred only to the similarities while

4

others expressed awareness of the difference: the child's frailty is temporary, for the child grows stronger and symbolizes the future, while the old person grows ever weaker and his weakness symbolizes the biological end. In a popular text from the thirteenth century, which was widespread in several languages, a wise man was asked why children and old people sleep so much. He replied that children sleep a great deal because they are green and sweet. They are like a delicate flower which could be blown off the tree by the slightest breeze. In sleep they rest and grow stronger. But the old, who are also weak, are like a ripe apple which is liable to fall from the tree at the slightest breeze. They do not grow stronger in sleep, but being weak they need the rest and benefit from it.[14] The comparison expresses the awareness of the difference, as well as the centrality of the body in both stages: the body is all engrossing, because it is not yet mastered, or no longer mastered.

In one of Petrarch's writings, in a dialogue between 'Reason' and 'Sorrow', Reason says that childhood is the best period of a man's life because it is furthest from death. Nevertheless, Reason maintains, no old man ever wishes to return to his childhood. The aged man wishes to return to the most dangerous stage in a man's life, the one in which he is most subject to temptations, namely, his youth,[15] which is the time of power and the opposite of old age. Reason was hardly accurate with regard to demographic reality. Child mortality in the Middle Ages was extremely high, and it was that which made for the low life expectancy. Indeed, the child was nearer to death than the young man, since anyone who achieved young adulthood had a better chance of reaching old age than did the child. Thus the statements which Petrarch puts in the mouth of Reason expressed the perceived resemblance between the old man and the child, who were both regarded as the powerless members of society. The analogy between children and old people persisted for a long time in Western culture. Where Medieval physicians and philosophers attributed the resemblance between old age and childhood to the changes in the humours taking place in the old body, the psychoanalysts ascribe it to the weakening of the Ego and the decline of the libido in old people.[16] When Erik Erikson was asked in an interview about the final phase of life (the eighth, according to his scheme), that of old age, he replied: 'It is perfectly obvious that if we live long enough we all face a renewal of infantile tendencies – a certain childish quality if we are lucky, senile childishness if we are not.'[17]

The analogy between the old person and the child, which was expressed in their low valuation, also had a pragmatic cause: the child did not yet fulfil any economic function nor did it contribute to procreation, while the old person was no longer capable of fulfilling these functions. In the Book of Leviticus, in the laws relating to vows (where a man vows to dedicate to God the value of a person), the highest valuation was placed on a man between 20 and 60 years of age – 50 silver shekels. The valuation of a woman of the same age was 30 shekels. At 60, a man's value went down to 15 shekels, five shekels less than that of a male between five and 20 years of age. A woman's value went down to 10 shekels, equal to that of a female between five and 20 (Lev. 27: 1–7). In the laws of the Barbarians (fifth to seventh centuries), the weregeld, i.e. the compensation paid to the family or the master of a person who was killed, depended upon the dead person's legal status (a freeman or a serf; a king's companion, or a freeman not of that standing), and the person's gender and age. According to the laws of the Visigoths, the weregeld of a freeman aged 20 to 50 was 500 solidi; aged between 50 and 60 it was 200 solidi; at 65 a man's value went down to 100 solidi, like that of a boy of ten. The highest weregeld of a woman was when she was between 15 and 40 years of age, when it stood at 250 solidi; between 40 and 60 it was 200 solidi, and after 60 it went down to 100 solidi.[18] The decline in the value of an ageing freeman was due not only to his poorer working capacity, that is to say, the altered ratio of his production as against his consumption, but due to his waning powers as a warrior (which also lowered his social standing). A woman's social standing was lowered by the waning (and in the final phase, the end) of her fertility, as well as of her working capacity. The family which lost a young man or woman stood to lose more than did the family of an old person, and had to be compensated accordingly.

The payment of weregeld disappeared gradually during the High Middle Ages, but in the slave markets of the Mediterranean during the Late Middle Ages the price of children and old persons was half that of young men and women.[19] The reason that children and old people were sold more cheaply was of course their limited working capacities. The child might compensate for its low productivity in later years, but this was uncertain. As for aged female slaves, their working capacity was less than that of the younger ones, nor would they serve as sexual objects for the master and his friends. In modern Western society as well there are various implicit tariffs for life. It is explicit in the earning-streams approach, which values a year of life proportionately to the earnings that flow from saving it. Younger years are thus worth more than older years.[20] And as Marian Rabinowitz, an authority on geriatrics, put it in an interview, in hospitals a young patient may be described as a 'longterm patient', while an old one is said to be 'taking up a bed'.

Contemporary Western society has often been described as gerontophobic, characterized by a profound anxiety regarding ageing and old age. This characterization is based both on the modern worship of youth and the significant increase in life expectancy. People believe they will reach old age, and they are afraid of it. In his book *Fear in the West, 14th–18th Centuries*, the historian Jean Delumeau discussed the collective fears felt by people during that period: real existential fears and imaginary fears; fears prevalent throughout society and fears which affected the lower classes or the ruling ones; perennial and cyclic fears; fears arising from the reality of the given state of scientific and technological knowledge, and fears which arose from religion, from the popular and the scholarly culture. The author dealt with fear of plagues, of famine and uprisings; fear of the Turk advancing in Eastern Europe and of the Indians in South America; fear of Jews, heretics and witches; eschatological fears of the end of the world and fear of ghosts which return to haunt the living. And over and above all these was the trans-historical, trans-cultural fear of death – the universal, spontaneous, gut-fear of annihilation, and the theological terror of the fate of the soul after death. The distinctive nature of the last-named fear was intensified by the Christian belief of that period and disseminated by the churchmen through all walks of society by a variety of methods.[21] The book, which unquestionably made a major contribution to the understanding of the state of mind of Western society in the past, made no mention of the fear of old age. But this, too, people feared in the past, both because of its proximity to death, and because of the troubles to which the old person was prone.

One of the problems of the historical study of marginal groups is that their own voices are rarely heard in the sources. Most of the writings of heretics were destroyed, and only a small part of their Medieval writings are extant. Peasants did not write; children did not write – only adults recorded selective memories and experiences from their own childhood; women wrote far less than men, and apparently only a part of what they wrote has survived, since it was not included in the period's canonical literature which was copied and preserved. Old men did write, as we shall see in the following chapters. However, except for some of the poets, in so far as they wrote about old age they rarely described their own personal experiences. As for what was written about old age and old people in general, only rarely is the writer's age known. Clearly, not all who wrote about old age were themselves old. Their writings could have been based on their personal acquaintance with, and observation of, old people. What they did was express the concepts, the attitudes, the images and anxieties surrounding old age that were prevalent in their culture. The authors of religious works dealt extensively with the manner in which an old person ought to prepare for death and repent, for the sake of his soul's salvation in the next world. At the same time, both the religious and the secular literature abounded in descriptions of the ills of old age: the body's increasing infirmity and ugliness, the ailments, the failing of the mental faculties, reasoning and memory, with the consequent physical and mental anguish suffered by the old person. In the writings which emphasized the insignificance and wretchedness of the human being from the moment of conception to old age, with the intention of arousing contempt for the world and resistance to worldly vanity, the authors paid special attention to the two extremes of life – infancy and old age. The descriptions of the deterioration of both body and spirit were quite merciless.[22] Old age was often numbered among the great evils to which mankind is subject in this life, such as pestilence, earthquakes, nightmares, depression and human viciousness.[23] Poets expressed their fear of ageing, and those who attained old age bewailed their condition.

The dream of prolonged youth recurred in legends and travel tales which combined reality with fantasy. The Medieval Arthurian and Alexandrian cycles depicted the blessed islands of Avalon, whose air preserved the dwellers from growing old. When they wished to end their lives they quit the place, grew old instantly and died. In John Mandeville's fourteenth-century travel book he described a fountain of youth found somewhere in the Indian jungle. Whoever drank its water never fell ill or grew old.[24] Flemish paintings of the fifteenth century showed men and women with slim, young-looking bodies swimming nude in a spring of youth, acquiring strength and youthfulness.[25] The alchemists searched for the means not only of prolonging life but also for the maximum postponement of old age and the extension of bodily and spiritual youth. In myths and legends, eternal old age and the extension of bodily and spiritual youth. In myths and legends, eternal old age was described as worse than death. In classical mythology the dawn goddess Aurora asked for immortality for her husband Tithonus, but she forgot to ask for eternal youth for him. He became a wretched, shrunken old man but could not die, until the gods took pity on him and turned him into a cricket. The moral of the mythological story is plain. It expressed the fear of old age and a warning against the unnatural desire for immortality. The penalty for such a wish is eternal old age, which is worse than death.

Similar stories with a Christian significance were also widespread in the Middle Ages. In the romance 'The Quest for the Holy Grail' (the Grail being the lost, sacred vessel from which Jesus drank at the Last Supper and which, according to Medieval legends and romances, would bring spiritual grace to whoever found it), King Mordren was condemned to live for 400 years as punishment for coming too close to the sacred vessel, despite warnings. He lived on, blind and covered with sores, his agonized longevity being both his punishment and penitence. Death was his salvation.[26] In 'The Pardoner's Tale' in Chaucer's *Canterbury Tales* there is an enigmatic figure of an old man whom the three young ruffians believe to be Death's agent. He longs to die, but is condemned to live and suffer as an old man.[27] In the Icelandic sagas, composed on the fringe of Medieval Western Europe, there is a description of old people who continued to set sail despite their great age, wishing to die at sea and believing that this would be their final journey. In this way they chose the manner of their death and also hastened its coming.[28]

It is known that groups which are socially marginal often occupy a central place in the symbolic order of their culture. But old people appear not only in symbolic contexts in the Medieval sources, and the fear of the body and soul's decline was not the only cause of the anxiety surrounding old age. The idea has been put forward in social gerontological research that, during the Middle Ages and later centuries until the nineteenth, people did not envision their own old age. In view of the high deathrate, especially of babies and children when parents saw half or even more of their offspring dying before them, they did not concern themselves with old age, nor did they take pains to secure themselves from want in later years since they did not expect to reach that stage. This idea is entirely erroneous. People were aware of the fact that old age was often accompanied by want. Didactic literature encouraged people to save for their old age, and whoever could afford to do so no doubt set aside as much as they could. People who did not save simply had not the means to do so. One of the negative qualities which were attributed to old people was stinginess, but even while denouncing it, writers would sometimes explain that it arose from the old person's anxiety at a time when he can no longer work and sees his property dwindling, and is afraid that he will be destitute in his final years.[29] In various discourses old age is frequently associated with poverty: 'old and poor'. In the second half of the thirteenth century, Roger Bacon proposed that the ruler create a special fund with some of the fines paid to the treasury, as well as the confiscated properties of rebels, to sustain those who for reasons of illness or old age could not support themselves.[30] The authors of Renaissance utopias (each of which implied some criticism of the existing social system), depicted the imaginary ideal state as a welfare state, wherein society was responsible for the proper care of its sick and old members. In the communistic utopias, such as the one described by Doni (who also proposed the abolition of the family), responsibility for the care of the aged fell entirely on the state; in other utopias, the offspring were responsible, but with the full assistance of the state.[31] One poet has an old man pleading with death to come and take him. His house is cold and draughty, his only food a little poor-quality bread. He begs death to close his tear-filled eyes, but death does not come and poverty does not loosen its grip.[32]

According to Simone de Beauvoir, in her book on old age, *La vieillesse*, the class struggle, rather than the conflict of the generations, has brought about today's ambivalent attitude towards old people. The young resent only those old people who wield economic and political power. The depreciation of old people in general is caused by the unwillingness of capitalist society to provide the necessary means to maintain them in dignity. And since the percentage of old people has grown considerably in the twentieth century, so that their presence cannot be ignored, they have become devalued.[33] But the explanation of the stinginess of old people, Roger Bacon's proposal, and the utopists' descriptions of ideal societies, all show that even while old people constituted a relatively small percentage of the population, and the prevalent social norm was that their offspring ought to care for them, there was a general awareness of the economic hardship endured by many old men and women. As we shall see in the following chapters, this awareness was expressed in various discourses and in the tiny assistance which people received from their employers and various institutions to help them in their old age. Even in the past it was impossible to ignore the problem because some old people had no off-spring, having been childless or because their children predeceased them; because the offspring of some old people had migrated elsewhere, and others were too poor to support their aged parents, or even refused to fulfil this duty although it was widely promoted in the normative literature.

Nor is the ambivalent attitude towards the old a product of the twentieth century, when their ratio in the population rose significantly (as indeed emerges from Simone de Beauvoir's own description of the attitude to the old in Western society in the past). What did not exist in the past was the institutional support for the old, or, in other words, there was no general policy of retirement pensions. The fact that there were no old-age pensions was due to the limited resources of pre-industrial society, as well as to its system of values. Allocating resources to the support of old people did not figure highly in the social order of priorities, neither in the Middle Ages nor in the following centuries, although the authors of the consti-tution of the French Revolution of 1793 listed respect for the aged as one of the cardinal civil virtues. They were also aware of the economic hard-ships of many old people. This is borne out by the clause dealing with the qualifications of foreigners who sought French citizenship, one of which is the claim that the applicant is 'supporting an old person'.[34] But this awareness did not produce a general programme of funding retirement pensions. As we know, the first such programmes came into existence towards the end of the nineteenth century, and became established only in the welfare state systems of the twentieth.

De Beauvoir's book is highly critical of the contemporary Western atti-tude towards the old, but she does not idealize the attitude held towards them in the past. Other writers, however, frequently produced such ideali-zed pictures. These rested on a number of assumptions: that in the past there were relatively fewer old people in the population and therefore, being rarer and distinctive, they were respected as the keepers of tradition and knowledge; that there was no obligatory retirement (which diminishes the person's own self-esteem); that old people were part of the extended, multi-generational family, in which their position as heads of the household was preserved and from which they received the necessary help.[35] These assumptions began to be revised following the research of historical demographers and social historians, who investigated the subject of old age in the past, mainly from early modern times. These researches have shown that it is not possible to deal in a general way with the status of the old and the attitudes towards them in pre-industrial society throughout

Western Europe (and the US) over hundreds of years. Some of the images and attitudes have changed in the course of time. Others, which were by no means unambiguous, persisted for a very long time, despite seculariz- ation. The real situation of old people was determined by the structure of the family, the patterns of property ownership, and the laws of inheritance, which varied from place to place; it was also evidently affected by the demographic and economic transitions which occurred in the course of the years.[36]

This book deals with the definition of the onset of old age, the image of old people and their place in the symbolic order, the attitudes towards the old, the norms concerning their behaviour, and that of their offspring towards them, their rights, and their real situation in Latin Europe during the High and Late Middle Ages (that is, from the beginning of the twelfth century to approximately the end of the first quarter of the fifteenth; a digression to the Renaissance, required by the subject matter, appears in the first chapter).

We might describe the first part of the book as a cultural history of old age in the said period. But whereas the cultural history was much the same in different parts of Europe, and changed very little during that period, the actual situation of old men and women varied not only according to their social status and gender but also according to the region and particular time in the long period of the High and Late Middle Ages. This book does not seek to exhaust the subject. The historical investigation of old age in Medieval Western society has only recently begun, and further research, which will no doubt be done and will concentrate on specific regions during this period, will provide a fuller picture. I have confined myself to presenting the most characteristic solutions to the phase of old age in a few regions (if only to keep the book to a reasonable size) since it is not possible to discuss the situation of old men and women outside the context of the demographic conditions and the socio-economic system.

Knowing a society's attitude towards its old people, like knowing its attitude towards children, broadens and deepens our understanding of its nature. Knowing the views and attitudes of Medieval society will help to shed light on its historical uniqueness, as well as on the issue of con- tinuity and change in Western society from an additional viewpoint. Per- haps this awareness will help us indirectly to distinguish between the universal, changeless aspects of old age and the relations between the gener- ations, which are part of the human condition, and those which are culture- bound and therefore liable to change.

1

WHO WERE THE OLD IN THE MIDDLE AGES?

Gerontologists and specialists in geriatrics have expressed reservations about fixing the onset of old age on a purely chronological basis. Their reasons are manifold. The process of ageing is a gradual one. There is no one biological event after which the person becomes old. Nor is it an even process: the organs and systems in our bodies do not all age at the same rate. Individuals also differ from one another both physically and mentally. In view of all this, Robert Butler (who coined the term 'ageism' to describe age-based discrimination) concluded that the idea of chronological ageing is a myth, because the advancing years intensify the individual differences more than making a broad similarity.[1] The geriatric consultant Marian Rabinowitz maintains that every elderly person has six ages: chronological, biological, cognitive, emotional, social and functional.[2] It has also been argued that in different economic, social, ethnic and cultural contexts, a man or a woman being 60 or 70 signifies different things, even in the same historical period. Hence the chronological age is only a marker showing where the individual stands in relation to time; or else, it serves as a convenient device for placing individuals in their social space. But the significance of age is a contingent, rather than an independent variable. One specialist in memory noted the relative and subjective nature of determining the onset of old age. In a discussion about the increasing likelihood of degenerative diseases of the memory among the old, he was asked, 'What age are we talking about?' He answered, smiling, 'An old person is one who is 15 years older than you.'[3]

Medieval scholars were likewise aware of the gradual nature of the ageing process, as well as of individual variations in its progress. Some also noted the subjectivity of determining the onset of old age. Vincent of Beauvais (c. 1190–1264) wrote: 'Amid the strains and labours of youth one does not notice old age creeping up one one ... It does not take over all of a sudden, but destroys by slow degrees.'[4] Arnold of Villanova (c. 1235–1311) pointed out the differences between human types. According to him, those of choleric temperament (namely, those whose dominant humour was the yellow bile), who had a sharp intellect, were prone to diseases in their

12

youth. But provided they survived that stage, they would enjoy good health in subsequent years, would age late and even live long.[5] Maimonides proposed a purely subjective yardstick for old age in a woman: 'Who is an old woman? One who is called old and does not protest.'[6]

Developmental psychologists who follow C. G. Jung's division of developmental stages throughout human life, and not only in childhood and adolescence, disagree on the question of whether continuity or change predominates through the stages of the personality's development; hence also on the question whether old age is a separate state of life entailing a significant personality change, or a continuation of a continuous self. For their part, old people reject the notion that old age is a separate stage in their lives and tend to emphasize the enduring, ageless self. This tendency was expressed in a series of interviews with 70 to 80–year-old men and women. In telling their life stories, they emphasized their continuous identity and interpolated symbolically significant elements from their past into their present self-images.[7] St Augustine of Hippo, who greatly influenced Medieval thinkers, was also conscious of the continuity of the ageless self as it was expressed by the old people interviewed. He voiced this awareness in his sermon *Ad competentes* in connection with his division of the lifecycle into six stages, in which old age began at 60.

> By means of these divisions or stages of age, you will not change from one stage to another, but staying the same, you will always know newness. For the second age will not follow so that an end may be put to the first; nor will the use of the third mean the ruin of the second; nor will the fourth be born so that the third may die; nor will the fifth envy the staying power of the fourth; nor will the sixth suppress the fifth. Although these ages do not come into being at one and the same time, they continue in harmony with one another in the soul, whose relationship with God is right, and they will conduct you to the everlasting peace and tranquility of the seventh stage.[8]

Like Augustine, developmental psychologists have also fixed on the age of 60 as the beginning of the final stage of life, that of old age.[9] Most geriatric specialists and gerontologists too, for all their reservations regarding an arbitrary chronological determinant, estimate that at 60 to 70 a person's abilities begin to decline to some extent, and the first signs of failure appear; that is, they too have recourse to chronological age as an indicator of competence.[10] In contemporary Western society, obligatory retirement at 65 marks the onset of legal old age. Modern retirement may be described as a rite of passage, complete with its three classical stages. It is a transition from the status of a working person to a liminal one, in which one is still working, but the conditions of retirement are already being discussed (the level of the pension and emoluments from the retirement funds). There is usually a little celebration, at which long or short speeches (depending on the person's position) are made, and gifts are given. The person now passes to the status of a pensioner. In the Middle Ages there was no such rite of passage, because there was no general policy of retirement or pensions. But in the Middle Ages, too, people were regarded as old from a certain age on, and thereafter enjoyed certain exemptions by law.

There is a widespread idea, to which a number of historians also subscribe,[11] that during the Middle Ages and the Renaissance men and women were deemed old at an earlier age than today. The popular notion is that people were regarded as old from their early forties. The idea is based mainly on the life expectancy in that period, which was considerably shorter than it is today. The historians who derived their opinion from Medieval and Renaissance sources were relying mainly on two kinds of sources: texts dealing with 'the ages of Man', or 'the stages of Life's course' (*aetates hominis; cursus aetatis*) and on the statements of people about their own ageing, as found in letters and in literary and philosophical writings. In this chapter we shall attempt to show that it is unsafe to draw conclusions from such sources regarding the earlier ageing (relative to our time) of Medieval and Renaissance people and also to propose a different kind of source, namely, legislative texts, from which to determine at what age people were defined as old in those days. Subsequent chapters will examine to what extent the cultural norm regarding the onset of old age, as depicted in the legislative texts, found expression in the social reality.

The division of life into stages, like the categorization of people by age group, was not unique to the Middle Ages and the Renaissance, but is apparently a feature of all cultures, including oral ones.[12] Divisions into all kinds of stages appear in a variety of Medieval texts: scientific, medical, didactic, homiletic and literary, and were even depicted in the arts. The various systems of division have been studied by several scholars from a variety of aspects, mainly in the past decade.[13] In this context we shall confine ourselves to a limited number of examples of the most popular schemes, without going into the physical and psychological traits which their authors attributed to each stage, or the expectations associated with them. Most of these schemes did not originate in the Middle Ages but were adapted, with some modifications, from Greek and Roman traditions, sometimes based on the Moslem versions of the ancient divisions. During the thirteenth century, writings began to appear in the vernacular languages and dealt with these divisions, thereby reaching a broader audience, so that even people who did not know Latin became familiar with the various schemes. Many who could not read heard about them (especially about the various expectations that concerned them at each stage) in sermons, and saw them depicted artistically in wall paintings and sculptures.[14] The commonest divisions were into three, four, six and seven stages, more rarely into five and twelve. Since our subject is the onset of old age, we shall refer only to those divisions which specify the person's age at the beginning and end of every stage. There were many divisions whose authors discussed each stage and its characteristics, but did not specify the age in question. The divisions into three, four and seven stages were considered to be scientific, since they all sought to offer a physical explanation and foundation for the processes of the individual's growth, development and ageing. The division into three stages was based on Aristotelian biology; the division into four on physiology, i.e. the theory of humours; and the division into seven stages, following Ptolemy, was based on astrology, namely, on the premise that man is subject throughout his life to the influence of the celestial bodies, presenting at every stage the characteristic traits of his dominant planet. However, as Burrow has already shown, not all the schemes based on three, four and seven stages rested on the above scientific theories. Some authors used a four-stage division which was not based on the theory of humours, but corresponded to the four seasons of the year; others used a seven-stage division corresponding to the seven cardinal virtues, or the seven canonical hours, and so forth. The most Christian was the division into six stages, based on the scheme of St Augustine of Hippo. It rested on a correspondence between six stages in the life of man and the six epochs of human history in its Christian version.[15]

An example of a three-stage division may be found in the work of a thirteenth-century physician, Bernard de Gordon, 'On the Conservation of Human Life' (De conservatione vitae humanae):

1 Aetas pueritiae – from birth to age 14
2 Aetas iuventutis – 14 to 35
3 Aetas senectutis – 35 to the end of life.

The first stage was further divided into several sub-stages.[16] In another work the author stated that the final stage, that of old age (senectus) ended at 60.[17]

Here are some examples of four-stage divisions. In Dante's Convivio:

1 Adolescenza – from birth to age 25
2 Gioventute – 25 to 45
3 Senetute – 45 to 70 (old age)
4 Senio (extreme old age) – 70 to death.[18]

In Philip of Novare's thirteenth-century didactic work Les quatre ages de l'homme:

1 Anfance – from birth to age 20
2 Jovant – 20 to 40
3 Moien age – 40 to 60
4 Viellece – 60 to 80

Philip stated that few lived to be 80, and whoever passed this point had better pray for death. He, too, like Bernard de Gordon, divided the first stage into sub-stages.[19]

In the thirteenth century Aldebrandin of Siena, in his book *Le régime du corps*, divided thus:

1 *Adolescentia* – from birth to 25 or 30
2 *Juventus* – 25 or 30 to 40 or 45
3 *Senectus* – 40 to 60
4 *Senium* (extreme old age) – from 60 to death.

Aldebrandin of Siena also subdivided the first stage.[20]

The treatise of Thomas of Cantimpré, 'On the Nature of Things' (*De natura rerum*), written in the middle of the thirteenth century, offers an example of a seven-stage division:

1 *Infantia* – from birth until the child begins to speak
2 *Pueritia* – from the beginning of speech to age 14
3 *Adolescentia* – 14 to 35
4 *Robor* – 35 to 50
5 *Senectus* (old age) – 50 to 70
6 *Etas decrepita* (decrepitude) – 70 until death
7 *Mors* – death.[21]

Another seven-stage division appears in a poem about love, youth and spring, 'The Fair Bush of Youth' (*Le Joli Buisson de jonece*), by Jean Froissart, written in the third quarter of the fourteenth century. The author notes the celestial body which dominates each stage: from birth to age four – the moon; four to 14 – Mercury; 14 to 24 – Venus; 24 to 34 – the sun; 46 – 58 – Jupiter (sometimes this stage continues for a few more years); from 58 until one passes into the hands of Atropos (namely, until death) – Saturn.[22] According to the poet, one is too old for love at 35, though actual old age begins at 58. Andreas Capellanus, the twelfth-century theoretician of courtly love, was more generous in apportioning years of love. In his view, men may love until they are 60, women until they are 50. His reasoning was physiological-psychological, not moral or social. He held that though sexual intercourse was possible after this stage, its sensual pleasure no longer aroused love, because of the cooling of the natural heat and the increase of evil external humours entering the body. These cause discomforts and ailments, with the result that at this stage a man must content himself with the pleasures of eating and drinking.[23] (Beyond defining the maximum age for love for women, Andreas concerned himself exclusively with the senses and feelings of men.)

Vincent of Beauvais, who wrote an encyclopaedia which contained different and at times even contradictory views on its various subjects, proposed two schemes of division: one, following Isidore of Seville, into six stages, and another, following Avicenna, into four. The six-stage division is:

1 *Infantia* – birth to age seven
2 *Pueritia* – seven to 14
3 *Adolescentia* – 15 to 28
4 *Iuventus* – 28 to 50
5 *Gravitas* – 50 to 72
6 *Senectus* – 72 to the end of life. The final stage had a sub-stage, of extreme old age.

The four-stage division is:
1 *Aetas adolescendi* – birth to 32
2 *Aetas consistendi* – 32 to 35 or 40
3 *Aetas diminuendi* (the stage of decline) – 35 or 40 to 60
4 *Aetas minuendi* (stage of enfeeblement) – 60 to the end of the life.[24]

Herlihy and Klapisch maintain that in the second half of the fourteenth century people's awareness of the sharply reduced life expectancy, due to the Black Death, found expression in their schemes of life's stages. They base their argument on a comparison between the scheme of Philip of Novare, in the thirteenth century, and that of the poet Eustache Deschamps. A ballad of Deschamps, written in 1384, presented four lifestages of 16 years each, with life ending at age 64.[25] (In an earlier ballad Deschamps put it even earlier, at 60.[26] By contrast, Philip of Novare proposed four stages of 20 years each, life ending at 80. But it is very doubtful that Deschamps based his scheme on the demographic reality. Bernard de Gordon, who lived in the thirteenth century, also put the end of life at age 60.[27] Pope Innocent III (1160–1216), writing in the later half of the twelfth century when the population was rapidly expanding and life expectancy was rising, expounding on the wretchedness of the human condition, stated that few reach the age of 40, and very few (*paucissimi*) the age of 60.[28]

In sum, we may say that with regard to the stage of childhood the various schemes were, if not in full agreement, at least in broad accord as to its span (either in the basic division or by means of the sub-stages), but with regard to the onset of old age the authors differed widely. The age at which old age sets in differs not only between the various schemes but often even between schemes based on the same number of stages. Even in the few examples given, old age begins at 35, 40, 45, 50, 58, 60 and 72. The schemes were developed in different contexts and related to different configurations of nature and time. They expressed the symbolic nature of every stage of life, as well as the writers' value judgements. Their divisions were not based on empirical evaluations derived from the biological or social realities. They were more interested in the qualitative change which took place in the transition from stage to stage than in the rate and age at which it happened. The fact that certain numbers had symbolic values also affected their choice of ages for the beginnings and endings of the different stages. It is also obvious that the Latin term *senectus* – old age – (or its equivalent in one of the vernacular languages) did not have the same meaning for all the writers. Some applied it to the period following the stage of youth (roughly equivalent to our 'middle age'), as well as to the elderly and senescent stages. Others applied it only to the 'middle-aged' and elderly stages, and applied the term *senium* for the stage of extreme old age. Still others applied the term *senectus* only to the elderly stage (again, using the term *senium* for extreme old age). There can be no doubt that the wide discrepancies between the ages defined in the various divisions as the onset of old age make it impossible to argue that people were considered old from their forties, or to use these divisions in support of this argument.[29] There can be no justification for relying on a particular scheme in which old age begins at 40, while ignoring all the others in which it starts later (or even earlier, 35!).

One question which the researchers of these schemes have hardly addressed is whether they were meant to represent the lifestages of both men and women, or of men alone. Indeed, it is difficult to answer this question unequivocally. Vincent of Beauvais, discussing the term *senectus*, pointed out that *senex* means an old man, whereas an old woman is designated by the word *anus*. He explained the etymology of the two words, and in passing hinted at the large proportion of widows among the old women.[30] It is difficult to judge from this comment whether or not his statements regarding the various stages, including that of old age, refer to women as well as men. But in his six-stage division he pointed out that the stage of *juventus* ends at 50, when a woman can no longer bear children. According to a certain nineteenth-century medical theory, when the sexual function is ended in old age the differences between men and women begin to blur and they grow more alike in condition and appearance, like children. But it is doubtful if a similar theory underlay Vincent of Beauvais' statement. Needing an obvious biological marker for the end of the youthful stage and the beginning of middle age, and finding none in men but only gradual processes, he used the marker which affected only women to define the end of the stage for all.[31] Indeed, it was widely believed in the Middle Ages that women stopped menstruating at 50, meaning that until that time they were capable of bearing children.[32] That is approximately five years later than the age which today is widely held to be the end of a woman's fertility. It is reasonable to assume that in the Middle Ages too women's fertility ended before the age of 50. In any event, women stopped bearing children at an earlier age, because childbearing was not predicated on the laws of biology alone, but was also affected by medical and socio-cultural factors. Klapisch-Zuber's research has shown that in the prosperous urban middle classes in Tuscany in the Late Middle Ages, in marriages which lasted throughout the couple's fertile years, women did not give birth after the age of 36. There were medical reasons for this: the women, who began to bear children at a very early age (the average age at marriage in this stratum in the Late Middle Ages was 17), gave birth many times (11 on the average), had natural miscarriages, bore dead babies, and suffered from complications and ailments following child-birth. Those who did not die in childbirth or soon after, while still fertile, could not always conceive again. Even when they could, it seems that family strategies prevented it from happening. Once there were enough male sons the couple would avoid producing additional offspring, either by sexual abstinence, or by various methods to prevent conception.[33]

Philip of Novare makes no reference to the woman's biology but, since he addressed his precepts regarding the various ages to both men and women, it may be inferred that he assumed that they passed through the same stages.[34] However, the comments of Vincent of Beauvais and Philip of Novare are not typical. None of the other writers stated explicitly that his scheme applied only to men but, whether or not they believed that women went through the same stages as the men, it is clear that they were concerned with men alone. When they described the waxing and waning of a person's physical and mental capacities, the emphasis was always on the physical powers, the power of doing, the power to command and to think – none of which qualities was attributed to women, who were assumed to be inferior to men at every stage of life. At any rate, Thomas Aquinas implied that at no stage did a woman reach the highest perfection possible, which was followed by the steady decline.[35]

Let us now turn to the second kind of source used by the researchers who argue that Medieval people were deemed old from their forties. These are the statements made by individuals about their own old age, in their letters and in their scholarly or literary writings. The historians Gilbert and Rosenthal quote in their articles a number of individuals from the Late Middle Ages and the Renaissance who, between the ages of 30 and 57, described themselves as old and some even referred to the approach of death. Gilbert quotes Pietro Aretino at 45; Erasmus of Rotterdam at 40; Michelangelo at 42, and François Villon at 30. (Regarding Villon, he notes that such a statement at 30 is exceptional.[36]) The individuals quoted by Rosenthal are older: Chaucer and Caxton at 50; Hoccleve at 53; Lord Scrope at 57.[37] I shall confine myself to only two statements, one by Petrarch (who does not appear in the above lists) and one by Michelangelo.

In the work known as *Secretum*, Petrarch conducted an imaginary dia-logue with St Augustine of Hippo, in the course of which Augustine tries to persuade the poet to renounce the desires of the flesh and realize that love and desire were unseemly at his age. Among other things he says, 'Believe me, yourself are not as much a boy as you perhaps think. The majority of men never reach your present age. You should be ashamed then, to be known as an aged lover, and to be such a long-standing subject of common gossip.'[38] Petrarch is referring to the years 1342–3, when he was about 40. In 1517 Michelangelo, aged 42, wrote a letter to Domenico Boninsegni, the Medicis' business agent, saying: 'Again, as I am an old man, it does not seem to me worthwhile wasting so much time in order to save the Pope two or three hundred ducats.'[39]

The *Secretum* expressed an inner struggle in Petrarch's soul, the tension between the opposite poles of his personality: the love of the world, and an inclination to Christian and Platonic asceticism. Augustine, representing the ideal of divine love as opposed to the loves of this world, calls on him to overcome his love for Laura. The author reinforces Augustine's arguments with the *topos* about the ridiculous old man who behaves inappropriately for his age (or, as the writers of the age put it, like 'a hundred-year old boy').[40] Petrarch could put these words in Augustine's mouth because there existed schemes in which old age began at 40 (the age at which he chose to present himself in the imaginary dialogue). He adopted this scheme also in his work *De remediis utriusque fortune* ('On the Remedies to the Two Kinds of Fortune'), which included encyclopedic knowledge, a catalogue of human conditions, as well as moral casuistry. In the dialogue between 'Reason' and 'Joy,' pessimistic Reason seeks to repress Joy's exhuberance and make him realize his foolishness. At one point Reason reminds Joy that his youth is drawing to a close. 'Old age follows closely upon the fortieth year. In darkness and silence it hits the unwitting man, and when he thinks it is yet far off, there it is upon his threshold.'[41] But in later times in his life, in texts written for diverse purposes and in various moods, he did not represent himself as old, though he had passed the age of 40. In his allegorical-epic work on the death of Laura (*Trionfo della morte Laura*), written when he was about 45, the poet addresses Laura thus: ' "Shall it be soon or late that I follow you?" And she, departing, said: "Tis my belief thou wilt be long without me on the earth." '[42] Here the poet, yearning for his dead love, does not represent himself as an old man whose days are numbered, but as one who can expect many more years of life. In a letter he wrote to Boccaccio when he was nearly 50, he noted that the ancient authorities held various views regarding the onset of old age, and pointed out the individual differences between people: 'Surely some people are older at 50 than others at 60.'[43] In a letter to a friend, written in 1361 when he was 57, Petrarch included some precepts which were meant for himself no less than for his friend. This letter was written at a time when the poet was determined to live and keep creating, so as to be remembered by posterity. He wrote: 'Faithfully, carefully, prudently care for it [life], and offer it all that is in you; drive away recurring diseases, postpone old age, which is subject only to death's power.' According to this letter, old age had not yet reached him.[44]

Unlike Petrarch's statements in the *Secretum* and the 'On the Remedies', Michelangelo's letters were candid expressions of his personal feelings. When he wrote in 1512, at the age of 37, to his family in Florence, 'Let it suffice that I shall be home before All Saints in case, if I do not die in the meantime', he was clearly filled with dread at the prospect of death. But a fit of anxiety about death at the age of 37 or a 40–year-old man feeling, at a time of exhaustion and stress, that he is growing old (a feeling which usually passes, if only partially) – are these unique to people in the Middle Ages and Renaissance? Numerous biographies, autobiographies, diaries, letters, philosophical writings and literary works, expressing the personal experiences of authors of the nineteenth and twentieth centuries, show that this is not the case.

Tolstoy's biography reveals an incident which his biographer Henri Troyat called 'the Night of Arzamas'. It happened in August 1869, when Tolstoy was 41, at the height of his vigour and in the fullness of his personal and creative life. He had been depressed and anxious for some months and, in order to escape the sense of emptiness that enveloped him, he set out on a journey to see an estate with a view to buying it. During the journey through the desolate steppe, his anxiety grew worse and reached its climax in an isolated inn in Arzamas, where he spent the night. He felt death behind his back and heard it whispering. After he returned home he recovered, but from time to time the terror of that night came back to haunt him.[46]

According to Schopenhauer (1788–1860), at age 40 a man begins to grow melancholy. This is because at this age he has not yet given up his desires and ambitions, but has no illusions left. He can already see death at the end of the road, which previously he ignored.[47] In her novel *The Curate in Charge*, Margaret Oliphant (1828–97) described the feelings and conduct of one of the characters who was 40 years old: 'He was just at the age when men are most careful of their lives, when awakening out of the confidence of youth, they begin to realize that they are mortal, and one day or other must die. He took fright. He consulted a kind of physician.'[48] Freud was haunted by his age from his forties. In 1890 he wrote: 'Yes, I am 44 already . . . an old, somewhat shabby Israelite.' Thanking his nieces in Berlin for their birthday wishes, he called himself 'an old uncle'. The following year he asked his family to stop doing anything about the birthdays of old folk, and said he was 'an elderly monument', not 'a birthday child'.[49] Samuel Beckett's novella *Malone Dies*, published in the French original in 1951 when the author was 45, was written in the first person and gives the impression that the narrator and the author are one. It opens with the words, 'I shall soon be quite dead at last, in spite of all. Then it will be the month of April or May. For the year is still young, a thousand little signs tell me so.'[50]

Developmental psychologists tell us that the forties crisis is not confined to philosophers and writers. According to them, *every person experiences* a crisis of greater or lesser intensity at about age 40. The developmental psychologist Daniel Levinson described it thus: 'A new season starts to make itself felt: he begins to realize that the summer of his life is ending and the autumn is fast approaching.' At this state a man is not yet near to death, nor does he feel a significant loss of physical vigour, but he senses a certain diminution of his youth vitality and an insult to his youthful narcissistic pride. He feels threatened by the changes which are taking place in him and becomes aware of his mortality. At times the crisis is accompanied by a sense of waste, a sense that time is running out and a desire to seek a new way to self-realization.[51] I do not claim that all men and women in their forties in contemporary Western civilization undergo a crisis. But there is no doubt that some people do go through such a phase at this time in their lives, experiencing a fear of death and a sense that their young days are over.

During the Middle Ages and the Renaissance life expectancy was much shorter than it is today, and many died young. The subject of death was not taboo. On the contrary, it was much discussed, with regard to the demise of the body, the departure from the pleasures of this world and the fate of the soul after death. The fear of death was expressed in writing, in sermons and, especially in the Late Middle Ages, also in art and in the 'dance of death'. The preachers urged people to be ready to die at any moment and not put off repentance until they were old, for death could come for them at any age. All these probably meant that the anxiety surrounding the awareness of death was sharper and more widespread than it is today, and that young people also were more intensely conscious of their mortality, and of the perishability of life. But despite the short life expectancy, and the frequent death of young people, people did not consider death at 35–40 a timely death. During the thirteenth to fifteenth centuries it was commonplace to describe the death of an aged person as a natural event, in contrast to the death of a young one. The death of a young person is bitter, it is comparable to the falling of an unripe fruit off the tree, whereas an old man dying was like a ripe fruit falling peacefully on the ground. The image of the ripe fruit (which recurred in popular literature, didactic and even scientific writings) was not applied to a man of 35–40, not even by Petrarch when he made use of it,[52] but to an old person. Albertus Magnus (1200–80) wrote in one of his scientific works that the death of an old man is not bitter, because of the cooling of the natural heat, the disappearance of the radical moisture and the penetration of harmful elements from outside. The old man feels next to nothing. He is like a lamp about to go out.[53] The extreme diminution of the natural heat was a sign of extreme old age, not of 35 to 40 years, and so was the physical and mental decline described by Albertus in the same context. Rosenthal (1990) points out, with regard to statements by men of 50 (or even 40) that they were old, that the educated were being dramatic when they made these assertions. But it is doubtful if, as he puts it, 'they adapted their feelings to the external literary model',[54] since men of 40 in the Middle Ages and the Renaissance were neither considered nor treated as old.

When, in the early thirteenth century, the monk Jocelin of Brakelond objected to the three candidates put forward by the abbot of his monastery of Bury St Edmunds for the post of prior, he described them as young men (*juvenes*) of 40, lacking knowledge and experience in the guidance of souls. Nevertheless, he wrote, 'these the abbot named, putting them above the sub-prior and many others who were older, superior and more mature men too, who were literate and had of old been masters of the schools'.[55] No doubt there were in those days 40–year-old priors, but the fact that Jocelin of Brakelond could refer to their age as a reason for rejecting their candidacy, maintaining that at such an age a man is not yet fully mature and experienced, undermines the assumption that in the thirteenth century a man of 40 was deemed old. Philippe de Commynes wrote in his *Mémoires* that he was presented to King Louis XI in 1468, when the monarch was 'in the flower of his age'; Louis XI was then 45 years old.[56] In the communal laws of Florence of 1415, a citizen had to be over 30 to qualify for election to one of the three great councils of the commune (Tre Maggiori), and only men over 45 could be elected to the commune's highest post, that of 'standard bearer of justice'.[57] (I have chosen an example from Florence rather than Venice, whose gerontocracy, it may be argued, was exceptional.)[58]

Let us now return to the letters of Michelangelo. After the letter he wrote at 37, in which he mentioned the possibility of dying, and the one he wrote at 42, in which he described himself as old, he again referred to his old age in a letter written in 1523, when he was 48, and in two letters written in 1525, when he was 50. In all these letters he expressed his weariness, the pressures he was under, the difficulties he had in meeting all his commitments, (he tended to accept too many commissions and struggled to carry them out on time), and his anxiety that he might not live to create all that he wished to create.[59] But these references to old age in five letters, out of more than 200, cannot be compared to his recurring mention of old age and death after 1540, when he was 65, with increasing frequency as he grew older. Now he mentioned his old age in dozens of letters. He wrote about his loneliness (most of his friends and relatives died before him), his special grief over the death of a brother, a close friend or a devoted assistant, his illnesses, the provisions of his will, and the meaning of old age and death.[60] Nonetheless, since these letters were written in a variety of moods and states of physical and mental health, from time to time he expressed the hope that he might live a few more years and produce some more works of art, the only things which gave meaning to his existence,[61] and described his artistic talent as God's gift to

23

him. After several letters in which he complained about his feebleness and age, he described, in a letter written when he was 74, an illness he was suffering from, and added, 'In other respects, I am almost as I was at thirty years of age.'[62] At 83 he was considering buying a house in Florence or a farm nearby, to which he would retire when he could no longer work (something that would happen in the future.)[63]

William of St Thierry (c. 1084–1148) began to write his biography of Bernard of Clairvaux, which he did not complete, at the age of 63. In the preface he wrote:

> Even now the sands of my life are running out, and my body, in the grip of illness and weakness, will soon be answering the call of death. I am certain that the time is not far off when I must leave this life and appear before my Creator. I fear that I may already be too late to start and finish a book that I dearly want to complete before my life ebbs out.[64]

In this, as in Michelangelo's later letters, is a genuine personal expression of a sick old man who knows that his days are numbered, a very different matter from a dramatic declaration of a 40–year-old that he is no longer young.

Before proceeding to the legislative texts it should be noted that in many areas the determining factor was the ability to function, rather than the chronological age (an issue to which we shall return). Nevertheless, chronological age played an important part in such matters as the minimum ages for marriage, for inheritance, for engaging in litigation, for election to certain posts in the secular administration, for holding ecclesiastical offices from sub-deacon to bishop, and for becoming a doctor of divinity (the minimum age for which was 35).[65] At the same time, throughout Western Europe, as well as in the Crusader kingdom of Jerusalem, men were entitled to various exemptions on grounds of age. This shows that the chronological age was of some significance, and the age threshold indicates at what age people were considered old in the Middle Ages.

In some of the legislative texts the only category eligible for exemption from certain duties is the old; in others they are mentioned alongside the sick and the disabled, and/or children. In the *usatges* of Barcelona in the twelfth century, the old alone are eligible:

> A knight who abandons his knighthood when he might have held on to it [namely] does not bear arms, keep a horse and a fief, does not go out with the army to war or raids, and does not attend public assemblies and the courts of law, as is the usage of knights, will neither be tried nor compensated as a knight, and will forfeit his knighthood, except when he is prevented by age [from the performance of these duties].[66]

24

The 1319 ordinance of Philip V of France allowed those of the king's vassals in Quercy and Perigord who were sick, impoverished or old to do homage to the local seneschal, instead of travelling north to do so before the king.[67] A 1341 ordinance of Philip VI of France abolished all the stipends of the royal officials, except for those who were sick or disabled, had served the king for many years, and the old. All these would continue to receive their stipends or, in other words, they were guaranteed a pension.[68] As in the former statute, the old are given the same privilege as the younger men who were either sick or disabled, but this statute included an additional category, that of long service: 'those who had served the king for many years'.

Decrees regarding compulsory labour included exemptions for the old as well as the sick, the disabled and children. In 1351 King Pedro I, the Cruel, issued a decree after the Black Death in the kingdom of Murcia, intended to prevent the migration of labourers and wage rises, in which he ordered all people to accept whatever work was offered them, except for the sick, the crippled, the very old and children under 12.[69] In England in the thirteen to fifteenth centuries, the bye-laws of the common field villages obliged all able-bodied men and women to work in the fields during the harvest. The sick, the disabled, children and the old were exempt from this duty and allowed to glean after the harvest.[70] The above statutes and bye-laws did not specify at what age people were considered old. They do show that the old were part of the society's self-image, and the object of a certain responsibility on the part of the legislator.

The laws and ordinances which specified the age for the exemption from certain duties and posts had to do with all forms of military service, with trial by battle, watch duty in the cities, positions in the various administrations, payment of taxes and compulsory labour. The threshold for these exemptions was 60 or 70 years of age.

In the Crusader kingdom of Jerusalem in the thirteenth century, a knight of 60 and over was exempt by law from personal military service for his fief.[71] By the 1285 Statute of Winchester, under King Edward I of England, the property of all men between the ages of 15 and 60 was assessed and they were obliged to equip themselves with arms according to the value of their lands and goods. Men over 60 were exempt.[72] Likewise, a statute of Henry VII, issued in 1503, discharged all men of 60 and over from the duty of 'fighting in the King's wars'.[73] The laws of Alfonso X of Castile and Leon, in the thirteenth century, set the age of 70 as the threshold for exemption from watch duty and war against the enemy. The clause then proceeds to assert, unusually for such a context, the traditional belief in the wisdom and experience of old men, adding that they were not all equally wise: 'This does not apply to those [over 70] with knowledge and skill, for it was the custom in antiquity to include in the ranks men who could no longer ride, for the sake of their wisdom and counsel.'[74] According to the chronicler Giovanni Villani, in Florence, too, there were warriors as old as 70. In his proud description of Florence in the second quarter of the fourteenth century, he writes: There were in Florence 25,000 men from the ages of 15 to 70 fit to bear arms, all citizens' (this in addition to 75 full-dress knights).[75] In twelfth-century Modena, too, men were deemed capable of bearing arms up to the age of 70,[76] while in Paris in the thirteenth century men of 60 and over were exempt from watch duty in the urban militia between sundown and sunrise (a duty to which the members of most guilds were liable).[77]

By all the laws of Scotland, Sicily under the Hohenstaufen, Northern and Southern France, Northern Spain and the Crusader kingdom of Jerusalem, men of 60 and over were exempt from the obligation to take part in trial by battle, and could send a proxy to fight in their stead. This was usually a professional champion (campio).[78]

The threshold for exemption from public and administrative positions was usually 70. In most cases the ordinances only permitted exemption, but some made retirement mandatory and barred men over that age from being elected or appointed to these positions. Under Edward I of England, in the Statute of Westminster II of 1285, among provisions designed to correct flaws and injustices in the functioning of sheriffs and bailiffs, men over 70 could not be compelled to serve on juries in the petty assizes.[79] In Florence, men of 70 and over could be excused from serving in the merchants' Council of Six. In Venice and Pisa too, citizens of 70 and over could be excused from serving in the councils, from filling certain posts, or serving as Venetian ambassadors abroad. The commanders of the Republic's army were also free, though not obliged, to retire at 70.[80] The laws of the city of Lucca barred men of 55 and over from being elected to public office. (This is the lowest age threshold that I have encountered in the various legislations, and it is exceptional.) On the other hand, citizens of Lucca who served as guardians were obliged to resign their guardianship only at 70.[81]

In Florence and Pisa in the early fifteenth century, a head-tax was imposed upon all men between 18 and 60. In the rural districts of the two states the tax applied to males between 14 and 70.[82] In 1355, during the Hundred Years War, a tallage was imposed on the citizens of Reims, to equip and maintain 30 armed knights. The ordinance explicitly included citizens under 18 and over 60, and it is evident from the wording that this was an unusual demand and that as a rule men over 60 were exempt from such a tax.[83]

The Statute of Labourers, which was passed in England in 1349 following the Black Death to meet the demands and interests of the landowners and the entrepreneurs in the cities, declared:

All able-bodied men and women of the Lord King's realm and below the age of 60, not living by trade or practising any specific mastery, or having his own land about the tilling of which he can occupy himself, not being the servant of another, if he should be required to serve ... shall be bound to serve him who requests, or else be committed to the goal.[84]

In Cyprus under the rule of Venice, the serfs were bound by the customary laws to perform personal service for the lord of the manor. From the age of 40 on they were gradually relieved of most of these duties, and only at age 60 were they entirely exempted from them, remaining liable to a nominal payment to signify their serf status.[85]

The idea that after the age of 60 a man was no longer able to carry out certain physical tasks, and found it hard to work for his living, also found other expressions. A statute of King Henry VII of England, dating from 1503, permitted the officers of the realm whose duty it was to punish beggars and vagrants, to lighten the punishment of those who were over 60 (as well as of pregnant women, and of the sick and disabled of both sexes.)[86] The rule of the *Scuola della misercordia* of Venice exempted the brothers who were over 60 from the obligation to scourge themselves. They were supposed to remain in the chapel and pray, while the other brothers marched in procession through the city and scourged themselves. It is reasonable to suppose that other fraternities which practised flagellation had similar exemptions for the men over 60.[87] Fasting was (justly) considered an easier form of mortification, and only those over 70 were exempted from it. This, at any rate, was the case in the 'Christian Laws' which were incorporated into the laws of Iceland in the twelfth century: 'People must keep the established fasts until they are 70.'[88]

Of all the statutes and ordinances cited above, the only ones which specified the age threshold for the exemptions and included women were the Statute of Labourers and Henry VII's law regarding beggars and vagrants. (The laws concerning harvest work, and probably also the one compelling acceptance of work offers in the kingdom of Murcia, applied also to women.) The translation of the differences between men and women into codes of behaviour and custom hardly extended to the lowest strata and so women under 60 were compelled to accept the work offered them, as were the men. Also, there must have been as many female beggars as male, and perhaps as many female vagrants. Other statutes made no reference to women, because they were not liable for military service; they were entitled at any age to send a proxy to stand in for them in a trial by battle; they filled no administrative or public positions; in the Italian republics the head-tax applied only to men; the tallage was paid by heads of households, who were generally men, except for a few widows, or independent female merchants and craftswomen, who also paid it; and the religious fraternities did not countenance public self-flagellation by women. (The women who practised it did so in private.)[89] However, a clause referring specifically to women, and a variety of references in other sources, suggest that 60 was held to mark the onset of old age in women as well as men.

Klapisch-Zuber, whose research has shown that in the Late Middle Ages Tuscan women in the prosperous and middle stratum did not give birth after the age of 36, also asserts that the end of childbearing marked a transition in the life of women, for which there was no male equivalent. She ceased to be a young woman fulfilling the procreative function. From this point on her role was to bring up her daughters, to maintain links with the extended family and to help the men find suitable matches for her daughters.[90] But this does not mean that from this age on the woman was considered old. According to Jean d'Ibelin's compilation of the laws of the Crusader kingdom of Jerusalem, widows over 60 who owned fiefs could not be compelled by their feudal lord to marry again (in other words, they were not fined for refusing to do so). The reasoning behind this law was based on the right of a knight to be exempted from certain duties at this age. Just as a knight over 60 was no longer obliged to perform military service on behalf of his fief in person, and did not have to take part personally in a trial by battle, so a woman of 60 and over was not obliged to marry. Another reason given was that a woman of that age could no longer bear children, while the purpose of marriage was sinless procreation. It would have gone against reason and the will of God, wrote Jean d'Ibelin, if the feudal lord were able to compel women of 80, 90 or 100, who were already 'half-rotten' (*demi-pourries*), to marry because they were liable to military service on behalf of their fiefs.[91] Needless to say, had the reason for this exemption been the woman's inability to bear children, she would have been exempted earlier, at least from the age of 50 when, according to most of the medical authorities, the menstrual cycle ended. Undoubtedly, it was in the interest of the Crusader kingdom, which was chronically short of fighting men, to set the highest age possible for freeing a fief-owning woman from the obligation to marry, thereby gaining the military service on behalf of the fief which would devolve on her husband. It was therefore set at 60, which was held to mark the onset of old age in both men and woman, after which the knight was also exempt from his military duties.

Medieval records rarely specified people's ages. As a rule, the age was given only in those cases where there were obvious practical implications which justified inquiring about it. Otherwise, the age was specified almost exclusively to point out that the person in question was either old or a child. It appears that the age of 60 was the earliest noted for this purpose. In a letter of remission granted in Touraine in 1410 to some youths who had held a rowdy charivari under the window of a newly betrothed widow, an event which ended badly, it was stated that the woman in question was very old, being over 60.[92] Whether or not the betrothed woman was indeed over 60, the explicit reference to 60 served to point out that she was an old woman. A letter addressed to the Bishop of Lincoln in 1338 concerning the Countess of Lincoln, Alesya de Lascy, stated that after her husband's death she took a vow of chastity and became a nun. But later she was abducted by a certain knight and subsequently agreed to marry him. The letter writer noted that she was 60 years old, and asked the Bishop to threaten to excommunicate the persons who had persuaded her to break her vow.[93] Her age was noted to emphasize the absurdity and sinfulness of her broken vow, and her willingness to marry at her advanced age. Similarly, the age of 60 was noted to show that a man was old. In one of the *exempla* (moral tales which were interpolated in sermons), the story is told of a man of 60 who repented, but lapsed and visited a brothel. Helped by St Andrew, he repented again.[94] Again, the age of 60 was noted to show that this was an old man who had little time left to repent of his sins. In Cypriot villages under Venetian rule certain men were appointed to act as 'jurors' (*zurati* or *giurati*, in the local Venetian dialect), whose duty it was to testify on oath in such matters as local customs, tenures and past events, whenever called upon to do so. Only men who had lived in the village for many years, remembered past events and knew the local customs, that is to say, old men, could be expected to fulfil this duty, and indeed it was decreed that they had to be 60 and over.[95]

There is no doubt that people in the Middle Ages were familiar with older traditions concerning old age: biblical, Greek, Roman and Barbarian. We have seen that in the biblical laws of vows, the value of men and women declined when they reached the age of sixty (Lev. 27: 1–7), while the Levites were supposed to retire from their priestly duties at the age of 50 (Num. 4:3; 8: 24–26). In Greece and Rome retirement was official and institutionalized only for military men. (This was during the period when the army was a citizens' army, i.e., in Greece until the conquests of Alexander the Great, and in Rome until the end of the Republic.) The age of retirement was 60. The commanders were not obliged to retire.[96] The New Testament advised: 'A widow should not be put on the roll under sixty years of age' (I Epistle to Timothy, 5: 9). By the laws of the Barbarians the value of a man declined at 50 and of a woman at 40.[97] We cannot tell to what extent medieval people were influenced by these traditions. If they were, they chose to follow those in which old age began at 60 rather than 50, and in some areas they extended it to 70.

It is known that as a rule Medieval people did not give their exact age. Some simply did not know how old they were. Moreover, there was a naive tendency to round the number up or down to the nearest decade, (a man of 63 would say he was 60; a man of 55 might say that he was 50 or 60). Some deliberately added or subtracted years; this is a known fact. Petrarch wrote to Boccaccio that young people subtract from their true age, while old people add to theirs. The young wish for more years and pleasures, while the old wish for respect and obedience.[98] There are indeed some known cases where young people subtracted from their true age, but it appears that the tendency of mature and aged people to add to their age was more widespread. The reason was probably psychological-social. Having once accepted the fact that they were old, and in any case being treated as old, by exaggerating their age they gained added prestige and what seemed like achievement. Perhaps some people, feeling weary and weak, honestly came to believe that they were older than they really were. Furthermore, people exaggerated their age so as to avoid paying taxes or holding public office (the kind which was considered onerous). Nevertheless, we need not exaggerate the difficulty of finding out a person's real age, and the limits of deception. When it was necessary to verify a person's true age – for example, when 'proof of age' was required to determine if an heir has reached the minimum age (21) to take over a feudal property (which was otherwise held by the feudal lord in his role as guardian of minor heirs), or when young men sought public office in the Italian republics – means were found to do so.

It was the same with people who sought exemption from duties on grounds of age. In the Letter-Books of the City of London from the last quarter of the fourteenth century and the first of the fifteenth, there are dozens of exemptions from serving on juries and assizes, and a number of discharges from watch duty in the city.[99] Generally, the exact age is not mentioned but where it is mentioned, together with the details of the inquiry about it, it apparently met the legal requirement (the 1295 Statute of Westminster II) which set the age of 70 as the threshold for exemption. In one application for exemption, an inquiry was ordered to find out if a man was in truth 70 and entitled to the exemption. The inquiry discovered that he was indeed 70 years old (and deaf to boot) and he was discharged. In another case, an explicit reference was made to the statute: 'A man may not be required to serve as juror if he be in truth 70 years of age, for that is the age prescribed by the Great Council as the limit for this service.'[100] In the county courts, too, it appears that men continued to serve as jurors until about the age of 70. One man served in the assizes of the hundred and of the county courts, at first together with his father and later as a head of household in his own right, for over 50 years.[101] People could also be discharged from other duties on grounds of age. And even if they succeeded in cheating and adding a few years to their true age, the age limit prescribed in the laws and ordinances remained relevant in reality.[102] Moreover, it would appear that people over 60 could be discharged from duties to which the law did not set an age limit. Rosenthal's research has shown that between 1350 and 1500, 30 per cent of the members of the English House of Lords passed the age of 60, and 10 per cent were over 70. In 1456 Lord Vescy, who was 66, was relieved of the obligation to attend the sittings of the House 'on account of his age and infirmity'.[103]

The Earl of Oxford was likewise relieved when he was only 52, due to his devoted service in the wars and his physical infirmity (not on account of his age). He was free to resume his seat in the House if he so wished.[104] Clergymen, too, who wished or were asked to retire, did so at age 60 or older.

However, it should be noted that the laws and ordinances which set an age for exemption did not do so for paid work. They applied, as we have seen, to military service, trial by battle and adminstrative and public offices (which brought no wages) or taxes. The only decrees which concerned work were the Statutes of Labourers and the manorial custom in Cyprus, which dealt exclusively with compulsory labour. Since there was no legally stipulated age for retirement from work, nor any pension schemes, and only a few people received a pension (mainly, though not exclusively, churchmen), it follows that the perceived onset of old age, namely 60 to 70, had limited practical social implication. The age at which people retired from salaried work and from agricultural or artisan labour depended on their functioning abilities, as well as on the demographic, economic and family circumstances, not on their chronological age. As for the high government offices, the determining factors were functioning ability and the political circumstances, again not age. We shall return to this problem when we come to the subject of ageing in the different social strata.

As for the self-image of men and women in the Middle Ages – that is to say, at what age they thought of themselves as old – this is not a question which can be answered with assurance. But the stipulation of 30 to 45 as the minimum age for election to certain posts and appointment to certain offices, and of ages 60 to 70 as being the threshold for exemption from certain duties and functions, as well as the frequent mention in various sources to age 60 as the beginning of old age, all suggest that people began to see themselves as old in their sixties and not in their forties, if only in the upper strata. They may have felt at 40 that they were passing into a new stage of life, and perhaps felt sad and anxious, but they did not see themselves as old. We do not know to what extent the self-image of peasants, or hired labourers, rural or urban, related to their chronological age or depended entirely on their functioning abilities and family circumstances (such as if they were married or widowed, or if they had offspring at home or not). The exemption of persons over 60 from certain duties in the Statute of Labourers, and in the Cypriot manorial customs, was decided by those who held political, economic and legal power. It was plainly in their interest to set the highest age possible for releasing workers from their duties, and they based it upon the idea of age which prevailed in their own social stratum. Yet it is reasonable to assume that even in that stratum different individuals internalized the cultural norms regarding old age in different ways, just as they do today. These differences are rooted in the individual personality, in the person's physical

31

and mental condition and in their particular circumstances, which determine both the sharpness of the transition in their personal relationships and their functioning ability.

We turn now to the life expectancy in the Middle Ages, and the percentage of old people (i.e. the over-sixties) in the general population. Although the extant Medieval records containing such demographic data are few and incomplete, preventing a full demographic investigation such as is possible for the Modern era, historical demographers have nevertheless determined the general demographic trend of the Middle Ages and the Renaissance. The general trend was of an increasing life expectancy from the twelfth century until the end of the thirteenth, a gradual decline in the first half of the fourteenth, a drastic decline in its latter half, and the beginning of an increase in the fifteenth century.[105] The demographic study of the Commune of Florence, based upon an almost unique record from the Late Middle Ages, a census book kept for tax purposes from the year 1427, reflects the general demographic trend of the period:

In 1300, life expectancy at birth: about 40
In 1375, life expectancy at birth: 18
In 1400, life expectancy at birth: 20
in 1427, life expectancy at birth: 28[106]

The same trend characterized other regions in Western Europe: a population increase and a rising life expectancy in the twelfth century, a gradual decline in the early decades of the fourteenth and a sharp decline in its latter half, due to the Black Death of 1348 and the subsequent epidemics, followed by a gradual recovery from the fifteenth century through the sixteenth. In some regions the recovery began in the first quarter of the fifteenth century, in others only in its last decades, or even at its end.

This was indeed a low life expectancy, but we must keep in mind not only that it represents an average, but that the highest rate of mortality was among babies and young children. The mortality rate began to decline slowly after the age of five, but remained high throughout childhood.[107] The epidemics took the greatest toll among the children and the high rate of infant and child mortality was the principle cause of the low life expectancy at birth. However, those who survived childhood had a fair chance of living to be 50 or 60, even 70 years of age. As a rough average, ignoring differences of time and place (and leaving out the period of the Black Death), in the High and Late Middle Ages (and later) the life expectation of a person of 20–25 was 30 years. In other words, in all social strata, from the nobility through the clergy and urban population to the peasantry, a person of 20–25 had a fair chance of living for another 30 years.[108] And given that at 20–25 a person had a life expectation of 30, that is to say, a median mortality age of 50–55, clearly there were some who lived to be 70, and there are known cases of people living to be 80 and 90.

Needless to say, life expectancy at birth in pre-industrial Europe was considerably shorter than it is today. (Nowadays Japan has the highest life expectancy: 79; followed by Iceland, Hong Kong and Sweden: 78; followed by Switzerland, Australia, France, Spain and Italy: 77; while in some of the countries of the Third World the average life expectancy is 42 or even less.) The same goes for the percentage of old people, that is the over-sixties, in the general population. The great increase in the percentage of old people occurred in the twentieth century. This is due to the higher life expectancy, as well as to the declining birth rate, which reduces the percentage of children in the population. Demographic historians estimate that the percentage of old people in pre-industrial Europe did not generally rise above 8 per cent, and in some regions at certain times not above 5 percent.[109] The assumption is that this was also roughly the percentage in the Middle Ages. (By comparison, in 1984 the percentage of old people in the developed countries stood at 14 per cent, and it is expected to rise to 20 per cent by 2030.) However, for a period of about 100 years, in the fifteenth century, the percentage of over-sixties in most of Western Europe was much higher than in previous times, and higher than in later periods up to the twentieth century. This was because the plague of 1348 and its subsequent outbreaks, which devastated Europe in the second half of the fourteenth and early fifteenth centuries, killed many children, and more young people than old.[110] Thus in 1427, 14.6 per cent of the population of Florence were over 60, and in Ravenna 15.9 per cent. The same increase in the ratio of old people was taking place in other parts of Europe. This high percentage gradually declined during the period of recovery and the steady increase of the population from the late fifteenth century.[111]

Medieval people were conscious of the high mortality rate among babies and children, and expressed their fears for their children's lives in a variety of ways.[112] And Petrarch (1304–74), whose book *On the Remedies* dealt with most of the problems and ideas of his time, who himself survived the Black Death and died at 70, offered a Malthusian explanation for the high infant and child mortality, which he believed to be inevitable. For, he argued, if all who were born were to survive, the earth would be unable to sustain them. He explained that he did not mean that this would happen if they all lived forever, since if they were immortal they would not be human, but simply if all who were born were to live to a ripe old age, or even reach maturity.[113]

The paucity of reliable demographic data from the High and Late Middle Ages is even more marked with regard to the ratio of men and women in the population, let alone their respective life expectancies. In all the records, women figure less than men. It may be said that throughout the Middle Ages there was a tendency to masculinize the data.[114] Less care was taken to register girls and women; the husband, as head of the family, represented his wife and, since women also owned less property than men, they figured less in the registers of property. Today in the developed countries women live longer than men. (In the United States male life expectancy is 73, and female 80, and women account for three-fifths of the older population.) It is assumed that the reasons for this are genetic rather than environmental. Some Medieval scholars believed that women lived longer than men. Aristotle held that men live longer than women thanks to their greater natural heat. However, he added, a man who fornicated or worked too hard died earlier than a woman.[115] By the thirteenth century all the works of Aristotle were widely known and had a decisive influence on the sciences of the age. Whether because of a mistranslation from Greek to Arabic or from Arabic to Latin, or because he really differed from Aristotle on this subject, Albertus Magnus wrote: 'By nature [naturaliter] men live longer than women, but per accidens women live longer than men. There were three reasons for this: women work less hard than men; their monthly cycle purifies their blood, and they expand less energy in sexual intercourse.'[116] A similar view was expressed in the satirical literature. A satirical work of the fifteenth century, The Fifteen Joys of Marriage, stated that in all social strata men age faster than women. This was so because the man toils and is responsible for everything. The hardships of pregnancy and childbirth cannot be compared to the toil, effort and thought that a man must expand in all his tasks. The hens, which lay fist-size eggs from a tiny hole, and which are only interested in food, are fatter than the cocks.[117] Needless to say, this scientific theory was not unrelated to the religious and secular views about the woman and her nature in the Middle Ages.

During the early Middle Ages the life expectancy of women was doubtless lower than that of men. But according to some demographic historians, their life expectancy rose during the High Middle Ages. Nutrition improved. With the increased consumption of meat the addition of iron in the diet was especially beneficial to women, who need it because of the loss of blood during menstruation, childbirth or miscarriage, as well as during lactation.[118] In the cities, which grew during the twelfth century, the work done by women was probably lighter than in the rural areas. At that time also the death toll rose among the men of the nobility. Boys of this class were killed in training for knighthood, and mature men in the Crusades and in the European wars (in which greater numbers took part than in the Early Middle Ages) and in the Late Middle Ages many men were legally executed. An analysis of the ducal families in England between 1330 and 1475 showed that at 20 the life expectation of men was 31.5 more years, and for women 31.1 years. But this held for natural death only. When violent death was taken into account, the life expectation of men of 20 was only 21.7 years.[119] As for the general population during the High and Late Middle Ages, it is known that the ratio of men to women in the different age groups varied from period to period, from place to place, and not only because of divergent life expectancies. By and large, however, it appears that women's life expectancy was shorter than men's. The decisive factors were environmental. Many women died in childbirth or soon after. In the rural areas they were worn out by work. Moreover, it was the women who looked after the sick, and were thus more exposed to infection.[120] The reason for the large number of widows, some old and some younger, in the High and Late Middle Ages, was the age gap between husband and wife (especially in the prosperous strata). Women who were married early outlived their husbands. It is also believed that at a later stage, once they stopped bearing children, the gap between the life expectation of men and women shrank, and sometimes women's life expectation exceeded that of men.[121]

2

THE OLD BODY

Discourse about the body, both from a physiological viewpoint and in a symbolic sense, increased gradually from the twelfth century on. One might say that the interest in the individual body in the various kinds of discourse, like the interest in the human body of Christ, climaxed in the latter half of the fourteenth and in the fifteenth century.[1] The concern with the body's physiology grew as part of the general interest in the concrete, in the phenomena and laws of nature, which from the thirteenth century on was strongly influenced by the natural philosophy of Aristotle and his Arab commentators. The body's partial rehabilitation was justified by its divine creation, the mystery of the Incarnation, and the belief in the resurrection of the body on Judgement Day. As the nun and mystic Hildegard of Bingen (1098–1179) wrote: 'Without the soul the body is naught, yet the soul cannot act without the body.' The soul is superior to the body, yet depends upon it. It is the microcosm in which the soul dwells. She went on to describe the beauty and intricacy of the human body, which was also the body of Christ when he was made flesh.[2] In Medieval culture the body was a multifarious symbol: it was a metaphor for the Church, for the polity, for society and the family. The four elements of the human body reflected and symbolized the four elements of the world. The body-microcosm was a symbol of the world-macrocosm. Even the souls departing from the body were depicted as bodies, as the naked bodies of small children. Despite the belief in the separation of the soul from the body at death, the torments of hell were described as bodily torments. The corpse of a saint whose soul had departed became, paradoxically, a holy relic. By a reversal the body also occupied a central place in the ascetic ideal. In scientific discourse and in symbolic contexts, reference was made to all types of bodies: to the child's body, the young man's and the young woman's body, and also to old bodies.

The image of the old person was not an unequivocal one in the Middle Ages. The old body was also variously interpreted, and various ideas were proposed regarding its implications for the person and its correct treatment. But the writings all described the old body in the same way. The self-same stereotype of the old body appears in the scientific and medical texts, in the moral writings and sermons, and in literary works. Those who believed in the rehabilitation of the body, who considered the preservation of its health to be legitimate, as much as those who viewed the body as the prison to which vain and sinful man devotes too much care and attention, used the very same stereotype. And whereas the bodies of young and mature men represented the social hierarchy – the body of a noble was described as magnificent, beautiful and strong, and that of the peasant as ugly and wretched – when it came to the old man's body no such distinctions were made. The old body was one and the same throughout the social strata. Those who described the beauty of the human body which was created in the image of God, and which was also the body of Christ when he was made flesh, did not envision the old body. The powerful and dignified old body belonged exclusively to the mythical heroes of the epics, those who transcended their age in body as well as in spirit.

THE NEUTRAL MALE BODY

Medieval scholars tended to combine medicine, psychology, theology and metaphysics. Thus medical texts sometimes included these aspects, as well as moral instruction addressed to the old person, side by side with words of compassion for his plight. As a rule, however, the descriptions in the medical and scientific texts were neutral, as opposed to the descriptions in the moral literature and in the symbolic discourse. This is how Roger Bacon (1214–92) described the signs of old age: 'White hair, pallor, wrinkling of the skin, excess of mucus, foul phlegm, inflammation of the eyes and general injury of the organs of sense, diminution of blood and spirits, weakness of motion and breathing in the whole body.'[3] Vincent of Beauvais, whose description closely resembles Bacon's, adds ironically that the hair either turns white or falls out altogether, but unlike the tree which sheds its leaves in the autumn and grows them afresh in the spring, or the fowl, whose feathers grow back after it has moulted, the man who has lost his hair will never grow it again.[4] The neutral description in the scientific and medical texts was incorporated either in a theoretical discussion of the process of ageing and the diseases of old age, or in the context of advice on the preservation of the old man's health, which sometimes also addresses younger people who do not take proper care of their health, warning them that they could age or even die prematurely.

Discussion about ageing and the diseases of old age appeared in the general compendia on pathology and therapy, which became common from the latter half of the twelfth century, with the spread of translations of medical texts from Greek and Arabic. It reflected the gradual rehabilitation of the body, and with it the legitimacy of the physician's calling, though it was still sometimes guardedly conceded.[5] Geriatrics, like pediatrics, had not yet become a distinct and separate medical profession. Advice for the old was usually incorporated in general health manuals (*Regimen sanitatis*), which offered guidance for all stages of life, from birth to old age, based on theoretical and practical medicine. To begin with, these texts were written only in Latin, but manuals translated from Latin, or written in the vernacular languages, became common from the thirteenth century on. The assumption in all these texts was that it is impossible to restore an old man to youth, or to rehabilitate what has already been impaired, since ageing is an inevitable and irreversible decline of the organism. The purpose of those manuals which clearly legitimized the care of the body was to delay as much as possible the deterioration of those parts which were still healthy and functioning, to enhance the old person's wellbeing, and to prevent premature death. At the same time, the medical scholars of the period were as aware as today's geriatric specialists of the difference between the normal afflictions of ageing, and pathological processes and diseases, though they were unable to cure them.[6]

It was commonly believed that the loss of immortality and the concomitant process of ageing were man's punishment for Original Sin. Opinions were divided on the question whether human life became even shorter after the Deluge (as described in the Old Testament), because of natural causes (mainly air pollution), or due to divine intervention.[7] As far as the medical texts were concerned, divine punishment following Original Sin, or divine intervention after the Deluge, were ultimate causes, while they were concerned with the process and the immediate causes of ageing. They followed the Classical authorities and the writings of Arab medical scholars in ascribing the primary cause of ageing to changes in the composition of the bodily humours. The natural heat, which is the source of the body's vitality, gradually diminished, consuming the natural moisture much as the burning lamp gradually consumes the oil. The old man is cold and dry, lacking radical inner moisture, though he does have external moisture, which differs from the inner kind. This 'bad' external moisture arises from the old body's many secretions: phlegm, mucus and tears,[8] which were sometimes described as 'bad' external humours. In other words, the old person is primarily cold and dry, but secondarily, he is cold and moist. These changes, namely, the diminution of the natural heat and the radical moisture, combined with the increase in the external humours, were the source of all the symptoms (*accidentia*) of old age, both physical and mental.

Roger Bacon, having listed the physical signs of old age, goes on to describe the mental signs: a decrease in the animal and natural powers of the soul, insomnia, mental restlessness, irritability and forgetfulness. Indeed, he continued, the royal Hali himself (presumably the Arab physician Hali Ibn Abbas) had already written that old age is the home of oblivion, and Plato wrote that it is the mother of lethargy.[9] The medical scholars of the

Middle Ages clearly adopted the Aristotelian theory about the connection between body and soul, or, in other words, the psychosomatic concept. According to Aristotle, a man reaches his physical and mental peaks at different ages. The latter takes longer to achieve, and begins to decline later. A man achieves his best physical strength at the age of 30–35, and his best spiritual and intellectual capacity at about 49. Some of the Medieval medical authorities agreed that the physical and the mental faculties did not begin to decline at the same time. Most of them held that the mental decline took place in extreme old age (generally denoted by the word *senium*). At this stage, the physiological changes occurring in the body – the diminution of the natural heat and the radical moisture, and above all, the increasing 'bad' humours – cause the old man to become childlike.[10]

By and large, the views of the Medieval medical scholars matched the conclusions of modern geriatric research. The psychoanalysts have not been alone in noting the psychological changes occurring in old age. Physiological and biochemical variables, as well as genetic ones, have been studied in connection with the psychological changes. Today, most geriatric specialists agree that in the process of ageing some cognitive faculties – such as memory, orientation, judgement and the discrimination between the relevant and the irrelevant – are affected and impaired, though with individual variations, and increasingly so with the advancing years. Likewise, the incidence of psychotic disturbances associated with old age (which are by no means universal) also increases in advanced senescence.[11]

In their detailed health regimens for every stage of life, as in general medical theory, the Medieval physicians followed Hippocrates, Galen and the Arab physicians of the tenth to twelfth centuries. As noted above, their aim was preventive and supportive, rather than therapeutic and rehabilitative. In the words of Maimonides (whose advice closely resembled that of the Christian writers): 'There is no preventing or postponing old age. But it is possible to prevent its speedy progress.'[12] Thus when the writers recommend that the old engage in some light physical activity, such as a daily walk or ride, they pointed out that whereas in the young such exercise serves to strengthen their limbs, the old cannot restore strength to their weakened limbs but may preserve the vitality of those organs which are still functioning and prevent their deterioration. It was inadvisable to strain a limb which was already impaired. And since the old man was held to be cold and lacking in the radical moisture, medical advice laid emphasis on the methods of enhancing his warmth and moisture. The correct diet was highly thought of, since it was widely believed that the humours were nourished by the 'useful' part of the food, which the stomach separated from the 'coarse and impure part'.[13] The old person was advised to eat and drink such foods and beverages which were thought to be warming, moisturizing and digestible, and the writers went on to recommend the appropriate kinds of food, drink and seasoning. Among other things, they recommended suitable meats and fish, insisting that it should always be the flesh of young animals, sucklings if possible; old red wine diluted with water; the milk of a well-pastured goat or donkey, blended with honey, and well-baked bread made from fine flour. The old man should eat three times a day, but only small amounts each time. He should sleep and rest a good deal in a sunny room which should be well heated in winter. Knowing that the old were inclined to catch influenza, bronchitis, pneumonia and other infections of the respiratory system, and that winter was a dangerous season for them, the writers repeatedly emphasized the importance of warmth for them. Some recommended scenting the old man's room with fragrant herbs. They stated that getting up in the night to pray was inappropriate for the old man's constitution. He should work little, have little sexual intercourse, and avoid excessive excitement, anxiety and anger. He should bathe quite often and oil his body afterwards. They listed the discomforts and mild ailments from which old people frequently suffer: colds, coughs, aches in the arms and legs, dizziness, noise in the ears, various itches, problems of digestion and difficulty in urinating. They recommended avoiding as much as possible drastic medical interventions, such as bleeding, strong enemas and emetics (which were the favourite methods of treating young people). Instead, they recommended using simple and natural methods, such as massage, hot compresses soaked in healing liquids, herbal beverages, warm baths and light exercise. When an old man suffered from constipation or difficulty in urinating, they recommended foods which promoted bowel movements (such as figs), or acted as diuretics. They emphasized the need to take into account individual differences between old people and their former habits, when prescribing the type of exercise, food and the like.

It should be noted that those authors of health manuals which referred to the stages of life and fixed the onset of old age (*senectus*) at 35–45 never addressed this sort of advice to people of that age, but to people over 60 or 65. With regard to the very old (over 72, according to Arnold of Villanova),[14] it was stated that they should follow the guidelines for the aged, but with greater stringency. They were to avoid all labour and all sexual intercourse, all anxiety and excitement; eat small amounts at frequent intervals, and they must never be bled. Believing as they did that the human being is a unity of body and soul, and that the mental state affects the body, these authors proposed ways of enhancing the person's happiness and contentment, and of avoiding anger, anxiety and melancholy, not merely for their intrinsic benefits, but because of their effect on the body's natural heat. Anger and melancholy could be prevented, and interest and joy could be awakened by means of aesthetic pleasure, listening to music, enjoyment of nature, intellectual discourse with friends, and of course, reading the Scriptures. In parallel, when they recommended certain food and drink (such as red wine), they noted that these could stave off melancholy. The learned surgeon Henry de Mondeville was especially convinced of the influence of the soul upon the body. In discussing various folk remedies which he held to be useless, he went on to say that if a person believed in them they might help, because the soul has the power to affect the body, and the imagination alone could cause the remedy to become efficacious.[15]

In the sixteenth century the Italian Alvise Cornaro wrote four *Essays on the Sober Life* (*Discorsi intorno alla vita sobria*). He wrote the first when he was 83, the second at 86, the third at 91 and the fourth at 95. He died peacefully at 98. In these essays he described his life in old age: his daily routine, his occupations, his aesthetic and spiritual pleasures. He also described in detail the health regimen which he followed, and which he believed combined with his sobriety and moderation in everything to enhance his pleasant and lengthy old age. He had been influenced by the works of Pliny the Younger and by Cicero's *On Old Age* (*De senectute*), but there is less apologetics in his own writing than in Cicero's. As for his health regimen, he was obviously familiar with the various manuals from antiquity, the Middle Ages and the Renaissance, but he claimed to be describing the health regimen which he actually followed. It bears a broad resemblance to the advice offered in the Medieval manuals. He emphasized the need to preserve the inner heat and the basic moisture, and his specific means for achieving this closely recall the ones which the Medieval manuals recommended. His medical theory is bound up with morality: moderation, the right measure in everything, and the observation of the moral precepts, are all essential conditions for the health of both body and soul.[16] In the early fifteenth century Alberti put a similar statement in the mouth of Giannozzo, one of the speakers in his *Family Book* (*Della famiglia*). Giannozzo is described as a healthy old man, still strong and handsome. According to him, the secret of his good health lay in his moderate consumption of easily digested foods, his personal cleanliness, sexual restraint and physical exercise.[17]

Cornaro was a nobleman. Alberti and the protagonists in his book belonged to the upper stratum of the merchants' class of Florence. Needless to say, the lower strata, even if they knew the health literature (which is doubtful), they could not observe the recommended regimens. The foods cited in them would have been beyond their means, their homes were very far from what the manuals described as ideal, and many of them were obliged to go on working as long as they possibly could. On the other hand, the genre of health manuals was clearly very popular in the upper social strata, since they gave rise to satirical works which made fun of their supposed efficacy. A ballad by the poet Charles of Orléans (1394–1465) mocked all medical advice, in particular the avoidance of sexual intercourse as a means of postponing old age and prolonging life.[18]

As for the treatment of sick old people, it was culturally determined, like all medical practice. It was inevitably influenced by social conventions and by conscious and unconscious assumptions. The treatment of the aged was not central in medical discourse. It would also seem that when it came to sick old people the physicians tended to do little treating. (This was probably for the best, since in any case they did not know how to cure most ailments.) The aim of the treatment was, as we have noted, primarily preventive and supportive, rather than therapeutic and rehabilitative. The old person had already lived his life, and there was no need to make desperate efforts to keep him alive, since in any case not much could be done. The physician of Francesco di Marco Datini (1335–1410), a wealthy merchant of Prato, instructed him to avoid excessive eating and drinking, not to go to bed directly after the meal, and to avoid anger and anxiety. He gave him almost no medicines, though he was suffering from fever, kidney stones and an inflammation of the bladder.[19] He seems to have been aware of his inability to help the old merchant. As for the advice to avoid anger and anxiety, it would seem that its usefulness was as dubious then as it is today. Since the physicians did not know how to cure most illnesses, many people, young and old, died of them. But there were no doubt disabled old people who needed care or at least regular help.

Various sources suggest that many old people were either partially or totally blind. (Louis IX established a special almshouse for poor blind citizens of Paris, with a capacity of 300.) Some were partially paralysed, and some were disabled by an accident which happened in old age. A fairly detailed description of the care of one such old man is found in the book of mystic Margery Kempe (c. 1372–c. 1439). She was married at 20 to a man about ten years older. When she was 40 they separated by mutual agreement, to enable her to live in chastity and contemplation. When her husband was in his early sixties he fell from the stairs and hurt his head badly. He was treated, and as she put it, the wound 'knitted'. But he remained disabled until his death some six years later. She was persuaded by the neighbours' gossip and the voice of God to return to his house and take care of him. She wrote:

> He turned childish again and lacked reason. He could not do his easement by going to a seat, or else he would not, but as a child, voided his natural digestion into his linen clothes where he sat by the fire or at the table, whichever it were; he would spare no place.

She was therefore hard at work washing and wringing out clothes, and her expenses on heating were excessively high. She resented the fact that the great deal of time she had to devote to his care caused her to curtail her prayers and contemplation. But she did her duty till he died. Margery Kempe's words and behaviour were unpopular in the community. She was critized and even accused of heresy. But it strikes me that she had a marked tendency to self-pity. As she put it, she consoled herself for the time she had to devote to caring for her husband, and the unpleasantness of the task, by viewing them as her atonement for desiring him in her youth.[20] She felt little compassion for him. It is reasonable to assume that there were women (for generally it was women who looked after the sick) who nursed their husbands or one of their parents with greater warmth and compassion, but the care could not have been made any easier thereby.

Returning to the representation of the body in the medical texts, we should note that the old body was described in a stereotypical way, but neutrally and without moral connotations. Nevertheless, given their view of man as a unity of body and soul, the authors of the scientific and medical texts who dealt with ageing could not but refer to the mental processes alongside the physical ones which affected the old person: the decline of the intellectual faculties and the tendency to irritability and melancholy. But these developments were depicted as resulting from the physiological changes, that is to say, not as a moral decline but as a process beyond the person's control.[21] Ageing was a part of the human condition. It was a law of nature that whoever goes on living and is not cut down prematurely would reach the degenerative stage of old age, the final stage of life.[22] Vincent of Beauvais, who included moral instruction in his encyclopedia, repeated the image used by the Roman poet Maximianus (c. 240–310), that compared old age to the 'breath of death' and to 'death in life'. (The idea behind the image was expressed in other words by Jean Améry: The death which threatens the young man in war, or even by sickness, comes from outside, but it threatens the old man from within. It grows inside him in 'the most revolting intimacy'.)[23] But Vincent of Beauvais' use of this image is free of theological connotations. It does not mean 'Remember death' (*Memento mori*), and the representation of death residing in the old man does not imply the approaching next world, in its religious or metaphysical sense, but a liminal state between life and death, and the beginning of the end of a biological process.

THE HARMFUL FEMALE BODY

During the Middle Ages there were a good many medical texts devoted to the ailments of women, chiefly to gynaecology, and there were manuals for the health care of the pregnant woman. But in the works we have cited so far, when it came to the description of the ageing process and advice on the preservation of health in old age, they evidently applied only to men. As in the divisions of life into stages, none of the authors stated explicitly that he was only concerned with men, but the texts make it clear that even if they did not exclusively consider men, men were their primary concern. In the Middle Ages (and even in later centuries), the term 'man' (*homo*) generally stood for the male, not for a human being.[24] In any case, women only rarely consulted the male physicians. But the authors of the medical texts did devote a separate discussion to one physiological change in the old woman's body, namely, the end of menstruation. In dealing with this physiological change the writers distinguished between women in the upper and lower social strata, a distinction which is absent in the discussion of the ageing male body. They ascribed the destructive effects of this change primarily to the old women who were poor. According to the theory about the effect of the end of menstruation, which was only implied in the learned scientific texts but was developed more crudely in the popularized ones, the old woman's body was capable of producing poison. We know that scientific literature and popular tradition alike held that menstrual blood was an impure and dangerous substance. These qualities were especially emphasized from the twelfth century on, a period when people were generally anxious about impurity in all areas.[25] However, with the cessation of the menstrual cycle the woman became even more dangerous, since she was no longer able to expel the superfluous substance from her system. This is how it is described in *The Secrets of Women* (De secretis mulierum), which is attributed to Albertus Magnus: 'the retention of menses engenders many evil humours. The women being old have almost no natural heat left to consume and control this matter, especially poor women who live on nothing but coarse meat, which greatly contributes to this phenomenon. These women are more venomous than others.'[26] According to this theory, the old woman's actual physiological mechanism makes her venomous. The old bawd who panders to fornication and crime, who prepares love philtres and deadly potions, is acting out the physiological changes taking place in her organism.

Since Medieval culture considered body and soul to be linked and mutually influential, it also tended to examine the body for signs of the state of the soul. The ugly body reflected a deformed soul. Conversely, a person who was believed to have a sinful and deformed soul was described as physically repulsive. The leper's appearance indicated his corrupt soul. And vice versa – the perverted soul of the Jew meant that he was seen as physically repulsive. It is uncertain if it was the appearance of poor old women which gave rise to the theory that their bodies could produce venom, or if the theory derived from the obsessive preoccupation with menstrual blood and other fantasies about the female body, not necessarily that of the old woman.[27] One way or the other, scientific theory invented a crude direct link between the physiological changes occurring in the old woman's body and her supposed personality and occupations. These writings did not represent her as an androgynous creature, as old men and women were sometimes depicted. Such a view would have disagreed with her allegedly harmful and dangerous nature.

THE OLD BODY AS A METAPHOR FOR THE TRANSIENCE AND VANITY OF THIS WORLD

In the sermons which centred on the 'contempt for the world' (*contemptus mundi*), with their denunciation of man's attachment to the vanities of this world and a call to repentance, the old body symbolized the transience and vanity of this world. Bernardino of Siena (1380–1444) described the old body thus: the head trembles; all the limbs shake; the hair is white; the belly swollen; teeth have fallen out; sight and hearing weakened; desire has cooled or altogether gone. (When Bernardino preached to the crowds in the city square he would spitefully mimic the tremulous head and shaking limbs of the old man who ignores his body's signals that the time is soon coming when he will be forced to leave this world.)[28] An English preacher described thus the old man who puts off repentence and denies his imminent death: 'See the wrinkled face, the snow-white head, the bent back, the failing of sight, hearing and limbs, the livid nose and nails, the evil breath, the hollow eye, the crazy mirth that seems to ignore its approaching death.'[29] Some of the details repeat the usual stereotype in the medical texts, but the description is crueller and more grotesque and the context gives it a different connotation.

Pope Innocent III, in a work which bears the influence of Horace and which itself influenced various genres from sermons to literature, in the later Middle Ages described the afflictions, torments, sins and vanities of this world, from conception to death. His description of the old man's body is detailed and ruthless: his heart is weakened and his head trembles; his hand shakes and his breath stinks; his face is wrinkled and his back bent; his eyes are dimmed and his joints feeble; his nose runs and his hair has fallen out; his teeth are rotten and his hearing is dull. He goes on: 'Young men, be not proud in the presence of a decaying old man; he was once that which you are; he is now what you in turn will be.'[30] Innocent III's description was not meant to arouse compassion, but to warn against pride and to arouse contempt for the world and the flesh. His address to the young is not a variation on the biblical injunction to honour the old, but a reiteration of the statement that old age is a part of the human condition that no one who lives long can escape. Here the old body does not merely signify the approaching end, as in the medical texts, but symbolizes the terror of the judgement in the next world, which man in his vanity and sinfulness avoids thinking about.

Petrarch did not compose sermons, but the author of the *On the Remedies to the Two Kinds of Fortune* also discussed the old body, though in a philosophical rather than religious context. 'Reason' tells 'Joy' that the old body, and the loss of pleasures associated with it, represent the fragility, transience and meaninglessness of this world: the golden locks will fall out; the single remaining lock will turn white; wrinkles will furrow the cheeks and brow; a dark cloud will dim the merry radiance and shining stars in the eyes. Even before the teeth fall out, they will lose their polish and white gleam. The neck and shoulders will lose their suppleness and become bowed. The old body suffers from scabies, gout and constant fatigue, wrote Petrarch. It can no longer run, jump, play ball games or dance. The young body is like a flower, but like a flower, its withering is inherent in its blooming. In the second part of the text, in the dialogue between 'Reason' and 'Sorrow', 'Reason' takes sly ironic pleasure in telling 'Sorrow' that he must accept reality and draw the right moral from the vicissitudes of fate, which are man's portion in this world, as well as from his advancing age. He must even learn to appreciate the benefits of old age, since it is a spiritual purification and an atonement of sins: 'Having lost your teeth you will eat less, talk less and bite less at another man's reputation . . . And if modesty does not restrain your wantonness and stop you from indulging in forbidden kisses', writes Petrarch, 'shame will restrain you . . .' The flesh and the body are part of the personality. In them dwell pain and 'temptation, pleasure and grief.' Regarding the feet, 'Reason' says to 'Joy': 'They will be so deformed that you will not know them as your own.'

This statement expresses a certain psychological truth – the old person's alienation from his/her body. This sense of alienation was also expressed by a fifteenth-century poet from South Tyrol, Oswald von Wolkenstein, in his poem 'I See and Hear' (Ich Sich und Hör). The poet addresses his old body as though it were something outside himself.[31] It is a *persona* that has been imposed on him. Present-day writers also describe the old person's inability to identify with his/her body. The image in the mirror appears to be a stranger: 'It is no longer I.'[32] Petrarch, conforming with the concept of body-and-soul unity, having enumerated the changes which take place in the old body and the ailments to which it is prone, proceeded to describe the old man's dulled wit, weakened memory and impaired speech.[33] Unlike the authors of the scientific treatises, other writers did not always draw a distinction between the first stage of old age, when only the body is weakened, and the later stage, when mental deterioration sets in.

'Reason', 'Joy' and 'Sorrow' are represented by male figures. Both the young and the old bodies described by Petrarch are male. He did not describe the body of the old mother who is close to death; he meditated on the brevity of life and the insignificance of man, on whence he comes and whither he is going: 'How narrow the place from which you have come, like the place to which you are going . . . from your mother's womb to the bowels of the earth, the mother of all.'[34] The image of the earth as the mother to whom the dead person returns, divested of all his worldly goods, was an ancient one and can be found in other Medieval writings. But Petrarch meant the actual mother's womb. The womb was extensively mythologized in both scientific and popular writings, and Petrarch also loaded it with symbolism. The mother is associated with sexuality and with death, with the giving of life and with extinction. Preachers and moralists only rarely used the female body as a metaphor for the transience and vanity of all things worldly. And when they did use it, they did not describe it as extensively and in such detail as they described the old male body. They generally contented themselves with noting that beauty is ephemeral, frequently adding sarcastic remarks about the vain efforts of old women to disguise the loss of their beauty with sumptuous clothes, cosmetics and affectations.[36] Likewise in the genre of urban literature called *fabliaux* – rhymed tales, with or without a moral, designed to amuse – the bodies described, whether young or old, were invariably male. The male was the active persona, the user. The woman's body was the object of that use, but it was not described. In these tales repulsive or ridiculous old men were described as hunchbacked, lame, cross-eyed, herniated or hairy as beasts.[37]

THE YOUNG/OLD OPPOSITION

The young/old opposition, like the male/female one, was a prototype binary opposition. Reductive as it is, it seems to feature in all human cultures. And the body plays a central part in the representation of the opposite poles of youth and old age. The opposition which appears in Petrarch's *On the Remedies* is found in metaphorical discourses in other literary genres of the Middle Ages. In these various texts the old and the young are contrasted both as symbols and the symbolized. Here are Jungian archetypes in which the youth stands for warmth, flowering, power, love, beauty and life, and is in turn symbolized by sunrise, fire, sun and spring. The old person stands for coldness, weakness, ugliness and death, and is symbolized by darkness, winter, 'Father Time' and the 'Grim Reaper'.[38] Old men and women were symbolized as well as symbolic. At times they signified the very same phenomena but it appears that unlike the sermons and *fabliaux*, which concentrated on the old male body, in these texts it was generally the old female body which symbolized or personified winter, the vices, old age itself and death. As Michel Foucault has amply explained, the link between the symbol and the symbolized is not merely a relationship, not merely descriptive, but a creative one. It imposed a constraining definition upon the body's potentialities.

In the thirteenth-century poem, 'Aucassin et Nicolette' there is a series of oppositions: the chivalric ideal and the monastic one; class opposites, as personified by the ugly ragged peasant contrasted with the handsome and splendidly dressed knight, Aucassin (as we have seen, the bodily distinction between the social strata was blurred in the description of old men); and the young/old contrast. The two poles, youth and old age, are represented by Aucassin and his father. The old father, though already feeble but still authoritative and harsh, is the source of the young people's troubles. Whereas Aucassin is a fearless knight, his weakened father employs the weapons of the weak – deceit and manipulation. His death puts an end to the young couple's suffering and they are free to marry. The younger generation has triumphed, and the reader is expected to identify with them. The old man's opposite number in the poem is the old woman, part companion, part jailer, whose duty it is to guard Nicolette when Aucassin's father imprisons her in the tower. The opposition young/old also runs through the descriptions of heaven and hell. Aucassin states that he is willing to go to hell after his death, if only he can win his beloved Nicolette here and now. And he adds:

> Moreover, in Hell dwell the goodly clerks and handsome knights that fall in tourneys and great wars, and stout men at arms and all men noble . . . . And thither pass the sweet ladies and courteous that have two lovers or three, and their lords also thereto. There goes the gold and silver and cloth of vair, and cloth of gris and harpers.

Hell is, therefore, power, beauty, grandeur, music, youth – the pleasures and joys of this world. By contrast, in heaven there is asceticism, ugliness, weakness, deformity, desolation and old age. And the recurring adjective in the description of its denizens and their surroundings is 'old' (viel in the French original): 'these same old priests; and halt old men and maimed, who all day and night cower continually before the altars, and in old crypts; and such folk as wear old amices and old clouted frocks'[39] (The word viel appears five times in this passage.) As Peter Dronke has noted, the author reduced both heaven and hell to mere figments of the imagination, which he used to draw a humorous description of the human condition, the heaven and hell on earth.[40]

The seasons also symbolized the stages of life and the transition from youth to old age.[41] At the same time, the seasons themselves were symbolized by feminine figures, typified by the opposition young woman/old woman. This was how John Lydgate described the seasons in one version of the fifteenth-century pseudo-Aristotelian work, Secretum Secretorum: In spring the world is like a ornamented young girl dazzling the eyes of the beholders; in summer the earth is like a richly apparelled bride, loved by many; in autumn she is like a respectable matron whose youth is behind her; and in winter the world is like an old hag close to death.[42] In Guillaume de Deguileville's The Pilgrimage of Human Life (Pèlerinage de la vie humaine) young, beautiful and well-dressed women personify the virtues, such as charity, mercy, wisdom, moderation, diligence and God's grace. By contrast, gluttony, lust, sloth, hypocrisy, envy, heresy, tribulations, disease, old age and death, are personified by ugly old women. Sloth is an ugly, filthy, hairy and smelly old woman. (Harsh modern descriptions of the ageing woman's body often mention the appearance of facial hair and/or moustache, while the hair on the head is sparse. This latter detail is absent in Medieval texts.) Pride is an obese woman of monstrous dimensions. Unable to walk because of her obesity and swollen legs she rides on Flattery. In one hand she holds a stick with which to spur on Flattery, and in the other a mirror into which she gazes. The figure of Hypocrisy is unclear, but she wears a cloak of the kind worn by old women who wish to hide their ugliness and deformities. Envy crawls on her belly like a snake; she is shrivelled and dry, lacking flesh and blood. Disease leans on crutches, and Old Age has legs of lead. Yet Mercy, who leads the pilgrim to the infirmary, is a young woman who bares one breast, so that she can nourish the hungry with her milk.[43] The old woman whose milk has dried cannot personify Mary, the Holy Mother, who suckles her child – the symbol of goodness and mercy. Caroline Bynum has demonstrated the association of woman and food in the Medieval culture; the view of the woman's body as food and the metaphor of food in the depictions of the feminine religious experience. This association could not persist in the description of the old woman's body.[44]

In the first part of *The Romance of the Rose*, written in the first half of the thirteenth century by Gauillaume de Lorris, who was on the whole kinder to women than his successor Jean de Meun, old women personify the enemies of love, which are: Hate, Felony, Villainy, Covetousness, Avarice, Envy, Sorrow, Hypocrisy, and Old Age itself. This is how he described Old Age:

> Shrunken at least a foot from what her height
> Had been in youth. She scarce could feed herself
> For feebleness and years. Her beauty gone.
> Ugly had she become. Her head was white,
> As if it had been floured. 'T were no great loss
> Were she to die, for shrivelled were her limbs,
> By time reduced almost to nothingness,
> And wrinkled foul that formerly were fair;
> Her ears hung pendulous, her teeth were gone.
> Years had so lamed her that she could not walk
> Four fathoms distance without aid of crutch.

Faithful to the scientific theory that the body's decline and degeneration in advanced age must be matched by a weakening of the intellect, Gauillaume de Loris goes on:

> ... she
> Had to her infancy again returned,
> No power she had and no more force or sense
> Than yearling child, although she did appear

49

Like one who in her prime was sage and wise,
Henceforth she would be nothing but a sot.[45]

During the Middle Ages there was a tradition in the Rousillon region
of France to fashion during Lent two effigies of ugly old women and burn
them at the stake at Easter. In rural regions of Italy and France, in the
ceremony of banishing winter and death, two effigies of the oldest and
ugliest women in the village were sawn in half. The effigies and their
destruction fulfilled the same function as the masks worn in religious
rituals of various cultures, namely, to express the fear, combat it and dispel
it.[46] In Petrarch's epic-allegorical poem on the death of Laura, death is
personified by an old woman in black.[47] In Medieval art, lust (*luxuria*) was
often depicted as an old woman being punished for sexual sins, for example,
the sculpture of a woman over the gate of the monastery of Moissac, who
has two snakes hanging from her withered breasts and a toad squatting on
her genitals.[48]

Only old men wrote in the first person; or, at any rate, the writing of
men only has come down to us. Feminine narrative in the Middle Ages
was rare. Even in the poetry which was written in the first person the
body occupies a central position. Sadness is the dominant mood of
the ballad of Jean Regnier (*c.* 1392 – *c.*1468). He is an old man of high
standing, but wishes he were a young valet. He recalls his childhood and
youth, how as a boy he used to go bird-nesting and as a young man he
went hunting in the spring. Now he must forsake the much-loved hunt.
He is weak, he suffers from gout; his hand holding the cup shakes. Soup
and milk are all he can consume. His nose runs. He suffers from the
cold and huddles by the fire. There is no more lovemaking. He studies
the theory of humours and is at the mercy of the physicians. None of the
past joys will ever return.[49] The ballad is full of sadness and a touch of
bitterness, but there is nothing grotesque about it. As A. Planche has
rightly pointed out, even these first-person descriptions are more stereotypical than individual.[50] They lay emphasis on the physical disabilities which
prevent the old man from doing the things he loves, lament his misery in
a form reminiscent of Maximianus' first elegy, and contrast his present
state with that of his young days. On occasion, though, the description in
the first-person poems is no less grotesque and merciless than in the
sermons that promoted contempt for the world. In his ballad 'An Old
Man's Regret' (Regrets d'un vieillard), Eustache Deschamps wrote: 'I am
bowed, humpbacked, shaky, my hair is white, my teeth are long, weak,
sharp and yellowed. My penis has become a soft tail serving only to piss.'
And he added the stereotyped description of the old man's mental defects:
he is impatient, miserly, short-tempered, grumbling, bored and boring,
hostile to new ways, to laughter and amusements.[51]

Georges Minois has noted the scorn and cruelty which animated the descriptions of the old woman's body in the art and literature of the six-teenth century. If the descriptions of the old man's body were scarcely flattering, those of the old woman's body were more humiliating and vicious. Susan Sontag (1979) has pointed out the double standard in the treatment of old men and old women in modern Western culture. Old women are censured and judged more severely than old men. The different attitudes are especially noticeable, according to Sontag, in the hostility and revulsion that the old woman's body provokes.[52] In the Middle Ages the descriptions of old male bodies were as merciless as those of old females. The figure of the upright, hoary, wise-eyed old man was as rare in Medieval writings as that of the white-haired, kind-faced, bright-eyed old woman. In his poem 'The Praise of Old Age', the fifteenth-century Scottish poet Robert Henryson described thus the song of an old man: 'Merry was the melody, sweet the voice and clear'. The old man enumerates the evils of youth and insists that nothing on earth would make him wish to be young again, for 'the more of age, the nerer hevynnis blisse'. The poet obviously empathized and identified with the old man, but although he endowed him with a clear and pleasant voice, he did not depict him as straight-backed or shiny-eyed. The first line of the poem describes him as 'ane old man and decrepit' who raised his voice in song.[53]

In their merciless descriptions of the old body, and its opposition to the young body, the Medieval writers in Western Europe were following a long tradition, going back to Ecclesiastes (Chapter 12) and the Roman writers Horace, Juvenal and Maximianus.[54] Presumably, the physical image of the old man or woman was also influenced by reality. Medical knowl-edge was limited, hygiene primitive, and there was no such thing as false teeth. Many old people were probably as toothless as babies. (People were much preoccupied with the problem of teeth, and dealt with it in medical, moral and legal contexts.[55]) Moreover, many of the old people were poor, which made their appearance all the more wretched. We may assume that many of them did indeed look pathetic. Nevertheless, it is unlikely that external appearances and literary tradition alone gave rise to the ugly and pathetic physical stereotype. According to Claude Lévi-Strauss, the language of the Nambikwara Indians of Brazil has one word for 'young' and 'beautiful' and one word for 'old' and 'ugly'.[56] The beauty which arouses our admiration is transient (which may be part of its appeal). The Nambikwara Indians express this fact in their language. But the descrip-tions of old age we have cited are notable not merely for the absence of beauty, but for the repulsive images of wretchedness and decay. Even today, when old people are healthier and look better than in the past, the degrad-ing image of decrepitude remains,[57] and the old body repels. It continues to do so because its appearance, with its symbolic charge, awakens anxiety in young and middle-aged people. The anxiety causes repulsion, and the repulsion in turn gives rise to a grotesque and humiliating image.

YOUNG AND BEAUTIFUL: THE SACRIFICIAL VICTIM, GOD THE SON AND THE RESURRECTED BODY

We have noted that there was a tendency to view the body and its move-ments as indications of the state of the soul. The ugly body reflected a deformed soul, and conversely, the virtues of the saint and his beautiful soul were reflected in his beautiful and radiant visage.[58] But there was a different approach, too. Explicitly, at least, beauty was a chivalric, rather than religious, ideal. In the chivalric epics and in the courtly literature the young protagonists, male and female alike, were always beautiful. On the other hand, the clergy tended to repress the admiration of beauty, and described it as a source of danger and seduction. The rehabilitation of the body in the High Middle Ages was not unequivocal.[59] Asceticism was a Christian value. The ugliness of certain saints was believed to result from the severely ascetic life they led.[60] Thus Aelred of Rievaulx (1109–1167) stated that the body was merely a vessel, whether rural or urban. A fine vessel may contain spoilt food, and vice versa, an ugly vessel may contain wholesome food.[61] Vincent of Beauvais wrote that a beautiful soul may reside in a wretched and deformed body. External beauty was a source of sin, and was only rarely accompanied by modesty.[62] This was the moral of the *exempla* about young men and women who not only tamed their bodies by ascetic means but actually disfigured their own beauty in order to avoid succumbing to their own sinfulness, or to prevent others from sinning, in thought or act. There were stories about a handsome youth who disfigured his face by scarring it with a knife, a young woman who cut off her lovely hair, a nun who put out her beautiful eyes which had aroused a king's lust. The young man who disfigured his face was said to have wished to be ugly in body so that his soul should become more beautiful.[63] The sacrificial victim, willing or involuntary, was always young – from Isaac and Jephthah's daughter, through the youths and maidens who were sacrificed to the Cretan minotaur, the female martyrs during the persecution of Christians, to Joan of Arc.[64] In the same way, the person who sacrificed his or her beauty was invariably young. Theology and aesthetics could not meet in the old person. The old man's ugliness is not the outcome of sacrifice. There is no sharp dramatic transition from beauty to ugliness or devastation. The old body could symbolize the human condition and its suffering, not the heroic sacrifice.

In the arts and writings of the Middle Ages God was always portrayed as young and handsome. Only in the Renaissance did God the Father begin to figure in the arts (at a time when individual portraits of old men also made their appearance). Renaissance art depicted God the Father as a powerful and dignified-looking old man,[65] but the image of God the Son continued to predominate. In the art and writing of the High Middle Ages the divinity depicted was Christ: as a baby, a small child or a handsome

52

young man. Whether he was shown as the suffering or the victorious divinity, he was always young. Sermons referred to the beauty of Christ. Aelred of Rievaulx, who stated that external beauty was like a fine vessel which did not signify its contents, lauded in his sermons the beauty of God the Son, which amazed the angels, the sun and the moon.[66] Male and female mystics, meditating on the body of Christ, his blood, wounds and sacred heart, envisioned a handsome young deity.[67] And whether the artists depicted Jesus' genitalia to emphasize his sexuality as a symbol of his humanity, as Leo Steinberg suggested, or only to point out his humanity without any erotic connotation, as Caroline Bynum argues,[68] they invariably showed him as young. The Virgin Mary was also depicted as a young and beautiful woman, suckling her baby or playing with him – a model for earthly mothers. She was even shown as young in some of the depictions of the *pieta* – the dolorous mother holding her son after he was taken down from the cross – which became common during the fourteenth century. Although chronologically she must have been at least 50 when he was crucified, she was often portrayed as a young woman, wearing dark garments and a headcloth. Gone were the blue mantle and golden hair, which characterized her image as a young mother in the miniatures and stained-glass windows. Her face was shown as haggard, but young.[69] Old men and women could not personify God the Son or his mother.

The denizens of paradise, too, were young, at least according to popular belief (though not according to the author of 'Aucassin and Nicolette'). In a popular religious text, the sage who was asked if people would grow old in heaven replied that they would be eternally young and merry as birds.[70]

As for the bodies which would be resurrected on Judgement Day, it was generally agreed, following St Augustine of Hippo, that they would be in their early thirties,[71] (some pinning it down to 30 years and two months). Whether they died younger or older, the righteous would be resurrected in bodies of the same age as the incarnated Christ when he chose to die, in the flower and vigour of youth. This belief was shared by orthodox theologians,[72] authors of popular religious texts, and even those heretics who believed in the resurrection of the dead on Judgement Day. According to Peter the Lombard (c. 1100–60), the risen bodies of the righteous would shine like the sun, and their earthly blemishes would vanish.[73] In the fourteenth and fifteenth centuries Lollard preachers promised their adherents that after the resurrection their immortal bodies would be agile, tenuous and radiant.[74] Paintings and sculptures depicting Judgement Day – for example, on the tympanum of the cathedral of Bourges, or in Signorelli's painting in the chapel of the cathedral of Orvieto – showed what youthful and handsome bodies the righteous souls would be resurrected in. As we shall see in the next chapter, there were some who searched for means to prolong youth in this world, but religion taught that man must accept old age as part of his condition, following Original Sin and the Fall. However, it legitimized the dream of perennial youth in the promise that would be fulfilled on Judgement Day.

THE OLD BODY AS AN OPPORTUNITY AND MEANS OF ATONEMENT

Parallel with the rehabilitation of the body in the twelfth century, some religious thinkers represented the body as a prison and a source of sin. Pope Innocent III quoted from the Old and New Testaments (Psalms 142: 8; Romans 7: 24) to describe the body as a prison which breeds sins and afflictions.[75] Bernard of Morlais, who was a monk at Cluny in the first half of the twelfth century, described the body in general and the female body in particular as a source of impurity and sin.[76] Alain of Lille (1128–1203), in the chapter 'On the Contempt of Self' (De contemptu sui) of his manual for preachers, wrote: 'O Man, remember that thou wert running semen, that thou art a vessel of filth and destined to feed the maggots', and went on to describe the different kinds of worms which would crawl out of the various organs of the cadaver, symbolizing the particular sin each organ was guilty of.[77] This was a didactic text, designed to humble man's arrogance, but it also expressed a loathing for the bodily aspect of the human being.

But some religious texts expressed a different attitude, one which could be of comfort to the suffering old person. It did not conflict with the concept of the body as part of the whole man, but differed in emphasis from the texts cited above. Here the emphasis is on the body as the focus of pain. As Caroline Bynum has shown, according to this view the body was not the enemy of the spirit, but a means and an aid to atonement and for drawing nearer to God.[78] As Bernard of Clairvaux put it: the body helps the soul which loves God. It helps by being weak, by dying and resurrecting. In the first instance (i.e. its weakness), it helps by promoting repentance.[79] The old body is weak, it brings one nearer to God by its suffering and pain, and because it has become free of lust. It is no longer the seat of temptation. It signals to its owner that he or she must prepare the soul for the next world, so that it will be ready when the time comes. It is a God-given opportunity, to be used or not. The old person who clings to this world and to his or her sins, who does not strive to save his or her soul and does not acquiesce with old age and the approach of death, will not draw near to God.[80] The old person does not need to mortify the body or to pray for illness, like the young ascetics who sought illness and suffering in order to atone for their sins, or the sins of others, and through suffering to draw nearer to God.[81] Old age itself was understood to entail physical suffering and almost to correspond to illness. This view of the weakening body as a means of uplifting the soul did not

54

conflict with the theory that the body and the soul, though separate entities, were interlinked. There was no body/soul dichotomy, but they were viewed as developing in different directions. John Bromyard, the fourteenth-century author of an encyclopaedia for preachers, put it thus: 'In so far as old age reduces the youthful vigour, it increases the soul's vigour in its devotion to God; that which is lowered in one is raised in the other.'[82] But this development was not seen as assured, only as a possibility. Its achievement depended on the person and on God's grace.

Some of the writers placed a greater emphasis on the atonement of sins; others stressed the spiritual elevation. Bernardino of Siena in his public sermons denounced the 'wicked' old men who resisted their old age. He expatiated on the inconsistency of human conduct: everyone wants to reach old age, but no one wants to be old. A man desires, strives and hopes to live as long as possible, but having grown old he complains. The old man must accept his age, examine his soul and strive to save it. And with a similar sarcasm to that of Petrarch in On the Remedies (as well as imagery and phrases used by the latter), he enumerated the sins that the old man is no longer capable of committing, on account of his weakness and impaired functions. Having lost his teeth he will laugh less, speak less, bite less at another man's reputation, and lie less. His weakened sight will free him of gluttony, greed and lust. If his hearing is diminished he will listen less to trivialities and instead read the learned books, write, and meditate in silence on the works of creation, in heaven, on earth and all that is in them.[83]

Dante emphasized the spiritual elevation. He likened man in the final stage of his life to a ship which gradually lowers its sails as it approaches the harbour. Calmly and gently, without bitterness, the soul which has grown noble advances towards its final fruition. Like other thinkers and scientific writers, Dante compared the old man's death to the ripe apple's fall from the tree. The scientific writers stressed the naturalness and painlessness of the event; Dante depicted it as the end of the road, resignation and a great serenity.[84]

Some who did not enumerate the sins which the old person could no longer commit, and did not ignore the body as Dante did, concentrated on the body's enfeeblement, due to both illness and old age, as a means of purifying and elevating the soul. Bernard of Clairvaux wrote in his manual for nuns, Liber de modo bene vivendi, that a healthy body could cause excessive attachment to the world, but the illness which attacks the body can purify the soul. The illness which sanctifies the soul is a good thing. It is not a punishment for sins, but it must be accepted without demur. In this world God sometimes shows mercy to the sinners and not to the virtuous, but it will not be so in the next world. Moreover, God chastises those he loves (II Corinthians 12: 9–10). Bernard wrote in this spirit to his friend Guerin, an abbot who had undertaken an extensive reform in his monastery at a very advanced age: the vigorous and powerful body always houses a feeble, compromising soul. By contrast, the infirm body (such as that of his aged friend) is animated by a stronger and more decisive spirit.[85] The attitude which valued bodily afflictions could view disease as a gift of God, and indeed some sought to become ill. (This contrasted with another prevalent attitude, which viewed disease as a punishment for sins and was hence an impure condition.) Old age, the body's decline and concommitant afflictions, were viewed as an inescapable process, not only in medical texts but also in didactic and moralistic ones. However, in some religious writings they are also described as a gift of God. On one level the gift was long life itself, seeing that so many died an untimely death, in childhood or youth; on another level, it was an opportunity granted to man, thanks to his weakened body and extinct desires, to draw nearer to God.

Those who saw the ageing body as an opportunity and a means of attaining a spiritual elevation and atonement for sins, and who described body and soul as developing in different directions, ignored the theory of humours. For according to the theory of humours, the physical decline (which was caused by the loss of natural heat and radical moisture) was accompanied by the decline of the intellectual faculties and even the development of negative qualities, such as irritability and melancholy. Vincent of Beauvais, whose writings generally included different and even conflicting attitudes, mentioned the two opinions of the ageing body's enfeeblement, and in this case attempted to reconcile them. He wrote about the virtues of old age, the growth of wisdom and the diminution of desires. He quoted St Jerome's statement that a Christian has no need of physical strength. At the same time, he proposed a healthy regimen for old people, and even suggested methods for preventing hair loss and greying. In the next paragraph he listed the symptoms of mental decline in old age: lack of energy, forgetfulness, gullibility and foolishness. Aware of the contradiction, he offered a solution based on the differences between people, arising from their disparate personalities. Just as not all young men are given to lusts and promiscuity, so too the foolishness known as senile dementia (*stultia que deliratio dicitur senium*) does not afflict all old men.[87] Unlike Vincent of Beauvais, who wrote an encyclopedia of natural philosophy and had to refer to physiology and the theory of humours, the authors of moral literature were not obliged to do so, at any rate in this context. They rejected determinism and stressed man's free will and choice, together with the grace of God.

Evangelical ministers in the nineteenth-century United States assured their congregations that if they followed the natural rules of health and morality they would enjoy a long life, a healthy old age and a natural death.[88] The Medieval authors of medical texts also upheld a medical theory which was inseparable from morality. The healthy body of orderly movements was also a metaphor for the polity, all of whose members functioned as they should. Roger Bacon attributed premature ageing *inter alia* to a failure to observe the moral laws.[89] But, needless to say, the view which held that the weakening of the ageing body was a value and a means of drawing nearer to God, did not link the spiritual elevation with the state of the body. Even the saints were not spared suffering in their old age. Bernardino of Siena, who had a realistic view of the old person, distinguished in his manuals between 'virtuous' and 'wicked' old men. After enumerating the mental failings of old men – impatience, melancholy, foolishness, mental blindness and distortion – he went on to say that these mainly affected the 'wicked' old men. However, he did not promise the virtuous old men, whose hearts turned to God and who willingly accepted their old age and atoned for their sins, that they would be rewarded with freedom from bodily suffering and disease. In one place in his sermon he compared the hoary head to white lilies or to the snowy stork, in contrast to the young man's black hair, which he compared to coal or a raven's wing. And he asked: Whose reason and judgement are so perverted, that he would not rather have the former than the latter, if he must change? But then he went on to say that white hair was a simile for the wisdom of age, and when interpreted literally (*ad litteram*), it stands for the old man's weakness, due to his cooling humours and the excess fluids draining from his body, whose colour is white.[90] The physiological processes in the body of the wise and virtuous old man were the same as those in the body of the foolish and wicked old man.

The authors of the lives of the saints (*Vitae*) described their infirmity and suffering in old age, and their strong spirit. One of the authors of the life of St Bernard of Clairvaux, who was close to him in his final days, Geoffrey of Clairvaux, wrote: 'His body which lay on the bed suffered great agonies, but his soul was free and strong'. Despite his pain he continued to contemplate and pray, to dictate and instruct his fellow monks, and he even consoled them.[91] Of Gilbert of Sempringham it was said that he derived fresh strength from his weakness, and in return for the loss of bodily light, was granted the enlightenment he deserved by the greater blessing of the spirit. Though he was infirm, sick and blind, he lost none of his spiritual energy.[92] These depictions of the weakening and suffering body coupled with spiritual elevation ignored the fact that a tormented body is an obstacle. It constrains and distracts, it is like an enemy who cannot be thrown off. As Maximianus wrote in his first elegy: 'I am conquered by an infirm body'.[93] The people of the period were, of course, aware of this fact. What Bernard of Clairvaux wrote in his manual for nuns on the subject of illness was meant to comfort and give meaning to the suffering it caused. But in practical advice to monks it was also said that while the body must not be pampered, neither should it be subjected to extreme asceticism that could cause illness, which is an obstacle to the spiritual exercises.[94] However, as a rule, when Church thinkers discussed the body as the adversary of the soul, they had in mind the lustful young body, not the infirm old one.[95] Geoffrey of Clairvaux described the physical agony of St Bernard, but did not depict it as something relentless and oppressive. Such a description appeared only in a letter Bernard himself wrote to his friend Arnald of Bonnevaux. He wrote about his abdominal pains; about his difficulties in bringing food and drink to his mouth and consuming the minimum amount he needed, especially of solid food. He described his sleepless nights on account of his pains, and the swelling of his legs. Devoting so much space to the description of bodily afflictions in a letter to a friend was in itself an admission that the body does not let up. He went on to say: 'Nothing pleases me any more, now that bitterness has conquered all'.[96] Geoffrey of Clairvaux included this letter in his *Vita*, but he did not repeat that phrase in his own description of Bernard's final days. It did not suit the hagiographical genre. Although in the twelfth century the *Vitae* became gradually more individualized than those of earlier saints, and included some non-iconographical details, nevertheless, this statement conflicted too much with the *topos* of the old age and last days of a saint.

This view of the body's ageing as an opportunity for spiritual elevation, coupled with the expectation of wisdom, serenity and resignation in old age, though without reference to bodily suffering, persisted for a long time in Western civilization and became secularized. The American author Lydia Sigourney (1791–1865) wrote: 'Among the highest accomplishments of age are its dispositions. It should daily cultivate the spirit to admire what is beautiful. To love what is good ... As the sensual pleasures lose their hold, the character should become more sublimated'.[97] According to Erik Erikson, 'only in old age can true wisdom develop in those who are thus gifted'. And in the final stage of the Ego's development, according to his scheme, the old person who has successfully completed the stages of life is expected to receive his approaching death with equanimity.[98] Diametrically opposed to the view that expects the old person to attain special wisdom, spirituality and renunciation, are such thinkers as Simone de Beauvoir and Jean Améry. The rejection of the view of old age as a time of serene meditation, and of the old people's supposed renunciation, runs throughout de Beauvoir's book on old age, (together with strong criticism of the disregard for the economic distress of most old people).[99] And Jean Améry wrote in the introduction to his book: 'All the advice given the ageing person to induce him to accept his decline, and where possible derive from it a variety of values – noble resignation, aged sagacity, a belated peace – struck me as a despicable deception, which I have felt compelled to protest against in every line.'[100]

As I have tried to demonstrate, it is not only in medical discourse that the body takes central place but almost in all other discourses about old age as well. The cruel description, primarily of the male body, serves as a metaphor for the transience and vanity of all worldly things while the female old body is used to personify all ugliness, evil and sin. It is the young body that symbolizes the beautiful, good and pure. However, there was also the conception that the old weak body was conducive to increased wisdom, inner peace and spiritual growth. Moreover, it was presented as an aid to the expiation of sin and to drawing closer to God. Despite the fact that the debilitating power of an ailing body was ignored, this conception gave meaning and offered consolation to an inevitable decline. Secularization deprived Western man of this consolation. Améry had no need to list it amongst the expectations and consolations he rejected.

3

TRANSCENDING AGE, TRANSCENDING THE BODY

THE POSTPONEMENT OF OLD AGE

Bernardino of Siena in his sermon to the aged said: 'If the ripe apple could reason and speak, it would offer thanks for having achieved the purpose of its creation,'[1] – that is to say, for having reached ripeness and fallen from the tree. So, too, must the old person accept his old age and confront his imminent death. Writers never tired of pointing out the naturalness and justice of the death of old people (as opposed to the dying of the young) in terms of the laws of nature, as well as in theological, moral and social contexts. This being a natural death, the 'art of dying' (*ars moriendi*), which evolved from the second half of the fourteenth century, scarcely referred to the aged. In the Dance of Death, both in the plastic arts and in writing, where Death is shown dragging away members of all the social strata, all the professions, both sexes and different ages, old people were hardly ever included. This, despite the emphatic use of oppositions in these depictions: man/woman; nobleman/peasant; layman/bishop and monk. The age contrasts were confined to child/young man, or young man/middle-aged man, where the latter was usually a great lord, one of the mighty of the land at the peak of his power.[2] Dragging an old man to his death and tomb would not have illustrated the power of Death, which could strike man at any stage of his life and before whom all were equal.

Likewise, the various miracle cures attributed to the saints only rarely included a miraculous cure of an old person.[3] Gerald of Wales expressed a truism often repeated today by the offspring of very old people. He wrote that a long senility (*diuturna nimis delira senectutis*) obliterated a person's entire past, the evil acts as well as the achievements. Proceeding from the physiological-psychological to the religious, he went on to say that a long life was desirable only to evil men and sinners, who wished to put off paying for their wicked deeds, and postpone the punishment awaiting them in hell (though the longer their sinful lives, the worse their punishment hereafter). For the virtuous, a short life was to be desired, the sooner to reach eternal joy in heaven.[4]

60

But the usual rhetoric of the didactic literature called on the old person to be ready to die, to prepare to die, not to fear death nor yet to wish for it.[5] While the Stoic philosophers accepted, and even praised, the suicide of a sick and suffering old man, Christian culture utterly forbade all suicide. Only Thomas More, in his *Utopia*, dared to voice the idea that in certain circumstances a self-inflicted death was permissible and even desirable. As he described it, a man who contracted an incurable and agonizing illness should be visited by a priest, accompanied by representatives of the public authority, who would suggest to him to commit suicide. The suggestion having come from a priest, who interprets the will of God, the man would be sure that it would be an act of piety. But if the patient should refuse to commit suicide by starvation, or by means of a painless potion, he should continue to be nursed as devotedly as before.[6]

Needless to say, people found it difficult to live up to the religious demand to resign themselves calmly to their old age and approaching death. Some expressed in writing their desire to put off as long as possible the rapid onset of old age and to extend their life span, and proposed ways of achieving this. They were not satisfied by the promise of eternal youth following the resurrection of the bodies on Judgement Day. As we have seen, the authors of the health manuals set themselves a modest enough purpose: to avoid as much as possible the body's deterioration and premature death. The proponents of extended youth and longevity, such as Roger Bacon and Arnold of Villanova, also favoured a good health regimen but, in order to extend the youthful state and life itself or actually to reverse the ageing which had already taken place, they proposed various means which were not included in the ordinary health regimen. According to Roger Bacon, in his day the first signs of ageing appeared at age 45 to 50, when a man was supposed to be in his prime. However, by means of the particular methods which Bacon proposed, a man would preserve all his powers until the age of 100, and only then would the first signs of ageing appear.[7] While the reference was to the ageing of mind and body, since both Arnold and Bacon thought of man as a psychosomatic entity, much emphasis was laid on the body, which would remain youthful-looking. Arnold even promised that his methods could restore lost sexual potency. (It appears that such promises were a good source of income also for the various charlatans who engaged in popular medicine. But on occasion they were sued by their disappointed patients for obtaining money with false claims.)[8]

Bacon based his ideas for extended youth and longevity on past ages, on the long lives of antediluvian men. He attributed the shortened lifespan not to divine intervention, but to air pollution, which did not exist in antiquity but was caused in his time by the increased population. Moreover, the human race was debilitated by its foolishness and immorality. Men in their foolishness did not observe the proper health regimen, and in their sinfulness they did not obey the moral laws. They grew feebler, and begot offspring who aged and died prematurely. Generation followed generation, and thus a weakened constitution was passed from parents to children and human life expectancy grew shorter 'as is the case in these days'.[9] To postpone old age and achieve longevity, said Bacon, it was necessary to observe the usual health regimen from birth on. At a certain stage (he did not specify exactly when), other methods had to be adopted. These could be learned from the scholarly magic and from the ancient tradition of occult wisdom, found principally in the astrological and alchemical writings of the Chaldees, through the Greeks, culminating in the Arabs. This occult tradition had been forgotten or deliberately hidden.[10] At the same time, one could learn from the ways of the animals, which use different herbs, stones and metals to strengthen their bodies, restore their youth and prolong their lives. The methods proposed by Bacon and Arnold[11] ranged from drinking gold solution as an elixir, to breathing the exhalations of healthy young girls. This last brings us back to the opposition old age/ youth. In this case, as Benoit-Lapierre put it, a balance was struck between the opposing poles of old age and youth but based on a parasitical or vampiric connection,[12] to the benefit only of the men who refused to grow old. As in other kinds of discourse, so too in developing the theory of postponing old age the authors thought only of men.

The hope of a connection such as the one Bacon proposed, though in a subtler form, may be found much earlier, in a poem by William of Aquitaine (1071–1127), known as the first troubadour. His poem 'Full of Joy, I Fall in Love' (*Mout jauzens me prenc en amor*) says:

> To refresh my heart in her,
> Renew my flesh in her,
> And so never grow old.[13]

The beloved is a means of preserving youth.

The idea of postponing old age and achieving longevity persisted in Western civilization through subsequent centuries, until our own time. (Today it rests on the belief that this could be achieved by genetic engineering.) From the time of Roger Bacon, medicine and alchemy remained linked in Western scientific tradition for hundreds of years. In the seventeenth century, the English Royal Society regarded the prolongation of youth and life as a major scientific endeavour. R. Browne, a member of the learned academy of medicine, translated Bacon's work *De retardatione accidentium senectutis* into English. In his introduction he wrote that only the wickedness and ignorance of his time prevented Bacon from carrying out his greatest experiment, the true extension of man's life expectancy.[14]

The Medieval supporters of the theory of postponing old age and prolonging life, such as Arnold and Bacon, did not promise eternal life or eternal youth. They sought to reach the impassable boundary, the utmost extension of life and postponement of death. Man forfeited immortality and eternal youth by his original sin. Man is fated to grow old because he is doomed to die. Thomas Aquinas wrote that our first ancestors went on living for many years after God sentenced them; but, he added, quoting Augustine of Hippo, 'They began to die when they received the sentence of declining into old age.'[15] In the part of the ceiling of the Sistine Chapel which depicts Adam and Eve eating the fruit of the Tree of Knowledge and being expelled from Eden, Michelangelo faithfully reflected the Christian conception of the history of humanity. Before the expulsion, Adam and Eve look young, whereas afterwards Eve is an old woman and Adam's face is haggard and he looks older than before.

TRANSCENDING ONE'S AGE

The idea of transcending one's age was familiar to the Epicureans, the Stoics and the early Christians. The ideal rested on the assumption that the human being, as a reasoning creature, can overcome life's course (*cursus aetatis*) and the laws of nature and time, and manifest the ideal qualities of all the natural ages[16] at every stage of his life. The reference was to the manifestation of the spiritual qualities of every age. As Augustine of Hippo wrote: 'In your body you cannot be both young and old. In your soul, however, you can: young through alacrity, old through gravity.'[17] But unlike Augustine, who believed in combining youth and old age in spirit, the idea of the Medieval thinkers was for the youth, or even the child, to transcend his natural age by developing the qualities of old age. In the lives of the saints, the *topos* of the 'boy old man' (*puer-senex*) occurred repeatedly. The boy/old man was grave, sagacious and pious from an early age. He personifies the supposed good qualities of old age: sagacity, chastity and piety. He resembles Samuel, Daniel and Jesus in their childhoods.[18] Thomas Aquinas wrote: 'A man may attain spiritual maturity in his childhood, because old age is not honoured for the passage of time, nor is it measured by the number of years.'[19] Extreme examples of aged characteristics in childhood were attributed only to saints-to-be.

However, the possibility of such characteristics appearing in youth was not confined to saints, and could also be cited in political contexts. Bernard of Clairvaux protested against the appointment of young immature candidates to high office in the Church, but he added that it had been known for young men, by the grace of God, to outdo old men in wisdom, understanding and moral conduct. In support, he quotes the verses from the Book of Wisdom (4: 8–9), that others also applied in this context: 'For venerable old age is not that of long time, nor counted by the number of years; but the understanding of man is grey hairs, and a spotless life is old age.'[20] Grey hair here is a circumlocution for the wisdom of old age, which not every old man possesses. Bernard of Clairvaux discussed the possibility that the positive qualities of old age might be found in young people, but he considered it to be a rarity. His contemporary, John of Salisbury, was less reserved when he discussed the choice of royal counsellors. 'Where such gravity of character is observed to exist, the question of bodily or physical age is not material.'[21] A blunter expression of this view is found in the sixth-century rule of Benedict of Nursia. Article 63 of the rule stated that the position of the brothers in the monastery should depend on the time they entered it, or on their virtue, or upon the abbot's appointment. Under no circumstances was the brothers' order and position to depend on their age since Samuel and Daniel, when still children, judged their elders.[22]

In the religious literature of the Middle Ages, youth's positive qualities did not figure in the ideal of transcendence. Augustine's ideal of combining youthful alacrity and aged gravity had disappeared. There was no equalization of spiritual ages, because the positive qualities of youth were ignored and never cited in opposition to the negative qualities of old men. By the grace of God, a man might transcend his age upwards. We have seen that the authors of scientific works compared the old, especially the very old man, to a child. In doing so they stressed the weakened intellectual faculties, the loss of discrimination and bodily control. Sometimes, though very rarely, the old man was described as knowing an important truth which is hidden from others. In this, too, the old man resembled the child, who was also sometimes believed to possess this faculty. This was the special privilege of the weak and marginalized, whose world was far removed from the centre. Some of the saints were described as being fond of the company of children, whose purity and innocence matched their own. Similarly, some saints were described by the authors of their lives as great favourites with the children, who felt naturally drawn to them.[23] But the classic form of the transcendence of age in the religious literature was for the person to rise above it, upwards. In so far as younger qualities were attributed to the ideal saintly Christian, they were childish qualities, not those of young men. All the texts we have cited thus far show that not all grey heads were believed to possess wisdom, spiritual maturity and piety. Moreover, both the popular and the learned literature referred to the *topos* of the 'hundred-years old boy' (*puer centum annorum*), which Petrarch, as we have seen, employed in the imaginary dialogue with Augustine.[24] The most notable folly of the 'hundred-years old boy' was his desire to continue to have love affairs, which was neither natural nor seemly at his age.

In the religious literature there was no spiritual equalization of the ages, and the only ideal it presented was of young persons who possessed the qualities of old age. But a different attitude existed in the didactic literature and in the myths which expressed universal-human, political and military ideals.

Aegidius Romanus (1247–1316) was a philosopher and theologian, who rose from an Augustinian hermit to become the Bishop of Bourges. Among other things he wrote a manual for the education of princes, which he dedicated to his former pupil and later king of France, Philip IV, 'the Fair'. In this work Aegidius deviated from the classic transcendence ideal in religious literature. He depicted an ideal which combined and balanced the archetypes of the young and the old; or, in his words, the development of the ideal qualities of the different ages at every stage of life. Following Aristotle, Aegidius enumerated the positive and negative qualities of young and old people, and the negative qualities of old men outnumbered their good ones. Among them he listed cowardice, stinginess, suspiciousness, shamelessness (because they valued utility above honour) and despondency. Thereafter, he agreed with Aristotle's conclusion, which was also adopted by other Medieval thinkers, that the ideal age for ruling and holding public office was middle age (*in statu*). At this stage the negative qualities of youth will have disappeared – such as a too-hot temperament, impulsiveness and excessive trust in any and every one – and the negative qualities of old age have not yet emerged. But in Aegidius' lifetime the French crown passed in the Capetian dynasty by inheritance, so that a young man or – at least in theory – an old man, might succeed to the throne. Aegidius' solution was to overcome age both upwards and downwards: 'Young and old alike can act in opposition to their [age's] inclination.' Those who were destined to rule had to shed altogether the old man's cowardice, despondency, shamelessness and stinginess, and find the golden mean between the impulsiveness, gullibility and passion of youth, and the timidity, vacillation and suspiciousness of the old. All the more, since a man's qualities at each stage of life were determined not only by his age, but also by fate (*fortuna*). In the category of *fortuna* Aegidius included a man's origin and the social estate into which he was born.[25] He did not argue that the higher qualities were confined to the nobility but, as we know, it was the dominant view that a person born into the nobility and suitably educated would evince noble qualities. In other words, given the right genes, the ruler could transcend his age and develop the appropriate qualities of the various ages.

An equalization of the ages, with a dramatic combination of the ideal qualities of youth and age as a vivid illustration of the ideal of transcending nature and time, appears in a poem by Adalbéron de Laon, 'A Poem for King Robert', composed *c.* 1020. Various antitheses occur throughout the poem: the holy and the profane, purity and impurity, a churchman and a layman, a nobleman and a serf, youth and old age. But the king combines in his person both youth and old age. He has wisdom and authority (*sapientia, potestas*). As an aged man of reason and understanding he knows the true Christian laws and social order. But his image is a youthful one (*imago iuventutis*), in form as well as in spiritual and body powers (*forma, virtus corporis, virtus animae*). His youthful image enables him to establish the correct relationships with the three orders of society, and even find favour with the masses (*vulgus*).[26] This contrasted with the fiction which grew in a later period, that the king was a single *persona* with two bodies – the natural one which was subject to the laws of nature and time, to the failings of childhood and old age, to accident and illness, and the political body, invisible to the eye, which was free of all the disabilities and imperishable.[27] In Adalbéron's theological-political monism, the king had a single body. It was not sacred, but it was capable, like the soul which inhabited it, of transcending the laws of nature and time.

Heroes overcoming their age both upwards and downwards also appeared in the heroic epics. The eponymous hero of *La chanson de Guillaume* personified the qualities of a young man in his physical might and his courage. He is a mythical figure. He is 350 years old, and riding his horse he fights like a lion against the Saracens. Beside him rides his nephew, a beardless 15-year-old. The boy arouses his uncle's admiration by his sagacity, like that of a mature man: 'Your body is a boy's body, but your wisdom is that of a man.' Despite his small stature, which makes it difficult for him to mount his horse, 'for Gui is small and the horse is big', he displays the fighting ability of a 30-year-old.[28]

In the lives of the saints, parallel with the *topos* of the 'boy/old man', there was also the 'old woman/girl' (*puella senex*). This was how the author of the life of Catherine of Siena described her at the age of six: 'From that moment on the little girl began to grow old. There was a marvellous maturity in her virtues and conduct. Her actions were not of a child or a young woman, but altogether marked with the dignity of old age.'[29] But the religious literature, which lauded spiritual transcendence over age and depicted it as an aspiration which, by the grace of God, could be attained by young men and not only by future saints, did not refer to young women. Likewise, in the heroic epics and the representations of the ideal king, where age was transcended upwards and downwards, both physically and mentally, there was no room for women.

Charlemagne was an historical figure, but by the time *La chanson de Roland* was composed in the twelfth century, he had already become mythical. In the epic poem he is 200 years old. Nevertheless, in contrast to the ahistorical figure in the heroic epic, he was not described as overcoming entirely the drawbacks of old age. He is still the leader of the knights and dispenser of justice. The Saracen king wonders and asks: Will old Charlemagne ever grow weary of fighting? But he is unable to crush the plot of Ganelon, despite being worried and conscious of the danger, nor can he avenge Roland's death until a knight is found who is willing to fight Ganelon. His weakness cannot be explained entirely by the limited power of the feudal monarch at the time of the poem's composition. He is an old man. His hair is white, his beard white and long, and he pulls on it compulsively. He is weary and the tears often flow on his old cheeks.[30] In modern literature, too, old men are sometimes described as weeping for no obvious reason, or at least as having moist eyes. Ernesto Sabato described thus the old men sitting in the public gardens: 'the tearful gleam that the eyes of oldsters have; we will never know if it is due to purely physiological causes, or if in some way it is the consequence of memory, nostalgia, a feeling of frustration, or the idea of death.'[31]

On the mental level, we still consider the integration of the young and old archetypes, if in different ways at different stages of life, as indicating a 'good' development of the personality. However, in contrast to the Medieval religious ideal of transcending age upwards, today the stress is on the integration of youthfulness in old age. The refusal to be reconciled to being middle aged, and the rejection of old age, are regarded as indicating impaired psychological development but what is really deplored is the 'old child', the 'elderly youth', the 'old middle aged' or 'old old person' – namely, those who aged before time, or those old people whose personalities have retained nothing of youth. When developmental psychologists describe the different tasks of the different stages of life, they refer to the need to strike a balance between the poles of youth and old age primarily to old people. The old are expected not to lose touch with the vitality of their youth, to preserve their youth in a manner which is appropriate to their age, and at the same time to accept the fact of their marginalization, both personally and as members of a generation whose time has come to step aside.[32]

THE EVER-RENEWED SOUL

One of the few female saints depicted in Medieval monumental art as an old woman was Elizabeth, who bore John the Baptist in her old age (Luke 1). Her features were sharp and her face was wrinkled. The artist emphasized her agedness and the miracle of her pregnancy. Her old body did not symbolize death but renewal, for she was about to give birth.[33] In the writings I have cited so far, the authors moved from psychosomatic determinism, that is the representation of the ageing body and the declining spirit as an unavoidable dual process, through the description of the ageing body as a means of spiritual elevation and drawing nearer to God, to the possibility of transcending the age. Or, in other words, to the possibility of integrating the archetypes of the old and the young at different stages of life, with the religious literature idealizing the 'old youngster'. Alongside all these was the idea of the ever-renewed soul. A divinely wrought miracle made it possible for Elizabeth's ageing body to conceive, yet it symbolized the gift of the soul's possible perpetual self-renewal. And the best and most beautiful soul, in the eyes of God and men, was the soul which remained young by perpetual self-renewal.

This idea was sometimes presented in a way similar to that of the writers who, regarding the body's ageing as a value and a means of expiation of sin and drawing closer to God, depicted the body and the soul as developing in different directions. Augustine described the 'exterior man' declining, while the 'interior man is from day to day renewed'.[34] In the twelfth century Aelred of Rievaulx too, described the soul as entirely free from the laws of nature and time, in contrast to the body which was subject to them. How marvellous is the soul, than which only God is more beautiful, wrote Aelred. The beauty of the soul is not corrupted, damaged or dimmed, by poverty, disease or old age, and death itself cannot destroy it.[35] In the sermon of Meister Eckhart (c. 1260–1327) which was devoted entirely to the soul's renewal, the ageing of the body is a given, though it is not described or directly referred to. This was his sermon on the verse in Paul's Epistle to the Romans (6: 4): 'Therefore we are buried with him by baptism into death: that like as Christ was raised up from the dead by the glory of the Father, even so we also should walk in newness of life.' God who created being from nothingness, who is ever present and ever active, is himself new. Life and renewal are his domain. All that is new comes from God and there is no other source of renewal. 'Therefore draw nearer to God, turn to God, return to God,' wrote Eckhart. All who draw nearer to God will be renewed and cleansed, will become virtuous and holy, as written in Psalms 103: 5: 'so that thy youth is renewed like the eagle's'. By living a life of grace a man is perpetually renewed, and the renewal is life. But those who move away from God will grow old (veterascunt), will sin and become lost: 'For the wages of sin is death, but the gift of God is eternal life, through Jesus Christ our Lord' (Romans 6: 23). The soul, which was created in the image of God, was created young. It might grow weary and worn in the life of the body, but it is capable of renewal and purification. Only the material and visible ages. Renewal is not a single act, but a repeated one. A man who draws upon his inner resources, detaches himself from the world and concentrates on the One, will by God's grace be renewed.[36]

John Bromyard states in one place in his work *Summa praedicantium* that old age, while diminishing the strength of the body, increases the soul's devotion to God. That which is depressed in the one is raised in the other. But he was not consistent in his statements. Elsewhere in the same work he wrote that the young are handsome, stronger and lighter than the old. The service of the young was beautiful and noble in God's eyes, because their souls are beautiful. The young offer the finest flour to God, while the old offer him the chaff. Even the penitent old men can only bring to God the dregs that are left in the cup.[37] Body and soul are one.

Meister Eckhart was consistent. The soul is free of the corporeal bonds, of the laws of nature and time. It can be renewed again and again. Whereas the old soul is a metonym of removal from God, of sin and loss. In this sermon Eckhart quotes repeatedly from the Psalms, as well as from St Augustine. It was, perhaps, no accident that he did not quote the verse of Psalm 92: 14, which says of the righteous that 'they shall be fat and flourishing', because it also referred to the body. Although the exegesis to the Vulgate (*Glossa ordinaria*) explained that its promise referred to the End of Days, nevertheless Eckhart chose not to quote it.[38]

The idea of renewal also underwent secularization and persisted for a long time in Western culture. Goethe believed that spiritual renewal was possible only to the geniuses, to those who possessed especially strong entelechy (entelechy: the complete realization of potentiality into actuality):

> As with all men of natural genius, then it will, with its animating penetration of the body, not only strengthen and ennoble the organiz-ation, but also endeavour with its spiritual superiority to confer the privilege of perpetual youth. Thence it comes that in men of superior endowments, even during their old age, we constantly perceive fresh epochs of singular productiveness; they seem constantly to grow young again for a time, and that is what I call repeated puberty.

But Goethe also expressed an awareness of the drawbacks of old age; the incapacitated and sick old body becomes the enemy of the spirit: 'Still, youth is youth; and however powerful an entelechy proves, it will never become quite master of the corporeal; and it makes a wonderful difference whether it finds in the body an ally or an adversary.'[39] Meister Eckhart referred neither to the young body nor to the old. But is it possible to discuss concepts such as 'young soul' and 'old soul' without some figurative association of the young and old body?

When we draw together the various discourses about body and age transcendence, four main ideals emerge: the ideal of prolongation of youth; the ideal of transcending one's age upwards; the ideal of equalization of ages, that is, the development at every age of the ideal qualities of all the natural ages; and the ideal of the ever-youthful soul. The first ideal negates old age completely, and expresses no sense of generational continuity – acceptance of the need to make room for the young – which might ease the pain of ageing and the approach of death. The second ideal promotes the positive qualities of old age, but also makes it clear that not all the elderly possess them. The ideal of the equalization of ages sometimes includes the negative traits of old age. The ideal of the ever-youthful soul offered the purest consolation. And it alone related not only to men but also women.

4

WHO AND WHAT IS AN OLD MAN, AND HOW HE SHOULD CONDUCT HIMSELF

The previous chapters should have provided the reader with a partial picture of the image of the old person, and what was expected of him. The first part of this chapter will try to complete the picture and to put it in its social rather than symbolic-religious context (though the two cannot be separated). The second half of the chapter will deal with the roles which were assigned to the aged as a group and as a category.

We have seen that the image of the old person was not unequivocal. The old man was believed to possess wisdom, an accumulated experience of life, cooler passions (as already noted by Plato and Aristotle), serenity and, though not as often as a child, the ability to see the unseen. At the same time, the old person was held to have feebler mental faculties and to tend to irascibility, melancholy, miserliness (this was mentioned very often), a complaining and grumbling disposition, cowardice, suspiciousness, despondency, shamelessness and a rejection of all things new (which nowadays is explained as the old person's lessened flexibility). Aegidius Romanus, who listed all these negative qualities, also described the old as merciful, free of avarice, less inclined to judge in doubtful matters, or to react impulsively and over-confidently. But even these qualities, which he defines as positive, are not unequivocally so. The mercy of the old, wrote Aegidius, arose from a different source to that of young people's mercy. Young people are merciful because they are sociable and friendly, and think that everyone is as kindly as are they, who have not had time to do wrong. Old people are merciful because, being weak and helpless, they want everyone to show mercy to all who are weak and helpless. Their reactions are cautious, because they are no longer sure of anything, since life has humbled them and made them wretched. (A gerontologist would describe this as a loss of self-esteem.) They are less avaricious, because all their desires and passions have subsided with the cooling of their bodies, so that they no longer crave what they do not possess. But they are stingy and guard jealously what they do possess.[1]

Other authors ascribed to the old both stinginess and avarice. According to Thomas of Cantimpré, while the other passions, such as the lust for power and honour, carnal desire and gluttony, decline in old age, avarice and stinginess grow worse. But some writers gave pragmatic reasons for the stinginess of old people. Unable to go on earning their livelihood, they are afraid that they might become destitute in their final days.[2] A modern psychological explanation is that the possession of property ensures the old man's identity. Since he no longer plays a part in society, he is no longer known by his office and function. He therefore needs possessions as a source of individual identity, a source of power and a refuge from anxiety.[3] Possession of property serves to expand the ego in the world, when one's personal being is diminishing in time and space. But then the fear of losing property gives rise to anxiety and suspicion.

Most Medieval authors who sought to explain the old people's miserliness contented themselves with the pragmatic reasons. Aegidius Romanus, however, explained it as resulting from their life's experience, by the fact that they no longer live in hope for the future, but only in memory of the past. Old people do indeed live more in memory of the past than in the present and in thoughts about their short future. But his linking this fact with the emergence of miserliness devalued the inner life of the old person and its significance. He also stated that because old people's bodies lacked vitality and moisture, they feared that they might lack everything.

We saw in the foregoing chapters that, together with the positive and negative qualities that were attributed to the ageing process, old age itself was often depicted as a source of suffering and misery, not only in a symbolic context, but also in the physical and social-psychological contexts. Philip of Novare wrote that there was no need to ask an old man, 'Are you suffering?' Old age always means suffering and afflictions. The older a man gets, the greater his pain and suffering. Therefore, whoever reached the age of 80 had better ask for death.[4] According to one fourteenth-century author who divided the life cycle into 12 stages corresponding to the months of the year, at the stage between 60 and 66 (which corresponded to the month of November) a man already knew that his end was near, and whether he was rich or poor, his relatives were waiting for the legacy. At the final stage, corresponding to the month of December, ending at age 72, he was as good as frozen and had no pleasures left.[5] And Bartholomaeus Anglicus described the feeble old man, coughing and spitting, as a general burden, judged and scorned by all.[6]

In a totally deterministic view there is no room for expectations of appropriate behaviour. It permits placing the aged in the social-political system, but it leaves no room for instruction concerning their proper conduct and the state of mind that they ought to cultivate. The deterministic attitude characterized the authors of scientific writings who adhered to the theory that the physiological changes were unavoidably linked to mental ones. They concentrated on the decline of the mental faculties and to a lesser extent on the old man's increasing irritability and melancholy.

But as a rule, these developments were attributed only to extreme old age (termed *senium* by most authors). In the previous, elderly stage the body was already weaker and, as we shall see, the man was expected to retire from social and political roles, but as yet there was no mental deterioration. This was the stage of old age to which was attributed wisdom and a life's experience.[7] In this way it was possible to reconcile the conflicting images of the old man, and to stipulate certain norms of conduct, chiefly for the first stage. Some writers, while adopting the scientific theory, did not distinguish between the stages of old age and extreme old age, but emphasized the individual differences between people, arising from their diverse personalities and temperaments (with or without references to the social stratum into which they were born), which enabled them to overcome the tendencies of their age.[8] They also noted the effect of the person's way of life in the earlier stages, before he was old. This determined to a large extent the manner of his ageing, and even helped to form his character.

In emphasizing the individual differences between old people these writers were following Cicero's *De senectute*, one of whose central arguments is that the quality of a man's old age is the product of the interaction between his age and character; in other words, the Ego persists. Against every common disparagement of old men – such as their poor memory, failing intellectual faculties, irritability and irascibility – which Cicero enumerated in order to refute them, he stated that these did not characterize all old people, and where they appeared, they owed more to the man's character than to his age.[9] The Medieval authors, who were less inclined than Cicero to idealize old age, were not so emphatic about the overwhelming effect of the personality. Even those among them who noted individual differences and, like Cicero, stressed that a man's old age was the product of his character and entire life, referred to what they regarded as the unavoidable changes of old age as a whole, and especially of extreme old age. At the same time, they never tired of emphasizing that a man's best defence against the development of negative qualities in old age was to lead a life of reason and morality, and strive to develop the positive qualities, most particularly from middle age. He must build up a treasury of appropriate action and Christian habits, because it is harder for a man to change his character and bad habits when he is old, let alone in extreme old age when his reasoning capacity and his memory grow even feebler.[10]

The failure of memory was and still is a source of shame and pain to the old person. In the learned culture of the Middle Ages it had a moral connotation. As Mary Carruthers has shown, 'memory' was both a literary and ethical concept. It indicated the strength of man's morality and humanity.[11] Its decline marked the diminution of the person's humanity. The writers of scientific works listed melancholy as one of the characteristics of old age. Gerontologists today also note that the incidence of depression increases in old age, ranging from depressed moods to what is termed clinical depression. But in the culture of the Middle Ages melancholy, like failing memory, was not only a source of suffering for the old person, but a sin. The low spirits were an expression of insufficient faith in God's grace and goodness. And while melancholy did not figure at the top of the hierarchy of sins, and was not mentioned as frequently in the public sermons as some other sins, nevertheless, it was not possible to attribute it to a person without a connotation of sin.

As a rule, even those who stressed the negative image of the old person did not refrain from addressing him with instruction and from defining what was expected both of his conduct and his frame of mind. And the expectations were high. Despite their awareness of the old person's weakness, the writers displayed none of the tolerance and understanding which were often shown to children and even to young people. As Bartholomaeus Anglicus said, 'Everyone judges the old man'.

The first expectation from the old man is described in the foregoing chapters: he must atone for his sins, accept his old age and his approaching death without a murmur, and strive to save his soul. Though didactic and moralistic literature called upon people of all ages to repent, since no one knows the hour of his death,[12] for the old person, who had achieved such an advanced age, this was clearly the primary duty.[13] In contrast to the fear of extinction, with which man was unable to contend, religion urged men to action against the theological fear, the anxiety about the fate of the soul in the next world. We are not concerned here with the final days or hours before death, nor with the concept of the good death, the model for which was the stereotypical death of a saint; that is a separate subject. We are concerned with a certain frame of mind and a particular conduct over a period of time. The cultural norm differed from that which prevails in Western culture today, when people are encouraged by their surroundings to ignore the approach of death. The friends of Francesco di Marco Datini urged him in the last three years of his life not only to take care of his will before it was too late, but actually to prepare for his death. His friend did not hesitate to compare him in a letter to a tree which is about to fall and can no longer be propped up. But it appears that Datini, like most people, did not accept his approaching end and did not achieve the necessary resignation. He increased his acts of piety. He prayed a great deal, fasted, went on pilgrimages to saints' shrines, donated generously to churches and monasteries and gave alms to the poor. But apparently he expected that all these would not only ensure his salvation in the next world but grant him a few more years of life. Before he died his friend wrote: 'He thinks that he has had a warrant of a long life from God.' After his death he wrote: 'it seemed to him very strange that he should have to die, and that his prayers should be of no avail.'[14]

The fears and behaviour of King Louis XI of France, as described by Philippe de Commynes, who was at his side in his final four years, after his first stroke, were much like Datini's. He paid a fortune to the one physician he trusted; he donated money to churches and monasteries; surrounded himself with clergymen and invited to his court a hermit from Calabria, who was known for his ascetic way of life and his great piety, so that they would pray for his long life. Unlike Datini, however, he was not only anxious, but also ridden with suspicions that people were plotting to seize him and harm him. He suspected everybody, from the servants who shut all the windows when he had his first stroke (when the doctor arrived he ordered the windows to be opened at once), through his noble favourites who held various state posts, to his son, daughter and son-in-law. He therefore did all he could to continue to run the affairs of state: he issued new ordinances and changed his decisions to show that he was still present and that his mind was unimpaired. He also surrounded himself with guards.[15] Datini died at 75; Louis XI at 60.

Quite different behaviour was attributed to the saints, who were supposed to serve as models and examples not only in the way they died, but in their conduct and frame of mind in old age. According to the author of one of the *Vitae* of Albertus Magnus, who died at 80, the saint continued to perform all his duties as a clergyman to his very last days, but in his final three years had secretly prepared for his death.[16] Aristotle tried to explain the particular fear that old people have of their approaching death. 'They love life,' he wrote, 'and all the more when their last day has come, because the object of all desire is something we have not got, and also because we desire most strongly that which we need most urgently.'[17] The Medieval writers showed less psychological understanding for this phenomenon. The separation from the life of this world, and even the dying agony, were not supposed to be as fearful as the sin which condemned a man to hell. Nor did writers in other periods show a greater empathy. In Euripides' *Alcestis* Admetus describes the old people who cling to life: their begging for death and moaning about their old age, said Admetus, signify nothing. At the moment when death approaches none of them wants to die and their age is no longer a burden.[18] So too La Fontaine, in the seventeenth century, mocked those who 'most resemble the dead', namely, the old, who deny their approaching end and cling to life more than those who are younger than they.[19]

Concerning those who put off repentance until their final days, the prevalent position of the authors of moralistic literature was, better late than never. In the popular literature there were tales about men and women who put off repentance until their final hours, but once they confessed wholeheartedly and in complete penitence, they were granted salvation.[20] According to Philip of Novare, however, those who repent in their final days and wish to die wearing a monk's habit would not go to hell, but would have to spend a long time in purgatory.[21]

Cicero in his work *De senectute* discussed in detail not only the importance of practising the virtues, but also the importance of spiritual and intellectual activity in old age, as protection against mental deterioration. He also mentioned some great minds, such as Isocrates, Sophocles and Plato, who produced their finest writings in old age.[22] During the Middle Ages the emphasis was on prayer and the study of religious works by way of repentance. Few Medieval writers discussed creativity and intellectual activity in old age, as did Petrarch and Bernardino of Siena, outside the purely religious context. The authors of books of medical instruction also recommended study and conversation with friends on intellectual and spiritual subjects, though not to prevent mental deterioration but to avoid the melancholy to which old men are prone.[23]

The expectation that the old person would concentrate on his salvation in the next world went hand in hand with relief from other duties, including the duty of caring for those nearest to him. Sometimes this relief was only implied, and sometimes it was stated explicitly and bluntly. Jean Gerson (1363–1429), in a brief essay which he said he had composed for an aged friend, alongside instruction about prayers, reading the Scriptures and concentrating on the approach of death, also urged the old man to stop concerning himself with the affairs of others and looking after their needs. When St Anthony grew old, Gerson wrote, an angel appeared to him and said: 'Think of yourself, Anthony, and let God manage the lives of others.' The old man who does not do so is mad.[24] In a secularized world some thinkers have termed this 'the liberation of the spirit', due to the old person's ability and right to observe current events from a certain distance, in freedom from personal interests or concern about the opinions of others about him. But only a thin line separates this 'liberation of the spirit' from complete withdrawal, indifference and insensitivity even to one's nearest. The psychoanalysts describe this reduction, and in extreme cases the complete dissociation from one's close environment, which are sometimes manifested by old people, as due to the weakening of the ego.[25] It is not clear from Gerson's words what kind or degree of emotional liberation he was seeking to legitimize. However, it is quite plain from his and other writers' statements, that this granting of relief from 'the affairs of others' had a social and political significance.

Philip of Novare declared that a man who has reached the age of 60 is relieved from serving. From this age on, having paid all his debts and discharged his duties to people near and distant, he need serve only himself, and if he has the means, avail himself of the service of others.[26] In view of the meaning of the word 'service' in Latin and in the French of Philip of Novare's time, it is clear that he was not referring to personal services only, but to serving in a public position. Vincent of Beauvais, too, stated that the old man ought to quit his occupations and the management of his estates.[27] In the thirteenth century feudal estates entailed administrative functions and sometimes also positions of government and command. Even a respected figure like old Giannozzo, in Alberti's *Book of the Family*, is described as having withdrawn to the margin of things. He helps, to the best of his strength and ability, those of his friends who are as old as he: he recommends them to the city authorities and aids them financially, while serving the younger members of the family as counsellor and arbitrator. But it seems that he no longer does any business and he is already removed from the centre of affairs. So, too, 64-year-old Piero, who in his forties and fifties was very active in political affairs at the service of princes, is shown as no longer filling a public position. This, despite the fact that Alberti was one of those who not only believed that honouring old people was a virtue, but expatiated on their wisdom, experience and valuable advice. According to him, the old members of the family were its soul, and to receive their instruction was to guard the family's welfare and prosperity.[28] Alberti did not release the old from emotional involvement and concern for those nearest to them, but he released them from political and economic activity.

Aristotle, too, thought that the old were unsuited to public office. In his *Politics* (Book II, Chapter nine), where he criticized the regime of Sparta, he censured the life membership of the Council of Elders (Gerousia), because the thinking power ages like the body. In a state ruled by the ideal constitution, according to Aristotle, the same citizens should be both the soldiers and the councillors (i.e. those who fill the positions of government) but at different stages in their lives. In their youth they should be the soldiers, and in middle age the councillors. This order was dictated by nature, which gave the younger physical strength and the older men greater wisdom.[29] Aristotle believed that such a system would also moderate the conflict of the generations; the young ones would know that their time would come. As for the old, he held that it is right to let people rest who have spent an active life in the service of the state. Moreover, since it is necessary to ensure that the worship of the gods is properly conducted, the priesthood should be entrusted to the old. So, too, Maimonides, who objected to the appointment of an 'excessively old' man to the Sanhedrin, held that all members of the Sanhedrin should be 'grey-haired and of upright stature',[30] that is to say, middle-aged.

It is known that images affect the formation of attitudes, and attitudes affect reality, that is, behaviour and action. However, the causal link between cultural attitudes and actual conduct and action is complex and by no means always direct. As we shall see in the following chapters, notwithstanding the cultural attitude which said that old people should retreat to the margins, there were men in the ruling strata in the Middle Ages who continued into old age to hold positions in the feudal territories, in the state and above all in the Church. They continued to do so despite the said cultural attitude, because there was no compulsory retirement age in most posts and offices, and a fief was granted to a man for life. Thus, whether a man remained active or retired depended on his personality, his physical and mental condition and the political circumstances. And where the management of a farm, a workshop or a commercial enterprise were concerned, the demographic realities, family circumstances and local custom also determined.

Christian ideals exalted humility as one of the virtues. It was mentioned in sermons for the community in general. But in the demand made upon old people to conduct themselves with humility was implied the assumption that the old man's status had declined, and with it came the expectation that he would retire to the margins. According to Philip of Novare, a proud old man was despicable. Even if he is great in wealth, he is weak in body and competence. He must therefore be modest and humble in all his ways.[31] A gerontologist has expressed a similar opinion: with the decline in the person's abilities, his attempts to maintain his former position at any cost can give rise to scorn and insult. Therefore his status must be reduced and restricted: a man's status may be defended so long as it is tolerated by the society, and it is tolerated only when it is diminished and restricted.[32] In other words, an ageing person must undergo a process of resocialization in order to contend with the reversal of roles: with his becoming dependent, to a greater or lesser degree, on those who are younger than he, and with his lowered status.[33] A modern observer of old people can see, besides those who are verbally aggressive and insist on their rights, or what they believe to be their rights, some old people whose eyes seem to apologize for their being here still. And the hero (or anti-hero) of a contemporary novel, *Autumn*, says: 'To be an old person here is almost a crime. Old people are forgiven if they behave quietly and humbly, but if they insist on their human rights they are harshly scolded . . . I try to keep my dignity, but not to overdo it, not to be ridiculous. . . . And it isn't easy.'[34]

A demand which was repeatedly made on the old man was not to try to behave like a young man: he must not be like the 'hundred-year-old boy'. The chief sin and foolishness of an old man who behaved like that was to keep seeking carnal relations. This denunciation of the wish for love in old age, and the expectation that the old avoid love and sex outside marriage, or even within legal marriage, was directed at men and women alike, more clearly and explicitly than in other areas, though with different emphases. The same ideas recurred endlessly in all types of discourses: in the scientific and the moralistic writings, through the various literary genres, to the proverbs. The scientific writings contradicted themselves. The accepted theory was that with the diminution of natural heat and the radical moisture an old man's desires cool, including the sexual desire. Yet again and again old men are warned to reduce sexual intercourse to a minimum, and the very old to avoid it altogether. This suggests that the writers were aware that the old man's sexual drive did not disappear altogether, that he still wanted sexual intercourse and might still be capable of it. The reason given for the advice to avoid it was that it caused a further reduction of the natural heat and radical moisture, and so shortened life. And since it was customary to bring in carefully selected examples from the animal world to illustrate the proper way for a man to live, Arnold of Villanova mentioned that the longest living war-horses were those which did not mate.[35] (This did not stop him from offering elsewhere in the same work advice on how to restore sexual potency, as we have seen.) In the scientific literature, the advice to refrain from sexual intercourse was directed at men alone. Albertus Magnus believed that one of the reasons women lived longer than men was that they expended less energy in intercourse. Comparing humans and animals, he noted the longevity of mules, which do not mate, and stated that hens which lay many eggs, like female animals which gestate and give birth frequently, did not live long.[36] It is not quite clear whether he also meant women who became pregnant and gave birth frequently. If that was the case, then the lives of women were shortened not by the act of copulation but by its outcome, namely, pregnancy and childbirth.

The writers of moralistic literature also believed that the sexual drive ebbed in old age. It ought therefore to have been easier for the old person, whose body was no longer a source of temptation, to avoid sin and to repent. Moralistic literature described the lustful old man as one who violated the laws of nature and behaved like a madman. According to the Franciscan Berthold of Regensburg, who preached all over Germany in the thirteenth century, people were prone to different sins at different ages, and the Devil tried to tempt them according to their inclinations. The sin of the old was avarice and miserliness. The old man tended to this sin because he was cold and belonged to the element of earth. He therefore desired to increase the crops, that is to say, to amass more and more possessions and to hold on to them. Sexual desire, however, did not arise from the old man's nature. That was why a lecherous old man provoked laughter and mockery, even in the Devil himself.[37]

Philip of Novare wrote that the old man's desire to make love was a wish without need or capacity.[38] Like other authors of didactic literature, he considered the *senex amans* (literally, a loving old man, but meaning an old lecher) a sinner who, instead of atoning for his sins when old age gave him the opportunity to do so by cooling his desires, persisted in sinning. According to a woman, Christine de Pisan (1364–1430), women's desires also cooled in old age. She phrased it delicately. Advising older women not to be censorious towards the young women and not to harass them, she wrote: 'If you are now free of the sins of youth, it is not thanks to your virtues, but because nature no longer inclines you to them'.[39] Philip of Novare stated that old women who continued to indulge in the sins of flesh were those who refused to acknowledge the fact of their ageing and kept sinning to prove themselves and to others that they were not yet old. When such women did not sin, it was not because they wanted to avoid sinning, but because the men did not want them and they humiliated themselves.[40] As in the case of men, the assumption was that women did not need sexual intercourse when they grew old. If they still wanted it, it was for an external cause: they wished to satisfy their vanity. As for the authors of the lives of the 'desert fathers' (that is the Christian hermits in the Egyptian and Syrian deserts in the fourth to seventh centuries) who wrote down the sayings and tales which were attributed to them, apparently neither they nor the desert fathers themselves knew that the sexual drive subsided or disappeared altogether in old age. The demons never stopped tormenting them and tempting them to carnal sin.[41] The Medieval writers who regarded the lustful old man as unnatural and mad did not quote those texts. The various literary genres, just like the folk sayings, mocked the *senex amans* as laughable and grotesque. Folk sayings often referred to the three types whom God hated: the stingy rich man, the proud beggar and the lecherous old man. The old man was mocked whether he sought love affairs or took a wife although canon law did not forbid old people to marry. Some canonists recommended the avoidance of sexual intercourse in marriage once the wife was no longer fertile but it was only by way of advice, not a prohibition.[42]

The main objection was to the marriage of an old man with a young woman, and also, though this was less frequently mentioned, the marriage of an old woman with a young man. The more moderate writers described such marriages as unseemly and compared it to the crossing of species.[43] Here and there this attitude was embodied in the law, or raised in court as an argument for the cancellation of an agreed marriage. In the thirteenth-century laws of King Alfonso X of Castile and León it was stated plainly: An old man must not marry a very young woman. The reason given was that there could be no love between them and they might not be able to procreate.[44] In a case of a breach of promise, which was brought before the *Parlement* of Paris following the bride's willing abduction, the lawyer who defended the girl argued that the first groom was an old man, whereas the man of her choice was young.[45]

In literature, the wealthy old man who married a young woman was depicted as pathetic and ludicrous: he coughs and he spits, he is hairy and ugly, he grumbles endlessly and is devoured by jealousy, yet his young wife nevertheless manages to cuckold him. Such were the three aged husbands of the Wife of Bath and Old January who married young May, in Chaucer's *Canterbury Tales*, the old husband in *The Fifteen Joys of Marriage*, the old husbands in many of Boccaccio's stories, old husbands in the Florentine carnival songs, and others.[46] These portrayals grew in a particular demographic and social setting. In the higher social strata, and in southern Europe also in the middle ones, already in the first marriage the husband was older than his wife. Widowers married again, and if they were widowed again, not infrequently they married for the third time, and so the age gap between the couple usually increased with every marriage. Some of the old men continued to produce offspring. Matteo Corsini married in 1362, when he was 40. In 25 years of marriage, his wife bore him 20 children. She died at about 50. He remarried (to a woman who was still fertile) and produced his last offspring when he was 77. There were, moreover, old men (68 and 70 in two cases) who had extra-marital relations, often with serving-maids, and occasionally bastards were born from such connections.[47] In some parts of Western Europe it was sometimes the custom for young men of the village or urban quarter to hold a charivari – a raucous band of percussive instruments with a yowling chorus – under the windows of a widow or a widower who was about to remarry. It was a hostile ritual, a form of controlled aggression, directed at those who violated certain communal rules. It voiced the economic and psychological concern for the children of the widow or widower by a previous marriage, as well as hostility towards those whose material resources enabled them to marry for the second time, thereby reducing the pool of eligible partners for the young people who were not yet economically independent enough to marry for the first time. Moreover, they were regarded as violating natural law, the proper sequence of time and the right balance in all things.[48]

Marriage between a wealthy old widow and a young man was apparently rarer than that between a rich old widower and a young woman, and was mentioned less frequently in the literature. The demand for property-owning widows, or for those who owned workshops, who were sometimes older than the men who asked for their hand, rose in periods of demographic pressure. In times of demographic decline people could make their economic way more easily, and the demand for widows went down, even for those who owned property. While the denunciations of marriage between an old man and a young woman stressed the old man's lasciviousness, when a young man married an old woman it was his greed which was emphasized. In either case little reference was made to the woman's motives. In reality, where a young girl, or even a young widow, was concerned, she did not as a rule have much say in the choice of husband. It was her parents who arranged to marry her off to an old man. According to one of the satirical writers, neither the young man nor the old woman would get much pleasure from their matrimony. Old women are jealous and suspicious of their young husbands, to a degree unknown in young wives. And the young man who must cleave to an old woman would grow ten years older within a year.[49] But the old woman who wanted to go on having extra-marital love affairs, or who acted as a panderer, was denounced more harshly than the old woman who married a young man. Sometimes she was portrayed as a grotesque figure, but more often she was described as possessing some secret knowledge which enabled her to bend others to her will, as a dangerous figure, more menacing than grotesque. And whereas the *senex amans* was usually a man of position and property, who competed with the less well-established young men, the old women who continued to engage in carnal activities, and who were expert in matters of love and sex, belonged to the lower social strata. They were also, as we have seen, the ones whom the popular medical texts described as feeding on coarse meat, which increased the amount of venom in their bodies. These repulsive old hags gave advice in matters of love and sex, prepared love philtres and acted as procuresses. At times they disguised themselves and, under cover of darkness, took the place of the young women whom the men expected. Others found pleasure in debauching innocent young women. Causing them to sin served the old women as substitute for their own sex lives.[50]

The charivari was usually held when there was an age gap between the widower and his young bride, or the widow and her intended, but sometimes it was also held when both parties were elderly. In such cases there was no loss of eligible young partners, nor was there a crossing of species, the young and the old. But it appears that although the Church did not ban marriage between two old people, it was regarded, at the very least, as unseemly. The same clause in the aforementioned ordinance of Alfonso X, which stated that an old man must not marry a very young woman, also stated that husband and wife must not be very old.[51] According to Philip of Novare, an old man who married a young woman lived in fear that a young man would steal her from him. If he married an old woman, 'two corruptions in one bed are insufferable'.[52] Another author compared the old couple to a pair of coffins.[53] For old people to fall in love or get married was to violate the laws of nature and break an aesthetic taboo. In *The Romance of the Rose* Old Age is one of the enemies of love. Love was meant for young (beautiful) people, not old (ugly) ones. Or, in the words which Jean de Meun put in the mouth of the Duenna, in the second part of *The Romance of the Rose*:

> While she enjoys her youth, she should pursue
> The joys of love; for when old age assaults
> She'll have no further part in lovers' bouts.[54]

Like the cruel descriptions of the old body, so too the satires and the denunciations in other literary genres of old men and women who pursue love and sex, have a long tradition in Western civilization, from the Greeks and Romans through the Middle Ages to our times, from the Greek Aristophanes and Menander, through the Romans Terence, Horace and Juvenal, to Thomas Mann's description of Aschenbach in *Death in Venice*, Marcel Proust's description of Charlus, or Kazantsakis' Madame Hortense ('Bobolina') in *Zorba the Greek* (though the latter did not even seek a connection with a young man but sought to fascinate a man as old as she.)

One rarely finds a sympathetic description of a love affair between two old people (yet without idealizing old age), such as in Garcia Marquez' *Love in the Time of Cholera*. In Western culture the very image of the old person, and especially the image of his or her body, causes anxiety. The thought of sexual intimacy between old people intensifies the anxiety, and where men are concerned, the fear of impotence. The idea that desire may disappear altogether in old age is less disturbing, because then there would be no disparity between desire and ability. At the same time, the picture of the impotent old man (or one who is believed to be impotent) still trying to copulate, reawakens in the young or middle-aged man his childhood fear of castration. Depicting him as grotesque is a way of overcoming that anxiety. Intimate relations between inmates in old-age homes are still regarded as unseemly, if not obscene, and provoke mockery and laughter. (Only in very recent years, as gerontologists determined that healthy old people do want sexual relations, have the cinema and television begun to portray attachments between old people in a favourable light, perhaps heralding the social legitimization of such relationships.)[55]

ROLES FOR OLD PEOPLE

One function which old men of all social strata performed in their position as old men was giving evidence on past customs and events. This function was not mentioned in the diverse normative literature, and did not rest on the assumption that old men possessed any special wisdom or experience nor, in that context, on their having a particular intuition or secret knowledge. They were called upon to fulfil this function because they had the necessary information on such matters as the custom in the feudal principality or the manor, on the ownership or tenure of a property, on the heir's age, or to which noble family did a certain coat of arms (which was displayed on shields, pennants, garments, books, walls and vessels) used to belong. Today it is known that people whose short-term memory is failing retain much of their long-term memory. Moreover, it appears that the memory of illiterate people (who formed the majority in the Middle Ages) is better than the memory of people who are used to relying on the written word. Men over 60 were not the only ones called upon to give evidence, but their number among such witnesses was high. As a rule, it was the elderly men who were called upon to testify, but occasionally women also gave evidence. As we have seen, people did not always know exactly how old they were, and when they did know, they did not deem it important to state it very precisely. Many rounded up their age, up or down, to the nearest decade. Some said that they were over 60 or near 60 (or 50). On the whole, churchmen and nobles knew their age more often than did the peasants.

The historian Jean Delumeau studied testimonies which were taken between 1177 and 1180. They were collected for the purpose of settling a dispute between the bishops of Siena and Arezzo concerning certain parishes and churches on the borders of the county of Siena, which both bishops claimed for their dioceses. The investigators were trying to find out what had been found and resolved in the years 1124–5, namely, some 50 years earlier, when an investigation had already been conducted in the matter. On this occasion the investigators were able to discover with some degree of accuracy the real age of at least some of the witnesses, and to compare them with the age they gave. It transpired that more witnesses deducted years from their age than added to it. On the other hand, the deductions were smaller than the additions. Most of those who exaggerated their age were quite old, and they added many years. Eight of them declared that they were 100 years old. An examination revealed that the 'youngest' of them was 75, and the oldest not over 90. Some linked the date of their birth to an event which their parents had told them occurred at that time: 'When the Crusaders took over the Sepulchre of our Lord, and the steward of the local hospital was captured by the Saracens.' Others could only state at what stage in their life they had been in the years 1124–5. One man said he remembered he had already been working in the fields. Another said that he was already then a merchant who travelled from place to place. Some of the knights said they had been squires, and some of the clergymen that they had been students at that time. Clearly, there were some inaccuracies in the stated ages, to a greater or lesser degree; however, most of the witnesses in an investigation of a 50–year-old affair were, naturally, old. (There were also some middle-aged witnesses, who had been small children, or had not been born, in 1124–5, but who testified what they had heard from their parents.)[56]

In 1265 King Henry III of England wrote to Loretta, the widow of the Earl of Leicester, who was then 80 years old and living as a recluse, telling her to report to the abbot of the Augustine monastery and the prior of Christchurch all that she knew about the rights and liberties of the stewardship of England attached to the earldom of Leicester.[57] In 1210, when the Count of Hainault wished to restore, as he put it, the ancient custom of his county and to record it in writing for future generations, he called on two old men, his bastard brother and the chaplain of the previous Count to come and give public testimony about it.[58] In England in the 1380s a dispute broke out between the Scropes and the Grosvenors about a coat of arms which both noble families claimed, and each sought to prove that it had been theirs for generations. The younger witnesses gave ages ranging from 40 to 56. (A very few stated that they were still younger – 32, 34, 42.) The many old witnesses gave ages ranging from 60 to 70. (One stated that he was 76 and another that he was 100 years old.) They stated that they had served in the armies as knights or squires for 40 or 45 years, and had seen such-and-such, or heard as much from their fathers.[59] (After hearing arguments and evidence for five years, the King decided in favour of Lord Richard Scrope.) In 1252 a dispute broke out between the canons of the Cathedral of Notre Dame in Paris and their serfs about the sum which the serfs were bound to pay as tallage. The mayor of Corbreuse, described as 'an old man over 70 and ailing', and the old archdeacon Jean were called upon to give evidence in the matter. The latter testified that he had seen the old records which listed the exact entitlements of the canons, and had also heard about them from his elders. (Both men testified in favour of the canons.)[60]

In English estates it was not uncommon to hold an investigation to verify the peasants' obligation to work for the lord of the manor so as to record those duties in writing. Thus, in 1315, in a Sussex estate belonging to the Bishop of Chichester, the peasants were asked if the tenants of certain plots were obliged to cart the dung of the manor's demesne. They gave an unequivocal answer that there had never been such an obligation, neither in theirs nor in their fathers' time. The ages of the witnesses are not given in the record, but their mentioning 'even in their fathers' time' suggests that the witnesses were elderly or old.[61]

The same goes for the testimonies of the jurors concerning people's tenure of particular plots of land. In one case the peasants testified that for the past 50 years none of them had seen any of the claimant's fathers or forefathers occupying that land.[62] In one inquiry into the right of a certain person to occupy a certain piece of land in return for feudal service, the witnesses did not mention how long the claimant had occupied the land, but stated that it had been held by three generations of his family – his grandfather, his father and he himself.[63] The old peasants were asked to testify on account of their age, while others, younger ones, were asked because of their standing in the rural community, being prosperous peasants and/or holders of various positions on the lord of the manor's behalf.[64] Likewise, in 'proofs of age' investigations, held to determine if the designated heir to the fief had reached the age of 21 and could succeed his deceased father, or if the lord should take it over as guardian until the heir reached majority, some of the witnesses were old men. In one case a man who stated that he was 60 years old testified that the designated heir was indeed 21. He stated that the heir was born in Bracewell on St Bartholomew's Day and was baptised there at the church of St Michael. He, the witness, remembered the occasion well, because his own son Patrick, who was born in the same year on the feast of the Exaltation of the Cross, was 21 years old on the last celebration of that feast.[65]

Fügedi's research has shown that in Hungary, in the fourteenth to fifteenth centuries, investigations were held not only to determine rights of ownership or tenure of properties, but also to find out if a person was entitled to the status of nobility. The lack of regular records of genealogy also made it difficult to prove the right to inherit the legacy of a distant relative. This too entailed formal investigations. Witnesses stated that they were 60, 66, 75 and 80 years old, and the investigators searched for old people. In 1380 two churchmen, assigned to investigate the ownership of a certain village, called on 'old men and women of the nobility' who remembered the relevant facts to come and testify before them.[66] In an earlier chapter we saw that the jurors in the Cypriot villages under Venetian rule, who were usually village dignitaries of 60 and over, were expected to testify about local custom and land tenure.[67] The importance of the testimony of old people also found expression in the law. According to the laws of Alfonso X of Castile and Leon, sick and aged witnesses could be questioned before the trial for fear that they would die before it was held.[68] Likewise, the compilers of family chronicles (*Ricordanza*) in fourteenth- and fifteenth-century Florence, who relied chiefly on public and private archives, also turned to old family members for information about the family's origins and early days, which they had heard from their own fathers.[69]

There is no doubt that from the twelfth century on both the authorities and the people in general made increasing use of written records to support and ensure the implementation of ordinances, acquisitions, sales and legacies. Laws were recorded in writing, and sales, purchases and transfers, as well as contracts and wills, were documented. In other words, regular forms emerged for giving orders, accepting obligations, contractual commitments and claims, based on written texts.[70] The very process of verifying existing customs in order to put them in writing illustrates this fact. At times this was stated outright: 'The acts and decisions of the fathers should be written down for the next generation, so that they will not be forgotten in the course of time and after the demise of the fathers.'[71] But the transition to the written record in all spheres was not completed until the end of the Middle Ages and after.[72] Old people continued to inform the younger generation about the past and served as living repositories of local history and civic ceremonial, manorial customs, electoral procedure and information regarding the origins and genealogy of individuals (despite the fact that failing memory characterized the stereotype of the old person).

The testimonies of old men and women were also required by the investigations of the papal commissions of inquiry appointed to look into the life, acts and personality of a candidate for canonization. Since they wished to know about the person's origins, childhood and youth, some of the witnesses were necessarily old people who alone could give evidence on the subject. Jean de Joinville (*c.* 1224–1317), who in his youth served King Louis IX of France, accompanied him on his first Crusade (1248) to Egypt and the Crusader Kingdom and became his close friend, was called upon at the age of 58 to testify before the committee of investigation which considered Louis' canonization.[73] (He wrote his book, *The History of St Louis* in his eighties, completing it when he was about 85.) Testimony about the childhood and youth of St Clare of Assisi (1194–1253) was given by lay men and women of Assisi, who described themselves as being in their sixties.[74] There are other examples of this kind of testimony given by old witnesses. The investigators who gathered material for the rehabilitation of Joan of Arc took testimonies from her fellow villagers. Joan was born in 1412, left her village in 1429 and was burned at the stake in 1431. Her contemporaries among the witnesses were in their forties, but others were 70 to 80 years old, men and women who were adults when she was a child.[75] There was no substitute for such testimonies as were given regarding Joan of Arc's early life and personality, or about the childhood and adolescence of candidates for canonization. Only those who knew the persons in question could testify. Even if parochial and other kinds of records were available in those days, they would not have shed light on the childhood, youth and personalities of those men and women.

One function of respectable elderly-to-old women of the middle stratum was to testify in court after examining the women who complained of rape, the widows who claimed to have been impregnated by their now deceased husbands (for if that was the case, and the child was born alive, the brother of the deceased could not claim the inheritance), and the women who were condemned to death whose execution would be deferred if they were found to be pregnant. They were also assigned to examine the breasts of women who were not suckling babies of their own, in a village or city quarter where a newborn baby was found murdered. (A lactating woman who did not have a baby was suspected of having given birth and committed infanticide.) None of these examinations could be carried out by men, and the function was entrusted to older women.[76]

Another role considered suitable for elderly-to-old women was to chaperone girls and young women. A prosperous Parisian merchant of about 60 married a 15–year-old orphan of a higher family than his own. In the years 1392–4 he wrote a guidance manual for her. It was an example of the kind of marriage which was denounced by the various texts. The manual was written with affection and empathy for the young girl who entered married life, and the author-husband even undertook to prepare her to be a spouse and housewife in her second marriage, after his death. He concentrated on the difficulties she would encounter as a young housewife, and in fulfilling her wifely duties. All the same, the old husband made no mention of the physical and mental suffering that often befell a young girl who was married off to an old man. (Nor, for that matter, did the satirists refer to that suffering. There was no room for it in that literary genre. The young wife was depicted as triumphantly leading her husband by his nose and cuckolding him.) In his manual he stated that she must not go about in public except in the company of an elderly Beguine by name of Agnes, who was known for her gravity and piety.[77] Less sympathetic was the portrait in 'Aucassin and Nicolette' of the old woman who was supposed to chaperone Nicolette and watch her when she was confined in the tower to keep her away from Aucassin. If in the old merchant's book the pious old companion was the opposite of the old bawd, in the literary work she was the opposite of the loving and beloved Nicolette (who, happily, succeeds in escaping from the tower and her old jailer).[78] One final function, in this context, was mentioned in the laws of Alfonso X, whereby a churchman might only have a resident housekeeper if she was (very) old.[79]

We have seen that Philip of Novare exempted men over 60 from service; women were not so privileged. In his manual, old women were not only called upon to pray, repent and give to charity, but also to go on with their traditional tasks: assisting the younger women by giving their help and advice, arranging marriages and bringing up the children.[80] It would appear that the legislator believed, as did Philip of Novare, that women could continue to fulfil their traditional functions in old age. And in reality, as we shall see in the following chapters, women did indeed continue to do so as long as they were able. As for the chaperones, in Italian cities these were usually the mother, an aunt or another female relative, mature but not necessarily old women.

5

'HONOUR THY FATHER AND THY MOTHER'

The biblical Commandment to honour parents (Exodus 20: 12; Deuteronomy 5: 16), repeated in the New Testament (Epistle to the Ephesians 6: 1–3), was interpreted in the Middle Ages as binding on the offspring for the rest of their father's and mother's lives; and even after their death, for then they were supposed to arrange for prayers and masses to be said for their souls. The duty of honouring the parents in childhood and adolescence was undoubtedly part of the inculcation of the social order, but as such it falls outside our present concern. Here we are concerned with the fact that the duty of honouring parents included nursing them when they were ill and providing for them, if necessary, in their old age. Much has been written about the symbolic significance of the story of Aeneas, who carried his lame old father, Anchises, on his back when they escaped from the burning Troy.[1] In the context of the present discussion, the idea of 'carrying the parents on the back' is a very real one, referring to that stage of life when the power-relations of father and son turn in the latter's favour, especially in the working strata, when the father's working capacity declined.

The Church limited the relations of natural kinship and in their place extolled the 'spiritual kinship', which was supposed to make for harmonious relations in society. At the same time, and in consequence of the above, the Church set the conjugal family above the family of origin, conforming with the verse, 'Therefore shall a man leave his father and his mother and shall cleave unto his wife and they shall be one flesh' (Genesis 2: 24), and St Paul's dicta (I Corinthians 7: 4 and Ephesians 5: 21–2).[2] But the quality of kinship relations (hence also of the relationship with the family of origin) was not dictated exclusively by the norms of the Church. In periods of insecurity kinship relations grew stronger. In northern Europe the nuclear became increasingly dominant from the twelfth century on. This process reflected the increased sense of security and the economic changes, such as the development of the land market, which served to weaken the link between the lands and the extended family,[3] while in southern Europe the extended family remained dominant. However, this difference between the northern and southern family structures, which was also reflected in the authority of the patriarch (greater in the south), found no expression in the normative literature that was written mostly by churchmen. The duty of honouring parents and supporting them materially was a basic norm everywhere.

In the commentary on the biblical precepts of honouring the father and mother two reasons were principally advanced: gratitude for the actual gift of life, and the duty of reciprocal giving. The author of a commentary on the Ten Commandments, written between 1405 and 1410, entitled *Dives and Pauper*, wrote: 'Man has two beginnings, the first in God, hence the first Commandment, and the second in his parents, hence the fourth Commandment'.[4] Another author described the role of the parents in the giving of life as a partnership with God in creating the offspring.[5] As for reciprocity – the parents had looked after their children when they were small, raised them, educated them and gave them all they could. Now that they are old, it is the duty of the offspring to look after them and to support them, as written in the New Testament: 'But if any widow have children or nephews, let them learn first to show piety at home, and to requite their parents: for that is good and acceptable before God' (I Timothy 5: 4). Alberti's Old Lorenzo, around whose bed are gathered the members of his family, says that the parents gave their children life, nursed them and brought them up, supported them materially and gave them their name. The parents having grown old, it is incumbent upon the younger people to help and support them. By acting thus, they can expect the same humane consideration and sense of duty to be shown them when they in turn grow old.[6] In stressing this reciprocal kindness Alberti was following the biblical precepts on honouring parents which, unlike any other Commandment, promised a reward in this world to all who obeyed them:[7] 'that thy days may be long upon the land which the Lord thy God giveth thee' (Exodus 20: 12); 'that thy days may be prolonged, and that it may go well with thee' (Deuteronomy 5: 16); 'Honour thy father and thy mother, which is the first commandment with promise. That it may be well with thee, and thou mayest live long on the earth' (Ephesians 6: 2–3). Alberti did not promise a long life, but kindness in the following generation; the offspring of the good sons will care for them when their turn comes.

Others, like Bernardino of Siena, did repeat the promise of long life, and expanded on the phrase 'it may go well with thee'. Bernardino enumerated all the good things which accrue to those who honour their parents, most of which were to take place in the here and now. They would gain a long life, material prosperity, a fine family with many offspring, above all sons who were healthy in body and spirit and of good character, a good reputation, paternal blessing, God's grace and eternal glory. The opposite would befall the bad sons who disrespected their parents and abused them. They would be punished with a short life, poverty, an unhappy family whose sons would be crippled, ugly, foolish and corrupt and would treat their parents hatefully and viciously, a bad reputation, paternal malediction, a heavy guilt and eternal torment.[8] In so far as any reference was made to the image of the aged in connection with the duty of honouring parents, it was exclusively to the 'positive' image: the old man's wisdom and experience, and the value of his advice, as in Alberti's book. Only the bad son speaks of his old father as a 'witless old fool'.[9] Only rarely (and gently) are the roles reversed, where the good son not only sustains his old father, but also helps him with advice.[10] If anyone considered the possibility that the parents might be responsible for their children's disrespect and offensive behaviour, the blame was never found in the parents' character and behaviour in old age, but in earlier stages of life. Bernardino of Siena, having enumerated the causes of sons' bad treatment of parents – viciousness, greed, pride (expressed in their contempt for the parents' wisdom and experience), carnal desire (expressed in the son loving his wife more than required by the verse in Genesis 2: 24, and taking her side against his father, and even more against his mother) – proceeded to refer to parental neglect, divine justice and justifiable revenge. By parental neglect he was speaking of the education of the children. The parents did not restrain them and did not correct them in time, so that they were corrupted, and treated their parents accordingly. By divine justice he meant punishment for past sins, and by justifiable revenge he meant reciprocity: the offspring treat them as they had treated their own parents, and just as they looked forward to their parents' demise, so now their own children look forward to their death.[11]

In most countries during the Middle Ages the duty of the offspring to support their aged and needy parents was not incorporated in the law. (By contrast, the English Poor Law of 1601 stipulated that it was the duty of the offspring to do so, and only those old persons who had no offspring, or whose offspring were too poor to support them, could claim assistance from the parish.)[12] In Italy, apparently some communes made it a punishable offence to neglect an aged parent.[13] But, as noted, the duty was a basic norm. As a rule, the various normative texts discussed only the duty to parents, not to other relatives. Where other relatives were mentioned, as in Alberti or Dante,[14] the requirement was to honour them and help them in a general, unspecified way, not to support them materially. The Great Council of Venice resolved in 1286 that only the illness of father, mother, brother, or wife and offspring, could release a man from the duty to serve as Venetian ambassador abroad. (The reference was to nursing care, not to material support – the parents of members of the Great Council not being among the needy).[15]

In reality, as we shall see, it was expected that well-off people would help not only their parents but also their poor relatives, or members of the family who were suffering a temporary distress. But as noted before,

90

normative literature, which was largely the work of churchmen, as well as folk tales and proverbs, mentioned only the duty of caring for old parents. The duty of providing for the aged parents, the representation of good sons as examples to others and the denunciation of undutiful offspring, recurred in all the texts which discussed norms of conduct, from manuals for confessors and moralistic literature,[16] through the genre of the *Bestiaries* (in which the habits of real or imaginary animals were described to teach a moral), to popular proverbs and tales. Likewise in the Icelandic saga, which was composed in the early thirteenth century, the positive hero provided for his aged father and mother. The hero of one of the sagas was not well off. He worked as a farm hand for a kinsman of his, but he owned sheep. Before departing on a long voyage he sold his sheep and gave his kinsman the sum required to feed and house his mother for three years. At the end of that period he resisted all the tempting offers of the King of Denmark, with whom he was staying, because he could not bear to think that while he enjoyed great luxuries, the money for his mother's sustenance would run out and she would be reduced to beggary.[17] Many of the texts laid direct emphasis on food and feeding, although they were addressing the sons, who were the heads of the households, whereas feeding clearly belonged to the role of the women, within the family or by way of charity. Yet in descriptions of what parents did for their young children, the act of feeding was always associated with the mother: she carried them in her womb, she bore them in great travail, and suckled them for a long time. Their crying often disturbed her sleep, her meals and pleasures, and after she weaned them she sometimes denied herself food in order to feed them.[18]

As a rule, the normative literature spoke of good sons and bad sons, but now and then the actions of a daughter were also extolled as examples to others. Thomas Brinton, Bishop of Rochester in the second half of the fourteenth century, recounted a story originally told by the Roman writer Valerius, about a woman prisoner whose daughter came and fed her with milk from her breasts[19] – an expression of limitless devotion and a role-reversal which expressed complete reciprocity. According to Bartholomaeus Anglicus, the word *pater* came from the word *pascendo* (to feed) because when the children are young the father feeds them and when he grows old they feed him, like the ravens.[20] It appears that out of all the animals, ravens and storks were chosen as models for mankind. The stork was often described as not only feeding its frail parents, but actually warming them under its wings (since like aged humans they suffered from the cold), and helping them to rise and fly. Sometimes the hoopoe and the pelican were similarly praised.[21] According to popular belief, the pelican nourished its young with its blood, and a parallel was drawn between it and Christ's sacrifice.[22] According to the prevalent medical opinion, the unborn baby was nourished by the menstrual blood which was not secreted during pregnancy and which after the birth turned into the nurturing milk. Thomas Brinton attributed to lambs a special sensitivity to their mothers' needs, of the sort usually attributed to the mothers, not to the children. The lamb knows its mother's cry out of a thousand sheep. When its mother is ailing, from heat or from exhaustion, the lamb stands between her and the sun, to shade her and cool her fever. (This contrasted with the future heirs, who cared only about the inheritance.)[23]

Medieval culture was as aware of the discrepancy between the love and devotion of parents to their children and vice versa, as were later periods.[24] (Perhaps that was why they expatiated so much on the duty of offspring to their parents.) The facts were stated ruefully, but with an acceptance of the nature of the human condition. The love and care of parents for their children were depicted as arising from a natural instinct,[25] not so the affection of offspring for their parents. According to Philip of Novare, God gave babies three kinds of knowledge and love. The first two came from the infant itself, and the third from those who tended it. The baby's first knowledge and love were its recognition of and love for the woman who suckled it – its mother or wet-nurse. The second was its recognition of the people who fondled it, played with it and carried it in their arms. The love of those who take care of children stems from nature, from pity and from the act of rearing them. But whereas the love of the carers, principally the father and mother, grandfather and grandmother, grows stronger with the passage of time, the child's love for them wanes.[26] Petrarch's 'Reason' not only speaks about the duties to parents, he also advises his interlocutor to spend as much time as possible with his father and to listen to him while he can. After the father's death he will miss his company and his advice. But he also states that a son's love cannot be compared with parental love (the father's love was greater, according to Petrarch, but the mother's more intense). It is a pity that this is so, but unlikely that it will ever be otherwise.[27]

In the collection of scientific and medical questions inspired by the medical tradition of Salerno there is the question why parents love their children more than their children love them. The answer is that this is so because the children incorporate something of their parents' substance (*substantia*), but the parents have none of their children's substance.[28] This attempt to explain the different degrees of love was by way of a scientific statement: the embryo is composed of its parents' substance. But in Christian civilization this statement had an added significance, that of selfless giving, if not outright sacrifice. The association with Christ's sacrifice in the sacrament was inevitable. In *Dives and Pauper*, Dives quotes II Corinthians 12: 14: 'the children ought not to lay up for the parents, but the parents for the children', to which Pauper, speaking for the author, replies that though the tree indeed receives its nourishment from its root, it also gives something in return – the tree refreshes the root with dew and rain and shades it from the sun. He does, however, admit that the root gives the tree more than it receives in return. Thus do parents care for their children, who are the future, who would live many more years and assure the continuation of the generations, more than their children care for them.[29]

Beside instructing the offspring to support their aged parents, the texts also advised people to make provisions for their old age. (Even Plato and Cicero, whose writings idealized old age, admitted that old age could never be easy, not even for the wise and decent old man, if he were destitute.)[30] The various didactic texts repeatedly urged people to save and put aside sufficient property for their old age, for the winter of their lives, when they would no longer be able to work and earn a living. They ought to prepare for that time from middle age (or, according to some texts, before they were 60), since nothing is as hard and as miserable as poverty in old age.[31] Literature also depicted the bitter fate of those who failed to save when they could.[32] In the French poem which was quoted earlier, in which the old, poor man begs to die, he also expresses remorse for failing to save in time and secure his old age materially.[33] The old bawd in *The Romance of the Rose* also expresses remorse for her grievous mistake: in her youth, when men lavished gifts on her, she was profligate and did not think to save for her old age. Now she is old and quite destitute.[34]

If people in general were advised to save and put aside for their old age, those who had property were urged not to transfer their property to their children in their lifetime, thereby becoming dependent upon them and their kindness. Early in the fifteenth century the Italian Paolo de Certaldo wrote: 'The son obeys his father so long as he is the head of the family, master of his house and property. Once the son has taken over the property and the authority, he begins to hate his father, to threaten him and to await his death. The father who trusted him has turned him from a friend into an enemy.'[35] This warning was also repeated in the *exempla* which were interpolated into sermons, in commentaries on the Ten Commandents and in folk tales.

The following story appeared in several similar versions. The father transferred his property to his son and moved into his house. The son and the daughter-in-law began to resent the old man's presence and to feel that he was living too long. At first he resided with them inside the house, but then they moved him to the cold porch. The old man caught a chill and sent his grandson to ask for a blanket for him. The son gave him not a blanket but an empty sack. Then the child said: You had better cut this sack in two, one half for Grandfather and the other half for you, when you are old. The tale was variously attributed to peasants and to burghers. Sometimes it ended with a caution – the son feels remorse, repents and promises from then on to treat his father respectfully: to take care that he had a well-heated room and warm clothes, and never to drink wine or taste a good cut of meat before giving better ones to his father.[36] In all the versions of the story the father is the injured party and the offender is the son, but he is prompted by his wife.

Petrarch also mentions the possibility of a son neglecting his mother as well as his father, but he too described the wife as hostile only to her father-in-law.[37] Bernardino of Siena must have been one of the few who described the daughter-in-law abusing her husband's mother.[38] The author of *Dives and Pauper* also wrote about the old father who was exiled to the cold porch, but then showed how he hoodwinked his son and daughter-in-law. One day he asked the daughter-in-law to give him a jar of the kind used to store grain. He put into it a few small coins and pebbles. When he was out of the room his son and daughter-in-law shook the jar and concluded that it contained a treasure. Fearing that he would disinherit them, they treated him well and looked after him properly until he died. After his death they broke the jar and found the coins and pebbles, as well as a stick and a parchment, on which was written: This stick is for beating the man who gave all his property to his children and became a beggar.[39]

During the Middle Ages the right of inheritance passed vertically, not horizontally. Sons took precedence over daughters, but a daughter preceded other male relatives (such as the father's brothers or nephews), and where there were no sons, the daughters inherited the entire property. This fact was not illustrated in the above *exempla*, but was evident in the various versions of the story of King Lear which were widespread in the Middle Ages: Lear's heirs are his three daughters. The basic plot of Shakespeare's play closely resembles one of the Medieval versions, including the speeches and behaviour of the bad daughters Goneril and Regan, and of the youngest, the good daughter Cordelia. The latter's honest words in the play, admitting that the duty of love and devotion to the father is not boundless – 'I love your Majesty according to my bond, no more no less' – which infuriate Lear and cause him to disinherit her, are an almost literal quote of a line in the Medieval version: 'I love you as mych as I owe to loue my Fadire'. Both in Shakespeare's play and in the Medieval version Cordelia speaks about her sisters' hypocrisy, but thereafter they diverge. In the Medieval version Cordelia says bluntly: 'As mych as ye han, so mych are ye worthe and so mych I louve you'. In other words, keep your worth, do not divide your kingdom in your life. In Shakespeare, however, Cordelia goes on to speak about the reciprocity of duties, expatiates on the role of the conjugal family, which limits the duty to the family of origin, and alludes to the verse 'Therefore shall a man leave his father and his mother'.[40] In contrast to the ending of Shakespeare's *King Lear*, the Medieval version ends happily. Cordelia's husband raises an army and defeats the armies of Goneril and Regan's husbands. Lear rules a few more years over Britain, dies at a great age and bequeaths the kingdom to Cordelia.

Tragedy was not one of the genres of Medieval literature. It had no such figures of old men as Oedipus or Lear. Such old persons as did appear in the courtly romance were not its protagonists. As we have seen, the Medieval texts which jeered at old men and women who wanted to have love affairs were following a long tradition in Western culture. In the same way, the texts which denounced thankless children and sympathized with the suffering old man were also part of a literary tradition. The subject persisted, in a variety of styles and degrees of intensity, according to the genre and the author's talent, from *King Lear* to the novels of Balzac and Zola.

What are we to deduce about the realities of life from the warnings to parents not to transfer their property to their offspring in their lifetime? Do they suggest that people tried to avoid this kind of arrangement, and sought other solutions when they were too old to run the farm or the workshop or to continue trading? Or do they suggest that in those cases where men chose to turn their property over to their offspring the latter failed to do their duty by them? The English historian Alan Macfarlane reached some far-reaching conclusions partly on the basis of these warnings and tales. In two of his books he presented a thesis according to which the English peasantry, unlike other peasant societies in Western Europe, individualized land-ownership as early as the thirteenth century. Land was deemed to belong not to the family, but to an individual. Once the land was legally transferred to the son, who was free from any family and community constraints, the father could no longer claim the income from the property, and the son was not obliged to support his aged parents. Therefore, Macfarlane argued, those men who transferred their properties to their sons in their lifetime took care to do so by legal contract, which itemized the sons' obligations to their fathers' maintenance: the exact amount of money, food, clothing, fuel etc., which had to be provided at regular intervals. Without such legal guarantees, the fathers could not expect their sons to support them after the transfer of the property. In his second book Macfarlane maintained (partly contradicting the previous argument), that most peasants did not transfer property to their sons and that there were few such contracts. When they grew old the peasants preferred to lease, mortgage or sell their land and to live on the proceeds.[41] I shall discuss the criticisms of this thesis by historians of English peasant society in Chapter 9 on old age in the peasantry. At this point, its relevance lies in Macfarlane's use, *inter alia*, of the warnings and tales which originated in England.

But if the warnings and tales indicated a uniquely English development in land ownership, as a result of which sons were no longer liable to support the parents who had legally transferred their property to them, then the warnings and tales, too, should have been uniquely English, which they were not. Anthropologists have noted that warnings not to bequeath property in one's lifetime are virtually universal.[42] Ecclesiasticus (Ben Sirach), wrote in the second century BC: 'As long as thou livest and hast breath in thee, give not thyself over to any. For better it is that thy children should seek to thee, than that thou shouldst stand to their courtesy' (33: 19–20). Such warnings and tales were widespread throughout Western and Central Europe, including Italy, France and Austria,[43] that is to say, both in regions where property transfers were relatively common (Austria) and in regions where it was not (southern France and Italy). They persisted in Western culture in the following centuries, including nineteenth-century America.[44] They do not indicate the existence or non-existence of the custom to transfer property to offspring. They express anxiety about old age, loss of status and dependency, and the pain caused by the asymmetry in the love and devotion between parents and their offspring, which are part of the human condition even when the offspring are 'good'. No doubt in regions where it was the custom for parents to transfer their properties to one of their offspring there were some cases where the sons mistreated their parents and failed in their duty towards them. But it is impossible to conclude from the warnings and tales that this was the general rule. Because those texts were meant to warn and denounce, they exaggerated the wickedness of the offspring. Bernardino of Siena, in a rhetorical flourish, described the son beating his father and dragging him by the beard (and that in a region where property transfer was uncommon). The conduct of the offspring towards their aged parents no doubt varied according to their personalities, the parents' personalities, and the relations which had existed between them before the parents were old – just as is the case today. There were no doubt offspring who looked forward to their parents' death (whether to be free of the obligation to support them, or to receive the inheritance); others undoubtedly felt their loss and mourned their parents when they died. And just as there were good sons and others who were not so good, so too there were good parents and others who were not so good. It seems that tension between generations competing for limited resources, which at times erupts into conflict, is a universal phenomenon. Different societies developed different methods, according to their particular socio-economic and cultural character, to limit and regulate this tension.[45] In some parts of Europe the method was to transfer the property to the offspring in the parents' lifetime. Significantly, perhaps, research into cases of homicide in England has shown that patricide and matricide were extremely rare.[46] That was the reason that Thomas Chobham, the thirteenth-century author of a manual for confessors, stipulated a longer and harsher penance for the murder of a wife than of a father. The reason, he explained, was not because the former was the greater sin, but because men more commonly murder their wives than their fathers.[47]

The transfer or non-transfer of property to the offspring in the parents' lifetime was determined by the family structure, local custom, demographic and economic conditions, as well as the particular family circumstances. A man might transfer his property in accordance with the custom of his time and place, yet feel sorrow and loss of self-esteem because of the fall in his status, from an independent head of the household to being his son's dependant, while the son, having become the householder or proprietor, gained a new social status. The sorrow, loss of self-esteem and chafing against the reduced status were expressed in popular proverbs in parts of Austria where it was the custom to make such transfers, for example: 'To sit on the children's bench is hard for the old'; and retirement was called 'to give up living' (*ableben*).[48] These were not complaints about the behaviour of the offspring, but expressions of grief over the change in status and way of life. The old people behaved in accordance with the social custom of the time and place. But we know that social mores and personal feeling do not always go hand in hand. Those proverbs expressed the personal feelings.

This chapter has dealt with the norm of the duty to honour and support one's parents in old age. In the following chapters dealing with the social reality, I shall try to show that despite the prevalence of this norm in moralistic and didactic texts, there was also an awareness that not all the elderly could be helped by their offspring.

6

CHURCHMEN IN THEIR OLD AGE

The previous chapters have dealt with old people as a group, and consequently with images, attitudes and norms. The following chapters will deal with sub-groups of the aged population, and hence with the lives of old men and women in the various social strata, their political and social status and their economic conditions. In the discussion about the working stratum special attention will be given to some solutions to the economic plight of old people who could no longer work, partly or entirely. Later, the discussion on the upper social strata will examine the extent to which their members looked after their aged subordinates, such as retainers, office-holders and male and female servants. The question of how property was passed on to the younger generation, with all its implications, will be examined with regard to all the strata. The present chapter concerns monks, nuns, the secular clergy and their servants. These did not face the problem of passing their property on to their offspring, but the Church system did have to deal with the issue of retirement (or non-retirement) of office-holders, and the transfer (or non-transfer) of those positions to younger persons in their lifetime.

Anthropologists have found that some oral cultures reserve the functions of religion and magic for old men. As women age in these societies they are, as a rule, only relieved of certain taboos, but not given any functions. The custom of appointing old men to religious and magic roles originates in the belief that as a man's physical strength dwindles, he acquires a passive affiliation with supernatural powers. This affiliation is believed to endow him with a special intuition, a gift of knowing the occult and an ability to influence the natural environment.[1] At the same time, these roles compensate the old men for the loss of other sources of status. It mitigates the cruel physical decline and loss of status by presenting the new role as a promotion to a higher and more dignified status. This phenomenon is especially prominent in societies in which age is the basic organizing principle,[2] but is not exclusive to them. Aristotle, who also proposed that the priesthood should be reserved for old men who could no longer serve as counsellors, that is wield power, saw it above all as a compensation for their being denied a share in government.

The Medieval Church, however, did not set a high minimum age for the holders of its various offices. The minimum age for a sub-deacon was 18; for a deacon it was 25, and after the Council of Vienne, 20; 25 for a priest and 30 for a bishop. And indeed, many were appointed to those offices at such early ages. But although old men were expected to retire to the margin, many who held high office in the Church, who had been appointed or elected in maturity, remained in place until they were very old. When they did retire, it was generally at a very advanced age; others never retired at all and remained in office until they died. As we have seen, one of Aristotle's arguments for entrusting the priesthood to old men was that those who had led a long and active life in the service of the state merited a rest in their old age, the implication being that he did not consider the office of priesthood to be a very taxing one. But the senior office-holders in the Medieval Church could not be said to enjoy a peaceful life, free of effort and challenges. In view of the power of the Church, its diverse activities, its involvement in every aspect of the life and culture of individuals and society, and its struggles with the secular power, the men at the top of its hierarchy had to possess initiative and strength and be capable of intensive activity. And, indeed, many of the old office-holders did manifest such qualities and abilities. This was true of the secular clergy, founders of religious orders, abbots, and the monks who were chosen to hold office in the secular Church.

MONKS AND NUNS

Monks and nuns forswore both family and personal property, but they were provided for in their old age, protected from want and from loneliness. They remained in their religious communities until they died. The Lateran IV Council (1215) abolished the official oblation, namely, the practice of offering young children to a monastery by their parents who vowed that when the time came, the child would take the habit or the veil.[3] The new religious orders which were established in the early twelfth century, such as the Cistercians and Carthusians, had already refused to accept children before the banning of the oblation. After the official ban children were still sometimes given to the old Benedictine monasteries, though without their being bound by a vow. The mendicants also gradually lowered the minimum age for joining their orders.[5] But mostly it was neither small boys nor the aged who entered monasteries, but young men. By contrast, all the female religious orders still accepted little girls who were destined to become nuns.[6] At the other end of the scale, throughout the High and Late Middle Ages there seem to have been more mature or elderly women who entered convents and became nuns than there were men who became monks in maturity. It would appear that many more widows than widowers chose the monastic life. There were also women who had always wanted to become nuns, but could not do so in their youth because their parents forced them into marriage.[7] In the High Middle Ages it happened that older men entered monasteries (and some did so literally in their final days, so as to die wearing a monk's habit). But, by and large, individuals who retired to a monastery in their old age, and certainly most of the men who did so, did not become monks or nuns, but only went in as pensioners. Some orders stated explicitly that old age, like sickness, was a barrier to joining their houses, because the person would be unable to withstand the way of life which the order demanded of its members. The 1252 rule of the Poor Clares stated that only such women would be accepted as were not disqualified by advanced age, ill health or 'fatuity'.[8] But as monks and nuns grew old they remained in their religious communities and were looked after till they died.

The few studies of life expectancy in the male orders in the Late Middle Ages show that it did not differ significantly from that of the general population, particularly not in the case of the mendicant orders. A study of the life expectancy of the Dominican friars at the convent of Santa Maria Novella in Florence showed that during the recurrent epidemics in the latter half of the fourteenth century it matched the life expectancy of the general adult population. The Dominicans mingled with the general population, they taught and preached, and the priests among them also administered the sacraments, including the extreme unction. Nor did they flee from the city to the country, like the wealthy laity. Inevitably, their life expectancy declined during the epidemics.[9] Hatcher's study of the priory of Christ Church in Canterbury, and Barbara Harvey's study of Westminster Abbey, revealed that the life expectancy of the Benedictine brothers also declined, nearly as much as that of the general adult population. The Benedictines mingled with the populace much less than did the Dominicans, but neither were they quite isolated from the town's inhabitants, and the epidemics of the fifteenth century were largely urban. The monastery housed servants and visitors, lodgers and pilgrims, who came and went, and some of the monks went into town in connection with their administrative duties, or studied at Canterbury College in Oxford. Since many of the monks of the period came from rural areas, they were especially susceptible to the urban epidemics. In the fifteenth century, when the plague broke out repeatedly, or at other times of unusually high mortality, people under 30 were the worst affected, in the monastic communities as in the population at large. The rate of infection must have been high in a monastery, where the monks ate in the common refectory, slept in a common dormitory and went in and out of the infirmary where they tended the sick. On the other hand, the monasteries of Christ Church and Westminster Abbey were among the richest in England and enjoyed a high standard of living. They had good food and clothing, and a higher standard of hygiene than among the populace at large (though far from what would be considered adequate today; monks, like most other people, did not bathe frequently). There was also in the monastery an infirmary with a physician and a dispenser constantly in attendance. When necessary, an additional physician or surgeon was sent for from London. The heavier work of the monastery was done by the lay brothers and servants. Men who wished to enter the monastery were examined and had to swear that they did not suffer from an incurable or contagious disease.[10]

As yet there has been no similar study of the life expectancy in the female convents, but it is reasonable to assume that it was higher than that of women in the outside world, and also of that of the friars. The fact that they did not bear children reduced their mortality rate in their fertile years. Even nuns of the female orders which were affiliated with the mendicants did not mingle as much with the general population, did not serve it as priests and did not preach. Nor did they study at the universities, like some of the mendicants and Benedictines. Therefore, except for the nuns of the Augustinian order, or the order of St John of Jerusalem, or those who belonged to the 'third order', which nursed the sick in the hospitals, the nuns were less exposed to contagious diseases than were the monks and friars.

By now it is clear that from the few studies which analysed the scant sources of demographic data it would be impossible to gauge the ratio of old persons in the various monasteries. But it is possible to learn about their presence in the religious houses from the rules of various orders, the chronicles and the lives of the saints. Already in the sixth century, St Benedict of Nursia referred in his rule to the aged monks. Orderic Vitalis (c. 1075–c. 1142), wrote about a frail and sickly boy who had been brought to the monastery at the age of five, and who at the time of writing was 57. Orderic himself died at the same house, St Evroult in Normandy, when he was about 67.[11] John 'Lackland', who opposed the election of Stephen Langton as Archbishop of Canterbury, exiled all the monks of Christ Church in Canterbury, whose duty it was to elect the Archbishop, except for those of them who were old and the sick.[12] There were also old men in the European houses of the order of the Templars, as appears from the testimonies of 115 Templars at the trial against the order which was held in Paris in 1307. Generally, men joined this order when they were young, particularly the knights among them. These were sent to the Crusader kingdom and the Christian principalities in the Near East, while the middle-aged and the old members of the order inhabited the houses in Europe. Among the witnesses at the said trial there was a very high percentage of men of 50–59, a marked percentage aged 60–69, and a small percentage of men over 70.[13] After the death of Clara of Montefalco, when her sister nuns testified about her humility and good deeds, they related that she always undertook the hardest and dirtiest chores, and nursed the sick and aged nuns.[14]

While there are no data about the percentage of old individuals in the religious communities as a whole, what is known is the age at which the leading ones took office, their age at retirement, if any, and the age of many of them when they died. Francis of Assisi (1181–1226), an outstanding model of the 'new' saint,[15] who founded what was in its time the most revolutionary order of Western monasticism, laid its groundwork when he was a young man. He wrote the first rule for his order in about 1211, when he was about 29. Likewise, St Clare (1194–1253), who followed in Francis' footsteps and founded the order of the Poor Clares at his inspiration and with his guidance in the (vain) hope that it would be as revolutionary as the male Franciscan order, was also very young when she laid its foundations – only 20 years old. St Dominic (1170–1221) founded the Dominican order in 1215, when he was about 44. The founders of other orders were much older. St Bruno (c. 1030–1101) founded the Carthusian order when he was 54. Robert of Molesme (c. 1027–1110) laid the foundation for the Cistercian order at Cîteaux when he was about 71. Gilbert of Sempringham (c. 1083–1189, who died aged about 100!) founded the Gilbertine order when he was in his early sixties. When he was about 80 he had to contend with a rebellion by the lay brothers of his order and with its bad reputation, and withstand the investigations of the Church authorities into the matter.[16] Some abbots and masters-general of the various orders retired at some stage, while others remained in office in old age until they died. The abbots of Cluny in the latter half of the tenth century and in the eleventh enjoyed exceptional longevity. (Some historians ascribe the order's rapid growth and stability in that period to, among other factors, its abbots' lengthy stay in office.) Odo (879–942) died at 63; Odilon (962–1048), died at 86, and Hugh (1024–1109) at 85. They all remained in office until they died. The poet Gilles Li Muisis (1272–1352), who was the abbot of the Benedictine monastery of St Martin in Tournai, remained in office until he died aged 80.[17] Those who retired apparently did not do so before the age of 60. Humbert de Romans (c. 1200–1277) retired from his position as Master-General of the Dominican order in 1263, when he was about 65, and devoted himself to his literary work until his death at age 77.[18] Raymond Penafort (c. 1180–1273), who was also an important canonist, retired from the same office in 1240, when he was about 60, but remained active for many more years, especially in proselytizing Jews and Saracens.[19] Another Dominican, Stephen of Bourbon (1272–1352), a tireless preacher and Inquisitor, who travelled in connection with his office through town and country far beyond the Dominican province of Lyons to which he belonged, did not retire until his final years, when he was nearly 80. He, too, devoted his last years to a great book, which he did not finish.[20] Gilbert of Sempringham retired from the headship of his order aged about

89. Hildegarde of Bingen (1098–1179) became the abbess of her convent at the age of 38. In 1150, when she was about 52, she founded a new convent near Rupertsberg and moved there with her nuns. In 1165, aged about 67, she founded another convent in Eibingen. All this was in addition to her extensive literary work and her activity on behalf of church reform. Heloise (c. 1100–1163) was the abbess of her convent until the day she died, aged 63. When Ella, Countess of Salisbury (c. 1191–1261) was widowed, she founded a Cistercian convent and served as its abbess for 20 years. She retired from this office at 68 and died at about 70. Juliana of Falconieri (c. 1270–1341) founded the female order of the Servites when she was 63, and headed her convent until her death at about 70. Another woman who was able to enter the religious life only when she was widowed was Frances of Rome (1384–1440). At the age of 52 she became the head of a community of religious women who adopted the Benedictine rule without a vow, and remained its head until she died at 56. There can be no doubt that old men and women occupied important positions in the monastic hierarchy. Their status was not based on their age, but on their social stratum, on their material means, which had enabled them (or one of their ancestors) to found a monastic house and acquire an education, as well as on their personalities. Many of them began their careers before they were old, but their advanced age did not prevent them from remaining in office and from functioning. They did not have to retire.

The abbots and heads of religious houses enjoyed the same privileges in retirement as they had while in office. Following a visitation by the bishop to one of the houses of regular canons in the diocese of Lincoln, a specific order was issued concerning the terms of retirement of the abbot, John of Grymesby. It stated that he should be assigned a suitable room with all his furniture and other appurtenances, and should receive twice as much as the other canons (that is to say, food, clothing, etc.).[21] The circumstances of this abbot's retirement are unclear. He may have been compelled to retire for some reason, and was dissatisfied with what he received. His age is also unknown. But the case suggests that when abbots retired voluntarily because of their advanced age, they enjoyed favourable conditions. John Cardinal entered the Hospital of St John the Baptist in Ely in 1350. By 1379 he had become its master, and in 1391 he retired. He was apportioned separate quarters in the hospital for himself and his personal servant, lighting, clothing, food and drink. He must have been in his early sixties at the time.[22] As for the general run of old monks, already the rule of St Benedict of Nursia stipulated that they must be relieved of some of the duties and restrictions which it laid upon the other monks. Benedict devoted a chapter to sick monks (Ch. 36) and another (Ch. 37) to the children and the aged. In the latter he stated that human nature itself is merciful to people at these stages of life, but the special consideration for them should be incorporated in the rule. With regard to food, the rule was not to be strictly applied to them, and they were to be allowed to eat before the fixed hours for meals.[23] In the rule of the Carthusian order of 1127, the prior Guigues justified the admission of lay brothers to the order by stating that some of the monks were weak and old and could not do the hard work. The Life of St Hugh of Lincoln (c. 1140–1200) described how, when his father grew old and weak, the prior of the monastery of Villarbenoît, where father and son were both monks, ordered the son personally to nurse his father, which Hugh did lovingly and devotedly. He made his bed, dressed and undressed him, and when the father grew too weak, he fed him.[24] The mystic Mechtild of Magdeburg (1210–97) entered the convent of Helfta when she was in her early sixties. She was admitted at such an advanced age both on account of her aristocratic birth and because she was already known as a mystic. (She had begun her religious life as a Beguine.) In one of her works she gave thanks to God for the nursing she received in the convent when she was old, sick and almost completely blind. She spoke of others in the convent as her hands and eyes. She died there aged 87.[25]

Some of the monastic rules, bishops' orders following visitations, and instructions issued to the monasteries following the church councils, referred only to the duty of looking after the feeble and the sick, but not the aged.[26] Presumably those of them who needed nursing were included among the sick and feeble. At the above mentioned Benedictine priory of Christ Church in Canterbury, the infirmary housed the frail and aged monks who were no longer able to follow the routine of the monastery, as well as the sick patients.[27] The order of the Templars maintained special small houses for its sick, disabled and aged members. Two such houses are known to have existed in England from the late twelfth century, one known as Denny Abbey in Cambridgeshire, and the other the Eagle in Lincolnshire.[28] Sometimes the old and disabled monks had personal servants, as did the Dominican Marculinus of Forli, who died in 1397. He was an ordinary friar who was not especially esteemed by his fellow friars (as evidenced by the fact that, unlike the lay people who gathered in the monastery chapel after his death, the friars did not regard him as a saint).[29] Only a monk who contracted leprosy was removed to a leprosarium with which the monastery had such an arrangement, and even that not invariably. Sometimes a leprous monk was isolated and nursed in his community.[30]

As we have seen, the rule of St Benedict of Nursia stipulated that the status of monks in their communities was not to depend on their age. The only position which the rule assigned to aged monks was that of gatekeeper: one who was a wise (sapiens) old man, who would know what questions to ask and answers to give, and who, being old, would not wander away.[31] His wisdom and experience as much as his physical weakness fitted him for this office. According to the rule, his advanced age made him unable, not unwilling, to wander. On the other hand, an order given following a bishop's visitation to one of the monasteries implied that the aged monk could be counted on not to wish to wander where he should not. According to this order, if one of the canons had to leave the monastery and go to the city to be bled, the abbot was to send him in the company of a monk of 'ripe discretion and age', who would stay at his side throughout the blood-letting and recovery, and would later report on his conduct.[32] Judging from a story recounted in *The Life of St Anselm of Canterbury*, older monks not only supervised the morals of their young fellows, but were also asked to solve personal problems, which called for maturity and tact. Eadmer told the following story: a young monk touched his genital organs and at once felt a very sharp pain, 'for his flesh felt so heavy, it was as if a great weight of lead were attached to that part of his body, drawing him downwards'. When Anselm, seeking to help him, asked to be shown the painful part, the young monk was too shy to do so. Anselm therefore took him to an old monk (*grandaevo fratre*), who was famous for his piety, to examine him discreetly, discover the nature of his ailment and help him as best he could.[33] Evidently, Anselm thought that the young monk would feel less embarrassed and threatened to reveal what he believed was a shameful condition to an old monk, who would be more detached from the conventions, than to a younger one.

The old monks were cared for, but they did not enjoy an honorable status on account of their age. In the manuals for monks and the monastic rules in the High Middle Ages the old monks had no special standing. There were only some generalized praises of old age as the stage of life at which it is possible to attain spiritual perfection, and the benefit which the young could derive from listening to the old.[34] It was the personality of the old monks, and the regard in which they were held in their communities, which determined their individual status.

In Chapter 10 we shall discuss the role of the monasteries in caring for aged paupers. Here I shall confine myself to the extent to which they secured the livelihood of their aged servants and other monastery employees. Some of the monasteries made provisions for the old age of the laymen and minor clergymen, who served in their houses. The beneficiaries of these pensions were clerks, squires, bakers, laundresses, male and female servants, who were not numbered among the monks. Sometimes the monastery granted the pension, and sometimes the employee purchased it from savings. One argument used by monasteries in resisting the demands of kings and patrons (the latter usually descendants of the original founders), to provide a pension for one of their people, was that it would reduce their ability to provide for their own clerks and servants.[35] The pension usually consisted of living quarters (inside or outside the monastery's periphery), food and clothing in accordance with the individual's standing, and pocket money. It was an acknowledgement of a moral obligation to secure the old age of those who had served the monastery for many years: it was not a legal obligation. We do not know how many of the bursars of monasteries acknowledged this obligation and provided any kind of pension, or how many of the employees of a given monastery benefited from it.

In some cases a prior agreement was made with an artisan that in return for his work he would receive a subsistence for the rest of his life, and a smaller pension would be paid to his widow. Again, we do not know how common this practice was. At the beginning of the twelfth century the French monastery of St Aubain in Angers made a contract with a certain gifted painter: the latter undertook to paint whatever he was asked in the monastery, as well as make 'glazed windows'; in return, the monastery undertook to grant him a house and a vineyard for the rest of his life. After his death the vineyard and the house were to revert to the monastery 'unless he had a son who knew his father's art and could serve the monastery' (like him).[36] A similar contract was drawn up between the monastery of St Remigius in Rheims and its victualler. The agreement specified in detail what he would receive by way of food, clothing and money for the rest of his life, and what his widow would receive if he predeceased her, for the rest of her life. Once they were both dead, the monastery had no obligation to their heirs.[37] Such an arrangement, granted for the worker's lifetime only, was most similar to a modern old-age pension. It differed from the military fief, which was originally a form of payment for services rendered, but in time came to be heritable. Unfortunately, as Rosenthal pointed out, in the Middle Ages, retirement with a pension was not a general institution, but only a 'sporadic practice'.[38]

THE SECULAR CLERGY

Popes were elected at an advanced age, whether they began their religious lives as monks or had belonged from the start to the secular church hierarchy. Very few were elected in their forties;[39] most were elected in their fifties or sixties, and some were even older. The following are some examples of popes whose birthdates are known, in a rising order of their age upon election. We include the dates of death, as popes remained in office till they died (except in cases where political conflicts broke out after the election, a pope was deposed or an anti-pope elected). Gregory VII (c. 1020–1085) was elected in 1073, aged 53, died aged 65; Victor III (1027–1087) was elected in 1086, aged 59, died aged 60; Nicholas IV (1227–1292) was elected in 1288, aged 61, and died aged 65; Callistus II (c. 1050–1124), was elected in 1119, aged about 69, and died aged 74; Innocent VI (1282–1362) was elected in 1352, aged 70, and died aged 80; Lucius III (c. 1110–1185) was elected in 1181 when he was about 71, and died aged 75; Gregory IX (c. 1155–1241) was elected in 1227, aged about

72, and died aged 86; John XXII (c. 1244–1334) was elected in 1316, aged 72, and died aged 90; Honorius IV (1210–1287) was elected in 1285, aged 75, and died aged 77; Celestine V (c. 1209–1296) was elected in 1294, aged about 85.[40] The Church could be said to be headed by elderly or old men.

Men were elected or appointed to other high offices in the church at various ages, and the rate of promotion in the hierarchy varied from one to the other. But those who lived long remained in office until they were very old. Some of them, like certain abbots and heads of monastic orders, did not retire at all, and those who did, retired at an advanced age, 60 being apparently the earliest. Some were elected at an advanced age. Here are a few examples of the ages at election and retirement (or death) of certain bishops and archbishops: Lanfranc (c. 1005–1089) was appointed Archbishop of Canterbury by William the Conqueror when he was about 65, and remained in office until his death, aged 84. St Anselm of Canterbury (c. 1033–1109) became Archbishop of Canterbury aged 60, and remained in office until he died, aged 75. His struggles during those years against the kings of England William Rufus and Henry I, his periods of exile and his intense activity in a variety of fields which entailed much travelling, were described by the author of his Life, Eadmer. Stephen Langton (c. 1150–1228) was elected Archbishop of Canterbury at the instigation of Innocent III when he was about 57, and died aged 78. These are examples of bishops who did not retire: Arnold of Rochester (1040–1124) was elected Bishop of Rochester in 1114, when he was 74, and remained in office until his death at 84. John of Salisbury (c. 1115–1185) was elected Bishop of Chartres in 1176, when he was 61, and died aged 65. Robert Grosseteste (c. 1175–1253) was elected Bishop of Lincoln when he was 60 and died in office, aged 78. Bishops who retired included Hato, Bishop of Troyes, who retired and entered the monastery of Cluny when he was about 69;[41] Marbode, Bishop of Rennes, retired to the monastery of St Aubain in Angers when he was about 80; Arnulf, Bishop of Lisieux, retired to the monastery of St Victor in Paris when he was 81.[42]

Throughout the Middle Ages there were many churchmen who not only held fiefs, but also served their kings in various offices, some as their close advisors. European kings in the Middle Ages were young, while many of their churchmen advisors were elderly or aged. Having taken most of the examples of old bishops and archbishops from England, let us look at some of the churchmen who served as advisors to the kings of France (though some of the above-named English churchmen also served as royal counsellors). One close advisor of Louis VI was Geoffrey of Vendome, a Benedictine abbot, who served the king until his death at 1132, aged 62. The best known royal counsellor was Suger (c. 1081–1151), abbot of the monastery of St Denis, who served as counsellor to Louis VI and Louis VII, and as the regent when Louis VII went on a crusade. He remained regent until he was about 68. A close advisor who served as chancellor to both Philip II Augustus and his heir, Louis VIII, was Guerin, who belonged to the order of Hospitallers, and was elected Bishop of Senlis. He served the king until close to his death in 1227, when he was 70. Other aged advisors of Philip II Augustus were Guillaume, who in 1200 at the age of 80 became bishop of Bourges, and his uncle, Guillaume 'of the white hands', who became successively Bishop of Chartres, Archbishop of Sens, Archbishop of Rheims and a cardinal. He headed the king's council, and when Philip II Augustus went on the crusade, served as co-regent with the queen mother, Adèle, who was then about 60 and he about 67. There are many such examples from all over Europe.

The European kings employed counsellors from among the churchmen, but it is well known that throughout the Middle Ages there were tension and conflict between the two powers, the Church and the state, over their respective standing and rights. (Churchmen in the service of kings who engaged in these power struggles were sometimes torn between the two loyalties.) Whenever this conflict broke out, young kings contended with elderly or aged popes. The four notable Medieval dramas of power contests between kings and popes point up the disparity between their ages. In 1077, at one of the high points in the struggle between the German emperor Henry IV and Pope Gregory VII (c. 1020–1085), Henry was 22 and Gregory 57. The age difference between Henry II of England and Thomas à Becket was less. Becket (1118–1170) was 52 when he was murdered in Canterbury Cathedral; the king was 37. But Alexander III (c. 1100–1181), the pope who, in the following year, set the terms for lifting the interdict which had been imposed on Henry's continental fiefs after the murder, was 61. Emperor Frederick II, *Stupor mundi* (1194–1250), was 34 when the 73–year–old Pope Gregory IX (1155–1241) excommunicated him in 1228. When the men of Philip IV 'the Fair' of France attacked Pope Boniface VIII (c. 1235–1303) in Anagni, the king was 35 and the pope 68. The cooperation and the conflict between the Church and the state were central factors in the history of Western Europe in the Middle Ages. Their causes were ideological, structural and power-driven, but the question remains, to what extent the age gap between the monarchs and the popes affected the conflict whenever it erupted. To answer this question it is not enough to examine the particular historical circumstances of each outbreak. It might be possible to do so after a thorough investigation of the personalities of the contestants, including the effect of the age variable on their actions and reactions.

The men who held high office in the Church – archbishops, bishops, wealthy rectors and vicars – did not suffer economic hardships when they retired. If they retired they had to give up their benefice but then they received substantial pensions, and some of them also owned property or other sources of income. The case of the lower clergy was less prosperous. Jean Froissart became a priest in his early thirties. In his poem 'The Fair Bush of Youth', which he wrote in 1373 when he had been a priest for some time, he described his economic circumstances: he did not have to engage in manual labour, and was assured of an annuity that provided him with a comfortable existence. Froissart had not engaged in manual labour before he became a priest, but having become one, he knew that his future welfare was assured and he need no longer look for patrons. He was given one of the wealthiest and most important rectorships of Cambrai, and received 40 pounds a year.[43]

A priest who received such an income was also insured against his old age. If he became incapacitated, he could obtain permission from his bishop to employ a curate or coadjutor, whom he would pay out of his own income; or he could give up his benefice and receive a substantial or at least a reasonable part of his former income as a pension until he died. Clearly, not all parish priests enjoyed an income large enough to employ a curate, or to share with a successor. Many minor clergymen did not even have a benefice, but received an annual salary. The Church recognized that aged clergymen who had to retire were entitled to a pension, but very often the men who retired from the lower ranks received only a tiny amount. There were, moreover, some who wanted to retire, and should have done so, being old, sick and sometimes senile, deaf or blind, but were not allowed to retire. That is evident from the complaints of parishioners, who frequently protested that their priest was no longer capable. The work of a parish priest was far from easy. In addition to the holy services in the church, he had to see to the religious processions and to march in them, and visit the sick and the dying throughout his parish. But the church authorities were not always quick to replace an old priest and appoint a successor.

The resources of the Church were not unlimited, and certainly not its willingness to spend them. Rosenthal and Orme have given examples of pensions which were paid to clergymen in England in the latter half of the fourteenth century and first half of the fifteenth. Some made for a comfortable life, some for a modest existence, and some were too small to secure life at all. They ranged from one to 20 pounds per annum, when the minimum income for a reasonable existence was five pounds. The sum was determined principally by the income from the retiring clergyman's benefice, which had to suffice for both his pension and his successor's salary.[44] The fate of unbeneficed clergymen, such as chaplains of private chapels or chantry priests, was still worse and so was the fate of other minor clergymen. Active priests who had to share the income of the benefice with their retired predecessors must have felt resentful, though we find no evidence of this in the source material. A rather unusual case concerning a fairly high churchman illustrates the problems which could arise in these situations. Gerald of Wales was an archdeacon. (He aspired to a bishopric, and was in fact elected bishop, but the election was not approved by the pope.) When he was nearly 60 he began to plan his retirement. He arranged with his nephew for the latter to succeed him as Archdeacon of Brecon, but without receiving the income thereof until the uncle's death. But the nephew disappointed him bitterly by failing to keep his word. Gerald eventually retired in 1207, aged about 61.[45]

In line with the general awareness, noted in previous chapters, of the economic distress of old people, the church authorities were also aware that retired clergymen who did not receive an adequate pension suffered want. Moreover, the church authorities viewed it as an indignity that old churchmen should be brought to the edge of starvation. Already at a church council in 816 concern was voiced for the fate of sick old secular canons, and a resolution was passed that, despite the fact that canons were allowed to own houses, the bishop would see to the establishment of a special house for the accommodation of sick and old canons, to be near the others' residence. It was also resolved that all the other canons would look after them lovingly and compassionately, visit them and read the Scriptures to them.[46] At the 1261 church council in Mainz it was resolved to devote the necessary resources to maintain almshouses for priests who, for reasons of age and debility, were unable to continue serving, as it disgraced the priesthood if those who had served God were reduced to beggary.[47] This awareness, as well as a sense of dignity and shame, led to the arrangements for pensions for retired clerymen, and for houses to accommodate them. But the church authorities stopped short of setting up a comprehensive and satisfactory system.

Those of the minor clergy who had an additional source of income could supplement their pension without having to resort to the asylums. In 1301, the manorial court of King Ripton dealt with a plea concerning an agreement for the transfer of a small plot of land by a chaplain to a couple of peasants. The problem arose because the agreement had not been drawn up before the court, as was customary – the reason being, according to the peasant plaintiff, that the chaplain had been far too ill to come to court. The plaintiff stated that the agreement was that he and his wife would cultivate the chaplain's land for the rest of his life. They would supply the seed, and give him the produce. In addition, they had under-taken to provide him with a coat of good quality every year. Furthermore, the peasant claimed, they had agreed that if the chaplain lived more than three years after they signed the agreement, they would pay him 40 shillings the first year, 26 in the second, 13 in the third, and no more thereafter. In return, the chaplain had agreed to bequeath the land to their children. When the chaplain died they came to claim the inheritance. The jurors rejected the claim, stating that they had never heard of the agreement.[48] We do not know when the chaplain acquired the land. In all probability, he did not cultivate it himself even before he fell ill. At any rate, it afforded him a small additional income when he was incapacitated.

Some patrons purchased pensions for the minor clergymen in their service, and clergymen who could afford it sometimes purchased such a pension in a monastery, or in one of the hospitals which were run by the Mendicants or religious communities.[49] Others who had no property, or whose property did not yield a sufficient income, and had not enough to purchase a pension, or whose patrons did not take care of them, entered one of those hospitals, (which were, in effect, almshouses). Some of the hospitals were established specifically for retired priests who had to give up their benefices, and for younger priests who had fallen ill; other hospitals accommodated them alongside needy laymen. It is known that such hospitals existed in the thirteenth to fifteenth centuries in Valencia in Spain, in Tournai in France and in several places in England.[50] Some were founded by laymen, some by bishops or other church authorities. The men who entered those houses were essentially recipients of charity, rather than possessors of a pension they had bought or that had been bought for them. They could make no prior agreement, such as was made with the purchase of a pension, stipulating what they were entitled to receive by way of food, drink, clothing and pocket money. The St Mary hospital in the county of York accommodated pilgrims, and blind or leprous priests resided there permanently. In some of the hospitals, such as the one founded by Stapledon, Bishop of Exeter in the early fourteenth century, the rule forbade the resident priests to bequeath their meagre property to their relatives. Two-thirds of it went to the almshouse and the remaining third was divided equally among the resident clergymen. Some of the residents had pensions and some had none. The small sums reveal their poverty. One resident left £13 when he died, five left a little over five pounds each, and 17 old clergymen left one pound or less.[51] As Orme's study has shown, the need for almshouses for retired clergymen varied with the demographic and economic conditions, which affected the ratio between the benefices (that the retiring priest and his successor could subsist on) and the number of retired priests. After the Black Death there were fewer priests, but the same number of benefices. Thus more priests could obtain a reasonable pension and fewer of them needed almshouses. We do not know how many received no pension at all, or whose pension was inadequate for their subsistence, and who did not find shelter in a hospice at a time of demographic pressure. As stated before, the Church had created something which approached, but never quite achieved, a pension scheme for retired clergymen.

As for the laymen and the minor clergy who served the senior clergymen, some of the latter left them something in their will, and some, like the monasteries and the laity, promised their dependants a pension of some kind for the rest of their lives. Bequests to manservants and maidservants, clerks and retainers, much less an assured pension, were a matter of good-will. We have no way of knowing how common either of these were. But an examination of wills from the Late Middle Ages has shown that bequests of small sums of money, household effects and clothing, to male and female servants (not necessarily old ones), were much more common than pensions for those who had served the testator for many years. It might be said that granting a lifetime pension was the exception. Sometimes the testator left an amount to be divided by, and at the discretion of, the executor of the will among all the servants. In other cases the will specified the sum or the object which each of the named servants, clerks or companions, would receive, according to the length of his service and the testator's estimation of his devotion.[52] Those wills reveal a certain personal relationship. In English wills from the fourteenth century and the first quarter of the fifteenth, the sums bequeathed by clergymen to their servants ranged from a few shillings to 100 shillings.[53] Similar sums were bequeathed by canons from the Lyonnais region of France in the latter half of the fourteenth century and the first half of the fifteenth. (In one exceptional case the amount was £25.)[54] Sometimes a squire received, in addition to a sum of money, his arms and horse.[55] In so far as clergymen took pains to obtain a pension for those who served them, it was in the form of payment to a monastery which would provide them with housing, food, clothing and pocket money within its periphery, or an allowance in kind.[56] Others contented themselves with leaving instructions in the will to pay the wages owed to their servants, with additional compensation. In 1420 a clergyman left his servant 40 shillings above his wages (*ultra stipendium*), as well as a coat, a hat, a sword, blankets and other covers.[57]

Gerontologists generally agree that intellectual activity in advanced age slows the decline of the intellectual faculties. The more active the intellect, the more efficiently are the memory, suppleness of thought and analysis preserved from deterioration. Cicero, too, noted this in his book on old age. As we have seen, the Medieval manuals made little reference to such activity. Nevertheless, this did not prevent many clergymen who were also active in the sphere of learned culture – such as historians, theologians, authors of philosophical and scientific treatises and poets – from continuing to engage in creative work in their old age, whether they retired or not. A list of all who produced at least some of their works between the ages of 60 and 70 would be too long, and we must again confine ourselves to a few examples. Orderic Vitalis (*c.* 1075–*c.* 1142) wrote most of the volumes of his *History of the Church* between the ages of 48 and 62. After a short interval, he resumed writing and continued until close to his death at about 67. The historian William of Malmesbury (*c.* 1080–*c.* 1143) began to write at an early age but worked on his last book, *The New History*, almost until his death, aged about 63.[58] Anselm of Canterbury wrote *The Procession of the Holy Spirit* and *Why God Became Man (Cur Deus homo)* during his exile when he was in his sixties. In the two years before his death at 75, he completed a book he had begun 20 years before.[59] Albertus Magnus, who died at the age of 80, continued to write almost to his dying day, and so did Vincent of Beauvais, who died aged 74, and Hildegard of Bingen, who died aged 81. She began to write her book, *De operatione Dei*, when she was about 68. The already mentioned Humbert de Romans and Stephen of Bourbon devoted themselves to their literary work after their retirement at a very advanced age. Likewise, Gilles Li Muisis, who has also been mentioned, remained at the head of his monastery and continued to write poetry at a very advanced age. It is possible to extend the list much further. In the past no less than in our time, the spheres of creative learning, art and literature, remain open before the old person who had those abilities and whose inner resources and faculties have not deteriorated. In the Middle Ages, much of the cultural heritage and historical narrative which were passed on to the younger generation were the work of old men.

The teachers at the institutions of higher learning were clergymen. We learn that a teacher's standing and authority were augmented by his advanced age, paradoxically, from Abelard's sarcastic remarks about his teacher Anselm of Laon (his birthdate is unknown; he died in 1117). Abelard, the arrogant and ambitious young man who came to conquer the centres of scholarship and education with his new method, stated that no one who asked Anselm a question ever received a satisfactory answer. He had many words at his command but what he said was meaningless. The fire he kindled with his words filled the house with smoke but did not illuminate it. Comparing him to the accursed tree which bears no fruit, with a flash of cruelty Abelard went on, 'Then I approached this old man . . . who owed his reputation more to long practice than to intelligence or memory . . .'.[60]

To conclude, though power was not based on an ascriptive criterion of age, it appears that the practice within the Church hierarchy was to favour age. Not only did prelates as well as abbesses continue to officiate in advanced age but many of them were elected or appointed when they were quite old, and had distinguished late-life careers. However, their status was not based on their age but on their roles and personalities. For minor clergymen (who were sometimes forced to retire despite the fact that there was no legal age of retirement) there were certain arrangements for pensions, but these were not always adequate. Monks and nuns as we have seen, were provided for their old age.

7

OLD AGE IN THE RANKS OF THE RULERS AND SOLDIERS

Not only the kings who contended with the popes were young. So were most of the European kings in the High and Late Middle Ages. Some were crowned in their minority, and regents ruled in their place for several years, and most became kings between their late teens and early thirties. Few reached the throne in their forties: Pedro III of Aragon began to reign in 1276, when he was 40; Alfonso VI of Castile and Leon in 1072, when he was 42, and the German Emperor Konrad III began to reign in 1138, when he was 45. All the others came to the throne at an earlier age. This was not a result of ideology, but a consequence of the dynastic principle. They became kings following the death of their fathers (or the death of another person from whom they inherited the crown), and kings did not live long.

Between the beginning of the eleventh century and the beginning of the fifteenth, the only European monarch to reach the age of 79 was Alfonso VI (1103–1109), king of Castile and Leon. None of the other kings of that kingdom reached the age of 70, and only two were over 60 when they died. (Alfonso IX [1166–1230] died aged 64, and Alfonso X [1221–1284] at 63.) Only three of the kings of Aragon were over 60 when they died. (James II [1264–1327] was 63; James I [1208–1276] and Pedro IV [1319–1387] were 68.) Only four of the German emperors were over 60 when they died. (Frederick I, 'Barbarossa' [1123–1190] drowned in a stream in Asia Minor en route to the Crusade, aged 67; Louis IV of Barvaria [1287–1347] died aged 60; Charles IV of Luxemburg [1316–1378] died aged 62, and Sigismund of Luxemburg [1368–1437] was 69 when he died.) Only three of the kings of England lived past their sixtieth year. (Henry III [1207–1272] and Edward III [1312–1377] were 65 when they died, and Edward I [1239–1307] was 68.) As for the Capetian dynasty of France, Louis VII [1120–1180] was the only king to reach the age of 60. This fact undoubtedly intensified Louis XI's anxiety in his final years. (He too died aged 60.) Very few women inherited the throne in the Middle Ages, and not all of them were allowed to reign. When Henry I left the throne to his daughter Matilda (1102–1176) it led to a civil war, in the course of

114

which, in 1148, she was forced to retire. (When her rival King Stephen died, her son succeeded and became King Henry II.) She died aged 65. Constance (1154–1198) who inherited the crown of Sicily, reigned very briefly. Other claimants to the throne won support for their opposition to her, and even more for their opposition to her husband, the German Emperor Henry VI. He was finally crowned in 1194, and died three years later. Even then, Constance was not acknowledged as queen, but only as the regent during the minority of her son, who became Emperor Frederick II, *Stupor mundi*. She died in 1198, aged 44. Only two queens actually reigned – the queens of Naples, Jeanne I (1326–1382) and Jeanne II (1371–1435). The first died aged 44 (thought she outlived four husbands), and the second when she was 64.

After the Golden Bull was issued in Germany in 1356, when emperors no longer inherited the throne from their predecessors but were chosen by the seven electors, the age of the candidate apparently did not affect the electors' choice. They were moved by political and dynastic considerations. Wenceslas (1361–1419) was elected in 1378 when he was 17, and Sigismund of Luxemburg in 1411 when he was 43. When Medieval kings were dethroned it was not on account of their age, and the few who did live to be old were not asked to abdicate. But if we believe one of the chroniclers, it was possible to ascribe to an aged king the same intellectual decline that was ascribed to any old man. The author of the Life of Edward the Confessor (1003–1066) related how the king told of a vision he had had, which was later interpreted as foretelling the Norman conquest. When the archbishop heard the king, he whispered in the duke's ear that the king was 'broken with age and disease, and knew not what he said'. Since the chronicler was writing after the Norman conquest, it is obvious that he did not approve of the archbishop's remark, and was implicitly critical of his short-sightedness. The old king clearly did know what he was saying.[1]

OFFICE HOLDERS IN THE ITALIAN COMMUNES

In the Medieval Italian communes, before the establishment of the rule of princes with its dynastic principle, those who had the vote were free to choose their rulers. It appears that both in theory and in practice the general preference was for middle-aged men, provided, of course, that they met the other necessary criteria. The Florentine Brunetto Latini wrote *The Book of Treasure* (*Li livres dou trésor*) in the 1260s, when he was about 40. He wrote it in French during his period of exile, but it was translated into Tuscan Italian in his lifetime, and was widely read. Intended as a manual for rulers, it is an encyclopedic work, containing summaries of all the various fields of knowledge, for the ruler was expected to be an educated person. The second part of the third book was devoted to political theory. It discussed principles, but it also referred to the political systems in the cities of Italy in general, and in Florence in particular. According to Brunetto, the best system is the one in which all the office holders are elected from among the qualified for a limited period, and regularly replaced. The chosen men should be old (*vieus*). He relied on Aristotle and applied to old men Aristotle's dictum about the middle aged, namely, that they were best suited to rule. He admitted that some old men were not wise, and it was therefore necessary to choose men who were old in wisdom as well as in years.[2] He used the term 'old', but though he set the minimum age for full citizenship at 25, he made no mention of how old the 'old men' had to be when elected to high office. In the first book he discussed the theory of humours, distinguished between different personality types due to the individual balance of their humours, and referred to the changes wrought by age on the temperament. His description of old people is much the same as in the scientific writings, and he also ascribed to them a decline of the intellectual faculties, without even distinguishing between the stages of old age and decrepitude.[3] It would seem, therefore, that despite his use of the word 'old', Brunetto had in mind not old but middle-aged men as most suited to rule, and above all, he wanted to show that young men must await their turn, and should not be entrusted with the most important positions. (He himself returned from exile in 1266, when he was in his mid-forties, and was elected to the city council.)

And indeed, most of the Italian republics enacted a minimum age for the various offices, to prevent the election of men who were too young. Men became full citizens of their republics at the age of 25, and provided they met the necessary criteria – including the right social background and economic status, suitable connections and personality – they could advance gradually through the ranks. We have seen that in Florence during the Late Middle Ages a man had to be at least 30 to be elected to one of the three major councils of the commune, and 45 was the minimum age for the highest office of all, that of 'standard-bearer of justice'.[4] The constitution of Genoa in 1363 set 33 as the minimum age for serving in the various councils of the Republic. The Doge had to be at least 40 years old. Some of the cities of southern France, which were merely autonomous, also promulgated ordinances which permitted only a very gradual rise in the local hierarchy, and there too a man had to be over 30 before he could enter the service.[5] As we saw in the first chapter, people were free to retire from public office between 60 and 70, but where there was no regular turnover in office they were not as a rule required to retire, nor were they disqualified from election (notwithstanding Alberti's description, in his book, of the retired family patriarchs). When the Genoese fleet sailed to attack Acre in 1257, it was commanded by Admiral de la Turca, who was then an old man of 73. He was accompanied by his son Mirialdo, described by the chronicler as a brave and honourable man, in whom the men had greater confidence than in his old father. But the son died during the

journey and the chronicler attributed the inaction of the fleet in the subsequent battle to the 'madness' which seized the old admiral after his son's
death.[6]

The minimum age required by Venetian law for various office-holders
and for service in the various councils was similar to that required by the
laws of other communes. The minimum age for serving in the Great
Council was 25, as it was for election to the office of councillor in the
Signoria. The minimum age for serving in the senate – the central council
of the Republic – was 32, and for service in the Council of Ten it was 40.
Men could retire from these offices at the age of 70. In reality, however,
men under 50 were rarely elected to the higher offices, to the military high
command, or any of the governing bodies: the senate, the Council of Ten,
the Signoria and the Collegio. Moreover, men took advantage of their right
to retire at 70 only from those offices which entailed much work and
brought little profit. The Doge was generally elected from among the
Procurators of San Marco. These Procurators were old men, experienced
in the politics of the Republic, who had already held high office and acted
as advisors to the Doge. The Doges who were elected from their company
were quite old. Between 1400 and 1600 their average age at election was
72. Some were elected in their sixties, and some in their late seventies or
even in their eighties. Their age and experience were regarded as ensuring
a wise and balanced government, and moreover, that their term in office
would not be excessively prolonged.[7] One of the most famous old Doges
was Enrico Dandallo. He was elected in 1192, aged about 85 and partially
blind. In 1204, aged about 97, he undertook to lead the Venetians on the
Fourth Crusade, which instead of reaching the Holy Land ended with
the conquest of Constantinople. According to the chronicler Villehardouin,
before setting off on the journey the Doge announced that he was old,
feeble and ill and in need of rest, 'but I see that no one could lead you
like myself, who am your lord'; therefore, if they so wished, he would
lead them. Hearing these words they all cheered, and some shed tears of
admiration for the great sacrifice he was making, who had every reason to
stay behind, but was moved by 'his great heart' to act as he did. In his
description of the journey Villehardouin repeatedly referred to the Doge's
wisdom, courage and shrewdness.[8]

The position of old men in the ruling stratum of Venice may be described
as a typical example of status based on two criteria: the age which confers
it ('ascribed criterion'), and personal attainment ('achieved criterion'),
namely, the men's social and economic standing and the network of connections they had built up. Yet in Venice, as we know, it was not based
entirely on personal achievements and age, but also on parentage and
origins. A person's origins 'ascribed' him status from birth. The well-
known 'myth of Venice' depicted it as a model republic, whose constitution
produced an ideal balance between might and right, order and liberty,

which was led by men who were moderate, modest and devoted to the general welfare. Historical research, especially in the past decade, has led to a revision of this image, and shown that in certain areas it was no more than a myth.[9] But, as Finlay's study has shown, the gerontocracy, which could only have arisen in an oligarchy and which it served to underpin, was a reality, for better or worse.

Comparison between human society and animal communities is always problematic, to say the least. But since we are dealing with the Middle Ages, when it was customary to draw analogies between humans and real or imaginary animals, I cannot resist the temptation to do so too. According to Konrad Lorenz, ethological observations have shown that the baboon communities represent an extreme example of geronotocratic order. The leaders are not the strongest males, but the old ones who are held to be the wisest. In one troop the unquestioned leaders, in peace and in danger, were a pair of toothless old males, who could have been easily overcome by any of the younger males. But they did show wisdom, astuteness and leadership.[10] By contrast, in Venice the rule of the old men was sometimes challenged by the young. There was constant tension between the generations, which now and then broke out into the open. But on the whole the struggle of the young against the dominant old in Venice lacked an ideological dimension and, where foreign policy was concerned, the divisions did not reflect the generational differences. The struggle was for power and influence, with the young men resisting the old men's monopoly on government, and the latter doing their best to hold on to it.

Historians and sociologists agree that in the various oligarchical, authoritarian and conservative regimes power is most frequently held by mature or old men. Moreover, it is characteristic of those who come to power in such regimes, even if they did so by way of rebellion or revolution, that they cling to it until their dying breath. Examples of this state-of-affairs may be found throughout history, from the oligarchical city-states of ancient Greece, through Venice in the Late Middle Ages and the Renaissance, to the Communist countries in our time, the USSR, China and North Korea, where after the revolution the regime became extremely authoritarian and conservative. Revolutions and uprisings bring to the fore young people with ideals, who believe in the possibility of political and social change and are bold enough to try to bring it about. In cases of conspiracies and rebellions, if their leaders are not motivated by ideals they anticipate at any rate a near future in which they and their followers would seize power. The old men are seen as responsible for the existing order, which the young seek to change or to overthrow. Vladimir Mayakovski expressed this idea in a poem in which an old man symbolizes the past which the revolution would smash: 'An old man – kill'; while the protest cry of the students in Tienanmen Square in Beijing in May 1988, 'We don't want a government of old men!', had a very concrete as well as symbolic significance. The Chinese regime was, and remains, headed by very old men.

Returning to the Middle Ages, we have little information about most of the leaders of rebellions, history's losers, hence at what age they led uprisings or plots. With regard to those whose age is more or less known, it appears that they were not young but middle-aged, in their forties. It is not known when John Ball, the leader of the English Peasant Revolt of 1381, was born, but it is known that he had been a priest in York and later moved to Essex. As far back as 1366 his heterodox sermons led to his being forbidden to preach, so at the time of the revolt in 1381 he must have been at least in his early forties.[11] Etienne Marcel (c. 1317–1358), who sought to bring about a thorough political reform in France which would reduce the privileges of the nobility and introduce urban federalism, was about 40 when he led his movement. His fellow leader, Robert Le Coq, was at least as old and probably older. His political career dated back to the reign of Philip VI, which began in 1328; in 1351 he became the bishop of Laon and one of the chief counsellors of King Jean II. Their opponent was the Regent Charles, who ruled on behalf of his father Jean, then held prisoner by the English, and who was 18.[12] Jacques Artevelde (1290–1345), who led the uprising of the cities of Flanders which erupted in Ghent in 1338, was then 48. He ruled Flanders for seven years, until he was murdered, aged 55. The 1354 conspiracy against the Venetian patriciate, which held the monopoly of power, was led not by one of the young men, but by the 76–year-old Doge, Marino Faliero. When the plot failed, he was executed as a traitor by the commune of Venice. Although the hero was an old man, the story fired the imagination of the young Lord Byron, who saw Faliero as a romantic figure and wrote a play based on the affair. The old Venetian must have been the doyen of the Medieval conspirators.[13]

FEUDATORIES

The Bavarian law concerning the dukes allowed a son to oust his father when the latter became incompetent. The law defined the criteria of competence: if he is neither blind nor deaf; if he can bear arms and mount his horse easily; go to war; take part in legal debate; judge the people, and obey the king's commands.[14] Feudal lords, big or small, faced no such danger in the High and Late Middle Ages. The centre of gravity of the feudal nexus had shifted from the person to the fief. The vassal was invested with the fief for life, and it could be passed on to his heirs only after his death. The life expectancy of men of the nobility was rather low, because of the prevalence of widespread violent death in that stratum.[15] But some of them did live to be old, and some continued to perform the military function of their social estate until quite an advanced age. Such were the knights and squires who testified in the dispute between the Scropes and the Grosvenors, and gave their ages as 60 and older though had not yet retired from service. (Even if they did add a few years to their true age, they were plainly no longer young.) Thus Frederick Barbarossa set out on the Crusade when he was 67, and so did Raymond IV of St Gilles (1042–1105), who went on the First Crusade when he was just over 60, and continued to take part in battles until his death at 63. In 1216 William Marshall, the perfect knight, aged 71, was appointed Regent of England when Henry III, while still a minor, inherited the throne, and at 72 he still took part in some battles.[16] Others like them, commanders and admirals of the Italian communes, some of whom were citizens and others mercenaries, also continued to serve and were killed in battle at an advanced age. Others who grew tired and weak, or fell ill, could send a substitute to carry out their military duties.

Women who inherited fiefs, and likewise minors and clergymen who held fiefs, also could not serve in person in the army of the king or the feudal seigneur. But whereas women and minors who inherited fiefs were subject to certain restrictions, none were imposed on men who could not serve because of their advanced age. The feudal lord might supervise the marriage of an heiress, since her husband would be responsible for the military service due from his wife's fief. If she refused to marry the man chosen for her by the feudal lord she could be heavily fined. During the minority of an heir to a fief the seigneur received all the income thereof, except for the amount needed for the heir's upbringing and education. But an old fief holder was liable to pay only for his proxy in the army, and could retain the rest of the income. In the thirteenth century the custom of paying compensation or a fine (scutage) in lieu of personal feudal service became another way of avoiding it. The custom began in England and was partially taken up in other countries.[17] The owner of a fief could permit his son and heir to pay homage to the feudal lord in his own lifetime (thereby ensuring that in the event that the heir died, his son, rather than his own younger brother, would inherit the fief). But even in these cases, the heir inherited the fief only upon his father's death.[18] Theoretically, the status of the fief owner was not diminished when he grew old. If his fief entailed gubernatorial functions, or only the administrative duties of the lord of the manor, he was free to hire clerks and other assistants. Moreover, just as fief holders could be freed from personal military service, so they could ask to be relieved of other duties, such as serving on a council, taking part in representative assemblies, or going on diplomatic missions. In Chapter 1 we saw that English peers who were unable, for reason of age or disability, to take part in the sessions of the House of Lords, were relieved of this duty by the king at their request.[19] They did not thereby forfeit their (hereditary) titles and status of peers. Nevertheless, it appears that the ageing feudal lords who retired from some of their duties did suffer a certain loss of status. (Philip of Novare, as we have seen, thought that this was how it should be).

Physical debility was and still is an important factor in lowering the old man's status. In feudal society, when the use of violence was not the monopoly of a central government, but the prerogative of many feudal barons, physical prowess, though not the only source of a man's social standing, was nevertheless a more essential factor than in modern society.[20] Though learning and knowledge also imparted power in the Middle Ages, they were not the basis of the feudal noble's power, even when some learning had become part of his education. It was possible, by means of payment or a proxy, to be relieved of the military duty which was an inherent in land holding in the Middle Ages, but the service, like the powers of command entailed in land holding, was an important element of the feudal ethos. The ethos of command, the honour and the service, were interlinked and interdependent. The service of the king created a common ground for the great nobles and the poor minor ones, and gave the latter the illusion of sharing the same lifestyle and status. A Medieval legend which satirized both the chivalric model, according to which a man's value is determined by his fighting ability, and the husband-wife relationship, and lauded filial devotion, told of an ancient law which exiled knights who were too old to fight. A devoted son kept his aged father in his house, despite the legal prohibition, and in the end received the king's approval of his action.[21]

In real life, it is clear that retirement from military duty, like the withdrawal from other activities – the council, the assembly, or specific functions – removed the person from the centre of events. Old nobles who withdrew into monasteries (a few to become monks, but most to live in the precincts), did not do so because of an official loss of status. They might have withdrawn because they felt weary and conscious that their standing was diminished, and perhaps from a desire to atone for their sins and to achieve that element of the chivalric ethos which they had failed to achieve during their career as warriors, namely, living according to Christian moral precepts.[22] In literary works and in the chronicles which described kinship groups, a nobleman valued his kinship group according to the power and standing of its middle-aged *seniores*, not the old ones. In these texts, the honour of the group and the representation of the *seniores* as a source of support and advice to the younger men, blur the conflict of the generations. It is in the literary descriptions of the old men that the raw tension is exposed. The old man is an object of contempt and derision. (Only when a stranger dares to taunt the old man does the grandson, who himself had mocked him earlier, confront the outsider, regarding the offence as touching on the honour of the kinship group.) The old man tries to do things he no longer can. He wants wars, when he himself can no longer fight. He is senile and feeble, but tyrannizes over his sons, and his commands are disastrous.[23] He is the polar opposite of the mythical old warrior in the heroic epic.[24] A poem by the troubadour Bertran de Born expressed his joy at seeing the lordship (*senhoratge*) changing hands, and the old leaving their houses to the young. Such changes renew the world better than the singing of birds and the blooming of flowers. He who replaces an old seigneur by a young one, and an old woman by a young one, is himself renewed.[25] This is another example of the binary opposite old/young in its symbolic connotation, but it also expresses the inter-generational conflict, the impatience and anticipation of the young, eager to replace the old men who last too long.

In the High Middle Ages certain offices in the service of the kings or great feudal lords were also held as fiefs, or as hereditary family possessions. Some entailed an actual function, and other were nothing more than an honorary position. The holder of such an office did not lose the income thereof when he grew old, even when the office entailed an actual function. Provided he had his lord's permission, he had the option of selling the office or leasing it out, substituting someone in his place and sharing the income with him, or passing it on in his lifetime to his heir, and dividing the income.[26] Some men followed one of these courses, and some of them retired to monasteries.[27] Others remained in office until old age, like those old clergymen who did not give up their positions in the church or in the service of the king. An extreme case of a man who lived to a ripe old age and retained his position until his final days, was Jean de Joinville (c. 1224–1317), the seneschal of Champagne. He not only testified, at the age of 58, before the committee appointed to consider the canonization of Louis IX, and wrote a biography of his king when he was in his eighties, he remained in office until he was over 90. The office of seneschal was passed on in his family since his grandfather's time, and he had inherited it before he was 20.[28] Needless to say, it is doubtful if another such example can be found.

SOLDIERS WITHOUT FIEFS, AND GOVERNMENT OFFICIALS

Real hardship was the lot of soldiers who managed to reach old age without being given a fief, whose contract covered only the period of their military service, or a fixed term. The number of noblemen who had not been granted a fief began to rise in twelfth century, with the growth of the population and the establishment of the principle of primogeniture. Some became the followers of a great feudal lord, the defence-force of his castle in peacetime and the first nucleus of his forces in war. Some were eventually granted fiefs by their lords, or married heiresses. But from the twelfth century on, some of these men became professional soldiers. The thirteenth century saw the spread of the fief-rente system which was, in effect, a wage that the employer could stop with relative ease. It was a transitional military institution between the traditional, unpaid, feudal service and the contractual, non-feudal, indenture system of the fourteenth century. It was one of the changes in military organization, methods of fighting and conscription, which took place in the fourteenth century. The need for mercenaries increased. It gave rise to a system whereby contracts were offered by a high-ranking commander (often a great feudal lord), who undertook to provide a given number of various kinds of fighting men for a limited period, or a specific military assignment. The system spread, with some local variations, through England, France, the Duchy of Burgundy, the Low Countries, and some of the German principalities. In England the contract was sometimes for life, with the commander retaining the soldiers and paying them something in peacetime. In France, on the other hand, the scene of the Hundred Years War, the contracts were always for a fixed term or a particular assignment.[29] The mercenaries (called *les grandes compagnies*) who had been discharged and received no more wages became the scourge of the land, and the death and destruction which they wreaked on France were far worse than those caused by the battles. Those men who survived and reached old age were forced to beg for a living, unless they were lucky enough to receive help from some quarter, since most of them had never married. In so far as kings and feudal lords looked after their old soldiers, they did so for their close retainers, who had lived in their courts in peacetime, in the same way that some of them provided for their long-time faithful servants. Several methods are known to have existed for securing the soldiers' old age. Some had been hired in advance on lifetime contracts, or received a promise, at some point in their career, of lifelong payment in recognition of their service until that moment.[30] Some lords willed the income from a particular property to their retainers for their lifetime. However, the latter did not always receive the promised amount, because of objections by the testator's widow, who was entitled by her right of dower to about a third of the income from her husband's entire estate during her lifetime.[31] (As a rule, the wills expressed the wishes and intentions of the testastor, but only the executor's account showed to what extent these were carried out.) Some of the lords obtained or bought a pension for their retainers or their widows in one of the monasteries.[32] Some provided for their accommodation in one of the almshouses. In 1378 there were at St Mary's Hospital in Staindrop, Durham, 18 gentlemen and a number of other poor men, probably retainers and servants of the hospital's founder, sheltering there in their old age.[33]

But it is evident that not all the retainers were provided for in old age, not even in an almshouse. The hospitals were small and could only take in a limited number of the needy. In the early sixteenth century, Thomas More in his *Utopia* put in Raphael's mouth, among other criticisms of the injustices and failings of contemporary society, a description of the sad lot of the retainers. These men, he said, had never learned a trade which would keep them and when their lord died, or when they became old or disabled, they were simply discarded.[34] In Venice low-ranking officers, and old or disabled common soldiers, received a small pension, or else were given a minor post. The high-ranking commanders received a generous pension, and sometimes their widows did too. But these, in all probability, did not really need their pensions to survive. They acquired properties in the course of their service; some also received fiefs, from which they could raise soldiers and enjoy an income and status.[35] As noted before, they were also less inclined to retire from service, and many of them fell in battle at an advanced age.

With regard to the offices which were not held as a fief, or as an inherited family possession, there is evidence that occasionally kings and feudal lords also provided for the old age of the men who had served them as salaried functionaries. One method was to continue to pay them when they could no longer work, as did Philip VI of France, who ordered that the salaries of his aged officials continue to be paid.[36] Sometimes an institution or a ruling body subject to the king's authority was ordered to pay the salary of one of the king's officials for as long as he lived. Thus the King of England ordered the mayor and aldermen of London to keep paying the salary of one Robert Flambard, a serjeant at arms, who had at some point been granted the lifetime office of mace-bearer of the city, although at that time he held a different office in the King's service.[37] In another case, the King had committed the city of London in advance to pay a salary (or guarantee the rent from a particular property) to one of his clerks; when the city failed to pay the man, the King ordered it to disburse all that was owing and to make sure that such delays would not happen again.[38] Furthermore, as in the case of retainers, though perhaps more consistently where office holders were concerned, the kings and feudal lords (who were also patrons of monasteries or hospitals) sometimes saw to it that their officials, when they grew old, would be admitted as pensioners by a monastery or a hospital run by the Mendicants or a religious community. In this way they guaranteed pensions for their aged clerks without having to pay them out of their own pockets.[39]

It is not possible, at this stage of the research, to estimate how widespread this practice was. Sometimes it is stated that a certain person retired, but with nothing to show if he did or did not receive a pension. John Russell, who served as an usher in the court of the Duke of Gloucester, wrote in the foreword to his manual that his advanced age obliged him to retire from the Duke's court, but he did not say if he received a pension.[40]. In the Middle Ages and the Renaissance, the Latin word *pensio*, like its cognates in several European languages, could denote a monthly or annual salary, an independent income, a student's grant, or a retirement income.[41] Therefore, even where it is stated that a person received a *pensio*, without further details we do not know what it actually entailed. Regarding pensions in the monasteries, John Fortescue wrote at the beginning of the sixteenth century that the institution of corrodies was originally created to secure the old age of the king's clerks and household staff; whereas now (that is at the time he was writing) it is given to other people, with the result that the king's officials are no longer secure in their old age.[42] Research done in the past decade has shown that the granting of corrodies by religious houses at the king's instance was less widespread than had been supposed.[43] It is therefore doubtful if in Fortescue's time many 'other people' enjoyed them, or that in the Middle Ages they were granted to all, or most, of the royal officials. It would appear that kings and feudal lords provided for the old age of those persons who had been close to them for a long time, whether as retainers, clerks, household staff or servants. The higher officials had other sources of income, and did not need pensions to survive in their old age. By contrast, the more-or-less anonymous minor functionaries in the various administrations were not provided for in their old age. Rosenthal's study has shown that in England from the second half of the fourteenth century to the middle of the fifteenth, scores of the king's coroners were compelled to retire, although in theory they had been appointed for life. These were minor royal functionaries, whose business it was to investigate cases of death in the shire and determine if it was caused by accident or murder, as well as civil matters in which the king had an interest, before they reached the courts. The justification for their dismissal was that they were too old or infirm to perform their work properly. They were not granted pensions. Rosenthal assumes that most of them had some other source of income, in addition to their salaries.[44] But the texts which describe their compulsory retirement offer no details about this matter, nor about how they lived in retirement.

Another unanswered question is, why some people chose to spend their old age in a monastery. Those whose patrons had bought or obtained a pension for them had little choice; some of them, at any rate, had none. They were no doubt pleased that their existence had been secured. But just as there were nobles who chose to retire to a monastery in their old age there were others, especially from the fourteenth century on, who purchased such a pension with a single payment or by promising a bequest to a monastery or a hospital,[45] and moved into it. In some of these institutions the pensioners participated in the religious life of the monks, or the religious community which ran the monastery or hospital. But it is unlikely that they all chose to live in this way for the same reasons which motivated some of the nobles, namely, awareness of their reduced status, and/or the desire to lead a truly Christian life and strive to redeem their souls. Were most of the men who did so childless? Or had their offspring died? Or did they prefer not to live with, or even near, their offspring?

125

WOMEN

Women were not mentioned in the discussion on the office-holders in the Italian communes, because with the establishment of communal government in the thirteenth century, and the demise of the political and military power of the feudal lords, the governing principle which rested on the hereditary fief also came to an end, and with it the family prerogative. Women had no part in the government of the communes. They could not hold any of the government offices. When widowed, whether young or old, a woman received her dowry (as a rule, in Italy in the High Middle Ages, her dowry was the daughter's only share in the family inheritance),[46] what she had been promised in the marriage settlement by way of income from a part of her husband's estate, and whatever the husband had left her in his will, if anything. Young widows were pressured by their families of origin to remarry.[47] In other European countries (and Italy, before the establishment of the communes), women who inherited fiefs which entailed powers of government exercised these powers fully and delivered the required services to their feudal lords, except for the personal military service. Because of the low life expectancy of the men of the nobility, women not infrequently inherited fiefs. Some of these women lived long and continued to head their feudal territories and to function until they were elderly or quite old. When married, they shared the powers with their husbands and, when widowed, they wielded them alone.[48]

An extreme example of an old woman, most of whose fiefs had already been transferred to her heirs but who continued to wield power and to support her sons, was Eleanor of Aquitaine (1122–1204). When she was widowed at the age of 67, she supervised the coronation of her son Richard the Lionheart, and went to Aquitaine to help him organize the Crusade. It was she who arranged his marriage, which entailed elaborate negotiations and journeys to Italy. When Richard was taken prisoner on his return from the Crusade, she supervised the strengthening of the fortresses in Normandy, returned to England to look into the activities of her son John, and to raise funds for Richard's ransom, after which she travelled to Germany to pay it in person. She was then 73 years old. When she was 74 she retired to the convent of Fontevrault but did not remain there long. She left it to journey to various places in France to receive the homage of the vassals on behalf of her sons, confirm city charters, negotiate with her sons' feudal lord in France, Philip II Augustus, and to make repeated, if unsuccessful, efforts to settle the dispute between her sons Richard and John, and between them and their nephew, her grandson Arthur. She returned to Fontevrault only in the last year of her life, and died there, aged 82. Matilda of Tuscany (1046–1115) headed her vast domains, which stretched from the Po Valley south beyond the Appenines to the Valley of the Arno, as far as the Pontifical State. Some of them she owned as allods and the rest she held as a fief from the German Emperor and she exercised her full powers of government. She was deeply embroiled in the struggle between the German emperors and the reforming popes, on the side of the latter. She sent an army to their aid, and engaged in extensive diplomatic activity. She remained at the head of her domains until she died at the age of 69.[49]

Margaret, Countess of Flanders and Hainault (1202–1280), inherited the county from her sister Jeanne in 1244, and headed it almost until she died, aged 80. She commanded her army to go to war and engaged in extensive diplomatic activity in the intricate relations between the kings of France, the German emperors, the counts of Flanders and the feudal lords of the Low Countries. She also put down urban uprisings. She conducted an economic policy designed to encourage international commerce, and removed some of the restrictions which had been previously imposed on the international traders under pressure from the local merchants anxious to preserve their monopolies. She withstood the pressures, extended the privileges of the foreign traders, and helped turn Bruges harbour into an international port. She also issued new coinage. Like her sister Jeanne (1200–1244), who had done much to promote the non-feudal bureaucracy (which was to last a long time) she also patronized writers and poets, took an interest in architecture and contributed to the construction of new public buildings in the cities of Flanders.[50]

It is possible that the status of women who inherited fiefs was less affected by their advanced years than that of old feudal lords. Physical prowess was not expected of them, since at no stage in their lives did they have to serve in the king's or feudal lord's army. In the new professional bureaucracies, which arose gradually in the High and Late Middle Ages (and in which noblemen also took part), women had no share at all. The same was true of representative assemblies. They had no part in them as elected representatives, as the king's appointees, or by right of inheritance. They did not need to ask to be relieved of this duty when they grew old. When feudal heiresses took part in the councils of their seigneurs, they did so by virtue of the family prerogative, which rested on the fief. Chivalric literature exalted the ideal of woman's youth and beauty, while the image of the old woman, as we have seen, was by no means unequivocal. A nobleman, himself no longer young, could refer to his wife contemptuously as 'old woman' (*vetula*).[51] But it is possible that once the woman was no longer a sexual object, she could deal more freely with the men of her stratum and with her subordinates, and that the latter were less offended by having to obey her commands than if she were a young woman. For women, even when they enter more public spheres, rarely find themselves in situations in which their ascriptive identity as females is irrelevant.

The women of the nobility married at an earlier age than their husbands, and thus, even when the men did not die a violent death, they often outlived them. Many lived longer than their husbands.[52] The same was true of the queens. Eleanor of Aquitane died at 82 and her husband, Henry II of England (1133–1189), when he was 56; Blanche of Castile (1188–1252), the wife of Louis VIII of France, died at 64, and her husband at 39; Margaret of Provence, the wife of Louis IX of France, died at 74, and her husband at 56; the Empress Matilda, the daughter of Henry I of England, died at 65, and her first husband, the Emperor Henry V of Germany, died aged 44. All these kings died a natural death, except for Louis IX, who also did not fall in battle but died of an illness contracted on his second crusade, while at the gates of Tunis.

Widowed noblewomen who inherited fiefs which did not entail political power but only manorial authority, and those who were not heiresses at all (and they were the majority), were nevertheless economically secure. Their economic condition varied according to the extent of their own property (inheritance and/or dowry), their husband's property, or the property which had been held by them as jointly owned. This was so because widows were entitled to the income from a third of their late husband's properties for the rest of their lives. The widow's dower right was legally recognized throughout the feudal world. (In the Italian communes the marriage settlement stipulated the widow's portion of the income.) It guaranteed the widow's right even if her husband had left debts or had bequeathed to a retainer the income of a particular property to which the widow was entitled, or willed a particular property to one of his offspring upon marriage, which would have deprived the widow of the income thereof. The feudal lord and the court were obliged to confirm the widow's right, even at the expense of debtors, knights or squires, or offspring. Her right superseded all others.[53] Some of the widowed noblewomen remained as such in the world; a few, as we have seen, became nuns; many more retired to convents without taking the veil, sometimes soon after the husband's death but more often at a later stage in their widowhood, that is to say, in old age. A young widowed heiress to a fief was pressured by her feudal lord to remarry and if she refused or turned down the man chosen by the seigneur, she had to pay a fine. Old widows were generally exempt from this duty. The Crusader kingdom, for all that it was chronically short of fighting men, set the age of 60 as the maximum at which an heiress-widow could be compelled to remarry. Only very rarely was an elderly widow forced to marry an elderly nobleman, or even a young one whom the king wished to benefit. Nevertheless, among the noble widows who remained in the world many married again, some for a third time, and a few at a very advanced age.

The inter-generational tension which the feudal literature reveals, openly or implicitly, was between fathers and sons: fathers and the sons they sent away at an early age to be brought up in the house of another nobleman;

fathers and younger sons, who would inherit a minute portion of the estate, most of which would go to the eldest son; ageing fathers and eldest sons awaiting their inheritance, and in general between the 'young' feudals and the *seniores* who held all the property, the power and the authority.[54] But in reality tensions could also arise between widowed mothers and their offspring or between them and other heirs of the younger generation, such as the children of the deceased husband from a previous marriage, or nephews when there were no direct heirs. Long-lived widows continued to enjoy the income from their dower property at the expense of the heirs. Special hostility and resentment were aroused by those widows who held additional properties given them by their husbands in their lifetime, and who remarried once or twice (they were naturally sought after) and yet insisted on their rights without yielding an inch, even at the expense of their sons and daughters. It happened that a dowager and her new husband damaged the landed property. Aware that it would not come to his own offspring, the new husband had no incentive to preserve the value of the property. Timber was cut down and buildings left unrepaired. Some of the dowered widows were very young and survived their husbands for many years – 20, 35, 40 and even 59 – while enjoying the income from their property, to the dismay of their heirs who watched their inheritance dwindling. Some of the widows outlived the sons and daughters who would have inherited the estate and then it was the next generation, that of the grandchildren, which awaited the inheritance. The matrimonial record-breaker was perhaps Katherine Neville. After her first husband died she married three more times, the last when she was in her sixties. Her husband was in his teens.[55] Women who outlived several husbands caused anxiety. In Medieval culture, both Christian and Jewish, a woman who outlived several husbands was regarded as a dangerous slayer of men.[56] (Men who outlived several wives were not similarly feared.) Katherine Neville was dubbed in her lifetime *maritagium diabolicum*.

It would seem that few of the widows of the king's minor officials and retainers ever received a pension. In general, they were expected to subsist on the property they had received as dowry, or inherited, and from their dower, even if the income from these was inadequate. An example of a pension given to a woman in recognition of her own, not her husband's services, is the one granted by the King of England to Lady Lovel, who had been a royal governess.[57] (Though apparently she did not need this pension to live on.) There is no telling if older noblewomen tended to live with one of their sons or daughters. They did not need to be supported by their offspring and they had servants to help them when they became infirm. Therefore, if they did live with their offspring, it was for companionship rather than from need. Possibly some of them wished to do so but circumstances created a physical, and perhaps emotional, distance between them and their children. This may also have been true of some of the women who retired to convents, as well as of the men. Their children might have died before them, or lived far away, especially the daughters who generally moved to their husband's abode. Only biographical studies of those noblemen and noblewomen about whom there is sufficient data to reconstruct their life-stories, particularly their family circumstances in old age, could shed some light on this question.

Clearly, though, it was not the common custom to grow old at the side of one of the offspring, nor was it always considered desirable for the old person. The wills left by peasants and nobles alike reflect this plainly. Since the widow's right to her dower was spelled out in the marriage settlement and required by law, the wills generally made no mention of it. But sometimes a knight stipulated in his will that his widow be entitled to live in the family house, and even specified what his heir would have to give her if the shared habitation became irksome or if she did not wish it. The will of one knight of the Lyonnais region in France stated that he realized his wife would want to leave the family house after his death, on account of their offspring's hardheartedness, particularly the son and heir's malevolence. Nevertheless, he asked her to remain in the house for the first five years after his death.[58] The success of such cohabitation depended on the personalities of the widow, the son and his wife, or daughter and her husband, and on the quality of their relations before the mother was widowed and grew old. However, it appears that where the dominant pattern was not one of joint residence of extended families – whether vertical (that is, aged parents, children and grandchildren), or horizontal (aged parents and several married siblings with their offspring) – neither was old age with or alongside one of the offspring widely accepted. The same may be said of the fathers (though this cannot be learned from the wills). An aged father did not live with his offspring as a matter of course, either, which is at least a partial explanation of why men withdrew to monasteries in their old age.

Noblemen provided for the old age of their manorial functionaries and male and female servants in much the same way as did the clergy.[59] As a rule, they left them small sums of money (rarely a generous amount), household items and clothing.[60] Very rarely did their wills promise an old-age pension, and there are few records of pensions bought for a male or female servant, or an assured place in one of the hospitals. It should be noted that many of the servants were young, and went into service for a period only. Moreover, some of them probably remained in the employ of the heir or heiress. In so far as people sought to secure the old age of one of their servants, it was for those who had served them for many years before the will was made, or who had served their parents before them. Sometimes the testator left a sum of money to be divided among his longtime servants;[61] or ordered that they be compensated for their long service, without specifying the exact amounts.[62] Sometimes a widow left in her will a fixed sum to be paid to a person who had been her husband's steward or personal servant.[63] There were few bequests of pensions. In 1418, a nobleman of the Lyonnais bequeathed a widowed servant of his a house to live in until she died. A noblewoman of the same region bequeathed a certain quantity of grain and a (very small) sum of money to her personal servant, to be paid annually until she died.[64] In 1411, an English nobleman left one of his servants a life income of 2 marks (1 *marca*: about two-thirds of a pound) a year from one of his estates.[65] In Tuscany the nobles sometimes ordered their heirs in their wills to accomodate and provide for their aged servants in the family house until they died.[66] But there can be no doubt that some of these had to subsist on charity, at least in part. The accounts of the almoner of the Duke of Burgundy list old ducal servants among the recipients of charity.[67]

8

OLD AGE IN URBAN SOCIETY

THE UPPER STRATUM IN THE CITY AND THE FREE PROFESSIONS

We have seen that Alberti, in his *Book of the Family* depicted the 64-year-old members of the family as retired from both political life and business activities,[1] whether because he thought that this was how it should be, or because he knew men who retired at that age. But like the office-holders in the Italian communes, who, as we have seen, remained in office until they were very old, so too they and burghers in other countries were disinclined to abandon their economic activities as they grew old. They welcomed their exemptions (in the Italian communes and in other European cities which enjoyed varying degrees of autonomy) from certain obligations, such as military service, watch duty in the urban militia, juror duty, or a part of their taxes.[2] But they did not hurry to withdraw from their occupations. It appears that those who retired did so from illness or disability. Bankers, merchants and artisans were independent, and could not be obliged to retire.[3] So, too, were physicians, lawyers and notaries. They could choose to retire partially and gradually, by transferring some of their work to their sons or other younger relatives, or to their hired staff.

It is known how old some of the great merchants of London and Florence in the Late Middle Ages were when they died. The average lifespan of 97 great London merchants in the years 1448–1520 was 49 to 50, but half of them died when they were over 50. Nineteen of them died between 50 and 60; 17 between 60 and 68; two between 69 and 70; four between 70 and 71; one died at 73, one at 75, and three between 77 and 78.[4] They engaged in their business activities almost until their last days. The great Florentine merchants, Gregorio Dati and Buonaccorso Pitti, died at 73 and about 78 respectively.[5] Matteo di Niccolo Corsini and Francesco Datini have already been mentioned: the former died at 79 and the latter at 75. Datini had been active in commerce from the age of 15, which means that his career lasted 60 years.[6] The great merchant houses in the Italian communes were generally run as family enterprises, either by the immediate family, that is, several brothers with their father at the head of the firm as in Venice, or as a larger company with other kinsmen as partners, headed by one of the family elders as in Florence. Thus, while some of the sons became partners, the fathers continued to head the company as long as they lived. Mirialdo, the son of the Genoese admiral della Turca mentioned in Chapter 7, was also a partner in his father's business but did not control it. Some fathers not only gave detailed instructions in their wills about how their sons were to run the company after their death, but actually demanded that the sons commit themselves in advance to follow these instructions.[7] Sons who did not join their fathers entered other commercial firms as junior partners, and the successful ones eventually set up their own companies. For them to be taken on as junior partners in a commercial enterprise they had to obtain their emancipation from their fathers, as well as part of their inheritance. By law, until a son was emancipated, he, his children and his property were subject to his father's authority (*patria potestas*), regardless of the father's age (even if the father was 60 years old, according to the jurist Azo), or that of the son.[8] Many, but by no means all, obtained their emancipation in their teens, and some when they were still children. Those who were not emancipated remained subject to their father's authority. It also happened that a son obtained his emancipation but went on living in his father's house, and the latter continued to dominate him and treat his property as his own.[9]

In previous chapters we noted other sources of inter-generational friction: the high minimum age for election to public office, which restricted the role of young men in government; likewise, the fact that many of the well-off older widowers married again and, if the second wife died, sometimes took a third – an outstanding source of both resentment and mockery – while the sons were obliged to postpone marriage until they were established economically. The father's marriage settlement guaranteeing his wife a portion of his property after his death, which inevitably came at the expense of the sons, was a source of tension between fathers and sons and sometimes led to bitter conflicts, as shown by the records of the notaries and courts. But, although the fathers continued to head their companies and everything – the jurists, the laws of the communes, the preachers – seemed to uphold the status of the patriarch in the Italian communes, the economic status of many of the great merchants declined in their old age and with it their social and political status.

In Florence in the Late Middle Ages lists were published of men who were disqualified from election to communal and guild offices because they had failed to pay the taxes levied on them. David Herlihy examined these lists from the years 1429 to 1435. It transpired that out of 6027 citizens who constituted the Florentine commercial aristocracy of the time, 1088 (i.e. 18 per cent) were disqualified. This means that at least once in their lives they were financially very embarrassed, if not altogether bankrupt. Upon examining the age of the disqualified men, it became clear that the stage of life at which these merchants were economically distressed was in their late fifties. There were a number of reasons for this. As noted above, emancipating a son entailed transferring some property to him. Without some property the son could not join a commercial company as a junior partner. It meant that he received part of his inheritance in his father's lifetime. Moreover, the father was sometimes obliged to emancipate his son even though the latter worked in his company. It was usually the son who went to the distant markets: Venice, Bruges, London. For him to be free to act on the spot, namely to invest or sell at the right moment, he had to have some disposable capital. The father was therefore obliged to emancipate him and provide him with some working capital.

The average age of emancipation in all the social strata of Florence was 20.09, but it was lowest among the merchants. Most merchants' sons who obtained their emancipation did so before they were 16 years old. Another reason for a father to transfer property to his son was that it would not be encumbered by his debts. Moreover, this reduced the tax levied upon the father by the commune. While such a step improved the chances of maintaining the status and the future of the lineage, it also exposed the ageing men to economic hardship. It could be said that the financial difficulties experienced by the great merchants in their old age were due not to misfortune or bad luck, but to a structural cause – the very nature of the commercial system which required considerable liquid capital, that had to be entrusted, at least in part, to the younger men for them to utilize with incentive and energy.

Other reasons for the reduction of the old merchants' assets derived from the structure of the family and the obligations of a patriarch. The great merchants had to give their daughters dowries, which in the Italian cities in the Late Middle Ages were very substantial. In their role as patriarchs they were also sometimes obliged to help provide dowries for their granddaughters. Furthermore, when they were well off they were expected to lend money to the younger members of their families who were starting their careers. Men in this stratum reached the height of their prosperity at about 50. Thereafter, their property began to decline, for all the reasons mentioned. The head of a family was poorer at 67 than he had been at 55, and as his financial difficulties increased, so did his debt to the commune. These men did not actually suffer want, but they were distressed and subject to pressure and insecurity. Appearing on the list of the disqualified amounted to a public pillory of grave ritual significance. It not only lowered their social and political standing, it also damaged their reputation as merchants with whom it was safe and profitable to do business.[10]

One partnership of father and son, or perhaps father and several sons, in thirteenth-century London, is suggested by the fact that they borrowed money jointly. The loan was recorded and they swore before the city authorities to repay it in time.[11] In another case the money was lent by father and son.[12] In the former case, we do not know if the fact that they took the loan jointly meant that they were business partners, or that one of them was guaranteeing the other's loan. In the other case, where father and son jointly lent the money, it is reasonable to assume that they were partners. But in northern Europe the development of business enterprises was not usually based on the family pattern. When young men completed their apprenticeship in a commercial firm (a longer stage than in the cities of Italy) which had been paid for by their fathers, they would begin to work as employees in some company until they had sufficient funds to set up their own business and become partners in one of the companies. They would acquire the necessary funds from savings, from their wives' dowries, by inheritance, and in some cases their fathers gave them the necessary amount out of their share of the inheritance. There were also merchants who retired at some stage and transferred the business to one of their sons. One such transfer agreement, made in London, spelled out the amount of money the son would pay his parents annually, plus the food, drink and clothing he would provide, the rooms which the parents would occupy and, in addition, the son undertook to provide a servant for each of his parents at his own expense whenever they wished to go outdoors.[13]

I do not know if an older notary or lawyer was preferred to a young one, on account of his greater experience. With regard to physicians, the German Konrad of Megenberg, the author of fourteenth-century didactic-encyclopedic work, stated that an old one was preferable since old physicians have acquired a great deal of experience. Where the young physicians had only theoretical knowledge, which they applied regardless of the individual case before them and sometimes caused their patient's death, the old physicians were better able to diagnose the ailment and hence choose the best method of treatment.[14] These statements made sense. Whatever medical knowledge was added in the course of a fourteenth-century physician's career, it could not have amounted to much, so that there were scarcely any changes in the methods of diagnosis and treatment. A popular proverb in the sixteenth century agreed with Konrad of Megenberg, that an old physician was to be preferred, but warned that a barber (who treated abcesses, wounds and broken bones, like a surgeon) should be young.[15] Midwives and female healers were sometimes called *vetulae* (old women).[16] While not necessarily an expression of respect, it does suggest that some of the practitioners were elderly or old women.

CRAFTSMEN WHO WERE GUILD MEMBERS

Artisans never retired. Labour in the workshop was not as arduous as agricultural work. Ageing peasants on rural estates were sometimes pressured to retire. The landowner feared that as their physical fitness declined his lands would be neglected, and he wanted to be sure of receiving the labour service that was his due as lord of the manor. The artisan was subject to no such pressure. The family constituted the production unit, with the man's wife, the children who had not yet left home, an apprentice or two and sometimes journeymen. The ageing artisan could thus leave the hardest tasks to others. Moreover, the rate at which a medieval artisan worked was not dictated by machines, or by management practices such as piece-rate work or time-bonuses. Such changes as occurred in the methods of production in a man's lifetime were small and gradual; they did not render his skills obsolete or inefficient and were not beyond his ability to adopt – as happens in modern production systems which undergo frequent and sharp changes.[17] Nevertheless, some artisans undoubtedly experienced economic hardships as their working capacity declined, and some were too ill or disabled to go on working. The problem was recognized. Already Jean de Joinville, listing the men whom Louis IX had helped with donations and charity, mentioned among them 'artisans who were unable to work at their crafts on account of old age or illness'.[18]

This awareness was also expressed in the statutes of many of the occupational guilds and religious fraternities. There are some extant statutes from the thirteenth century, but the great majority date from the fourteenth. Helping members in distress was neither the sole nor the principle purpose of these guilds and fraternities. The prime purpose of the guilds was to protect the interests of their members who were in the same occupation, and to supervise their economic activity. The prime purpose of the fraternities was the maintenance of a religious framework for the laity. They were connected with parishes, religious houses or non-parochial churches. Some of the fraternities consisted of members of the same craft, while others admitted men of diverse crafts. In contrast to the occupational guilds, very few of which admitted women to full membership, the fraternities accepted women. They also provided their members with a social circle. Every fraternity had its own patron saint, and paid for a religious procession on the saint's day. Some fraternities maintained their own chapels and chaplains. Some guilds and fraternities also subsidized theatrical performances in the city. Rich and well-established guilds and fraternities also supported outside charities and made regular donations to poor people who were not of their membership, founded a small hospital or school, or paid for the refurbishment of a church or the repair of a bridge.[19] But many of the guilds and fraternities also assisted their own members. It should be emphasized that the recipients were not the poorest. The members of the occupational guilds were established artisans (as opposed to those who failed to be admitted into a guild and were obliged to work for others). Even the poorest members of fraternities were not indigent, but belonged to the lower-middle stratum. Fraternities charged admission fees and collected dues from their members, and were careful not to accept persons who appeared likely to become dependent on charity. Some rules stipulated that persons suffering from a 'loathsome' or incurable disease could not be admitted, but only persons who were 'healthy of body and capable of supporting themselves by their labours'.[20] Other rules stated that only persons who had been members of the fraternity for at least seven years could qualify for assistance.[21]

The guilds and fraternities assisted in a variety of cases, and in a variety of forms. It was commonplace to help a person on his last journey and beyond it, in the next world, by providing a seemly Christian burial and the saying of prayers and masses for his soul. This kind of aid was of particular concern to people following the Black Death and the later epidemics, in which many children perished, or as a result of which they moved when the demographic decline opened opportunities for land purchases or for better-paid work away from their native place. In this world, the occupational guilds and fraternities provided legal aid when their members were prosecuted, lent them money, and in rare cases helped them to get out of prison. Assistance was also commonly given to members' widows, and so was help in financing the dowry for a member's daughter (whether to be married or to enter a nunnery), and an orphaned son's apprenticeship; a member in financial difficulties caused by loss of merchandise in a fire or a shipwreck was helped, and likewise sick and crippled members who could no longer support themselves. Our concern here is with the last category, which included the aged. It was not assumed that every old person was necessarily sick or disabled, nor that every old person *per se* was entitled to help. References to the old did not imply that they were automatically entitled to a pension, but only the sick and disabled among them. The regulations of the Parisian guild of cooks, in the latter half of the thirteenth century, were unusual in showing particular concern for the old, unlike the regulations of other guilds and fraternities. They stipulated that a third of the fines that it collected were to go into a special fund 'for the maintenance of old men of the craft who lost their standing owing to a [failed] transaction, or old age'.[22] The rule expresses the awareness that old people were liable to run into financial difficulties, but it did not stipulate that they should be helped because they were old. Other guilds did not create special funds for their old members and did not refer to them as a separate category but lumped them together with the sick and disabled.[23]

Most of the statutes did not specify the amount of aid to be given. In many cases they only stated that distressed members were entitled to assistance, adding that certain office-holders in the guild or fraternity could determine the amount to be given depending upon the person's need, his standing before the problem arose and the financial state of the guild or fraternity.[24] Sometimes a single donation was made, together with an exemption from the dues to the guild or fraternity.[25] Or a daily payment was made, usually of half a penny (*denarius*), at times combined with the right to dine each day at the house of a different member (provided the needy person was not bedridden) and the 'brothers' were instructed to show hospitality and provide the same food as was served to the head of the household.[26] But the commonest form of help was a weekly payment, which ranged from four to 14 pence.[27] In the period following the plague the minimum wage in agriculture was one penny with a daily meal, or two pence without.[28] It is assumed that a quarter of a penny a day was enough to avoid starvation, being the price of a loaf of bread of about 1kg. Hence a penny a day could cover a modest subsistence: bread, beer and sometimes meat.[29] Some of the rules, having stipulated the amount, went on to state that if there were many needy persons each one would receive a smaller sum, until the fraternity acquired additional funds or the masters and wardens of the guild or fraternity decided on the amount.

In 1330, the Venetian fraternity of John the Apostle established a small hospital of four beds for their sick members. Another Venetian fraternity had four members who were physicians, whose duty it was to treat sick members for free.[30] The weavers guild in Valenciennes in France kept a room with several beds in one of the city's hospitals, and so did the tailors' guild in Paris.[31] It is not known whether these beds were meant for temporary hospitalization or to provide a final refuge, as in the case of aged and indigent clergymen, servants and retainers. The tailors' guild in Strasbourg, at any rate, viewed the hospital as the least satisfactory solution. Its rules stipulated that a member was to be helped 'as long as was necessary, so that he would not have to go into hospital'.[32] This assistance was provided from the funds of the guild or fraternity, or from members' bequests, and sometimes a special collection was made for the purpose or each member was asked to contribute as much as he could. This was assumed to be temporary assistance until the person was again able to provide for himself, as many of the rules made plain: 'so long as the brother is in need'. This proviso was omitted with regard to people who had leprosy, or a chronic illness and to cases of disability due to old age – presumably because in such cases assistance would be needed for the rest of the person's life.[33] The mention of annual payments or, where the payment was on a weekly basis, the stipulation that the recipient was also entitled to a garment or a hat each year,[34] suggests that the need for continued assistance was recognized. Only rarely did the regulations state explicitly 'for the rest of his life'.[35] So much for the statutes of the guilds and fraternities. We do not know to what extent they were actually observed. Moreover, it should be kept in mind that only the big and relatively wealthy fraternities could afford to assist their members. We cannot conclude that all the craftsmen of the occupational guilds or fraternities were secure from want in their old age, but we may assume that they were not abandoned, and that the needy among them were less dependent on the charity of the church or the city, the demand for which greatly exceeded the means.

WOMEN

The women of the prosperous urban stratum were as secure in their old age as the noblewomen. The right of dower, or the marriage settlement, the dowry and sometimes an inheritance from the husband or the family of origin, all ensured a comfortable existence.[36] The problem of retirement from economic activity did not obtain in the case of women of this social stratum. Women did not engage in banking, international commerce or domestic wholesale trade. In this stratum, as in the nobility, women married men who were older than they, especially in the Italian cities. Many of them outlived their husbands and there were many widows in the cities. The young urban widows were not subject to pressure from a feudal lord to remarry as were the heiresses or fiefs. In so far as such pressure was applied, it came from their family of origin. But a widow's remarriage depended not so much on her wishes, or the amount of pressure applied by her family, as on the demographic and economic conditions which determined the demand for widows.[37]

By and large, the marriage prospects of an older widow were fairly restricted, especially in the Italian cities, where older men definitely preferred to marry virgins or women who were much younger than they. By contrast, the old Parisian merchant who wrote a manual for his young wife assumed that she would remarry.[38] Social realities meant that all husbands assumed that this might happen, but not all took it for granted. A burgher of Lyons stipulated in his will that his widow, if she wished, could live in the eldest son's house for the rest of her life. If she did not, the son would have to compensate her financially, as would the younger sons, who would also have to set aside a room for her use in their house. Apparently, the testator assumed that if his widow did not choose to reside with the son it would be due to disagreement between them, or because she remarried. He left her the freedom to choose. In the Italian cities husbands on their deathbed sometimes asked their wives to promise that they would not remarry (and thereby reclaim their dowry and have to leave their offspring with the late husband's family). A wealthy Florentine stated in his will that he was leaving his widow the considerable sum of 500 florins, to be paid her by their sons if they failed to show her the respect due to a mother. This arrangement revealed concern for the widow, some uncertainty about the sons and the assumption that, if relations between mother and sons were harmonious, she would reside with the eldest son who would inherit the family house and become its head. In the early thirteenth century a prosperous Genoese burgher left the bulk of his estate to his widow (in addition to her dowry and the portion agreed in the marriage settlement), on condition that she did not remarry. If she did, she would be entitled only to her dowry and the portion agreed in the marriage settlement.[39]

Evidently, the women of this class were secure in their old age but there is no doubt that once widowed they had less property than the men of their social stratum. Moreover, they too lost some property as they grew old, because like the men they transferred some of it to their sons in their lifetime. A widow was expected, and sometimes pressured, to give her sons their share of her dowry in her lifetime.[40] In England it happened even in the cities that a widow transferred to one of her offspring land she owned in the environs, which she herself had not cultivated. The reason for such a transfer could not, therefore, be that she wished or needed to retire from work, which was the chief reason for the transfer of landed property to sons (or strangers) in the peasant society. In 1288 a widow in Leicester signed an agreement transferring her main landed property and the income from another land to her daughter and grandson (the daughter's son), in return for which the daughter and her heir undertook to provide her with food, clothing and all her needs for the rest of her life. They were also obliged to give her a proper Christian burial, and the daughter undertook to educate her son at 'the school of clerks'.[41]

While women represented a considerable proportion of the urban labour force, there is scant reference to them in the sources concerning production in the city. This was because their work was subsumed under that of the family workshop.[42] As unmarried girls they worked for their fathers, and once married they worked with their husbands. The fathers and husbands were the heads of the households and it was their names which appeared in the various records. Some women also did other work (usually in one or another stage of textile production) to supplement the family income; some took in work given out by a contractor and worked at home; others engaged in retail trade, chiefly in foodstuffs; and some were wage-earners. Very few women were full members of mixed male-female craft guilds, and all-female guilds were extremely rare.[43] Thus the nature of women's employment caused little trace of it to appear in the records. It is difficult to investigate the length of their working lives, except for the two occupations which biology has reserved for women, namely, those of wet-nurse and prostitute. The working life in both occupations was naturally limited, especially in the case of wet-nursing. In all probability, prostitutes who did not save enough to retire on continued to work until a fairly advanced age, earning less and less. As for other urban female workers, whether married, unmarried or widowed, they probably went on working as long as they were able, within the limitations imposed upon them. The craftsmen's guilds generally assisted the widows of their members (some rules made the assistance conditional on the widow behaving properly or not remarrying).[44] But few of the guilds permitted the members' widows to continue working at their late husband's crafts. Some of the widows married craftsmen who had worked for their husbands as journeymen. This was one way for such employees to be admitted into a guild and the prospect made it an attractive match, even when the widow was older, despite the warnings of the normative and satirical literature.

As noted above, some of the religious fraternities admitted women, but their rules concerning assistance to needy members always referred to 'a brother', never 'a sister'. Although the poorest female members of the fraternities worked all their lives, not only in their homes but also at the craft, bringing in an income or a wage, they were not assisted if they were distressed through their own inability to go on working. In old age, if the woman was still married and her husband was incapacitated, the couple were assisted because of his disability. If widowed, the woman received some help, not because she would no longer work, but because she was a widow. It was an important element in the model of Christian charity to help the widows, whether they were old, or young and burdened with children.

HOUSING

In his *Book of the Family*, Alberti makes Gianozzo praise the common residence of the extended family as the ideal model: it is a proper and desirable thing for brothers and their families, parents and their sons and their families, to dwell together under one roof, and warm themselves at the same hearth, under one head of household. In other European countries old parents did sometimes reside with a son or a daughter, but it was not the sole pattern, nor was it represented as such. (The agreement between the woman of Leicester and her daughter and grandson made no mention of common residence.) But in the Late Middle Ages Alberti's ideal was not commonplace in the Italian cities either. The 1427 Florentine census reveals that the average number of persons per household was 3.8, and only 3.6 per cent, of all households were family homes of more than 10 persons.[45] Such households could be found only in the upper propertied stratum.[46] Even in these households the large number of residents did not necessarily mean that brothers, parents and children lived together. The wealthy urban households included many servants and minor clerks employed by the head of the family, much as in the castles and noble residences of northern Europe. Poor or solitary relations, of various degrees of kinship, often lived there too. It was one of the duties of a prosperous patriarch to take care of poor, solitary and/or aged relatives. The number of solitary old people was especially high from the mid-fourteenth century on, since the epidemics killed mainly children and young people. We have already observed that the percentage of old people greatly increased during this period.[47] The poorer the household, the fewer were its members. The smallest households, those of one or two persons, were usually headed by women, mostly widows. During that period the families in the lower social strata were broken up not only by the high rate of mortality, but also by the mobility of people seeking work where the demographic decline made for a labour shortage. Clearly, not all the aged widows chose to live alone. Many of them were condemned to solitude by the demographic and economic circumstances. Some of the widows with means, whose families had not entirely dispersed, lived with a son and his family, sometimes with a daughter and her family. Those who were widowed early and never remarried did not move into a son's house when they were old, but went on living where they had always lived, helping to run the household and bring up the children. The widow of Francesco Datini of Prato did not live to be as old as he, but died in her fifties. After his death she lived mainly in Florence, with Datini's daughter and her husband. She had raised this illegitimate daughter of his from infancy and regarded her as her own child. The widowed mother of Datini's notary lived in a village not far from Prato, on a tiny farm which Datini had put at her disposal. It enabled her son to visit her often (being country-born, he also liked to stay there).[48]

In 1370 one of the wealthy citizens of Florence founded the Orbatello, an asylum for widows of all ages from the lower-middle stratum, to lodge in for the rest of their lives. This was partly a kinship establishment, partly an almshouse supported by the commune. It also admitted fatherless girls, or girls orphaned of both parents, who were the daughters, granddaughters, sisters and nieces of the widows' families. There they lived until they were married, and the institution provided their dowries. In the fifteenth century the administration of the home passed to the commune, but its internal management was dominated by the matrons, who ran it wisely, efficiently and humanely. The Orbatello retained this character until the sixteenth century.[49]

Some men and women did the same as the nobles and retired to monasteries or purchased a pension in a hospital. Christine de Pisan was born in Italy, but lived in Paris from childhood. She was widowed at 25 and never remarried. At 54, after an extraordinary literary career, she retired to a nunnery where she died at 66. The custom of buying a pension in a hospital was already widespread in the thirteenth-century. The late thirteenth-century statutes of the city of Lille stipulated the manner of taxing the property of persons who had retired to a monastery or a hospital and donated the bulk or the whole of their property in return for care and accommodation for the rest of their lives; or who had promised to bequeath their property to the monastery or hospital. They were taxed in the same way as persons who had taken their property out of the city.[50]

Some chose to retire to a religious establishment which they had helped to found or to maintain, or with which they had had business dealings, as in the case of the burgher who retired to the Hospital of St John the Evangelist in Cambridge, together with his manservant. In late fourteenth-century England, most of the people who bought pensions in the Benedictine monasteries were burghers of the middle stratum, often craftsmen and traders who had had dealings with the monastery or had been in its employ. The standard of living in the monastery or other institution to which these people retired depended on their standing, namely, the amount paid or promised as a bequest. In the twelfth and thirteenth centuries most of the pensioners resided in the monastic precinct or nearby and ate their meals in the monastery, or else they received prepared food (as well as other things, such as clothing or fuel). In later times more pensioners went on living at home and received regular rations of uncooked food. From the late fourteenth century pensions generally took the form of money, and the pensioner remained at home.[51]

In the cities of Austria as well the purchased pension gradually ceased to entail residence in the establishment but could be converted to an annuity which was paid to the purchaser, who continued to live at home. Some men purchased such pensions for themselves, and others for their wives, to secure their subsistence in old age. This custom gradually spread beyond the religious bodies, to include the city council or one of the corporations.[52] The men who bought such pensions for themselves presumably retired, if only partially, from their occupations, while the annuity secured them from want in their old age, even if they ran into financial difficulties. The same questions which arose with regard to the nobles who retired to monasteries or other religious institutions arise with regard to the burghers who purchase pensions and moved into the institutions. Did men and women who had offspring, and whose circumstances would have permitted joint residence, also prefer this sort of retirement, even though it reduced their offspring's inheritance? Christine de Pisan had a son and a daughter, but the daughter was a nun, and the son apparently lived in England, having been sent at 13 to be brought up in the court of the Earl of Salisbury.

WAGE-EARNERS

Some wage-earners were hired for life. It was customary for a lay school to hire a teacher for a period of several years, but in fourteenth-century England some schools hired them for life.[53] The 1310 records of the Fraternity of St Mary in Cambridge show that the summoner, whose task it was to summon all the members to gatherings and various events 'whenever called upon to do so', was hired for life.[54] Presumably such persons continued to receive their modest wages (a teacher's wages in a primary school was quite low, as no doubt were those of the summoner), even when they could no longer carry out their duties. But as a rule, urban labourers were not hired for life. Journeymen who were not admitted into an occupational guild, or whose craft was not organized in a guild, were taken on for a limited period or a specific task and received daily or weekly wages. They went on working as long as they could, if not longer. In Venice the wall-crack fillers and the carpenters succeeded in forcing their employers to hire, for every six artisans, one of their veteran colleagues who was over 55. The records of the City of London refer to an accident which happened to an old workman. He fell when he climbed a ladder to examine the wall, was injured and died that night.[55] That the laconic factual record mentions that he was old suggests that those who reported the accident attributed it to his age. He had gone on working when it was too much for him. Likewise, the workers at the evil and despicable occupation of judicial torturers, continued to work until they were old. When the procurator of the court of Châtelet in Paris was summoned by the *Parlement* to answer claims that he had been overdoing the torture, he stated that the work was carried out by experts, one of whom had a professional experience of 40 years.[56]

Most wage-earners were unable to save enough for their old age during their working years, or to acquire an income-bearing property, or a pension at one of the hospitals. Most lived from hand to mouth. Those who had the means to pay the admission fee to one of the fraternities and to keep paying its membership dues probably received some assistance when they were old and could not work. We have seen that the widows of the prosperous urban strata were provided for in their old age, but had less property at their disposal than had the men of the same strata. The same applies to the wage-earners. The men were not provided for, but the widows and spinsters were worse off. Wage-earner husbands could not assure a subsistence for their widows. The women worked in less well paid occupations than the men, and where they did the same work they still earned less than the men. Consequently, they were even less in a position to save for the future than the men of their social stratum. In fifteenth-century Nuremberg some journeymen, and more particularly their widows, as well as spinsters from the working stratum, contracted with a particular family or hospital to leave them their tools, beds, household utensils and clothes, in return for board and lodging until they died. Their accommodation and food must have been extremely modest. The people who made these agreements were poor, but not the poorest. The latter were paupers, whereas these had some property. Meagre as was the property they promised the family with whom they lodged, or the hospital, nevertheless their offspring, who presumably belonged to the same stratum, wanted it for themselves. Sons and daughters opposed these agreements of their parents as depriving them of their rightful inheritance. The court records of Nuremberg show that offspring tried to prevent their parents from making these arrangements, or, after the parents' death, attempted to obtain the property which was bequeathed in this way.[57] Evidently, their own plight made them inconsiderate, if not cruel. Their housing and economic conditions probably made it impossible for them to care for their aged parents at home. Nevertheless, they opposed the arrangement made by the parents, though it was not one alternative among several but the old people's only way of warding off solitary want.

The burghers, like the clergymen and the nobles, left bequests to their male and female servants: a small sum of money, clothing, household utensils, and sometimes a horse for a manservant.[58] Some single women made the bequests conditional upon the maidservant remaining with them until they died.[59] Some servants were promised a small plot of land, or the annual income from a plot of land, a house or a shop.[60] Such bequests were left to faithful servants who had been especially close to the testators. Francesco Datini, who was obviously a generous person, left the widow of his devoted manservant, who had herself worked in his household for a while, a house and an annual income 'so that she may lack none of the things without which one cannot live in comfort'. A prosperous Genoese instructed his heirs in his will to provide food, drink and a room in the family house for a maidservant for the rest of her life, and that 'no one would have the right to disturb her'.[61] We have already mentioned the old Cambridge burgher who retired to a hospital together with his manservant. The servant survived his master and remained in the hospital after his death. His master must have purchased a pension for him too.

9

OLD AGE IN THE PEASANTRY

Work on the land was more arduous than in the workshop. Peasants who lived to be old could not go on working as before, even if they were not sick or disabled. Arrangements for their retirement, full or partial, varied from region to region in western Europe, depending on the local inheritance laws and customs, the family structure and the nature of the peasant economy. While primogeniture was the dominant principle of inheritance in the fiefs, and partible inheritance predominated in the cities, in peasant society several principles obtained. We know of primogeniture, ultimogeniture, partible inheritance, and impartible inheritance descending jointly to all the offspring, or only the sons. In some regions customs allowed the father to choose which of his sons would be his heir. As a rule, where there was neither a demesne estate cultivated by the tenants' labour, nor a strong peasant community, arrangements for retirement were based on the local custom, but concerned only the family in question. It was not so in regions of demesne estates. There the lord of the manor, to protect his own interests, could intervene in the peasants' retirement and even determine when an aged peasant might retire. Where the rural community was strong, as in the regions of the common field villages, its representatives were sometimes involved in the arrangements for retirement; above all, they supervised the execution of the maintenance agreements between fathers and sons. But underlying the different laws, customs and local conditions, there were two fundamental models of retirement. In one, when the father grew old and was unable to work as much as before, he did not transfer the holding to his son (or sons), but remained the head of the household and controlled the funds, even though he was no longer the main workforce on the land. In the second model, the aged peasant retired and transferred the holding to one of his sons, who then became the head of the household (in spite of the warnings of the popular proverbs and the didactic literature). So much for the social custom. Needless to say, its practice was affected by the particular demographic conditions of the time and the place, as well as by the specific family circumstances. The sharp demographic decline caused by the epidemics which erupted in the mid-fourteenth century led to changes in patterns which had seemed normative before the plague. In this chapter we shall see some examples of arrangements based on the two said models, and consider their effects on the lives of the older and younger generations which had to share the resources.

In most regions of southern Europe the ageing peasant remained the head of the household and the farm, whether the laws of inheritance designated the eldest son as the heir or all the sons who remained in the place. Only the sons who left the family estate were no longer subject to the father's authority. In certain regions (e.g. Périgord), they had to be emancipated before they were free to leave. In others, such as Gascony, it was not necessary. The only property which the sons obtained in their father's lifetime, exclusively or in partnership with him, was that which they inherited from their mother.

In Tuscany there was a marked difference in the status of the old father in the rural areas and the cities. In the rural areas the family holding was not divided, except in extraordinary circumstances, and the father continued to head it until he died. If a son married and established his own family and household nearby, he and his property remained under the father's authority. Sons who left the family estate received a sum of money, furniture and household utensils. Such was also the dowry given to the daughters, which was generally smaller than in the cities. Heads of families did not sell portions of their land to assist their departing sons or to provide dowries for their daughters. In contrast to the great merchants in the cities, whose properties diminished in their fifties, in the rural areas the older a man became, the larger was his property; at any rate, it was not diminished. Though their life expectancy was low, some peasants lived to be old and many households, especially after the Black Death, were headed by men in their sixties. In the rural areas, men who had families (some remained unmarried because they could not afford a family) started them at an earlier age then the men in the cities. They were younger when their children were born, and the children reached maturity before the fathers were old. The fathers, who had become heads of households and acquired authority only when their own fathers died, were in no hurry to relinquish their position, and generally held on to it until they died. And so the members of the new generation also had to wait many years before they could head the household. The Florentine *Catasto* of 1427 shows that very few peasants retired and transferred their estate to their sons, who became financially responsible for them. While in the Tuscan cities of the Late Middle Ages there was a relatively large number of one- or two-person households, in the rural areas, despite the demographic decline, the families had reorganized on an extended basis and the number of persons per household was larger. Some of the households included parents with sons and their families, or brothers with their families, and sometimes even uncles and other lone relations. A peasant woman who was widowed early or late in life, and did not remarry, stayed on in the family house which was headed by the heir. Nonetheless, some households were headed by solitary widows, or contained only two persons. The 1427 census shows that these constituted 9.1 per cent of the households in the rural region of Florence, while in the city they constituted 14.3 per cent. By and large, these were poor households of childless widows, or widows whose offspring had died or migrated, and had no relatives with whom they could reside.[1]

In the region of Languedoc, as early as the twelfth to thirteenth centuries, it was a common practice for married brothers to live together and cultivate their land jointly. (This was called a *frèrèche*.) Le Roy Ladurie has shown that, after the Black Death of 1348, families throughout Languedoc reorganized themselves on an extended basis, both vertically and horizontally. This was a reaction to the collapse of many families during the great mortality, and to the moral and physical insecurity caused in France by the Hundred Years' War and the devastation wreaked by the mercenaries. This formation also spread in other regions, such as Cevannes, Velay, Auvergne, Haute Provence and the Dauphiné, including areas which before the plagues had seen the development of the nuclear family. The extended family persisted in most of these regions until about the middle of the sixteenth century.

Another reason for the amalgamation of the extended family was the manpower shortage. The number of hired labourers declined, the demand for them increased and so did their wages. (Worst hit were the mountain regions, where the need for manpower was greatest.) The extended family could supply the needed labour and reduce the dependence on hired hands. These households were headed by the father of the family throughout his life. When a man joined his wife's family he too became subordinate to the patriarch, and so were his children. He was obliged to serve, honour and obey the head of the family. His property became part of the joint family property, controlled by its head, and so were the daughters-in-laws' dowries. Sons and sons-in-law could not spend more than a few coins without the father's permission. Le Roy Ladurie has shown that the father's bed was sacrosant, as was his regular portion of food, and woe betide the daughter (or granddaughter) who presumed to sell the old man's bed, or even its covering, or who tried to reduce his portion. The young couple (or couples) had no privacy at all. Such a way of life inevitably gave rise to tension and resentment, which were no doubt aggravated if a widowed father added a stepmother to the household which included his sons and daughters-in-law, daughters and sons-in-law, and their children. The marriage settlements of the offspring, drawn up by notaries, were designed to reinforce and sustain the arrangement. Various clauses were put in to secure the head of the household against any possible deviation or revolt on the part of the younger generation. While the legal contracts allowed in theory for the dissolution of the arrangement, if one of the sons wished it, in practice this was hardly possible. The yoke remained on the son's shoulders until the father became decrepit or died – and not always then. Whereas in Tuscany, when the father died the son and heir became head of the household, in Languedoc his place was often taken by the widow. (Hence Le Roy Ladurie's suggestion to describe this regime not as a patriarchy, but as 'the rule of the older generation'.)[2]

No human system ever suits everybody to the same extent, and this is true not only of those arrangements which favour particular interest groups, political and economic. The structure which was headed by the ageing father of the family until his dying days provided economic security for both the older and the younger generation, but it was patently favourable to the older. No doubt the internal relations within the extended family were affected by the personalities of the sons and daughters, and above all by that of the father. Only sons who were emancipated and had departed, and the daughters who received their dowries and left, were freed from their father's authority. Presumably, the departing sons were more independent and rebellious, and chafed under the father's domination. They preferred to lose the protection and security of the family framework in order to be free of the pressure and oppressiveness, which was the price paid by the remaining sons for those benefits. We have no way of knowing if the remaining young (or not so young) people retaliated against the father when he became helpless, by treating him badly and contemptuously, or continued, from force of habit, to obey and respect him. In any event, the period of decreptitude could not have lasted long – in the fourteenth to sixteenth centuries there were no means of prolonging the life of the very old, as there are today.

In some regions the re-formation of the extended family took place soon after the great demographic decline, and in others later. In the early decades of the fifteenth century, in certain regions of south-western France and the rural regions of Navarre, extended-family households existed side by side with solitary old people living alone, or two-person households. Some of the latter were pauperized and became beggars. Those who owned land sold it, being unable to cultivate it themselves, their offspring having died or migrated. Others combined the fragments of former families into a new household. Thus one household included two widows with three orphaned grandchildren and one married son. This phenomenon of joined family-fragments appeared in the early fifteenth century in other regions of France, including areas where the nuclear family had been predominant before the epidemics (e.g. Rheims), and others where the extended family, vertical or horizontal, had predominated.[3]

The second model, whereby the ageing peasant retired at a certain stage and turned the holding over to one of his sons, was characteristic of north-western Europe, where the nuclear family predominated, but it was also customary in some central European countries (e.g. Austria),[4] and a few regions in the south. One such southern region was the Pyrenees. The pattern of retirement was not uniform throughout the region. In Béarn the dominant system of inheritance was primogeniture. When the father retired, he shared the control of the property with the inheriting son or daughter. (In Béarn an elder daughter's claim took precedence over younger sons – an absolute exception to the general rule.) An agreement determined the part of the property the income of which would go to the father, who also retained exclusive control over the possessions which had accrued to the family in his lifetime and which he was free to bequeath to whoever he wished. But he could not transfer or sell any part of the family property without the heir's approval.

In Haute Ariège, on the other hand, the father was free to choose one of his sons as his heir. When the father retired, this son became the head of the family and the farm, and the father (or both parents) stayed on with him in the family house. The other sons became shepherds, or received something and left. A man who had no sons had reason to fear his old age. A peasant woman of the local village of Montaillou recounted in the court of the Inquisitor Jacques Fournier how an aged peasant reacted to his son's death: 'When my son Raymond died, I lost everything I had. From now on, I shall have no one to work for me.'[5] But for a man who had several sons, the absence of an inheritance law meant that he could prefer the son who was closest to him, and to whom he felt he could entrust the property with the minimum damage to himself. Yet the testimonies of various peasants before the same court show that this freedom of choice did not always lead to the retired peasant feeling comfortable in the house he had turned over to his son. One retired peasant related that when a neighbour asked him for a loan of an implement or a draught animal, he was obliged to say that he no longer dared to do anything without his son's permission. A widow who lived in her son's house related that she had been forced to sell her property and was living a life of misery and humiliation, and 'feared to make a move'. This peasant woman clearly was unhappy in her son's house, but Le Roy Ladurie deduced from the testimonies before the same court of the Inquisition that, by and large, ageing and aged women in the region of Haute Ariège were more respected than were aged men. Occasionally an old husband referred to his wife (who was usually younger than he) as a 'cracked old woman', (*vetula trueia;* unlike the local noble, who, as we have seen, contented himself with calling his wife *vetula*). But her standing in her family and village was higher than in her youth. She helped her daughters or daughters-in-law to manage the household and bring up the children, and was usually well-liked by them, by her sons and her grandchildren.

Anthropologists have observed that in traditional societies ageing women do not lose status as much as the ageing men. However, they do not agree on the reason for this. Some argue that old age is less disruptive in a woman's life than in a man's, and others that, on the contrary, old age significantly changes her position. Proponents of the former view point out that since the traditional occupations of the female were less physically demanding, the women did not have to give them up as they grew old. There was also greater continuity in their emotional relations with their children than there was in the relations of the men and their children, which were never as strong. The anthropologists who support the latter view suggest that in patriarchal and patrilocal societies, where a young bride enters her parents-in-law's house, her status definitely changes when her mother-in-law becomes decrepit or dies; then the daughter-in-law, herself no longer young, becomes mistress of the house. They also point out that since a woman's biological function is punctuated by biological changes throughout her life (menarche, loss of virginity, pregnancy, childbirth and lactation), she copes better than the man with the physical changes of old age. Furthermore, they note that when a woman grows older she ceases to be a sexual or a procreative object, and can therefore be freer in her conduct in male society.[6] In reality, there were both continuity and change.

In the Haute Ariège, as in most other regions, the woman's husband was the head of the household, and when the son took over, the position of the old woman whose husband had either died or retired did not undergo a great change, as did that of the man who retired. This was so even if her relations with her daughter-in-law were less harmonious, since the head of the household was the son and not his wife. A real change occurred in the peasant woman's life when she retired from agricultural work. Women were an important part of the labour force of the Medieval peasant society, and by no means confined to household occupations. We have seen that the statutes which were passed after the Black Death, ordering people to accept whatever work was offered, applied to men and women alike. A peasant whose wife died married again not merely for emotional reasons, or to get a housekeeper, but because he needed the woman's labour in the cultivation of the land. Since at no time in their lives did women hold any official position in the manor or village community, in this sense, too, old age made no difference to them. A significant change of status occurred only in those regions, like Languedoc, in which the widow, rather than the elder son, became the head of the household. But this was not the custom in most regions. As for the biological changes, when a woman ceased to be a sexual object her social position did indeed become somewhat freer. On the other hand, as noted earlier, there was the popular belief, backed by popular medical literature, that the old woman's body produced venom, and that she had an 'evil eye'.[7] Former prostitutes, or women who were known as procuresses, were regarded as the most dangerous, but even an ugly old peasant woman, especially if she was solitary and impoverished, could be similarly regarded. Many of the women who were accused of witchcraft in Early Modern times were poor and lonely peasant women. The status of the male peasants in the centre of the marginal group of the old was obviously lower than it had been when they were younger. In the Haute Ariège the depreciation occurred when they were in their fifties, when their physical strength, energy and voluntary responsibility were diminishing. The men of the leading families in the village who held such positions as the lord's bailiff, head shepherd or even local priest, assumed them at an earlier age than urban men assumed important offices. By the time they were 30 they had usually reached the top of their status and power, and began to decline in their early fifties. They generally retired from heading the household before they were really old but rather when the son and (chosen) heir married, or not long afterwards. Their retirement and the transfer of authority to the son sharpened the loss of status. Nor could the ageing man rule his wife as he had done in the past. He could insult her, but whereas in his youth she did not dare to defy him, she did so when he was old and had lost status. In the Icelandic saga one old man says to another, when the women laughed at him when he stumbled and fell: 'The women took us more seriously when we were young'.[8] In the Pyrenees the system provided for the older generation and at least one of the younger men and his family. The older generation gave a piece of land in exchange for part of the income from the younger people's labour.

The records of Jacques Fournier's Inquisition court are a unique source in that they convey the voices of the peasants themselves about areas of life which are absent in other records, including those in which they are the speakers (as, for example, the records of the secular and church courts which dealt with civil, criminal and marital cases). As we know, the priesthood of the Catholic Church was not reserved for the old; even the *Perfecti* among the Cathars were not necessarily aged. Nevertheless, the peasants' testimonies bear out the anthropologists' conclusions regarding the popular attribution of spiritual wisdom and knowledge of the mysterious to the aged – at least in the region in which they lived and testified. For all their reduced status, the aged peasants were not only the principal speakers in the 'evenings at the fireside' (*veillées*), being the living archives of past events and ancient traditions, but in matters of faith and the secrets of this world and the next, their words carried weight with the younger folk.[9]

In the Haute Ariège there was no demesne estate, and the rural community did not intervene in the retirement arrangements agreed between fathers and sons. Not so in England, where there were demesnes, and where in the regions of common fields the rural community had some supervisory powers. Extant manorial court-rolls provide data about these retirement and maintenance agreements. (Similar medieval records did not survive in other European countries.) Already in the thirteenth century there were in the English manors peasants who retired and transferred their holdings to their sons, but this was not the general custom. In less populous regions, such as the Midlands, prosperous peasants helped their sons to get established and start their own families by giving them a portion of the family holding, or buying land for them. The 'middlings' – i.e. the peasants who owned medium-sized properties, and belonged to the middle rank of the peasantry – tried to do the same. The poorer peasants whose holdings were small, had not enough to set aside for their sons, nor the means to help them buy their own land. The thirteenth century was a period of demographic pressure and land shortage, so the sons of the well-off and middling peasants were in no hurry to leave their villages. The parents' assistance and the young people's dependence upon them ensured that the latter remained with them as they grew old. Those who left the villages were the offspring of the poorest peasants.

On the other hand, in densely populated regions, where it was difficult to acquire land (e.g. East Anglia), already in the thirteenth century sometimes when the son and heir married, the father retired and transferred the holding to the heir, and such retirement agreements were more common. Furthermore, widows, not necessarily old ones, transferred their farms to their sons, or to a daughter and son-in-law, when they could not cultivate the land by themselves and render to the lord of the manor the labour services that their holdings were charged with, and in the common field regions also meet the demands of the village community. Sometimes they retired of their own volition, announcing that they were incapable (*impotentes*) of running the farm on their own, and sometimes they were pressured to do so. Others solved their problem by marrying again.[10]

So much about the period prior to the Black Death of 1348. Thereafter, retirement agreements proliferated everywhere, agreements with offspring, with kinsmen and with strangers. The offspring of many peasants died before their parents, and others migrated. An examination of the court rolls of Halesowen in the Midlands revealed that 48 per cent of the offspring who were known from the records for the years 1350–1400 died or moved out of the village in their parents' lifetime.[11] The survivors were mobile to a degree that was unknown before the plague. Holdings fell vacant and young people were able to obtain land from landowners who were anxious to repopulate their estates, or else they inherited holdings from relatives without offspring. They no longer depended on their parents' assistance. Peasants who still had a son or a married daughter in the village were anxious to keep them there, in order to assure the cultivation of the land and their own subsistence in old age. They therefore retired and transferred the holding to them. Widows found it harder than ever to work their holdings on their own, since after the Black Death there was a shortage of hired labour and the labourer's wages rose. Moreover, with the

153

great availability of land, the demand for propertied widows declined.[12] We have seen that Alan Macfarlane argued (in his second book) that once the son obtained the legal title to the holding, the father was no longer entitled to any of its income. Therefore few peasants transferred their holdings to an offspring and most of them preferred, when they could no longer work the holding, to sell, lease or mortgage it, and live on the proceeds.[13] However, the research of Zvi Razi and Richard Smith has shown that a large number transferred their properties to one of their offspring.[14] Transferring the holding to kinsmen was the second option, and to strangers the third. In Halesowen in the period 1350–1400, retirement arrangements made with offspring still constituted 46.5 per cent of all maintenance agreements; 44.2 per cent were made with kinsmen, and only 9.3 per cent with strangers. In the period before the Black Death, two-thirds of the maintenance agreements were made with sons, daughters or grandsons and one-third with kinsmen.[15] Sometimes the father retired and transferred the holding to one of his offspring with a verbal maintenance agreement, without registering it in the manorial court. Some agreements were recorded long after the transaction had been carried out. Parents preferred to make agreements with one of their children, because it was the custom, and because they expected to be better looked after by them than by strangers. The increase in the number of agreements with kinsmen and strangers was due to the heavy mortality of young people, and above all the migration of the survivors. While it is not certain that every man who concluded such an agreement with a stranger had no offspring left in the village, it stands to reason that this was usually the case. Some of the maintenance agreements made with strangers gave them the holding out-right, for them and their heirs to inherit, but often the holding was transferred only for the lifetime of the retired peasant, or for the other party's lifetime. Thus when one or the other party died, if the retired peasant had offspring who had migrated from the village, they could return and claim their inheritance.[16]

There were two kinds of retirement and maintenance agreements: the first was for the immediate transfer of the holding to the son, or the daughter and her husband, with whom the agreement was made; the second kind was 'delayed devolution', meaning that the property was promised as a bequest to the offspring with whom the agreement was made. The promise was given in public in the manorial court, by which time the future heir could have already paid the lord of the manor the 'entry fine', due from every person who received a holding in the manor. Under the latter type of agreement, which was commoner in the thirteenth century, the elderly person retained more authority than under the former. After the Black Death, agreements to transfer the land became more common. Both kinds of agreement entailed paying the retired peasant a pension, in kind or money. (After the plague, agreements entailing payments of money multiplied).[17]

These contracts also obliged the person who obtained the holding to render to the lord of the manor the services which were due from the possessor of the holding. Some peasants agreed to transfer the entire holding, and others only a part thereof. Those who transferred the bulk of it sometimes retained a few strips of land for cultivation and a small vegetable garden near the house for their own use.[18] The records of the coroners include the case of a peasant 'of more than 50' who climbed a ladder to pick his peas, fell, and three days later died of his injuries.[19] He may have been a peasant who retained a few strips for cultivation. We have seen that Macfarlane argued (in his first book) that once the son had become the legal owner of the holding, the father was not entitled to any part of its income, and therefore the fathers took pains to itemize in the agreements exactly what the offspring would be obliged to provide for their subsistence.[20] But an examination of the agreements showed that not all the peasants did so. They contented themselves with stipulating that all their needs would be met, or that they would be supported, or that the son would support the parent 'honourably to the best of his ability' (*honorifice pro posse suo*).[21] Evidently they trusted their children. Sometimes the itemized list was a codicil to the original, general, agreement because the original agreement stipulated that the retired parent would receive all he or she needed 'according to his/her station', and if they were dissatisfied with what they got (presumably, while living in the new owner's household), they would be entitled to such-and-such things, which were itemized.[22] In some cases the agreement stipulated only what portion of the grain the retired peasant was entitled to, on the assumption that an appropriate portion of the dairy products and vegetables from the holding would be given without being specified. However, there were also many agreements which included a detailed list from the start. These lists illustrate the parent's expectations from their children according to their standing in the village community. Some of the lists are extremely detailed, suggesting that the parties did not wish to leave anything to chance, or to the whim of the offspring, implying that they did not trust them fully. (In some cases agreements spelled out what would be done in the event that the daughter died, leaving the son-in-law in charge of the holding, or the death of the kinsman who had taken it over.)[23] The more substantial the holding, the greater was the retiring peasant's bargaining power, and the more he could demand in return. The items which were listed in these agreements as due to the elderly peasants included: grain (wheat and/or barley and oats), beans, ale, coal or firewood, specific garments (to be provided every year or two), sometimes bedding, and sums of money to be paid at regular intervals. The more prosperous retired peasants were also promised regular supplies of dairy products, meat, eggs and honey; or they could keep farm animals within the holding at their own expense and for their own consumption. The amount of grain specified in some of the agreements exceeded the needs of a single peasant or a couple. It was probably intended that the excess would be sold in the market, as an additional source of income for the retired persons. Dyer's research suggests that, as a rule, the items promised in the agreements reflected the living standards of peasants of the same rank (prosperous, middling or poor) who did not retire.[24]

The accommodation which the recipients of the holding promised the retiring peasants also varied according to the size and quality of the property. Some asked only for a corner of the house to put their bed in, and a place beside the hearth in winter. Others demanded a room of their own (in some cases stipulating access to the kitchen, the pantry, the barn, the latrine, etc.). Some, mostly couples, demanded a separate house. Widows or widowers generally asked for a room. A room in the house generally meant a side room, or they were given the attic. The central room was for the son and daughter (or the stranger) who obtained the holding. When the retiring couple demanded a house they were given a cottage, or if necessary one was built for them within the boundary of the holding, but the main building was always for the incumbent.[25] The author of *Dives and Pauper*, we recall, warned fathers against turning their properties over to their sons in their lifetime. However, with regard to joint residence, he wrote that it was better for old people to dwell with their offspring and not with strangers – but only if they knew them to be kind and generous.[26] Unfortunately, in most cases the problem of the joint residence came up only after the holding had been transferred (until then most of the married sons and daughters lived separately); and evidently it was no easier in those days than it is today to know in advance how well such an arrangement would work. Consequently, many of the retiring peasants secured themselves against this contingency, and stipulated that if conflicts arose as a result of the shared residence, the son would be obliged to provide an alternative accommodation.[27] A similar clause was included in the wills of many English and French peasants.[28] They stipulated that the widow would be entitled to reside in the family house with the son and heir but if she did not wish to do so, or if the experience proved uncomfortable, the son would have to provide her with a house of her own. As the earlier chapters showed, the same clause was common in the wills of the burghers and the knights. In north-western Europe the joint dwelling was not regarded as an altogether ideal solution (the author of *Dives and Pauper* notwithstanding).

The foregoing examples indicate that the lords of the manor recognized the right of elderly peasants, even the bondsmen, to transfer their holdings to an offspring, a kinsman or a stranger, and to conclude agreements to provide them with a pension in their old age. Otherwise the contracts could not have been made. Moreover, as noted before, they had an interest in making the older peasants retire, and sometimes put pressure on the ageing peasant, or the widow who did not remarry, to retire and make way for someone who could cultivate the land properly and carry out the labour obligations in the demesne owed by all the peasants.[29] Confirmation of the title to the holding entailed payment to the lord of the manor ('entry fine'), and in some cases so did the registration of the agreement. However, the manorial court, which functioned on behalf of the rural community, protected not only the interests of the lord of the manor. Though it was not free from the latter's influence, and that of the prosperous peasants, it unquestionably also looked after the interests of the aged peasants who retired. Their records contain complaints of retired peasants about delays in payments of money or in kind; about being barred from the vegetable plot or the barn to which the agreement had stipulated free access; about bad treatment, and the like. These complaints were investigated by the court and, if found to be justified, the jurors denounced the violators, warned them and sometimes helped the two parties to reach a settlement (in cases of delayed payments). In more severe cases they fined the culprits, and where the agreement appeared to have been grossly violated declared it to be null and void and that the holding reverted to the retired peasant, who could then transfer it to someone else.[30]

The agreements were thus not merely a matter between the aged peasants and their offspring, kinsmen or strangers. The old parents were not left at the mercy of wicked sons or daughters, as described in the moral tales which exhorted people not to give up their properties in their lifetime, or powerless in the hands of strangers who took advantage of their frailty. We saw in earlier chapters that various texts expressed awareness of the hardships endured by old people. But the secular rulers only exempted them from certain obligations, and the Church only looked after some of its clergymen. The English rural community did not assure the old peasants a pension either, but recognizing that old age was a social-economic problem, it sought to protect their interests.[31]

As in the regions where the father did not retire but remained the head of the household, so in the regions in which he retired and transferred the headship to his son, the quality of their relations undoubtedly depended on their personalities and their mutual experience in the past. If some of the offspring failed in their obligations, or offended the retired parent (and these were the cases which came up before the court), others fulfilled their obligations and treated their aged parents well. And if some of the offspring were 'wicked sons', there were doubtless also domineering fathers, who could not accept their sons' new status as masters, meddled in the running of the farm, or made excessive demands. The court records include disputes with widowed mothers, who wanted to get the maximum dower at their offspring's expense and remarry.[32]

But even when everything went smoothly, the retired elderly peasant could not avoid the loss of status. This was not a unique feature of the

Pyrenees. He was no longer the master, and having to vacate the main building, or its central room, symbolized painfully the change in his position. As the folk proverb put it, 'It is hard for old people to sit on the children's bench.' Once retired, the elderly peasant could no longer hold any position in the village community or the manor (the community elected people to some of the positions, and the lord of the manor appointed the others). These included: jurors, pledgers, court assessors who evaluated the damage caused by one villager to another, ale tasters, foresters and the lord's bailiffs. The sole function left to the aged as a group was to testify about past events, primarily with regard to tenure claims and labour obligations as they have been 'since time immemorial'. The institution of 'evenings at the fireside' did not exist in northern Europe. Fair treatment by the son or daughter who had taken over the property could not alleviate the loss of self-esteem. Those whose children died or migrated made agreements with kinsmen or strangers. Bereavement was painful, and the offspring's migration and abandonment of their aged parents was also hurtful. The offspring who migrated did not wish to hurt their ageing parents, but the urge to make the most of the newly opened opportunities after the plague was stronger than the desire, or call of duty, to remain at their side. The pain and insult crossed the gender division, and could affect men and women alike.

But as with the peasants of Haute Ariège as well as other social strata, so too in the English manors, the women apparently did not suffer the same loss of status as the men. During their married life, even where the couple's principal property was based on the woman's dowry or inheritance, it was not she but her husband who headed the household. If the husband died and she retired, her status remained largely unaltered. In any case, women were barred from holding any position in the community or the manor, but they could continue to fulfil their traditional functions so long as they were able, helping the daughter or daughter-in-law, whether they lived under the same roof or not. But it seems that sometimes they over-exerted themselves. Among the records of the coroners there is a case of a woman in her seventies who one morning climbed a ladder to get some straw for kindling, slipped, fell and was killed. It was her husband who found her.[33] In another case, an old woman (90 years old, according to the record, but she might well have been younger and the age of 90 was given to emphasize that she was very old) died in a fire in the attic in which she slept. Her candle had fallen on the straw and set it alight. It was said that she was so exhausted by her day's work that she did not notice when the straw caught fire. That this was a completely destitute woman is evidenced by the fact that not a single object was found that could be donated to the church (*deodans*), as was customary when a person died suddenly, without confession and extreme unction. She probably lived alone, as the record makes no mention of other residents, but this is not certain. Retired peasants were often given the attic.[34] Petrarch's statement, that in old age, 'there is no more room for physical labour and material worries', has a ring of bitter irony about it, witting or unwitting.[35]

So far we have dealt with peasants who possessed a holding, of whatever size, which sustained them and which they could transfer to others, thereby securing themselves at least a subsistence in their old age. The situation was much worse for the landless cottagers, or smallholders whose holdings were insufficient to maintain them, who hired themselves out as labourers to the landlord or prosperous peasants to supplement their income. There were many such peasants in all the regions.[36] When they grew old they could no longer work as hired labourers, though some of them had no land at all and no possessions but their muscles. These former agricultural labourers belonged to the stratum of paupers, in the strictest sense of the term. In regions where the rural community was relatively strong, such as those of the common fields in England, these people received some assistance. The common law allowed paupers to enter any field after the harvest and glean whatever they could, and many of the local bye-laws made the same allowance. The paupers could glean in the cornfields or peas plots, and gather straw for roofing and pallets, and in some cases for kindling. The peasants were forbidden to pasture their animals in those fields for several days after the harvest, to leave something for the gleaners. Once when the brothers of the Hospital of St John in the manor of the Bishop of Ely let their sheep graze in the field too soon, the manorial court fined them for doing so.[37] The laws of Louis IX of France, in the latter half of the thirteenth century, also forbade letting the animals graze in the fields for three days after the harvest, to enable the paupers to glean.[38] But the local bye-laws not merely allowed for gleaning, they controlled it. Only children, the sick, the disabled and the old, whom no one would hire even at the minimum wage of the period, were allowed to glean. The following formula recurs in the bye-laws: Gleaning may be done only by such persons as cannot earn one penny a day with victuals, or two pence without; or: only a person whom none would hire (at this wage).[39] Since at harvest-time there was always a great demand for labour, the old men and women in question must have been really enfeebled if no one would hire them. The control not only determined who was entitled to glean, but also the manner of the gleaning. The would-be gleaner, or gatherer of leavings of peas, had to obtain permission from the owner of the holding; if he failed to do so, his gleanings would be confiscated and he would have to pay the lord of the manor a fine. With regard to peas, the gatherer was to stand in the corners of the field and not in the centre. Some of the bye-laws also stipulated the hours of the day when gleaning was allowed.[40]

In some East Anglian estates the community kept a charity fund for the poor. In others, a third of the fines collected from persons whose pigs broke into other people's plots were set aside for the local poor. (The sums were minute. Out of a three-penny fine, one penny went to the poor).[41] Some villagers in England, Tuscany and southern France established alms-houses for sick and old local paupers, and in Tuscany there were urban charities which established branches in the rural environs of the cities (*contado*), though fewer and smaller than in the cities.[42] Church charities were also rarer in the countryside, which might have prompted the migration of paupers, including aged ones, from the village to the city, both in Tuscany and England.[43] The religious fraternities, too, were generally poorer in the country than in the city. They provided their members with a religious framework, and assured them a Christian burial when their time came, but they could neither assist them materially nor contribute to other charities. Some peasants who made testamentory provisions for their widows and young children also left instructions that a portion of the holding was to be sold and the proceeds given to the local paupers. Some wanted the sale to be carried out directly after their death, and others only after the death of their widows, or even children.[44]

Some lords of the manor also left in their wills sums of money to be distributed among their customary tenants, the hired labourers, or the poorest tenants on their estates. There is no telling how much the beneficiaries received from such a bequest (assuming that it was carried out faithfully by the executors), because we do not know how many they were. Some peasants were bequeathed a cottage upon their retirement. But as a rule these were not individual bequests but sums of money to be distributed to the needy or, in some cases, instructions to reduce the rents of the poorest peasants (without specifying for how long).[45] In the very rare case of a peasant receiving a pension from the landowner, it was a partly employed man, one who had a small holding but worked principally as a servant of the lord of the manor and was granted the pension as such (like the few other pensioned servants described in earlier chapters). When a peasant of the manor of Hales retired, his holding reverted to the lord of the manor (namely, the abbey), and in return was guaranteed the following pension: two loaves of bread (one of fine flour and one of brown) daily, three gallons of mixed ale a week, five shillings a year, and the right to have his daily meals with the servants of the abbey.[46] However, it was not clear either what led to the decision to grant this peasant a pension. Was it because he had been a servant at the abbey, or because he was willing to surrender his holding? Monasteries favoured such arrangements, which enabled them to recover land for the demesne estate.[47] In Austria and Norway, ageing hired labourers were usually not sent away and the prosperous peasants who employed them kept them on in their house, or moved them from house to house.[48] No such custom is known to have existed elsewhere. Needless to say, the assistance of the rural community could not cover the needs of all its poor inhabitants, or only the aged ones.

As we know, it was widely accepted that the care of old people was the duty of their offspring. While the normative literature referred only to the duty to parents, in at least some regions until about the mid-fifteenth century, the extended family also helped its aged members, as part of its overall mutual responsibility, even though northern European households generally comprised of the nuclear family.[49] But the offspring and relatives of poor people could not help them much. Furthermore, already in the thirteenth century poor peasants had fewer kinsmen in the village than did the prosperous ones, and it was chiefly the sons and daughters of the poor who migrated. After the Black Death, in the latter half of the fourteenth century, many more opportunities opened before the survivors. Lands fell vacant and wages rose. The old people could not benefit directly from the demographic and economic changes. If they had offspring who did well they could benefit indirectly but, as noted earlier, in many families the young died before their parents and many others migrated away. This happened not only in England, where the nuclear family predominated, but also in regions where the extended family was predominant. There, too, families disintegrated after the epidemics. This state of affairs, in which offspring were unable to support their aged and needy parents, persisted in England into the early seventeenth century, when this filial duty was incorporated in the Poor Law. By this law, only those aged people who had no offspring, or whose offspring were too poor to support them, were entitled to assistance from the parish. It transpired that there were many such people, and the people who were responsible for administering the Poor Law in the parish had to contend with this fact. The great mobility of the peasantry meant that many of the offspring had migrated; others were unable to support their aged parents because they themselves were poor and at the stage when they had young children of their own to support.[50]

The situation was much the same in the Late Middle Ages, (although the women's earlier marriage meant that when they were old and widowed, many of their offspring no longer had young children to support). Offspring and relatives helped the needy. These were kinsmen who could stand surety for the old and impoverished, and if they came from another village, could accommodate them in their homes. Those who had relatives in the village were no doubt better off than the solitary strangers. People did not want beggars in their village. A stranger who had no one to stand surety for him was expelled. Whoever accommodated an unwanted stranger in his house was fined.[51] The strange paupers who were not driven out of the village subsisted by begging, minor theft and gleaning. If they were caught stealing, or breaking the gleaning rules, they were expelled.[52] It is doubtful if many lived long in this manner and some grew old and froze to death in a ditch, or died in an accident. The solitary ones were undoubtedly the worst off. But evidently the presence of a son in the village did not in itself assure an old widow's subsistence. In one village an old female beggar drowned, and it was her son who went to look for her and found her body.[53]

While in the legislative texts there is some distinction between the sub-groups in the elderly population (not all concessions and exemptions apply to all strata of society), in all the other texts they are represented and addressed as one group. However, as the last four chapters have shown, it is clear that there was a great diversity in their lot. The status and partici-pation of the elderly in Medieval society varied according to gender, social stratum, position, regional custom, level of functioning and personality. It was also affected by the demographic conditions of time and place as well as by specific family circumstances. What they all shared was a common image. General attitudes towards them prevailed despite the diversity of their lives.

10

THE OLD AND THE CHARITABLE ORGANIZATIONS

In previous chapters we discussed the limited extra-familial assistance which ageing persons received from various economic and occupational institutions: churchmen from the Church (somewhat better provided for than the laity); churchmen's servants and officials from their employers; officials and servants of kings and nobles from their patrons and employers; artisans from their guilds or fraternities; urban servants from their employers, and peasants from the lord of the manor and the village community. The present chapter will discuss the position of the poorest old people in the context of the normative and charitable systems of the period, alongside the other poorest groups, namely, those who were utterly destitute. Clearly, it is not always possible to distinguish the aged poor who obtained something from the above-named bodies from the destitute who depended on public charity. As we have seen, the assistance which peasants received in the manorial and communal frameworks, or urban labourers from their employers, did not always suffice for subsistence.

We know that in the Middle Ages there was no government-administered relief, neither in the kingdoms and the feudal territories nor in the Italian city-states. The only assistance given by governments to the needy took the form of tax exemptions for the poorest and, in times of famine or war, deferment of taxes and debt repayments, prohibition of the export and hoarding of grain, and the supervision of its market price. (In the Italian city-states all the over-sixties were exempted from head-tax, and in France from the tallage, regardless of their economic situation.)[1] The public body which organized poor relief and incorporated it in a legal code (i.e. canon law) was the Church. Giving to charity from the surplus – that is to say, from whatever was not needed for the maintenance of a person's living standard according to his status, and that of his family and dependents – counted as an act of justice (*iustitia*). Only that which was given not from the surplus counted as an act of Christian love and mercy. The theological view that this world is essentially flawed, being the outcome of Original Sin and the Fall of Man, coupled with the limited means of production

163

and resources, meant that poverty was seen as an unavoidable component of human society. 'Ye have the poor always with you.' Society was hierarchical, the resources were in the hands of a privileged minority, of which the Church was a part, and no attempt was made to deal with the immediate causes of poverty, such as the low wages of labourers or the fact that the holdings of many peasants were too small to provide a subsistence. Hired labourers did not count as deserving poor, whom it was a Christian duty to assist, except in periods of extreme economic hardship or if they had small children to feed. The awareness of poverty was coupled with the duty of charity.

The Church as an institution, as well as individual churchmen, contributed to charity. The Church also administered the obligatory alms-giving by the laity (one third of the tithe they paid to their church had to be allocated to the poor of the parish), and one third of the movable property bequeathed in a will was set aside for the redemption of the testator's soul, namely, for charity. And wills were administered by the Church. Moreover, the Church administered the voluntary contributions of secular bodies (e.g. the city council, a guild, the inhabitants of a particular parish) and of individuals who endowed and maintained the various charitable institutions. The staff which ran the various almshouses, orphanages and leper houses, including those founded by laymen, were usually members of a religious community (mainly the 'Third Order' of the Mendicants). The demand for charity and its availability depended on the demographic and economic conditions. But, as in all societies, the willingness to supply, that is, to give alms, was determined by religious-moral, social and cultural factors. Almsgiving in the Middle Ages stemmed from its perception as one of the duties of the Christian man to his brother in God and the belief that it would promote his redemption in the next world. It had a penitential value and indicated the giver's moral condition. Although according to the New Testament poverty was a surer way to salvation than wealth, views on the subject wavered in the Middle Ages. Eventually the dominant theological position concluded that there was nothing wrong in a person being rich, provided he was a 'good' rich man, that is to say, pious and merciful, donating to churches and monasteries and giving alms to the poor. His opposite was the 'wicked' rich man, proud, merciless, greedy, miserly and gluttonous. Almsgiving was also undoubtedly an indicator of socio-economic status.

The Medieval concept of charity was a sweeping one. It did not necessarily mean poor relief. It included donations to monasteries and religious orders, to the construction and maintenance of churches, to the purchase of candles and of works of art for churches, to bridge building and road mending, to the establishment of hostels for pilgrims and ransoming captives. People contributed to all these no less than to poor relief, both in life and in their wills. These contributions were considered to be as efficacious in discharging one's Christian duty and leading to redemption, as almsgiving; and they were also a good socio-economic indicator. Such bequests reflected not so much a personal decision on the part of the testator, as the social norm represented by the clergyman who counselled him and drew up his will. Already in the late eleventh century people bequeathed property to churches and monasteries for masses to be held for their souls' salvation. Such bequests became commonplace with the spread of the belief in purgatory. During the fourteenth century it became customary to endow special chantries, whose priest's chief duty was to hold masses for the souls of their founders and their families. (A chantry priest had no benefice but was paid a salary. As such, his subsistence in old age was not assured.) All these donations greatly reduced the amounts which might have been used to alleviate poverty.

The aged as such were not counted among those whom the Scriptures defined as deserving of assistance. Scriptural tradition referred to widows and orphans, the sick and the disabled. These were the unfortunate (*miserabiles personae*) whom the Church was supposed to protect. When the idea of the role of the monarch became established, the king, too, was presented as the protector of the weak and the helpless, i.e. the same categories. Clearly, not all the widows and orphans were impoverished (the great feudal widows, for example!), nor were all the sick and disabled without means. But the patronage of the Church consisted not only in material support but also in judicial defence, which was supposed to be given without regard to economic status. Only during the pontificate of Innocent IV (1244–1254) did canon law begin to distinguish between those members of the said categories who had means and those who had none, with a view to legal assistance. Pope Innocent IV ruled that poor widows, orphans, cripples, lepers, prisoners and poor old people could bring their cases directly to the ecclesiastical court. Those who had means, that is to say, who counted as *miserabiles* in the technical sense only, would be allowed to appeal to the ecclesiastical court only after their cases had been dealt with by a secular court, if they believed that justice had not been done because of negligence, or because it had been deliberately perverted by the judge.[2] This papal legislation listed the aged among both the poor and the technical *miserabiles*. It reveals an awareness that not all the aged were supported by their offspring (accounting for their inclusion among the poor), and the assumption that they were enfeebled, mentally, physically or both (hence their inclusion among the technical *miserabiles*). One of the secular jurists who held that legal aid must be given to individuals who did not know how to press their case, or how to defend themselves in court, also included the aged among them, alongside the women and children.[3]

However, despite the fact that Innocent IV listed the aged among the poor *miserabiles*, other kinds of texts did not usually count them as a deserving category, nor did testators who left charitable bequests. As a rule, when the diverse normative writings and sermons itemized the various kinds of poor people deserving of Christian charity, rather than subsuming them all under the heading *pauperes*, they mentioned widows and orphans and the disabled, but not old people. Likewise, in stories about the acts of charity and mercy done by saints for poor people, the same three groups are mentioned, but not the old. (The story about Clare of Pisa who befriended an old woman, visited her regularly and nursed her in her dying days, is an exception.)[4] Nor as a rule did old people as such figure in the lists of potential recipients of alms in the monasteries and noble houses. The accounts of the almoner of the Duke of Burgundy record distributions to widows, poor scholars, old ducal servants, large families and the 'shamed poor' (i.e. people who had fallen from comfort to poverty).[5] The Duke's old servants figure as a specific group, not as old people *per se* (like widows and orphans). When testators left a certain amount of money not for the poor in general but for a particular category, it was for blind people, prisoners, women in childbirth, lepers, orphans, widows, young women needing dowries, or large families,[6] but not for the aged as such. And yet, in other contexts we have seen that the aged did figure as a group. The reason was that while it was known that old age was often plagued by economic distress, the basic assumption remained that it was the duty of the offspring to support their aged parents and look after them. The frequent references to widows and orphans, the scriptural deserving poor, stemmed from the fundamental perception of the role of the family. Some women were widowed early and had no grown-up children, and some had small children to support. Women being considered physically and mentally weaker than men, they were seen as needing protection. And indeed, given the legal and social restrictions that constrained them, widows often did need legal assistance, regardless of their economic condition. Likewise, children whose fathers died were also seen as helpless, being without a man to defend their interests.

Nevertheless, it cannot be said that in practice old people received less assistance than other needy groups. Accounts of actual almsgiving, such as the daily or weekly distribution of charity, or the lists of almshouse inmates, mention the aged among the recipients. The list of the recipients of a daily bread ration at the monastery of Cluny in the eleventh century included children, widows, cripples, blind people, old men and women; the charitable distribution in other Benedictine monasteries of the period was much the same.[7] (In addition to bread, the monastery of Cluny also distributed beans four times a week and vegetables three times. On the major holy days and anniversaries, meat, wool and shoes were also distributed.)[8] Old people are mentioned in the records of hospitals, and there were also special almshouses for the aged poor.[9] A person who contributed to a hospital, either to the institution itself or for distribution among its inmates, was also helping the aged poor. Likewise, the donations to other bodies by the prosperous guilds and fraternities doubtless reached the aged poor too.[10] And old needy people had one advantage over young ones. An old person begging for alms could not but be treated as an honest and deserving poor man, unable to support himself by work. He was not suspected of being one of those lazy rogues who would rather beg than do an honest day's work. These were defined as the dishonest and undeserving poor. We referred earlier to Roger Bacon's proposal, in the latter half of the thirteenth century, that the ruler establish a special fund, financed in part by fines collected by the authorities and the confiscated properties of rebels, for the support of those who for reasons of illness or old age were unable to work, and for special shelters to house them. At the same time, he proposed that the able-bodied be compelled to work. If they failed to do so, they were to be expelled from the country.[11] The statutes of the Cistercian order in the latter half of the thirteenth century stated that during the harvest season, when there was plenty of work available, alms were to be given only to pilgrims, children, cripples and old people incapable of working.[12]

This distinction between the genuinely needy and the impostors grew much stronger after the Black Death of 1348, as the various discourses as well as the legislation showed. Landowners and urban entrepreneurs alike were anxious and angry about the great mobility of the labourers and the rising wages. The authorities sought to protect their interests by setting a maximum wage and ordering landless persons without a regular occupation to accept whatever work was offered them at the fixed rate, on pain of imprisonment.[13] The over-sixties were exempt from this obligation. Laws were passed against vagrancy. King Jean II of France ordered the Mendicant preachers to warn their flocks against giving alms to the able-bodied vagabonds, idlers, rogues and gamblers, and to encourage almsgiving to the blind, the amputees and other unfortunates. The wardens of almshouses were ordered to refuse to shelter vagrants, but only cripples and sick people, and to grant a single night's lodging to poor travellers.[14] At the same time, he ordered the expulsion of all the healthy idlers, male or female, from Paris. The order stipulated that if they were caught for the second time they would be jailed, the third time pilloried, and on the fourth time they would be branded on the forehead.[15]

In the long intervals between battles in the Hundred Years War in France, in addition to the companies of professional soldiers who, discharged and without pay, lived by plundering the population, there were also many gangs of robbers. These attracted people whose homes had been ruined and whose harvests destroyed. Their presence intensified the fear of poor vagrants as potential robbers and murderers.[16] The aged poor aroused no such fears. In Florence after the plague one of the leading charitable institutions, Or San Michele, redefined its policy in view of the demographic decline and the collapse of many families. As de la Roncière's study has shown, whereas before the plague the bulk of the aid was given to hired labourers with large families and to the unemployed, after the plague it was directed principally to widows, orphans and the needy old. In the years after the Black Death these constituted the largest proportion of the institution's regular listed recipients of assistance (as distinct from the small alms which were given indiscriminately, as in other institutions, to all who begged at the gate). During that period wages rose and the number of unemployed fell. The aged, the widows with young children and the orphans were seen as the most vulnerable sector of the population. However, the amounts given to these regular listed recipients did not suffice either. They were by way of supplementary income for such people as had some means of their own. Those who were entirely dependent on charity (many of whom must have been old), either obtained alms from more than one institution, or resorted to the distributions at the gates of the many monasteries and other institutions which handed out small change, bread and soup and sometimes apparel.[17]

It has been argued that Medieval almsgiving, inspired and supervised by the Church, was insufficiently discriminating, meaning that it was not necessarily given to the neediest. It emphasized the spiritual benefits to the giver, not the needs and wellbeing of the recipient or the society to which both of them belonged. It is true that in addition to the view that God allows poverty to exist, which therefore is necessary, it was held that the poor man conduces to the rich man's salvation by his existence, and his need of alms, which the latter provides. But as for lack of discrimination in almsgiving, Pullan has already shown in his study of Venice, that the argument is overstated. The Decretists, the commentators on canon law, maintained as early as the latter half of the twelfth century that charity must be given selectively, with careful consideration of the recipients. When in sixteenth-century Venice the secular authorities took over the supervision of charity, they made no significant changes in the system.[18] Barbara Harvey's extensive research on the English Benedictine monasteries reveals that they too tried to avoid distributing indiscriminately the resources they allocated to charity. They did hand out food to all comers at the monastery gates – at first daily and from the thirteenth century mostly three or four times a week, as well as on the anniversaries of deceased monks, founders and patrons. The secular patrons whose anniversaries they commemorated stipulated this in their wills. However, from the twelfth century onwards the monasteries also contributed to the establishment of hospitals, regularly aided the disabled poor who could not come to them in their homes, and provided food and shelter to the poor in their almonries. Some of these poor people became their servants, or lay brothers, thereby earning their living.[19]

The real problem stemmed from the highly unjust distribution of resources, which were concentrated in the hands of a narrow, politically powerful stratum, whose members would not even consider the causes of poverty. Welfare systems and old-age pensions had not been dreamed of. In so far as the condition of the working strata improved from time to time, it was due to changes in the labour force and land market, not to an ameliorating social policy. The fact that contributions to other causes than poor relief also counted as charity reduced the available means which might have helped the needy within the existing framework. For example, the population of the town of Worcester in the first half of the fifteenth century numbered about 4000. Only some 3 per cent of the inhabitants, 120 persons, received regular assistance from the various charitable bodies in the town. They included sick people, cripples, widows, orphans and the aged. There can be no doubt that the actual number of poor people in all these categories exceeded 3 per cent of the population.[20] They had to subsist on the distribution of alms at the various institutions, and the occasional distribution at the funerals of rich people. As we have seen, the regular alms given to old people in Florence did not suffice for their subsistence, because the same bodies also supported orphans, widows with children, sick and disabled people, and provided *ad hoc* assistance to poor women in childbirth and girls needing dowries. Most almshouses were small, and even those which were meant for the aged only (or also for the aged), could take in but a few.

In the period following the Black Death there was, on the whole, less willingness to help the poor than before. The ideal of voluntary absolute poverty, which certain religious groups sought to follow, was treated as akin to heresy while involuntary destitution (which concerns us here) was viewed as a source of social danger. In the latter half of the fourteenth century, the uprisings of peasants and urban labourers intensified the fear and rejection of the poor, the paupers in the broad sense of the term. While in earlier centuries involuntary poverty also carried a certain spiritual value, in keeping with the New Testament (provided the poor man was 'good', i.e. was humble, submitted to his fate and prayed for his benefactor), by the Late Middle Ages this positive image had largely disappeared. After the plague, people who wished to help the needy generally chose to help those who were nearest to them, such as poor kinsfolk or dependents (as in the bequests to servants and retainers or to peasants of the manor, as described in previous chapters), or fellow members of their guild or religious fraternity.[21] More money was spent on chantries for the holding of masses and prayers for the soul of the donor and his family, and on magnificent funerals (though this custom was denounced by the preachers). Those who could afford such funerals specified in their wills how many poor people were to take part in the procession (often with the instruction to have them wear black), how many candles they were to carry, and the meal and the alms which they were to receive. The poor played a symbolic part in the ceremony. Their presence symbolized the moral condition of the deceased, as well as his socio-economic status, which the funeral demonstrated. For their part, the poor, including the old, were eager to assist at such funerals for the sake of the alms and the meal. The almshouses also encouraged the inmates who were capable to take part in the funerals of the great.[22]

The problem of the distribution of means between the generations is both historical and contemporary. It recurs in all societies within the family. In the modern welfare state the distribution of resources between the different age groups is also a social problem. It is not easy to establish criteria for allocating resources to the young and the old. Should the state spend more on old-age pensions, medical care for the aged and geriatric institutions, or should it invest more in medical care for premature babies and children as a whole, in child allowances and in subsidizing higher education?[23] In previous chapters we looked at the way in which the various social strata in the Middle Ages dealt with the problem of inter-generational division of resources. The Church, in its charities, gave no thought to the just distribution of alms between the generations. In the final analysis, the principal criteria of worthiness were the family status and biblical tradition. Except for certain periods when assistance was also given to large families, to women in childbirth and to poor scholars, the bulk of the funds went to people who had no families or whose families were incomplete, i.e. widows, orphans, the sick and disabled who had no kinsfolk to take care of them and to solitary old people. Though not every person could count on his or her family for subsistence, the basic assumption was that needy persons who had families should be supported by them. Though the aged *per se* were not one of the theologically approved objects of charity, they were not deprived in comparison with the other needy groups. (In Florence after the Black Death there was as much emphasis on helping old men and women as on helping orphans.) Those aged persons who belonged to the margins of their marginalized group, who received no assistance and suffered great privation and even hunger, were not the victims of a deliberate policy of discrimination in favour of other needy groups. They suffered worse because they were unable to take advantage of changes in the land and labour market, as did the younger people, and because charity was never sufficient for the needs of any of the groups.

POSTSCRIPT

It is not proposed in this postscript to summarize the status and condition of old people in the Middle Ages. I dealt with this to the best of my ability in the body of the book. I also believe there is no need to elaborate on the by now acknowledged fact that the 'golden age' for the elderly in 'the past' is a myth. Here I should like to concentrate on what appear to me the most significant similarities and differences between old age in the Middle Ages and in present Western society.

In the Middle Ages, as today, people were regarded as old when they reached the age of 60 or 70. The low life expectancy and the high infant- and child-mortality caused even young people to be acutely conscious of possible extinction, of the sense that life could end at any moment. However, people also feared the ageing process because of its concomitant physical, mental and social changes, as well as its nearness to death. In Medieval times, too, there were various solutions to life in old age, and the family was not the only known framework. There were also various ways of dividing the limited resources between the older and younger generations, though they could not prevent tensions. Tensions of an economic nature, no less than political and social tensions, existed between the generations in all systems. In regions where old people were forced to retire and withdraw to the margins, they felt the loss of self-esteem keenly. Where they maintained their status, it was the younger people who felt constrained and sometimes resentful. Then, as much as in later periods until today, people voiced their awareness of the lack of symmetry in the love and concern between parents and their offspring.

One fundamental difference between the Middle Ages and the present is the existence in today's Western societies of the institution of retirement and old-age pensions. Since there was no compulsory retirement in Medieval society (nor indeed until the end of the nineteenth century), some people continued to function, to work at their occupations and to hold office until ripe old age, and sometimes to their dying day. Their knowledge and skills did not become obsolete as they do today. But the price of the freedom from compulsory age-linked retirement was the absence of pensions. We saw in previous chapters what were the implications of this lack for people who were unable to go on working and had to retire having no assets but the power of their hands.

There have been few changes in the image of the old person and the attitude towards the aged. Beside the 'positive' image there was the 'negative' one, often accompanied by expressions of rejection. Beside insights (no less profound and illuminating that those of later thinkers and gerontologists) and perceptions of individual differences among old people and empathy with their distress, there were widespread stereotypes and some difficult expectations concerning the states of mind and conduct, as well as the expectation that the old man should withdraw to the margin. The obvious improvement in the condition of old people has come about as a result of technological developments and the general rise in the standard of living in Western society, the extraordinary expansion of medical knowledge and the widening of welfare services. In the most pragmatic terms, the high proportion of old people in society (higher than ever before) means that they represent a significant sector of the consumer society. In addition to the old men and (even more) women who live on or below the poverty line, there are many old people with means, who constitute the 'third age market'. This group is catered for with a vast array of goods, from numerous offerings of the latest technology designed to improve the elderly person's quality of life, to expensive old-age homes and special cruises and tours. But despite the concrete changes, and the efforts of geriatricians and gerontologists not only to advise the welfare authorities how best to cope with the problem of the increasing elderly population but also to readjust social values accordingly, there have been few changes in the images, expectations and attitudes, although they have undergone secularization. In this area there has been more continuity than change. This can also have a tangible effect.

However, secularization also entailed change. Secularization eliminated the meaning of the old person's disabilities and suffering, and took away the consolation. It deprived him of the belief that his bodily affliction brought him closer to God, that suffering is atonement and a means of salvation in the next world, and that the devout soul is eternal and can be rejuvenated. According to the geriatric specialist and author Marian Rabinowitz, 'Suffering can make one younger, not only older. Some people are stirred by it to wonder and to ask questions. Curiosity is a youthful characteristic.' We respect the questioning, searching individual, particularly if he is old, but freedom of thought and mental questing exact a price. It is undoubtedly harder for a person to wonder and to seek a meaning and significance in life and the world, including one's own ageing, than to accept and internalize the significance proffered by the religion in which one has been brought up and which is part of one's being. The belief in the afterlife and in reward and punishment in the next world did not (and does not) do away with the fear of death; indeed, for the believer it was (and still is) an added source of anxiety, but it did and still does offer meaning and hope.

Some anthropologists have suggested that old age can serve as a laboratory for the examination of the interaction between the universal-human and the cultural-distinctive elements, and the tension between them. They argue that beside the pragmatic ways which old people develop to satisfy their essential needs, they may also be searching for pure significance, because they are less constrained by their social-cultural context. For the old person, the significance of things is not necessarily found in immediate experience. He can think a-historically, because his sense of time is different. He is post-cultured, as a child is pre-cultured. The idea is intriguing, but testing it would require a comparative analysis based on prolonged conversations with old people from a variety of cultures, (few of which have remained uncontaminated by the 'global village'). But if the experiment ever gets under way, it in itself would have purpose and dignity, because it would entail listening to the old people, while the search for the universal would inevitably also disclose the individual.

Elderly people refuse to see old age as a separate stage in their lives, in which their personalities undergo a significance change, and they tend to emphasize the continuity of the ageless self. This view conflicts with the position which stresses the dominance of change in old age, and it certainly rebuts the stereotype of the elderly. From personal observation of old people (and without laying claim to a scientific assessment), I would say that there is as much individuality in old age as in other stages of life, and that the continuity of the self predominates. Yet in extreme old age, which nowadays more people live to than ever before, the personality in most cases does undergo significant change, and the resemblance between the individuals gradually increases. Similar mental states appear, and characteristic behaviour is manifested.

The reader will have seen that the aim of the present book is more modest than that of the said anthropologists. The historian, unlike the anthropologist, cannot interview the subjects of his research, and the voice of the old person is rarely heard in the Medieval sources. Such a voice might have told us more, and in a direct way, about the experience of the elderly in that society, and to what extent he outgrew the constraints of his specific culture, if at all. I can only hope that this book has helped to illuminate the issue of change and continuity in Western culture from another angle, that of the aged, their position and the attitudes towards them. If it has helped to point out the universal and unchanging aspects of old age and of the relations between the generations, which are part of the human condition, so much the better.

I conclude with an extract from an essay by Patrick White, one of my favourite authors, who died some years ago. It was first published in 1988, when White was 76. This is a personal description of his thoughts and feelings as an old man, but it may express what other old people think and feel. The reader of the present work may find in it some insight into the question of continuity and change in the general view of old age, and of the aged person's view of his own place in the world.

I would like to believe in the myth that we grow wiser with age. In a sense my disbelief is wisdom. Those of a middle generation, if charitable or sentimental, subscribe to the wisdom myth, while the callous see us as dispensable objects, like broken furniture or dead flowers. For the young we scarcely exist unless we are unavoidable members of the same family, farting, slobbering, perpetually mislaying teeth and bifocals. Some may Christian Science their disgust if they see death as a handout, then if the act is delayed, remember the gouging they have suffered in the past.

Some of us become vegans to atone for the soft cruelties we've inflicted on our fellow animals – parents, children, lovers, friends – though our eyes continue to conceal knives ready for strangers we pass in the street if they don't recognize our right of way.

Prayer and vegies ought to help towards atonement. But don't. There is the chopping to be done. Memories rise to the surface as we hear the whimper of a frivolous lettuce, the hoarse-voiced protest of a slivered parsnip, screaming of the naked potato in its pot of tumbled water. So how can an altruist demonstrate his sincerity? Could we perhaps exist on air till the day we are returned to earth, the bed in which potatoes faintly stir as they prepare sightless eyes for birth?

O Lord, dispel our dreams, of murders we did not commit – or did we?

Patrick White, *The Screaming Potato* in *Three Uneasy Pieces*
(Penguin Books, 1990)

NOTES

INTRODUCTION

1 R. Trexler, *Public Life in Renaissance Florence* (New York, 1980), pp. 368–71; N. Orme, 'Children and the Church in Medieval England', *The Journal of Ecclesiastical History* 45 (1994), pp. 582–6.

2 'si puer vel adolescens, si vir vel estate senex', *Bartholomew of Exeter, Bishop and Canonist, With the Text of Bartholomew's Penitential*, ed. Dom A. Morey (Cambridge, 1937), XXV, p. 194. See also: *Councils and Synods, with Other Documents Relating to the English Church*, eds M. Powicke and C. R. Cheney (Oxford, 1964), Vol. II, part 1, p. 224; John Myrc, *Instructions for Parish Priests*, ed. E. Peacock (London, 1868), p. 44.

3 *Analekten zur Geschichte des Franciscus von Assisi*, ed. H. Boehmer (Tübingen and Leipzig, 1904), pp. 24–5.

4 Regarding societies based on the age system: M. Almagor, 'Charisma Fatigue in an East African Generation Set System', *American Ethnologist* 10/4 (1983), pp. 635–49.

5 See J. Keith, 'Age in Anthropological Research' in R. H. Binstock and E. Shanas, eds, *Handbook of Aging and Social Sciences* (New York, 1985), pp. 231–63.

6 *Annales S. Iustinae Patavini*, M.G.H.S., Vol. 19, p. 179.

7 Matthew Paris, *Chronica majora*, ed. H. R. Luard (Rolls Series, London, 1877), Vol. 57/4, p. 134.

8 Thomas Aquinas, *Summa theologiae*, 3a, q. 72, art. 8 (Blackfriars, London, 1974), Vol. 57, pp. 212–15.

9 M. Lauwers, 'La mort et le corps des saints. La scène de la mort dans les *vitae* du Moyen Age', *Le Moyen Age*, 94 (1988), pp. 37–8, note 110.

10 'ou par aage, ou par viellegnere ou par nature ou par fame', *Les Livres de jostice et de plet*, ed. L. N. Rapetti (Paris, 1850), L. II, C. XIV, p. 98.

11 Tractate *Sanhedrin* 36: 3; Maimonides, *Mishneh Torah* ('The Repetition of the Law'), on the Book of Judges, Rules of Sanhedrin B(3); also B(9), according to which a stranger is also barred from serving in the Sanhedrin. In the Old Testament too, alongside the precept 'Thou shalt rise up before the hoary head, and honour the face of the old man', (Lev. 19: 32), and the role of old men in the society, they were on occasion numbered among the marginalized groups to emphasize the social whole, when the centre of power – i.e., the adult males – was taken for granted and needed no mention, e.g. Genesis 19: 4 (referring to the men of Sodom): 'both old and young, all the people from every quarter'. Or in the prophecy of Zechariah: 'There shall yet old men and old women dwell in the streets of Jerusalem, and every man with his staff in his hand for

175

very age', (Zech. 8: 4–5). Or, 'cause to perish all Jews, both young and old, little children and women, in one day' (The Book of Esther 3: 13).

12 T. Smith, ed., *English Gilds* (London, 1870), p. 148.

13 Honorius Augustodunensis, *De philosophia mundi libri quatuour*, P. L. Vol. 172, L. IV, col. 9. This was actually the work of William of Conches in the twelfth century, which was mistakenly attributed to Honorius; Albertus Magnus, *Parva naturalia, de aetate sive de juventute et senectute*, Tractatus I, in *Opera omnia*, ed. A. Borgent (Paris, 1890), pp. 306–14.

14 *The History of King Boccus and Syndracke*, trans. H. Caumpeden (London, 1530), q. CCXXV.

15 Francesco Petrarca, *De remediis utriusque fortune* (Rotterdam, 1649), pp. 556–7.

16 See G. M. Hamilton, 'Changes in Personality and Psychological Phenomena with Age', in *Problems of Aging*, ed. E. V. Cowdry (Baltimore, 1942), pp. 810–31; P. L. Assoun, 'Le vieillissement saisi par la psychoanalyse', *Communications* 37 (1983), pp. 167–79.

17 R. T. Evans, *Dialogues with Erik Erikson* (New York, 1967), pp. 53–4.

18 *Leges Visigotorum*, M.G.H., *Leges*, Sectio 1, ed. K. Zeumer (Hanover, 1902), Vol. 1, VIII, 4, 16, pp. 336–8.

19 J. Heers, *Esclaves et domestiques au moyen-age dans le monde méditerranéen* (Paris, 1981), p. 273.

20 N. Daniel, *Am I My Parents' Keeper? An Essay on Justice between the Young and the Old* (Oxford, 1988), p. 94.

21 J. P. Delumeau, *La peur en Occident, XIVe-XVIIIe siècles* (Paris, 1978).

22 Innocent III. *Lotharii Cardinalis (Innocenti III) de miseria humanae conditionis*, ed. M. Maccarrone (Lugano, 1955).

23 Francesco Petrarca, *op. cit.*; L. II, Dialogi 83, 86, 95–103, 113–15.

24 *Mandeville's Travels*, ed. P. Hamelius (E.E.T.S. London, 1919), p. 113.

25 G. Vigarello, *Concepts of Cleanliness. Changes in Attitude in France since the Middle Ages*, trans. J. Birrel (Cambridge, 1988), p. 29.

26 *La Queste del Saint Graal*, ed. A. Pauphilet (Paris, 1923), pp. 82–7, 262–3.

27 Geoffrey Chaucer, *The Canterbury Tales*, ed. W. W. Skeat (Oxford, 1947), 'The Pardoner's Tale', pp. 284–5; for interpretations of this tale, see A. K. Nitecki, 'The Convention of the Old Man's Lament in the Pardoner's Tale', *Chaucer Review* 16 (1981–2), 76–84; Jonathan Swift wrote a merciless and bitter description of eternal old age. Gulliver meets creatures who were condemned to live forever as old men. Their frightful appearance and disgusting character have cured all their countrymen of the desire for immortality. In this sharp satire Swift ascribes to them all the bad qualities which were attributed to the old in the Middle Ages, enlarged and sharpened as though by a magnifying glass. They are despised and detested by all, and have had all their privileges withdrawn: Jonathan Swift, *Gulliver's Travels* (Everyman's Library, 1966), pp. 220–8. The book was first published in 1726.

28 *Njal Saga*, trans. M. Magnusson (Penguin Books, 1960), p. 254.

29 'quia laborare se ulterius pose desperans ea, que iam in futuris necessitatibus aggregavit, quasi cotidie minoranda et non cumulanda conservat.' Thomas Cantimpraetensis, *Liber de natura rerum*, ed. H. Boese (Berlin-New York, 1973), pp. 81–2; Philippe de Navarre, who divided life into four stages, held that in the third stage, i.e. between the ages of 40 and 60, a man should economize and save, so as to have means of subsistence in his old age. Woe to the man who failed to do so, for he would suffer degradation and hunger: '*Les quatre ages de l'homme*', ed. M. de Fréville (Paris, 1888), 102, pp. 56–7; see also Aegidius Romanus, *De regimine principum* (Rome, 1607), L.I, pars 4, C. 3,

pp. 195–9; Gilles li Muisis, *Le lamentation* in *Poésies*, ed. Kervyn de Lettenhove (Louvain, 1882), Vol. I, p. 23.

30 Roger Bacon, *Opus majus*, ed. J. Bridges (Frankfurt/Main, 1964), Vol. II, pars 2, p. 251; *Opus majus*, trans. R. B. Burke (Philadelphia, 1928), Vol. II, part 2, p. 661.

31 M. Eliav-Feldon, *Realistic Utopias. The Imaginary Societies of the Renaissance* (Oxford, 1982), pp. 47–55, 84, 101–3.

32 Michaut le Caron dit Taillevent, *Le pauvre vieux* in *Anthologie poétique Française. Moyen Age*, ed. A. Mary (Paris, 1967), Vol. 2, p. 232.

33 S. de Beauvoir, *La vieillesse* (Paris, 1970).

34 *Les constitutions de la France depuis 1789*, présenté par J. Godechot (Paris, 1970), De la garantie de droit, art. 23, p. 92; Acte constitutionel, art. 4, p. 83.

35 I. Asimov, *Of Time and Space and Other Things* (London, 1967), p. 196; D. H. Fischer, *Growing Old in America* (New York, 1977).

36 P. Laslett, 'Mean Household Size in England since the 16th Century', in *Household and Family in Past Times*, eds P. Laslett and R. Wall (Cambridge, 1972), pp. 125–58; *idem*. 'History of Ageing and the Aged', in *Family Life and Illicit Love in Earlier Generations* (Cambridge, 1977), pp. 174–213; L. Stone, 'Walking Over Grandma', *New York Review of Books* (12 May 1977); *idem*. 'Family History in the 1980s. Past Achievements and Future Trends', *Journal of Interdisciplinary History* 12 (1982), pp. 69–70; P. N. Stearns, ed., *Old Age in Preindustrial Society* (London, 1982), pp. 1–18; the chapters concerning the Middle Ages in G. Minois, *Histoire de la vieillesse. De l'antiquité à la Renaissance* (Paris, 1987); some articles in the volume *Life, Death and the Elderly. Historical Perspectives*, eds M. Pelling and R. M. Smith (London, 1991); and the entire volume *Aging and the Aged in Medieval Europe*, ed. M. M. Sheehan (Toronto, 1990); the particular articles which I consulted, concerning old age in the Middle Ages, are specified in the notes and in the bibliography.

CHAPTER 1 WHO WERE OLD IN THE MIDDLE AGES?

1 Cited in T. Cole, *The Journey of Life, A Cultural History of Aging in America* (Cambridge, 1992), p. 229.

2 M. Rabinowitz, *A Man's Age* (Hebrew), (Tel Aviv, 1985).

3 An interview with Professor Amos Krochin, *Haaretz*, 19.10.1990 (in Hebrew).

4 'In studiis autem et laboribus iuventutis non intelligitur quando senectus obrepit . . . non subito frangitur, sed diurnitate extinguitur', Vincent de Beauvais, *Speculum naturale* in *Biblioteca mundi seu speculum quadruplex: naturale, doctrinale, morale, historiale* (Douai, 1624), Vol. I, L. 31, C. 88, col. 2361.

5 Arnaldus de Villanova, *De regimine sanitatis* in *Opera omnia* (Basel, 1585), col. 824.

6 Maimonides, *Mishneh Torah, Hilkhot Issurei Bi'ah*, Chapter 9 (5).

7 S. Kaufman, *The Ageless Self. Sources for Meaning in Late Life* (Madison, Wisc., 1986).

8 Augustinus, *Sermo ad competentes*, P.L., Vol. 38, C. 8, col. 1081; trans. M. Dove, *The Perfect Age of Man's Life* (Cambridge, 1986), pp. 48–9.

9 E. Erikson, 'Eight Stages of Man', in *Childhood and Society* (New York, 1963); D. Levinson, *The Seasons of Man's Life* (New York, 1979). Erikson divided life into eight stages, Levinson into four. According to him, there may be another transition at about age 80, but he has not studied it. His book contains a summary of the views of previous developmental psychologists.

10 M. Rabinowitz, *op. cit.*, p. 24.

11 See, *inter alia*, I. Asimov, *Of Time and Space and Other Things* (London, 1967), pp. 195–6; C. Gilbert, 'When did a Man in the Renaissance Grow Old?', *Studies in the Renaissance* 14 (1967), pp. 7–32; R. Finlay, 'The Venetian Republic as a Gerontocracy. Age and Politics in the Renaissance', *The Journal of Medieval and Renaissance Studies* 8 (1978), p. 158; R. Trexler, 'A Widows' Asylum of the Renaissance: the Orbatello of Florence', in P. M. Stearns, ed., *Old Age in Preindustrial Society* (London, 1982), p. 127; M. W. Labarge, 'Three Medieval Widows and Second Careers', in M. M. Sheehan, ed., *Aging and the Aged in Medieval Europe* (Toronto, 1990), p. 159.

12 See J. Keith, 'Age in Anthropological Research' in R. H. Binstock and E. Shanas, eds, *Handbook of Aging and Social Sciences* (New York, 1985), p. 241 f.

13 J. de Ghellinck, 'Juventus, gravitas, senectus', in *Studia Medievalia in hon. R. J. Martin* (Bruge, 1948), pp. 39–59; E. Sears, *The Ages of Man. Medieval Interpretations of the Life Cycle* (Princeton, 1986); M. Dove, *The Perfect Age of Man's Life* (Cambridge, 1986); J. A. Burrow, *The Ages of Man* (Oxford, 1986).

14 E. Sears, *op. cit.*, 5, 18, 19, 24, 43–8, 71–8. The many other plates are illuminations.

15 J. A. Burrow, *op. cit.*, pp. 5–11, 66–72, 80–5.

16 Bernard de Gordon, *De conservatione vitae humanae seu de regimine sanitatis* (Leipzig, 1570), p. 105.

17 Found in the work known as *Liber prognosticorum*. See L. Demaitre, 'The Care and Extension of Old Age in Medieval Medicine', in M. M. Sheehan, ed., *Aging and the Aged in Medieval Europe* (Toronto, 1990), p. 8, note 23; other examples of three-stage divisions: J. A. Burrow, *op. cit.*, pp. 5–11, 66–72; E. Sears, *op. cit.*, pp. 88–9, 90–3.

18 Dante, *Convivio*, in *Opere di Dante*, ed. M. Barbi (Florence, 1921), IV, pp. 21–8.

19 Philippe de Navarre, *Les quatre ages de l'homme*, ed. M. de Fréville (Paris, 1888), pp. 1–5, 102, 105.

20 Aldebrandin de Sienne, *La régime du corps*, eds Landouzy and R. Pépin (Paris, 1911), pp. 79–82. Other examples of four-stage divisions can be found in J. A. Burrow, *op. cit.*, pp. 5; 12–36, 57–8, 74–5, 84; E. Sears, *op. cit.*

21 Thomas of Cantimpré, *Liber de natura rerum*, ed. H. Boese (Berlin-New York, 1973), L.I, LXXVIII-LXXXIV, pp. 80–2.

22 Jean Froissart, *Le joli buisson de jonece*, ed. A. Fourrier (Geneva, 1975), 707–1611, pp. 73–105.

23 Andreas Capellanus, *On Love*, trans. P. G. Walsh (London, 1982), L.I, C.5, pp. 38–9; other examples of seven stage divisions: J. A. Burrow, *op. cit.*, pp. 5, 19, 37; E. Sears, *op. cit.* pp. 38–53, 105–6, 124–44, 149–51, 153.

24 Vincent of Beauvais, *Speculum naturale*, Vol. I, L. 31, C. 75, cols. 2348–9; also Bartholomaeus Anglicus, the thirteenth-century author of a very popular encyclopedia which was translated from Latin into several European languages, proposed two possible divisions, one into three and the other into six stages; Bartholomaeus Anglicus, *Liber de proprietatibus rerum* (Strasbourg, 1505), L. IV, C. 1: *de etate; On the Properties of Things, John Trevisa's Translation of Bartholomaeus Anglicus*, ed. M. C. Seymour (Oxford, 1975), Vol. I, pp. 291–2.

25 Eustache Deschamps, *Oeuvres complètes*, ed. Le Marquis de Queux de Saint-Hilaire (Paris 1878–1903), Vol. II, Ballade CXXVIII, p. 151; D. Herlihy and Ch. Klapisch, *Les Toscans et leurs familles; Étude du catasto Florentin de 1427* (Paris, 1978), p. 202.

26 Eustache Deschamps, *op. cit.*, Ballade LXXXIX, p. 181.

27 See note 17.

28 Innocent III, *Lotharii Cardinalis (Innocenti III), Di miseria humanae conditionis*, ed. M. Maccarrone (Lugano, 1955), VIII: *De brevitate huius vite*, p. 16.

29 For example, C. Gilbert, *op. cit.*, pp. 11, 32, and note 65.

30 'Senex vero tantum generis est masculini, sicut anus foeminini.' 'Nam dicitur mulier sola quasi anosa, senectum quida multa secum.' Vincent de Beauvais, *op. cit.*, Vol. I, L. 31, C. 87, col. 2360.

31 Concerning the cited medical theory, see H. J. von Kondratowitz, 'The Medicalization of Old Age. Continuity and Change in Germany from the Late 18th to early 20th Century', in *Life, Death and the Elderly. Historical Perspectives*, eds M. Pelling and R. M. Smith (London, 1991), pp. 147–8.

32 Other ages were mentioned as the time when menstruation stopped: 35, 40, 45, 60 and 65 (if the woman was moist). However, the most widely accepted idea was that the cycle ended at age 50. See J. B. Post, 'Ages of Menarche and Menopause: Some Medieval Authorities', *Population Studies* 25 (1971), pp. 83–7; D. W. Amundsen and C. J. Diers, 'The Age of Menarche in Medieval Europe', *Human Biology* 45 (1973), pp. 363–9.

33 Ch. Klapisch-Zuber, 'Le dernier enfant: fécondite et vieillissement chez les Florentines XIVe-XVe siècle', in *Mélanges offerts à Jacques Dupâquier*, (Paris, 1993), pp. 277–90.

34 'de touz ceus et de toutes celes qui vivent tant qu'il deviennent viel'. Philippe de Navarre, *op. cit.*, pp. 52–3, 84.

35 Discussing the sacrament of confirmation, Thomas Aquinas points out the frailty of children, women and the aged. However, the weakness of children is temporary, and men are frail only in the last stage of their lives, whereas the frailty of women is their lifelong condition. All this referred to the wars of this world. In spiritual battles women displayed great courage, and some had even become martyrs. Thomas Aquinas, *Summa theologiae*, Tertia Primae, Q. 72, art. 8 (Blackfriars, London, 1966–74), Vol. 57, pp. 212–13.

36 C. Gilbert, *op. cit.*, pp. 10–11, 15–16.

37 R. T. Rosenthal, 'Retirement and the Life Cycle in 15th Century England', in M. M. Sheehan, ed., *Aging and the Aged in Medieval Europe* (Toronto, 1990), pp. 185–6.

38 *Secretum*, in Francesco Petrarca, *Prose*, ed. G. Martelloti (Milan, 1995), p. 182. The *Secretum* deals with the years 1342–3, but was probably written in the late 1340s, and edited again by the author in the 1350s. In this connection, see J. D. Folts, 'Senescence and Renascence: Petrarch's Thought of Growing Old', *The Journal of Medieval and Renaissance Studies* 10 (1980), p. 231 and note 87.

39 *The Letters of Michelangelo*, trans. E. H. Ramsden (Stanford, 1963), Vol. I, Letter 116, pp. 105–6.

40 The following are but two examples of texts which show that there were, as Burrow put it, social sanctions against people who did not behave appropriately for their age. These texts were based on Seneca's statement regarding the old man who behaved this way, and on the erroneous Vulgate translation of Isaiah 65: 20. *Walafridi Strabi Fuldensis Monachi Glossa Ordinaria*, P.L., Vol. 113, col. 1311; *The Book of Vices and Virtues. A 14th Century English Translation of the Somme le Roi of Lorens d'Orleans*, ed. W. N. Francis (E.E.T.S. London, 1942), p. 287; J. A. Burrow, *op. cit.*, pp. 141–62.

41 *Francisi Petrarchae de remediis utriusque fortune* (Rotterdam, 1649), L. I, Dialogus 1, p. 15; this work was widely popular and already in the fourteenth century was translated into French and in the sixteenth century into English; *Phisicke Against Fortune by Francis Petrarch. Englished by Thomas Twyne* (London, 1579), f. 1v.

42 'Al credar mio, tu stardi in terra senza me gran tempo.' Francesco Petrarca, *Canzionere, trionfi, rime varie e una scelta di versi latini*, eds C. Muscetta and D. Ponchiroli (Torino, 1958), II, V. 187–9, p. 516; translated as *The Triumphs of Petrarch*, trans. E. H. Wilkins (Chicago, 1962).

43 Cited in J. D. Folts, *op. cit.*, p. 223.

44 See S. K. Cohn Jr, *Death and Property in Siena 1205–1800. Strategies for the Afterlife* (Baltimore, 1988), pp. 87–94; the quote from the letter appears on p. 90.

45 *The Letters of Michelangelo*, Vol. I, L. 79, p. 71.

46 Troyat's description of this episode was based on Tolstoy's diary and letters, and on the diary of his wife, Countess Sonia Tolstoy, as well as on an unfinished story of Tolstoy's in which he described that night. Fearing that the readers would find it hard to believe the story as a true life experience, he entitled it 'Notes of a Madman'. Henry Troyat, *Tolstoy*, trans. Nancy Amphoux (New York, 1969), pp. 388–93.

47 Cited in S. de Beauvoir, *La vieillesse* (Paris, 1970), Vol. I, p. 321.

48 Margaret Oliphant, *The Curate in Charge* (reprint Gloucester, 1987), p. 3.

49 P. Gay, *Freud, A Life of Our Time* (New York, 1988), pp. 134, 156.

50 Samuel Beckett, *Malone Dies*. A novel translated from the French by the author (New York, 1956), p. 1.

51 D. J. Levinson, *The Seasons of Man's Life* (New York, 1979), pp. 18, 21, 26, 322; F. Sheehy, *Passages. Predictable Crises of Adult Life* (New York, 1977), pp. 6, 11, 13, 350.

52 *De remediis utriusque fortune*, L.II, Dialogus 83, p. 563; *Phisicke against Fortune*, f. 266 v; see also Dante, *Convivio*, IV, 28.

53 Albertus Magnus, *Parva naturalia, de morte et de vita*, in *Opera omnia*, ed. A. Borgent (Paris, 1891), Vol. IX, T. II, C. 7, p. 363; see also Vincent of Beauvais, *op. cit.*, Vol. I, LXXXI, C. 87, col. 2360.

54 J. T. Rosenthal, *op. cit.*, pp. 185–6.

55 *The Chronicle of Jocelin of Brakelond*, ed. trans. H. E. Butler (London, 1942), p. 127.

56 'en fleur de son age', Philippe de Commynes, *Mémoires*, ed. J. Calmette (Paris, 1965), L. IV, C. 12, p. 325.

57 D. Herlihy, 'Age, Property and Career in Medieval Society', in M. M. Sheehan, *op. cit.*, p. 145.

58 R. Finlay, 'The Venetian Republic as a Gerontocracy: Age and Politics in the Renaissance', *The Journal of Medieval and Renaissance Studies* 8 (1978), pp. 157–78.

59 *The Letters of Michelangelo*, L. 155, Vol. 1, pp. 144–5; L. 173, Vol. 1, p. 162; L. 174, Vol. 1, p. 163.

60 *The Letters of Michelangelo*, Vol. II, L. 206, p. 6; L. 219, p. 21; L. 237, p. 37; L. 251, p. 51; L. 262, p. 58; L. 265, p. 61; L. 266, p. 61; L. 271, p. 64; L. 279, p. 72; L. 280, p. 75; L. 281, p. 76; L. 287, p. 79; L. 299, p. 86; L. 306, p. 92; L. 312, p. 94; L. 314, p. 95; L. 316, p. 96; L. 322, p. 100; L. 326, p. 104; L. 327, p. 105; L. 341, p. 113; L. 343, p. 118; L. 344, p. 119; L. 347, p. 120; L. 364, p. 133; L. 366, p. 134; L. 368, p. 135; L. 376, p. 140; L. 378, p. 141; L. 389, p. 146; L. 391, p. 147; L. 399, p. 154; L. 402, p. 155; L. 403, p. 156; L. 407, p. 159; L. 408, p. 160; L. 409, p. 160; L. 410, p. 161; L. 414, p. 163; L. 417, p. 164; L. 419, p. 165; L. 428, p. 170; L. 431, p. 172; L. 432, p. 173; L. 433, p. 174; L. 435, p. 177; L. 436, p. 177; L. 448, p. 186; L. 450, p. 191; L. 451, p. 192; L. 454, p. 194; L. 455, p. 194; L. 458, p. 195; L. 459, p. 196; L. 462,

p. 197; L. 464, p. 199; L. 468, p. 200; L. 469, p. 202; L. 470, p. 202; L. 476, p. 203.

61 Vol. II, L. 208, p. 8; L. 212, p. 12.

62 Vol. II, L. 323, p. 102.

63 Vol. II, L. 413, p. 1662; L. 445, p. 184.

64 *Vita Prima*, P.L. Vol. 185, col. 225; trans. A. Walker, *St Bernard of Clairvaux* (London, 1960), p. 10.

65 H. Rashdall, *The Universities of Europe in the Middle Ages*, eds F. Powicke and A. B. Emden (Oxford, 1963), Vol. 1, p. 472, note 1.

66 'nisi senectum eum detineret'. *Usatges de Barcelona. El codi a mitjan segle XII*, ed. J. Bastardas (Barcelona, 1984), 7 (us. 9), p. 58.

67 *Recueil général des anciennes lois françaises depuis l'an 420 jusqu'à la Revolution de 1789*, eds A. J. L. Jourdan, Decrusy and F. A. Isambert (Paris, 1822–33), Vol. III, no. 567, p. 222.

68 *Ibid.*, Vol. IV, no. 109, pp. 465–6.

69 This edict was published on pp. 286–92 of the article by J. T. Fontes, 'El ordenamiento de precios y salarios de Pedro I al reino de Murcia', *Anuario de Historia del Derecho Español* 31 (1961), pp. 281–92.

70 W. O. Ault, *Open Field Husbandry and the Village Community* (Transactions of the American Philosophical Society. New Series 55, part 7, Philadelphia, 1965), pp. 13–15, and Appendices 15–18, 61; B. Harvey, ed., *Custumals and Bye-Laws (1386–1526) of the Manor of Islip* (Oxfordshire Records Society Ser. XL, 1959), p. 105.

71 *Livre de Jean d'Ibelin. Assise de la haute cour* in *Recueil des historiens de Croisades*, Lois, ed. M. Le Comte Beugnot (Paris, 1841), C. 226, p. 358.

72 *The Statutes of the Realm*, eds A. Luders, T. E. Tomlins and J. Raithby (London, 1810–28. Reprint, 1963), Vol. I, p. 97.

73 *Ibid.*, Vol. II, Statute 19, p. 649.

74 *Las siete partidas del Rey Alfonso el Sabio*, ed. G. Lopez (Salamanca, 1555; reprint Madrid, 1974), P. II, t. XIX, ley 4, p. 66.

75 *Chronica di Giovanni Villani*, ed. F. G. Dramagomanni (Florence, 1845; reprint Frankfurt, 1969), Vol. III, XI, C. 94, p. 324.

76 A. Pertile, *Storia del diritto Italiano della caduca dell'Impero Romano alla codificazione* (Torino, 1892–1902), Vol. III, p. 253 and notes 45, 46.

77 *Règlements sur les arts et métiers de Paris rédigés au XIIIe siècle et connus sous le nom du Livre de Métiers de Etienne Boileau*, ed. G. B. Depping (Paris, 1837), II, p. 20; VIII, p. 31; XIV, p. 43; XV, p. 45; XVI, 48; XVII, 51; XVIII, 52; XIX, p. 55; XXI, p. 59; XXXI, p. 76; XXXII, p. 76; XXXIV, p. 80; XXXVII, p. 87; XLII, p. 97; XLIII, p. 99; LI, p. 125; LVII, p. 147; LVIII, p. 149; LIX, p. 152; LXIII, p. 161; LXVII, p. 171; LXVIII, p. 174; LXX, p. 180; LXXI, p. 184; LXXII, p. 187; LXXVI, p. 203; LXXX, p. 220; LXXXII, p. 223; LXXXVII, p. 239; LXXXIX, p. 246; C, p. 274, and pp. 422–27.

78 *Regiam maiestatem* in *The Acts of the Parliament of Scotland*, eds T. Thomson and C. Innes (Edinburgh, 1844), Vol. I, L. IV, C.2, p. 632 (268); *Usatges de Barcelona. El codi a mitjan segle XII*, 51 (us. 55), p. 88; *Die Konstitutionen Friedrichs II Hohenstaufen für sein Konigreich Sizilien*, eds H. Conrad, T. von der Lieck-Buyken and W. Wagner (Vienna, 1973), Vol. II, L. II, t. xl, pp. 230–32; Philippe de Beaumanoir, *Coutumes de Beauvaisis*, ed. A. Salmon (Paris, 1900), Vol. II, c. LXI, no. 1713, p. 377; concerning the discharge from duty at age 60 according to the *Libre de costumas* of Bordeaux, see G. D. Guyon, 'La Procédure du duel judiciaire dans l'ancien droit coutumier bordelais', in *Mélanges Roger Aubenas. Recueil de mémoires et travaux d'histoire du droit et des*

institutions des anciens pays de droit écrit, 9 (1974), pp. 385–409; *Assises de la haute court. Livre de Jean d'Ibelin*, C.CVI, p. 176; C.CCXXVI bis, p. 359; C.CCXXVIII, p. 363; the editor cites two manuscripts in one of which the discharge was given at age 60 and in the other at age 40. It seems to me that we can readily accept age 60, both because this was the age of discharge throughout Europe, and because in the Crusader kingdom age 60 was also the age of discharge from personal service on behalf of the fief, and a woman who inherited at age 60 was not obliged to marry at the behest of her feudal lord: see notes 71, 91. Concerning the trial by battle, see R. Bartlett, *Trial by Fire and Water: the Medieval Judicial Ordeal* (Oxford, 1988), C. 6, pp. 103–26.

79 *The Statutes of the Realm*, Vol. I, c. 38, p. 89.

80 A. Pertile, *op. cit.*, Vol. III, p. 253, and note 47; R. Finlay, *op. cit.*, p. 172; D. E. Queller, 'The Civic Irresponsibility of the Venetian Nobility', in D. Herlihy, R. S. Lopez and V. Slessarev, eds, *Economy, Society and Government in Medieval Italy. Essays in Memory of R. L. Reynolds* (Kent, Oh., 1969), pp. 223–35; D. E. Queller, *The Venetian Patriciate: Reality versus Myth* (University of Illinois Press, 1986), p. 130.

81 A. Pertile, *op. cit.*, Vol. III, p. 253 and note 48.

82 D. Herlihy and Ch. Klapisch, *Les Toscans et leurs familles. Étude due catasto florentin de 1427* (Parish, 1978), pp. 332, 336; Ch. Klapisch, 'Household and Family in Tuscany in 1427', in P. Laslett and R. Wall, eds, *Household and Family in Past Times* (Cambridge, 1972), p. 269 and note 5; D. Herlihy, 'Property and Career in Medieval Society', in M. M. Sheehan, ed., *op. cit.*, pp. 143–58.

83 Ph. Contamine, *Guerre, état et société à la fin du Moyen-Age. Étude sur les armées des rois de France 1337–1494* (Paris, 1972), p. 35, and note 39.

84 *Statutes of the Realm*, Vol. I, p. 307.

85 B. Imhaus, 'Un Document démographique et fiscal Vénetien concernant le casal du Marethasse (1549),' Μελεταιχαι υπμ-νηνατα 1 (1984), p. 513; B. Arbel and G. Veinstein, 'La Fiscalité véneto-cypriote au minoir de la legislation ottomane: la qānūnnāmē de 1572', *Turcica* 18 (1986), pp. 18, 19. My thanks to Dr Benjamin Arbel for these references.

86 *Statutes of the Realm*, Vol. II, C. 12, p. 657.

87 B. Pullan, *Rich and Poor in Renaissance Venice* (Oxford, 1971), p. 51 and note 82; see also pp. 72, 34–40.

88 *Laws of Early Iceland. Gragas*, eds, trans. A. Deunis, P. Foote and R. Perkins (Winnipeg, 1980), Vol. I, Christian Laws Section, p. 49.

89 A chronicler from Padua described the Flagellant movement in 1260. While the men scourged themselves in public, some of the women did so in the privacy of their chambers. *Annales S. Iustinae Patavini, M.G.H.S.*, Vol. XIX, p. 179. Concerning women in the fraternities which practised self-scourging, see G. Cecchini, 'Raniero Fasani et les Flagellants', *Mélanges de l'École française de Rome. Moyen-Age – Temps Modernes* 87 (1975), p. 347.

90 See note 33.

91 *Assises de la haute court. Le livre de Jean d'Ibelin*, C.CCXXVIII, pp. 362–4.

92 R. Vaultier, *Le folklore pendant le Guerre de Cent Ans d'après les lettres de rémission du Trésor des Chartes* (Paris, 1965), p. 33.

93 J. T. Rosenthal, *Nobles and the Noble Life*, 1295–1500 (London, 1976), Document 69, p. 184.

94 *Mirk's Festial. A Collection of Homilies*, ed. T. Erbe (London, 1905), p. 6.

95 V. Lamansky, *Secrets d'etat de Venise. Documents, extraits, notices et études* (St Peterburg, 1884), Vol. II, p. 015.

96 M. I. Finley, 'Les personnes agées dans l'antiquité classique', *Communications*

37 (1983), pp. 31–4; the Romans had a saying, 'Sixty-year-olds – off the bridge' (*sexagenarii de ponte*). According to the anthropologist Gavazzi, the saying went back to times when old people were killed off. M. Gavazzi, 'The Tradition of Killing Old People. Prolegomena to a Revised Methodological Treatment of the Subject', in L. Dégh, ed., *Folklore Today. A Festschrift for Richard M. Dorson* (Bloomington, Ind., 1976), p. 178.

97 See note 18 to Introduction.

98 Cited in J. D. Folts, *op. cit.*, p. 226.

99 *Calendar of Letter Books of the City of London. Letter Book H. 1375–1399*, ed. R. R. Sharpe (London, 1907), pp. 6, 328, 329, 331, 349, 351, 361, 390, 396, 397, 398, 405, 420, 421, 422, 423, 427, 431, 434, 435, 437, 438, 442, 443, 445, 449, 451; *Letter Book I. 1400–1422* (London, 1909), pp. 5, 7, 8, 9, 10, 11, 12, 13, 14, 16, 20, 24, 25, 26, 27, 28, 29, 30, 35, 36, 39, 47, 48, 49, 53, 56, 62, 64, 65, 66, 67, 68, 70, 72, 74, 79, 81, 83, 85, 86, 87, 88, 90, 91, 93, 95, 97, 98, 99, 100.

100 *Calendar of the Letter Books of the City of London, Letter Book K*, ed. R. R. Sharpe (London, 1911), pp. 86–7, 271–2, 304–5, 307, 308, 313–14, 326, 382.

101 H. Cam, 'An East Anglian Shiremoot of Stephen's Reign', *E.H.R.* 39 (1924), p. 570.

102 Examples of legel procedures for the verification of age: an example of such an investigation, as well as additions and substractions from the true age, 'estas racionabiliter probetur per legales homines de visneto et per eorum iuramente', *Regiam maiestatem*, L.II C.XXXVIII, in *The Acts of the Parliaments of Scotland*, Vol. I, eds I. Thomson and C. Innes (Edinburgh, 1844), p. 616 (252); Glanvill, *Tractatus de legibus et consuetudinibus Regni Anglie qui Glanvilla vocatur*, ed. trans. G. D. G. Hall (London, 1965), L.XIII, C. 16, pp. 83, 159–60; *English Historical Documents*, ed. H. Rothwell (London 1975), Vol. III, p. 826; J. P. Delumeau, 'La mémoire de gens d'Arezzo et de la Sienne à travers des dépositions de temoins' in *Temps, mémoire, tradition au Moyen Age*, Actes du XIIIème congrès de la Société des Historiens médievistes de l'enseignement superieur public (Université de Provence, 1983), pp. 45–67; D. Herlihy, 'Age, Property and Career in Medieval Society', in M. M. Sheehan, ed. *Aging and the Aged in Medieval Europe* (Toronto, 1990), p. 146; M. T. Clanchy, *From Memory to Written Record. England 1066–1307* (London, 1979), pp. 175–6; D. Herlihy and Ch. Klapisch, *op. cit.*, p. 337.

103 J. T. Rosenthal, *Nobles and the Noble Life*, pp. 50, 128.

104 J. T. Rosenthal, 'Retirement and the Life Cycle in 15th Century England', in M. M. Sheehan, *op. cit.*, pp. 177–8. Rosenthal notes that in view of the fact that the Earl of Oxford was executed two years later, the permission given him to resume his seat in the House of Lords was not very practical.

105 T. Hollingsworth, *Historical Demography* (London, 1976), pp. 378–87.

106 D. Herlihy and Ch. Klapisch, *Les Toscans et leurs familles*, pp. 199–201; D. Herlihy, 'The Generations in Medieval History', *Viator* 5 (1974), pp. 351–2; the same trend took place in certain English estates, see Z. Razi, *Life, Marriage and Death in a Medieval Parish* (Cambridge, 1980), pp. 109, 128; B. M. Campbell, 'Population Pressure, Inheritance and the Land Market in a 14th Century Peasant Community', in R. M. Smith, ed., *Land, Kinship and Life-Cycle* (Cambridge, 1984), pp. 87–134; an example of a demographic increase which began only in the second half of the fifteenth century: P. Desportes, 'La Population de Reims au XVe siècle d'après un dénombrement de 1422', *Le Moyen Age* 72 (1966), pp. 463–509.

107 E. A. Wrigley and R. Schofield, 'Infant and Child Mortality in England in the

Late Tudor and Early Stuart Period', in C. Webster, ed., *Health, Medicine and Mortality in the 16th Century* (Cambridge, 1979), p. 65; T. H. Hollingsworth, 'A Demographic Study of the British Ducal Families', *Population Studies* 11 (1957), table 5; J. Kirshner and A. Molho, 'The Dowry Funds and the Marriage Market in Early Quattrocento Florence', *The Journal of Modern History* 50 (1978), p. 421.

108 J. Hatcher, 'Mortality in the 15th Century: Some New Evidence', *The Economic History Review* 39 (1986), pp. 19–38; T. H. Hollingsworth, 'A Demographic Study of the British Ducal Families', *Population Studies* 11 (1957), pp. 4–26; J. T. Rosenthal, 'Medieval Longevity and the Secular Peerage 1350–1500', *Population Studies* 27 (1973), pp. 287–93; R. Fossier, *La terre et les hommes en Picardie jusqu'à la fin du XIIIe siècle* (Paris-Louvain, 1968), Vol. I, p. 280; Z. Razi, *op. cit.*, pp. 43–5, 130–1; E. B. DeWindt, *Land and People in Holywell-cum-Medingworth: Structures of Tenure and Patterns of Social Organization in an East Anglian Midlands Village* (Toronto, 1972), pp. 180–1; Ch. Dyer, *Standards of Living in the Later Middle Ages. Social Change in England c. 1200–1500* (Cambridge, 1989), p. 182; S. Thrupp, *The Merchant Class of Medieval London* (Ann Arbor, 1976), pp. 194–195.

109 P. Laslett, 'History of Aging and the Aged', in *Family Life and Illicit Love in Earlier Generations* (Cambridge, 1977), Ch. 5; M. Mitterauer and R. Sieder, *The European Family. Patriarchy to Partnership from the Middle Ages to the Present*, trans. K. Osterveen and M. Hörzinger (Oxford, 1982), p. 146; P. M. Thane, 'The Debate on the Declining Birth-Rate in Britain: The Menace of an Aging Population, 1920–1950s', *Continuity and Change* 52 (1990), p. 283; *idem*, 'Old Age in English History', in *Zur Kulturgeschichte des Alterns (Towards a Cultural History of Aging)*, eds, C. Conrad and H. J. von Kondratowitz (Berlin, 1993), pp. 18–19.

110 G. N. Biraben, *Les hommes et la peste en France et les pays européens et méditerranéens* (Paris, 1975), Vol. I, pp. 218–25; J. Heers, *Le clan familial au Moyen-Age. Étude sur les structures politiques et sociales des milieux urbains* (Paris, 1974), p. 70 and note 3; D. Herlihy and Ch. Klapisch, *Les Toscans et leurs familles*, pp. 459–61; Z. Razi, *Life, Death and Marriage in a Medieval Parish. Economy, Society and Demography in Halesowen 1270–1400* (Cambridge, 1980), pp. 129, 151; M. Zerner, 'Une crise de mortalité au XVe siècle à travers les testaments et les rôles d'inscriptions', *Annales E.S.C.* 34 (1979), pp. 571–8; R. Trexler, *Public Life in Renaissance Florence* (New York, 1980), p. 362.

111 D. Herlihy and Ch. Klapisch, *Les Toscans et leurs familles*, pp. 370–1 and note 143; Ch. Dyer, *op. cit.*, p. 253; J. C. Russell, 'How Many of the Population Were Aged?' in M. M. Sheehan, *op. cit.*, p. 123; Z. Razi, *op. cit.*, p. 151; Ch. Klapisch, ' "A uno pane e uno vino": The Rural Tuscan Family at the Beginning of the 15th Century', in *Women, Family and Ritual in Renaissance Italy* (Chicago, 1985), p. 41; G. Minois, *Histoire de la vieillesse. De l'antiquité à la Renaissance* (Paris, 1987), p. 296.

112 S. Shahar, *Childhood in the Middle Ages* (London, 1990), pp. 150–1.

113 *Francisci Petrarchae de remediis utriusque fortune*, L.I, Dialogus 78, p. 225; *Phisicke Against Fortune* f. 102 r-v.

114 A. G. Carmichael, *Plague and the Poor in Renaissance Florence* (Cambridge, 1986), pp. 39–40.

115 Aristotle, *Parva naturalia*, ed. trans. W. S. Hett (The Loeb Classical Library, London, 1986), vol. 8, p. 405.

116 Albertus Magnus, *Quaestiones super de animalibus*, ed. E. Filthaut, L.15, q. 8, in *Opera omnia* (Cologne, 1955), Vol. XII, pp. 263–4.

117 *Les XV joies de mariage*, ed. J. Rychner (Paris, 1963), p. 57.

118 D. Herlihy, 'Life Expectations for Women in Medieval Society', in R. T. Morewedge, ed., *The Role of Woman in the Middle Ages* (London, 1975), pp. 1–22; V. Bullough and C. Campbell, 'Female Longevity and Diet in the Middle Ages', *Speculum* 55 (1980), pp. 317–25; according to Fossier, improvements in midwifery led to a rise in women's life expectancy: R. Fossier, *op. cit.*, pp. 279–80.

119 T. H. Hollingsworth, 'A Demographic Study of the British Ducal Families,' *Population Studies* 11 (1957), pp. 5–26; see also J. T. Rosenthal, 'Medieval Longevity and the Secular Peerage 1350–1500', *Population Studies* 27 (1973), pp. 287–93; G. Duby, 'Dans la France du nord-ouest au XIIe siècle: les jeunes dans la société aristocratique', *Annales E.S.C.* 19 (1964), pp. 839–43.

120 D. Herlihy, *Medieval and Renaissance Pistoia. The Social History of an Italian Town* (New Haven, 1967), pp. 90–1, 283–8; D. Herlihy and Ch. Klapisch, *Les Toscans et leurs familles*, p. 200; Ch. Klapisch-Zuber, 'Demographic Decline and Household Structure. The Example of Prato, Late 14th to Late 15th Century', in *Women, Family and Ritual in Renaissance Italy* (Chicago, 1985), p. 27; Ch. Klapisch-Zuber, 'Le Dernier enfant, fécondité et vieillissement chez les florentines XIVe-XVe siècles' in *Mélanges offerts à Jacques Dupâquier* (Paris, 1993), pp. 281–2; T. H. Hollingsworth, *Historical Demography*, pp. 290–1, 376; J. Russell, 'The Effects of Pestilence and Plague 1315–1385', *Comparative Studies in Society and History* 8 (1966), pp. 464–73; J. Russell, 'How Many of the Population Were Aged?', in M. M. Sheehan, *op. cit.*, p. 126.

121 J. T. Rosenthal, 'Aristocratic Widows in 15th Century England', in B. J. Harris and G. K. McNamara, eds, *Selected Research from the Fifth Berkshire Conference on the History of Women* (Durham, 1984), pp. 36–47; R. E. Archer, 'Rich Old Ladies. The Problem of Late Medieval Dowagers', in T. Pollard, ed., *Property and Politics: Essays in Later Medieval English History* (Gloucester, 1984), pp. 15–35; G. Z. Titow, *English Rural Society 1200–1300* (London, 1972), p. 87; Ch. Klapisch, 'Fiscalité et démographie en Toscane (1427–1430)', *Annales E.S.C.* 24 (1969), pp. 1313–37; in early Modern times, too, the number of widows was greater than that of widowers, though the age gap between husband and wife was smaller, as girls were married off later than in the Middle Ages. The reason was that more widowers than widows found someone to marry for the second time: P. Laslett, 'A History of Aging and the Aged', p. 200.

CHAPTER 2 THE OLD BODY

1 See A. Boureau, *Le Simple corps du roi* (Paris, 1988), pp. 43–70.

2 Hildegard of Bingen, *Scivias sive visionum ac revelationum*, *P.L.*, Vol. 197, Visio 1, col. 427; *Liber divinorum operum simplicis hominis*, *ibid.*, Visio 4, cols. 813, 899.

3 Roger Bacon, *Opus majus*, ed. J. H. Bridge (Frankfurt/Main, 1964), Vol. II, p. 206; Roger Bacon, *Opus majus*, trans. B. B. Burke (Philadelphia, 1928), II, p. 619.

4 Vincent de Beauvais, *Speculum naturale* in *Biblioteca mundi seu speculum quadruplex* (Douai, 1624), L. 31, C. 90, col. 2363; see also Bartholomaeus Anglicus, *Liber de proprietatibus rerum* (Strasbourg, 1505), L. 6, C. 1.

5 According to the resolutions of the Church Councils of the thirteenth century,

a patient who wished to see a physician had to consult a priest first, as the soul was considered to be more precious than the body. At the same time, the priest was often called 'the soul's physician', and texts devoted to repentance employed medical metaphors. See J. D. Mansi, *Sacrorum consiliorum nova et amplissima collectio* (reprint Graz, 1961), Vol. XXII, C. 22, cols. 1110–11; *Les status synodaux français du XXIIIe siècle*, ed. O. Pontal (Paris, 1971), Vol. I, pp. 184, 190, 191 & note 7; *Councils and Synods with other Documents relating to the English Church*, ed. M. Powicke and C. R. Cheney (Oxford, 1964), Vol. II, part 1, pp. 173, 705, part 2, pp. 1060–1; Humbert de Romans, *Sermones* (Venice, 1603), Sermo 66, pp. 65–6; Arnaldus de Villanova, *De regimine sanitatis*, in *Opera omnia* (Basel, 1585), Col. 838; John of Salisbury, *Policraticus*, ed. C. C. Webb (reprint Frankfurt, 1965), Vol. II, L. 2, C. 29, p. 168; the learned surgeon of the fourteenth century, Henry of Mondeville, implied that the surgeon's profession was more important than the priest's. See M. Ch. Pouchelle, *The Body and Surgery in the Middle Ages*, trans. R. Morris (Oxford, 1990), p. 46; the contemporary existence of satirical criticism of the medical profession (and others) also shows that it was already well established. See, for example, a thirteenth-century text, *La Bible Guiot*, in Ch. Langlois, *La vie en France au Moyen Age d'après quelques moralistes du temps* (Paris, 1907), pp. 66–8.

6 L. Demaitre, 'The Care and Extension of Old Age in Medieval Medicine', in M. M. Sheehan, ed., *Aging and the Aged in Medieval Europe* (Toronto, 1990), pp. 3–22.

7 This issue was dealt with at length in Engelbert of Admont (1250–1331), *Liber der causis longevitatis hominem ante diluvium* in *Thesaurus anecdotorum novissimus*, ed. B. Pez (Augsburg, 1971), Vol. I, cols. 439–502; the author ultimately attributes the shortening of human life to natural causes, primarily air pollution. Roger Bacon, too, attributed the shorter life span and early ageing to air pollution, as well as to failure to observe an appropriate health regimen and disregard for moral laws: R. Bacon, *Opus majus*, Vol. II, pp. 205–6; trans. p. 618.

8 Albertus Magnus, *Parva naturalia. De morte et de vita* in *Opera omnia*, ed. A. Borgent (Paris, 1891), Vol. IX, Tractatus II, C. 8, p. 365; Vincent de Beauvais, *op. cit.*, L. 31, C. 91, cols. 2364–5; *The Prose Salernitan Questions*, ed. B. Lawn (Oxford, 1979), q. 186, p. 101.

9 Roger Bacon, *Opus majus*, II, p. 206; trans. II, p. 619; idem, *De retardatione accidentium senectutis cum aliis opusculis de rebus medicinalibus*, eds A. G. Little and E. Withington (British Society of Franciscan Studies 14, Oxford, 1928), pp. 9, 29, 31, 80.

10 Aristotle, *Rhetoric*, Bk. II, C. 14; *Honorii Augustodunensis de philosophia mundi libri quatuor*, P.L., Vol. CLXXII, L. 4, C. 36, col. 99; Vincent de Beauvais, *op. cit.*, L. 31, C. 87, col. 2360; Arnaldus de Villanova, *De regimine sanitatis*, col. 372; Albertus Magnus, *Parva naturalia de aetate sive de iuventute et senectute* in *Opera omnia*, ed. A. Borgent (Paris, 1890), Vol. IX, Tractatus 1, C. 6, p. 314; Gabriele Zerbe, *Gerontocomia: On the Care of the Aged and Maximianus' Elegies on Love and Old Age*, trans. L. R. Lind (Philadelphia, 1988), C. 1, pp. 30–1.

11 In this connection, see J. C. Coleman and W. E. Broen, *Abnormal Psychology and Modern Life* (Glenview, Ill., 1972), pp. 547–53; regarding the views of the psychoanalysts, see notes 16 and 17 to Introduction; similarly, Medieval Jewish exegetical literature also held that forgetfulness and a diminution of the intellectual faculties took place parallel with the physical decline. See M. A. Signer, 'Honour the Hoary Head. The Aged in the Medieval European Jewish Com-

munity', in M. M. Sheehan, *Aging and the Aged in Medieval Europe* (Toronto, 1990), p. 43–4.

12 *Pirkei Moshe Berefuah* (Hebrew), trans. R. Nathan Hameati, commentary by Z. Muntener (Jerusalem, 1970), article 17, p. 217.

13 In this connection, see M. Ch. Pouchelle, *op. cit.*, p. 75.

14 Arnaldus de Villanova, *op. cit.*, col. 671.

15 Roger Bacon, *De retardatione*, pp. 6–9, 34–40, 79, 178; Aldebrandin de Sienne, *Le régime du corps*, eds L. Landouzy and R. Pépin (Paris, 1911), pp. 79–80; Bernard de Gordon, *De conservatione vitae humanae seu de regimine sanitatis* (Leipzig, 1570), pp. 100, 117–24; Vincent de Beauvais, *op. cit.*, L. 31, C. 89, cols. 2361–2; Arnaldus de Villanova, *op. cit.*, cols. 669–73; M. Ch. Pouchelle, *op. cit.*, p. 65.

16 Alvise Cornaro, *Discorsi intorno alla vita sobria*, ed. P. Pancrazzi (Florence, 1946); concerning the popularity of this work until the nineteenth century, its translation and an analysis of its sources and character, see G. J. Gruman, *A History of Ideas about the Prolongation of Life* (Transactions of the American Philosophical Society 56, pt. 9, Philadelphia 1966), pp. 68 f; T. R. Cole, *The Journey of Life. A Cultural History of Aging in America* (Cambridge, 1992), p. 147.

17 Leon Battista Alberti, *I libri della famiglia. The Family in Renaissance Florence*, trans. R. N. Watkins (New York, 1969), Bk III, pp. 170–1.

18 Charles de Orléans, *Ballade farcie de regimen sanitatis* in *anthologie poétique française. Moyen age*, ed. A. Mary (Paris, 1967), Vol. II, p. 217; examples of statements of physicians and scientists concerning the harm to the old man who does not give up sexual intercourse: Albertus Magnus, *Parva naturalia. De morte et de vita*, Tractatus II, C. VIII, p. 365; Arnaldus de Villanova, *op. cit.*, cols. 823–4.

19 I. Origo, *The Merchant of Prato. Francesco di Marco Datini* (Penguin Books, 1963), pp. 305–8.

20 *The Book of Margery Kempe*, eds S. B. Meech and H. E. Allen (E.E.T.S. London, 1940), pp. 179–81.

21 As, for example, Pierre Bersuire wrote in the fourteenth century: 'Senes enim deficiunt in caloribus, et spiritibus vitalibus, quae sunt causa dilatationis cordis et laetitiae, et ideo propter frigiditatem constringentem necesse est quod faciliter irascantur.' Petrus Bertorius, *Dictionarium*, in *Opera omnia* (Cologne, 1730), pars. III, p. 86.

22 Albertus Magnus, *Parva naturalia. De morte et de vita*, Tractatus 2, C. 12, p. 370.

23 'Quid enim est senectus? Optatum malum, mors viventium, incolumis languor, spirans mors.' Vincent de Beauvais, *op. cit.*, L. 31, C. 88. col. 2361; Jean Améry, *Du vieillissement. Révolte et resignation*, trans. A. Yaiche (Paris, 1991), p. 181.

24 Even present-day gerontology has devoted more research to ageing men than to ageing women, though the latter are more numerous. And even in feminist criticism, the ageing of women has been studied only marginally. See R. Barnet and G. Baruch, 'Women in the Middle Years: Conceptions and Misconceptions', in *Psychology of Women: Selected Readings*, ed. G. H. Williams (New York, 1979), pp. 479–87; S. Reinharz, 'Friends or Foes: Gerontological and Feminist Theory', in *Radical Voices*, eds R. D. Klein and D. L. Steinberg (New York, 1989), pp. 222–39.

25 Not only the woman's menstrual blood was believed to be unclean and harmful. According to both popular and scholarly opinion, the foetus in the mother's womb was nourished by her menstrual blood, which was not excreted during

her pregnancy. Thus the blood which nourished the unborn child was also unclean. According to Pope Innocent III, menstrual blood was so vile and impure, that its very touch could cause the grass to wither and fruit to perish on the tree. Dogs that lick it become rabid, and a child conceived by a menstruating woman becomes a leper. In the questions and answers of the medical scholars of Salerno it was stated that a newborn baby cannot sit, stand or walk, unlike newborn animals, because it has been nourished in the womb by its mother's menstrual blood, which is not easily purged, whereas animal foetuses are nourished by purer substances while in the womb. *Lotharii Cardinalis (Innocenti III), De miseria humanae conditionis*, ed. M. Maccarrone (Lugano, 1955), L. I., C. 4, pp. 11–12; *The Prose Salernitan Questions*, q. 228, p. 155; Bartholomaeus Anglicus, *op. cit.*, L. 6, C. 4; *Summa decretorum de Magister Rufinus*, ed. H. Singer (Aalen, 1963), p. 16.

26 D. Jacquart and C. Thomasset, *Sexuality and Medicine in the Middle Ages*, trans. M. Adamson (Oxford, 1988), p. 75; during the fifteenth century, when the *fascinatio* (the process by which certain people could harm others by looking at them) was discussed by the medical academics, they concluded that women acquired this power naturally as they grew older. The entire discussion was based on the premise that the bodies of menstruating women contained an actual or potential venom, and so did the bodies of post-menopausal old women. These last were thought to be especially dangerous. Their effect was not always voluntary, but it could be even more dangerous when coupled with the desire to hurt. The victims of the old women were mainly children. This theory was developed by Diego Alvarez Chanca (*Tractatus de fascinatione*, 1499) and Antonio Cartagena (*Libellus de fascinatione*, 1529): F. Salmon and M. Cambré, 'Fascinating Women: The Evil Eye in Medical Scolasticism', paper presented at Barcelona Conference, Cambridge 1992 (unpublished).

27 See C. Thomasset, 'The Nature of Woman', in C. Klapisch-Zuber, ed. *A History of Women in the West* (London, 1992), pp. 43–69; in certain non-literate societies post-menopausal women are believed to be free of the curse of their sex and of some of the harmful natural powers. They are freed of certain social taboos and enjoy a freedom denied to the younger women. See Simone de Beauvoir, *La vieillesse* (Paris, 1970), Vol. I, p. 81; J. Griffen, 'A Cross-Cultural Investigation of Behavioral Changes at Menopause', in *Psychology of Women: Selected Readings*, ed. J. H. Williams (New York, 1979), pp. 488–95.

28 Bernardino de Siena, *Sermo de calamitatibus et miseriis humanae vitae et maxime senectutis* in *Opera omnia*, eds P. P. Colegii S. Bonaventurae (Florence, 1959), Vol. 7, Sermo 16, pp. 254–6, 260; concerning his movements while preaching: D. Herlihy and Ch. Klapisch, *Les Toscans et leurs familles. Étude du catasto florentin de 1427* (Paris, 1978), p. 607.

29 G. R. Owst, *Preaching in Medieval England* (Cambridge, 1926), p. 342.

30 Innocent III, *Lotharii Cardinalis (Innocent III), De miseria humanae conditionis*, L.I., C. 10, p. 16.

31 G. F. Jones, 'The Signs of Old Age in Oswald von Wolkenstein's "*Ich sich und hör*" ', *Modern Language Notes* 84 (1974), pp. 767–87.

32 J. Améry, *Du vieillissment*, pp. 85, 190; Simone de Beauvoir, *The Woman Destroyed*, trans. P. O. Brian (London, 1984), p. 17; Penelope Lively, *Moon Tiger* (Penguin Books, 1988), p. 192.

33 Francesco Petrarca, *De remediis utriusque fortune* (Rotterdam, 1649), L. I., pp. 18–19, L. II, pp. 94–5, 353, 564–6, 597–9; *Phisicke against Fortune by Francis Petrarch. Englished by Thomas Twyne* (London, 1579), f.3v, 284v-285v, 162r, 267r-268v.

34 *Ibid.*, L. I, p. 427; f.106r.

35 Popular medical writings stated that the size of an old woman's womb differed from that of a young woman, and the wombs of lustful women differed in size from those who were less lustful. Some authors described the womb as a 'wild animal' which has its own characteristics and desires and moves about in the woman's body. See: R. Barkai, *Les infortunes de Dinah ou la gynécologie juive du Moyen Âge* (Paris, 1991), p. 41 and note 20.

36 See, for example, Giraldus Cambrensis (Gerald of Wales), *Gemma ecclesiastica*, ed. J. Brewer (Rolls Series XXIb, London, 1862), pp. 182, 184; Philippe de Navarre, *Les quatre ages de l'homme*, ed. M. de Fréville (Paris, 1888), p. 90; *Les enseignements d'Anne de France à sa fille Suzanne* in A. A. Hentsch, *La littérature didactique au Moyen Age s'adressant spécialement au femmes* (reprint, Geneva, 1975), p. 204; M. Laigle, *Le livre de trois vertus de Christine de Pizan et son milieu historique et littéraire* (Paris, 1912), pp. 351–2.

37 In this connection, see M. T. Lorcin, 'Le corps a ses raisons dans les fabliaux', *Moyen Age* 90 (1984), pp. 443–53.

38 D. J. Levinson, *The Seasons of Man's Life* (New York, 1979), p. 211.

39 *Aucassin et Nicolette. Chantefable du XIIIe siècle*, ed. M. Roques (Paris, 1954), p. 6; *Aucassin and Nicolette*, trans. A. Lang (London, 1905), p. 13.

40 Peter Dronke, 'Profane Elements in Literature' in *Renaissance and Renewal in the Twelfth Century*, eds R. L. Benson and G. Constable (Oxford 1985), pp. 588–9.

41 Eustache Deschamps, *Adieux á la jeunnesse*, in *Oeuvres complètes*, ed. Le Marquis de Queux de Saint-Hilaire (Paris, 1878–1903), Vol. 1, p. 250; *The Sermons of Thomas Brinton*, ed. M. A. Devlin (London, 1954), p. 286.

42 Cited by J. A. Burrow, *The Ages of Man* (Oxford, 1986), pp. 30–1; other translation of the work: R. Steele, *Three Prose Versions of the Secretum Secretorum* (E.E.T.S., London, 1898).

43 William of Deguileville, *Le pèlerinage de la vie humaine*, ed. J. J. Stürzinger (London, 1893), pp. 229, 251–2, 255, 374, 407, 414.

44 C. Walker Bynum, *Holy Feast and Holy Fast. The Religious Significance of Food to Medieval Women* (University of California Press, 1987).

45 Guillaume de Lorris and Jean de Meun, *Le roman de la rose*, ed. F. Lecoy (Paris, 1968), Vol. I, V. 338–60, 389–97, pp. 11–13; *The Romance of the Rose by Guillaume de Lorris and Jean de Meun*, trans. Ch. W. Robbins (New York, 1962), pp. 9–10; another description of the loss of the woman's beauty in her old age is in Conon de Béthune, *La vieille amoureuse* in *Anthologie poétique française: Moyen Age*, ed. A. Mary (Paris, 1967), Vol. I, pp. 216–18.

46 G. Minois, *Histoire de la vieillesse de l'antiquité à la Renaissance* (Paris, 1987), p. 243; J. Delumeau, *La peur en Occident XIVe-XVIIIe siècles* (Paris, 1978), p. 11.

47 Francesco Petrarca, *Trionfo della morte* in *Canzioniere, trionfi, rime varie e una scelta di versi latini*, eds C. Muscetta and D. Ponchiroli (Rome, 1958), pp. 54–5.

48 Ch. Frugoni, 'L'iconographie de la femme au cours des Xe-XIIe siècles', *Cahiers de Civilization médiévale*, Xe-XIIe siècles 20 (1977), pp. 180–2, 184.

49 Jean Régnier, *Ballade de la vieillesse* in *Anthologie poétique française*, II, p. 205.

50 A. Planche, 'Le corps en vieillesse. Regard sur la poésie du moyen-age tardif', *Razo* 4 (1984), p. 54.

51 Eustache Deschamps, *Regrets d'un vieillard* in *Oeuvres Complètes*, Vol. 6, pp. 225–30; Vol. 7, MDV, V. 25–8; for an English version of Maximianus on his old age, see A. K. Nitecki, 'Figures of Old Age in Fourteenth Century English

Literature', in M. M. Sheehan, ed. *Aging and the Aged in Medieval Europe* (Toronto, 1990), pp. 110–11.

52 G. Minois, *Histoire de la vieillesse*, pp. 345–7; S. Sontag, 'The Double Standard of Aging', in *Psychology of Women: Selected Readings*, ed. J. H. Williams (New York, 1979), pp. 462–78.

53 *The Poems of Robert Henryson*, ed. D. Fox (Oxford, 1981), pp. 165–7; the title 'In Praise of Age' was only given to the poem in the eighteenth century. See pp. 449–52.

54 Regarding the influence of and borrowings from Roman authors, see G. R. Coffman, 'Old Age from Horace to Chaucer: Some Literary Affinities and Adventures of an Idea', *Speculum* IX (1934), pp. 249–77; Gabriele Zerbi, *Gerontocomia: On the Care of the Aged and Maximianus' Elegies on Old Age and Love*, trans. L. R. Lind (Philadelphia, 1988), pp. 309–18, 321.

55 *The Prose Salernitan Questions*, pp. 120, 251–2; Francesco Petrarca, *De remediis*, L. II, Dialogus 94, pp. 597–9; *Phisicke Against Fortune*, fol. 284r-v; see also L. Demaitre, *op. cit.*, p. 11; there were various remedies for toothache, and some of the pilgrims who visited the shrines of the saints were seeking cures of their own and their children's aching teeth. By contrast, Alvis Cornaro boasted that at age 80 he still had all his teeth. In the twelfth century in a legal compilation known as 'The Laws of Henry I', the section dealing with compensations for bodily injuries includes all of Isidore of Seville's discussion of dentistry in his *Etymologia*, and different compensations were stipulated for the loss of molars, incisors and canine teeth. *Leges Henrici primi*, ed. trans. L. J. Downer (Oxford, 1972), pp. 294–5.

56 C. Lévi-Strauss, *Tristes tropiques*, trans. J. and D. Weightman (London, 1989), p. 376.

57 In this connection, see P. Thompson, C. Itzin and M. Abendstern, *I Don't Feel Old* (Oxford, 1991), ch. 6.

58 A. Vauchez, *La sainteté en Occident au derniers siècles du Moyen Age d'aprés les procès de canonization et les documents hagiographiques* (École française de Rome, 1988), pp. 508–10.

59 See J. Le Goff, 'Corps et idéologie dans l'Occident médiéval', in *l'Imaginaire médiéval*, (Paris, 1985), pp. 123–48.

60 A. Vauchez, *op. cit.*, p. 512.

61 Aelred of Rievaulx, *Speculum caritatis* in *Aelredi Rievalensis opera omnia*, eds A. Hoste and C. H. Talbot, (Corpus Christanorum Continuatio Medievalis, Turnhout, 1971), L. 3, C. 19, p. 126.

62 Vincent de Beauvais, *Speculum naturale*, L. 31, C. 86, cols 2359–60.

63 R. E. Marsan, *Itinéraire espagnol du conte médiéval VIIIe-XVe siècles* (Paris, 1974), pp. 227–33.

64 In this connection, see N. Warner, *Joan of Arc. The Image of Female Heroism* (Penguin Books, 1983), Ch. 13.

65 See, for example, Tintoretto's 'The Creation of the Animals', in the Venice Academy and, of course, Michelangelo's 'The Creation of Adam' in the Sistine Chapel. God the Father is also depicted in paintings by Masaccio, Titian, Filippino Lippi, Raphael, Lucas Cranach, Cosimo Roselli and others; there are also paintings and sculptures of 'the Throne of Grace' – God the Father seated, holding his Son's body. See L. Steinberg, *The Sexuality of Christ in Renaissance Art and in Modern Oblivion* (London, 1984), figs. 243, 254.

66 Aelred of Rievaulx, *In annuntiatione Beate Marie de tribus tunicis Ioseph*, in *Sermones ineditii B. Aelredi Abbatis Rievallensis*, ed. C. H. Talbot (Rome, 1952), p. 84.

67 *Le héraut de l'amour divin. Révélations de Saint Gertrude*, trans. Pères benedictins de Solesmes (Paris-Poitiers, 1898), L. 3, C. 15, p. 175; *Le livre de l'experience des vrais fidèles par Sainte Angèle de Foligno*, eds J. Ferré and L. Baudry (Paris, 1927), p. 62.

68 L. Steinberg, *The Sexuality of Christ*; C. Walker Bynum, 'The Body of Christ in the Later Middle Ages: A Reply to Leo Steinberg', in *Fragmentation and Redemption. Essays on Gender and the Human Body in Medieval Religion* (New York, 1991c), pp. 79–117.

69 Examples of the Pièta as a young woman: A. Kutal, *Gothic Art in Bohemia and Moravia* (London, 1971), figs. 65, 111, 128; G. Ring, *A Century of French Painting 1400–1500* (London, 1949), plates 85, 113, 114, figs. 37–9, pp. 224, 228; Michelangelo's Pièta was so young and beautiful that already in his time someone asked why he made her so young looking: R. S. Liebert, *Michelangelo* (New Haven, 1983), pp. 67–70, fig. 6(4).

70 *Le roman de Sidrach*, in Ch. Langlois, *La connaissance de la nature du monde au Moyen Age d'après quelques écrits français à l'usage de laïcs* (Paris, 1911), pp. 257–8.

71 St Augustine, *De Civitate Dei* (Corpus Christianorum Series Latina, 48, Turnhout, 1955), L. 22, C. 15, p. 834.

72 See, for example: Albertus Magnus, *De resurrectione*, in *Opera omnia*, ed. W. Kübel (Aschendorf, Münster, Westf. 1958), Vol. XXVI, tractatus 2, Q. 6, p. 264.

73 Petrus Lomardus, *Sententiae in IV libros distinctae*, eds Collegium S. Bonaventurae a Claras Aquas (Rome, 1981), L. 4, D. 44, pp. 516–19.

74 *Lollard Sermons*, ed. G. Cigman (E.E.T.S., London, 1989), pp. 110, 238; concerning the belief of the Waldenses in the resurrection in 33–year-old bodies, see *Registre de l'inquisition de Jacques Fournier (1318–25)*, ed. J. Duvernoy (Toulouse, 1965), Vol. I, p. 88.

75 Innocent III, *Lotharii cardinalis (Innocenti III) De miseria humanae conditionis*, L. I, C. 20, pp. 28–9.

76 Bernard of Cluny, *De contemptu mundi*, ed. H. C. Hoskier (London, 1929).

77 Alain of Lille, *Summa de arte paedicatoria*, P.L., Vol. 210, cols 116–17; Alain of Lille expressed different views in different contexts. In the work known as *Anticlaudianus*, for instance, he expressed what Curtis called 'Optimistic naturalism'. See E. R. Curtius, *European Literature and the Latin Middle Ages*, trans. W. R. Trask (New York, 1963), pp. 117–22, 198.

78 C. Walker Bynum, 'The Body of Christ in the Later Middle Ages: A Reply to Leo Steinberg', pp. 79–117.

79 Bernard of Clairvaux, *Liber de diligendo deo*, P.L., CLXXXII, C. 11, col. 993.

80 John Bromyard, *Summa praedicantium* (Antwerp, 1614), pars. 2, C. 5, p. 354; Vincent de Beauvais, *Speculum naturale*, L. 31, C. 87, col. 2360.

81 C. Walker Bynum, 'The Female Body and Religious Practice in the Later Middle Ages', in *Fragments of the History of the Human Body*, ed. M. Feher (New York, 1989), I, p. 166.

82 'ut quantum senectus a iuvenili vigore distrahit, hoc maior mentis devotio suppleat, et quod ille qui in uno gravatur, in alio sublevetur', John Bromyard, *op. cit.*, pars. 2, C. 5, p. 355.

83 Bernardino de Siena, *op. cit.*, pp. 253, 256–62.

84 Dante, *Convivio* in *Le opere di Dante*, ed. M. Barbi (Florence, 1921), C. 4, p. 28; the image of the ship lowering its sails as it approaches the port, as a metaphor for the final stage of life, also appears in the *Divine Comedy*, The Inferno, 27, lines 79–81.

NOTES

85 Bernard of Clairvaux, *Liber de modo bene vivendi*, *P.L.*, CLXXXIV, C. 43, cols 1264–5.
86 *Idem, Ad abbatum guarinum alpensem epistola*, Epist. 254, *P.L.*, CLXXXII, col. 461.
87 Vincent de Beauvais, *Speculum naturale*, L. 31, C. 89–90, cols 2359–61.
88 Cited by T. R. Cole, *The Journey of Life*, p. 131.
89 Roger Bacon, *Opus majus*, Vol. II, pp. 205–6; trans. Vol. II, p. 618.
90 Bernardino de Sienne, *op. cit.*, pp. 245–6, 258; see also John Bromyard, *op. cit.*, pars. 2, C. 5, pp. 355–6.
91 *Vita prima auctore Gaufrido*, *P.L.*, CLXXXV, L. 5, C. 1, cols 351–5; see also Guillaume de St Thierry, *Vita prima, ibid.*, col. 225.
92 *The Book of St Gilbert*, eds, trans. R. Foreville and G. Keir (Oxford, 1987), C. 27, pp. 86–9; see also *The Life of St Anselm, Archbishop of Canterbury by Eadmer*, ed. trans. R. W. Southern (London, 1962), p. 141.
93 Gabriele Zerbi, *Gerontocomia On the Care of the Aged and Maximianus' Elegies on Old Age and Love*, trans. L. R. Lind (Philadelphia, 1988), Elegy 1, line 257, p. 325.
94 *Guidonis quinti majoris Carthusiae epistola seu tratatus ad fratres de Monte Dei*, *P.L.*, Vol. 184, C. XI, col. 328.
95 Thomas Aquinas, *Summa theologiae*, 2a 2ae, Q. 164, art. 2 (Blackfriars, London, 1974), Vol. 44, pp. 178–81.
96 'Quae enim voluptas ubi sibi totum vindicat amaritudo?' Bernard of Clairvaux, *Epistola* 310, *P.L.*, CLXXXII, col. 514.
97 Cited by T. R. Cole, *op. cit.*, pp. 147–8.
98 R. I. Evans, *Dialogues with Erik Erikson* (New York, 1967), p. 54; E. Erikson, 'Eight Stages of Man', in *Childhood and Society* (New York, 1963), pp. 247–73.
99 Simone de Beauvoir, *La vieillesse*, I-II (Paris, 1970).
100 J. Améry, *op. cit.*, p. 11.

CHAPTER 3 TRANSCENDING AGE, TRANSCENDING THE BODY

1 Bernardino de Siena: *De calamitatibus et miseriis humanae vitae et maxime senectutis* in *Opera omnia*, eds P. P. Collegii S. Bonaventurae (Florence, 1959), Vol. VII, Sermo 16, p. 262.
2 J. M. Clay, *The Dance of Death in the Middle Ages and the Renaissance* (Glasgow, 1950); A, Tenenti, *La vie et la mort à travers l'art du XVe siècle* (Paris, 1952); H. Rosenfeld, *Der Mittelalterliche Totentanz* (Münster/Köln, 1954).
3 Several cases of miracle cures involving old people were attributed to Bernard of Clairvaux, and two of the main cures attributed to Gilbert of Sempringham appear to have involved an old man and woman: *Vita prima*, *P.L.*, Vol. 185, cols 339, 343, 345, 350, 389, 393; *The Book of St Gilbert*, eds R. Foreville and G. Keir (Oxford, 1987), pp. 98–9, 276.
4 Giraldus Cambrensis, *Speculum duorum*, eds Y. Lefèvre and R. B. C. Huygens, trans. B. Dawson (Cardiff, 1974), Distinctio II, C. 8, pp. 206–7.
5 See, for example, Gabriele Zerbi, *Gerontocomia: On the Care of the Aged and Maximianus' Elegies on Old Age and Love*, trans. L. R. Lind (Philadelphia, 1988), C. LVII, p. 305.
6 Thomas More, *Utopia*, ed. trans. R. M. Adams (New York, 1975), Vol. II, p. 65.
7 Roger Bacon, *De retardatione accidentium senectutis cum aliis opusculis de rebus medicinalibus*, eds A. G. Little and E. Withington (British Society of Franciscan Studies 14, Oxford, 1928), pp. 10, 80; *idem, Opus majus*, ed. J. H. Bridge

(Frankfurt/Main, 1964), Vol. II, pp. 206–13; Roger Bacon, *Opus majus*, trans. B. B. Burke (Philadelphia, 1928), Vol. II, pp. 619–26; the work known as *Liber de conservatione et retardatione senectutis* was attributed to Arnold of Villanova. As for the question how much Arnold (or another writer, if the attribution was incorrect) copied from Roger Bacon, see Roger Bacon, *de Retardatione*, pp. XLII-XLIII; Arnold also incorporated several chapters on this subject in his *De regimine sanitatis*, in *Opera omnia* (Basel, 1585), cols 818–38.

8 Arnaldus de Villanova, *De regimine Sanitatis*, cols 819, 825; on a lawsuit brought in 1326 against a surgeon who promised to cure his female patients of their barrenness, and his male patients of sexual impotence: J. Shatzmiller and R. Lavoie, 'Médicine et gynécologie au moyen age: un exemple provençal', *Razo* 4 (1984), pp. 133–43.

9 Roger Bacon, *Opus majus*, Vol. II, pp. 205–6; trans. Vol. II, p. 618.

10 Roger Bacon, *De Retardatione*, p. 3.

11 Arnold of Villanova, in the chapter 'Wine in which Gold was Quenched' in his book *On Wine*, explained how to prepare a potion of gold. See *The Earliest Printed Book on Wine, by Arnold of Villanova*, trans. H. E. Sigerist, with facsimile of the original German edition of 1478 (New York, 1945), pp. 36–7.

12 N. Benoit-Lapierre, 'Guérir de vieillesse', *Communication*, 36, (1983), p. 15.

13 *Les chansons de Guillaume IX, Duc d'Acquitaine 1071–1127*, ed. A. Jeanroy (Paris, 1913), lines 34–6, p. 23.

14 R. Browne, *The Cure of Old Age and Preservation of Youth, translated with Annotations and an Account of his Life and Writing* (London, 1683), p. 4; on the search for methods of prolonging youth and life in other cultures, and in the West from the Renaissance on, see G. Gruman, *A History of Ideas about the Prolongation of Life* (Transactions of the American Philosophical Society, 56, pt. 19, Philadelphia, 1966). The Chinese emperor K'ang-hsi (1661–1722) attacked the Taoists who claimed to be able not only to postpone old age, but even to achieve immortality. He denounced them as shameless mountebanks who aged and died like everyone else. See J. Spence, *Emperor of China. Self-Portrait of K'ang-hsi* (New York, 1975), p. 101; there was a gradual transition from the view based on the longevity of antediluvian men that could be renewed, to the idea that the postponement of old age would be achieved in the future by science and technology. One of the most recent methods to be tried has been the injection of growth hormones. One current research project seeks to slow down the biochemical processes which cause the ageing of the body's cells by reducing the body's temperature.

15 Thomas Aquinas, *Summa theologiae*, 2a 2ae, Q. 164, art. 1 (Blackfriars, London, 1971), Vol. 44, pp. 172–3.

16 See J. A. Burrow, *The Ages of Man* (Oxford, 1986), pp. 95–139.

17 St Augustine, *Retractationum libri II* (Corpus Christianorum Series Latina, Turnhout, 1984), Vol. I, C. 26, p. 80.

18 See S. Shahar, *Childhood in the Middle Ages* (London, 1990), pp. 15–16; J. A. Burrow, *op. cit.*, pp. 137–42; on the *topos* of the old child in the classical literature and the myths of different religions, see E. R. Curtis, *European Literature and the Latin Middle Ages*, trans. W. R. Trask (New York, 1952), pp. 98, 105; by contrast, there was a popular saying, 'Young saint, old devil'. Burrow interprets this rejection of untimely maturation as a protest against the authors of the lives of the saints and moralistic literature, in the name of the laws of nature. See J. A. Burrow, *op. cit.*, p. 49.

19 Thomas Aquinas, *Summa theologiae*, 3a, q. 72, art. 8 (Blackfriars, London, 1974), Vol. 57, pp. 214–15; and Pierre Bersuire wrote in the fourteenth century:

'Sic vero moraliter possible est quod homo iuvenis corpore, canus tamen, senex prudens et maturus sit in mente', Petrus Berthorius, *Dictionarium*, in *Opera omnia* (Cologne, 1730), pars. 3, p. 86.

20 Bernard of Clairvaux, *De moribus et officio episcoporum seu epistola XLII*, P.L., Vol. 182, C. 7, cols 826–7.

21 John of Salisbury, *Policraticus*, ed. C. C. Webb (London, 1909), Vol. I, L. 5, C. 9, p. 321; *The Statesman Book of John of Salisbury*, trans. J. Dickinson (New York, 1963), pp. 111–12.

22 *Le règle de Saint Benoit*, eds, trans. J. Neufville and A. de Vogüé (Paris, 1972), Vol. II, C. 63, pp. 642–44; rabbinical literature, too, discussed this question, whether the verse in Leviticus 19:32, 'Thou shalt rise up before the hoary head, and honour the face of the old man' referred to a scholar of whatever age, or to any old man whether a scholar or not. Rabbi Shlomo Yitzhak of Troyes (second half of the eleventh century) argued that the text meant any old man, while Rabbi Yitzhak of Dampierre, in his twelfth-century talmudic exegesis, interpreted 'old man' to mean a 'scholar', regardless of his chronological age. See M. A. Signer, 'Honour the Hoary Head. The Aged in Medieval European Jewish Community', in M. M. Sheehan, ed., *Aging and the Aged in Medieval Europe* (Toronto, 1990), pp. 41–5.

23 *Acta Sanctorum*, eds J. Bollandus and G. H. Henschenius (Paris-Rome, 1836–1940), March I, pp. 553, 574; March III, p. 193; *Liber exemplorum ad usum praedicantium*, ed., A. Little (British Society of Franciscan Studies, Aberdeen, 1908), p. 107; *Magna vita sancti Hugonis*, eds, trans. D. Douie and Dom. H. Farmer (London, 1986), Vol. I, p. 219; *The Golden Legend of Jacobus de Voragine*, trans. G. Ryan and H. Rippenger (New York, 1948), p. 687.

24 See note 40 to Chapter 1.

25 'possunt enim contra illam pronitatem facere', Aegidius Romanus, *De regimine principum* (Rome, 1607), L. 1, pars. 4, C. 1–4, pp. 188–203; Aristotle on the qualities of young men, old men and men of middle age, when they reach the peak of maturity: *Rhetoric*, Bk. II, C. 12–14; on the subject of the bad qualities of old men, see also his *Ethics*, Bk. IV, C. 1, 1121b, Bk. VIII, C. 3, 1156a, C. 5, 1157b.

26 *Carmen ad Robertum regem*, ed. trans. C. Carozzi (Paris, 1970).

27 E. A. Kantorowicz, *The King's Two Bodies. A Study in Medieval Political Theology* (Princeton University Press, 1957); A. Boureau, *Le simple corps du roi* (Paris, 1988).

28 'Cor as d'enfant e si as raisun de ber.' 'Petit est Gui e li cheval est grant.' *La chanson de Guillaume*, ed. D. McMillan (Paris, 1949), Vol. I, lines 1436–43, p. 61; line 1479, p. 63.

29 *Acta sanctorum*, April III, p. 870; there is a similar description of the eight-year-old girl Maria, who wishes to become a recluse, in Hrotsvitha's play *Abraham* in *Hrotsvithae opera*, ed. K. Strecker (Leipzig, 1906), pp. 162–78.

30 *La chanson de Roland*, ed. Bédier (Paris, 1947).

31 Ernesto Sabato, *On Heroes and Tombs*, trans. H. R. Lane (London, 1981), pp. 25–6.

32 In this connection, see D. Levinson, *The Seasons of Man's Life* (New York, 1979).

33 G. Zarnecki, *The Art of the Medieval World* (New York, 1975), p. 403, fig. 421; W. Sauerlaender, *Le siècle des cathédrales 1140–1260* (Paris, 1989), pp. 100–2, figs. 92–3; in later periods, too, she was portrayed as an old woman, as, for example, in a fourteenth-century painting by an unknown artist at the 'little

palace' in Avignon, in which she is shown seated in her bed after having given birth.

34 Augustinus, *De diversis quaestionibus octaginta tribus* (Corpus Christianorum Series Latina LXIV (Turnhout, 1975), C. 58, De Iohanne Baptista, pp. 105–6.

35 Aelred of Rievaulx, *Speculum caritatis* in *Opera omnia*, eds A. Hoste and C. H. Talbot (Corpus Christianorum Continuatio Medievalis, Turnhout, 1971), L. 1, pp. 4043.

36 Meister Eckhart, *In novitate ambulamus* in *Die Deutschen und lateinischen Werke*, eds E. Benz, B. Decker and J. Koch (Stuttgart, 1956), IV, Sermo 15/2, pp. 145–54, especially: pp. 149–50.

37 John Bromyard, *Summa praedicantium* (Antwerp, 1614), part 1, C. 3, p. 5, part 2, C. 5, p. 356.

38 'Adhuc multiplicabuntur' (id). 'Ecclesia magis incipiet esse uberrima, cum ad finem saeculi erit perducta tunc enim passionibus electorum cito implebitur numerus beatorum. Et accipitur hic aliter senectus, quam supra', Walafridus Strabo, *Glossa ordinaria*, *P.L.*, Vol. 113, col. 1001. (This compilation of interpretations was edited in the twelfth and thirteenth centuries, and was mistakenly attributed to Walafrid Strabo.) Pierre Bersuire quoted this passage to justify the fate of the virtuous man in old age: Petrus Berthuis, *Dictionarium*, pars. 3, p. 86.

39 J. P. Eckermann, *Conversations with Goethe*, trans. J. Oxenford (London, 1930), pp. 249–50.

CHAPTER 4 WHO AND WHAT IS AN OLD MAN, AND HOW HE SHOULD CONDUCT HIMSELF

1 Aegidius Romanus, *De regimine principum* (Rome, 1607), L. I, pars. 4, C. 1–4, pp. 188–203.

2 Geoffrey Chaucer, *The Canterbury Tales*, ed. W. W. Skeat (Oxford, 1947), p. 100; *Les XV joies de mariage*, ed. J. Rychner (Paris, 1963), pp. 101–2; Thomas Cantimpraetensis, *Liber de natura rerum*, ed. H. Boese (Berlin-New York, 1973), L.1, LXXII, p. 81, LXXXIII, p. 82; *The Early English Version of the Gesta Romanorum*, ed. S. J. Herrtage (London, 1879), p. 47; Berthold von Regensburg, *Vollständige ausgabe seiner Predigten*, ed. F. Pfeiffer (Wien, 1880), Vol. II, p. 142; Francesco Petrarca, *Secretum* in *Prose*, ed. G. Martelloti (Milan, 1955), p. 88; Aegidius Romanus, *op. cit.*, p. 195.

3 See Simone de Beauvoir, *La vieillesse* (Paris, 1970), Vol. II, pp. 291–3.

4 Philippe de Navarre, *Les quatre ages de l'Homme*, ed. M. de Fréville (Paris, 1888), 173, p. 95; 194, p. 105.

5 *Les douze mois figurez*, ed. J. Morawski, *Archivum romanicum* 10 (1926), p. 362.

6 Bartholomaeus Anglicus, *Liber de proprietatibus rerum* (Strasbourg, 1505), L. VI, c. 1, de etate; *On the Properties of Things. John Trevisa's Translation of Bartholomaeus Anglicus' De Proprietatibus Rerum*, ed. M. C. Seymour (Oxford, 1975), p. 290.

7 See, for example, *Honorii Augustodunensis de philosophia mundi libri quatuor*, P.L. Vol. 172, L. IV, C. 36, Col. 99; Philippe de Navarre, *op. cit.*, 166, p. 92; on the wisdom of the aged: Bernard de Gordon, *De conservatione vitae humanae seu de regimine sanitatis* (Leipzig, 1570), pp. 5–6; Arnaldus de Villanova, *De regimine Sanitatis* in *Opera omnia* (Basel, 1585), col. 672; Leon Battista Alberti, *I libri della famiglia. The Family in Renaissance Florence*, trans. R. N. Watkins (New York, 1969), pp. 39–40.

8 See statements of Vincent of Beauvais and Aegidius Romanus: note 87 to Chapter 2, note 25 to Chapter 3.

9 Cicero, *De senectute*, in *Cicero in 28 Volumes* (The Loeb Classical Library, Harvard, 1971), Vol. 20, III-XIV, pp. 16–58; this was also Plato's opinion. See Plato, *Republic*, trans. R. Waterfield (Oxford, 1994), 329, pp. 5–6.

10 Bernardino de Siena, *Sermo de calamitatibus et miseriis humanae vitae et maxime senectutis* in *Opera omnia*, eds P. P. Collegii S. Bonaventure (Florence, 1959), Vol. 7, Sermo 16, pp. 245–6; Vincent de Beauvais, *Speculum naturale* in *Bibliotheca mundi seu speculum quadruplex: Naturale, doctrinale, morale, historiale* (Douai, 1642), L. 31, C. 89, col. 2362; Philippe de Navarre, *op. cit.*, 97–9, pp. 53–5; 121–5, pp. 68–70; 127–9, p. 72; 166, p. 92; John Bromyard, *Summa praedicantium* (Antwerp, 1614), pars. II, C. 5, pp. 354–6.

11 M. Carruthers, *The Book of Memory. A Study of Memory in Medieval Culture* (Cambridge, 1993).

12 Among others: Giraldus Cambrensis, *Speculum duorum*, eds Y. Lefèvre and R. B. C. Huygens, trans. B. Dawson (Cardiff, 1974), D. II, C. 8, pp. 199–205; Humbert de Romans, *Sermones* (Venice, 1603), Sermo XCVIII, pp. 118–19.

13 In addition to the sources quoted in previous chapters, the same expectation occurs in other literary genres. See William Langland, *Piers Plowman*, B text, ed. A. V. C. Schmidt (London, 1978), Passus XII, 3–11; *The Early English Version of the Gesta Romanorum*, ed. S. J. Herrtage (London, 1879), LXXXVI, pp. 406–7.

14 I. Origo, *The Merchant of Prato. Francesco di Marco Datini* (Penguin Books, 1963), pp. 341–2.

15 Philippe de Commynes, *Mémoires*, ed. J. Calmette (Paris, 1965), Vol. II, L. VI, C. 6–11, pp. 280–322.

16 P. Loë, 'De Vita et Scriptis B. Alberti Magni', *Annalecta Bollandiana* 10 (1901), pp. 274–310.

17 Aristotle, *Rhetoric*, Bk. II, C. 13, 1389b.

18 Euripides, *Alcestis* in *Euripides IV*, trans. A. S. Way (The Loeb Classical Library, London, 1964) Vol. 4, 1. 672–99, p. 461.

19 See: Ph. Ariès, *L'homme devant la mort* (Paris, 1977), p. 17.

20 *The Early English Version of the Gesta Romanorum* LXXX, pp. 400–4, XCV, pp. 425–6.

21 Philippe de Navarre, *op. cit.*, 126, p. 71.

22 Cicero, *op. cit.*, V/13, p. 22, VII/22, pp. 30–2; Plato, too, had old Cephalus describing the pleasure of intellectual conversations with friends in old age, when there are no longer any physical pleasures: Plato, *Republic*, 328, p. 4.

23 S. K. Cohn Jr, *Death and Property in Siena 1205–1800. Strategies for the Afterlife* (Baltimore, 1988), p. 91; and see notes 15, 83 to Chapter 2.

24 Jean Gerson, *À un vieillard* in *Oeuvres complètes*, ed. Mgr Glorieux (Paris, 1960), Vol. II, XIX, p. 76.

25 In this connection, see G. V. Hamilton, 'Changes in Personality and Psychosexual Phenomena with Age', in E. V. Cowdry, ed., *Problems of Aging* (Baltimore, 1942), pp. 810–31.

26 Philippe de Navarre, *op. cit.*, 194, p. 105.

27 Vincent de Beauvais, *Speculum naturale*, L. 31, C. 89, col. 2362.

28 Leon Battista Alberti, *op. cit.*, Bk III-IV, pp. 35–42, 156–7, 167, 170.

29 Aristotle, *Politics*, Bk. VII, Ch. 9; in contrast to Aristotle, Plato thought the old men among the philosophers were the most suitable to act as judges and rulers: Plato, *Republic*, 409, p. 110; 411–12, p. 115.

30 Maimonides, *The Repetition of the Law, Book of Judges, Rules of Sanhedrin*, B (3).

31 Philippe de Navarre, *op. cit.*, 174, pp. 95–6.

32 M. Rabinowitz, *A Man's Age* (Hebrew, Tel Aviv, 1985), p. 59.

33 In this connection, see R. Payne, 'Some Theoretical Approaches to the Sociology of Aging', *Social Forces* 38 (1960), pp. 359–62.

34 Renata Jablonska, *Autumn, In the King Albert Square and Other Stories* (Polish).

35 Arnaldus de Villanova, *op. cit.*, cols 823–4.

36 Albertus Magnus, *Parva naturalia. De morte et de vita* in *Opera omnia*, ed. A. Borgent (Paris, 1890), Vol. IX, Tractatus II, C. 8, p. 365.

37 Berthold von Regensburg, *op. cit.*, pp. 142–3.

38 'de volanté sanz besoing; la volantez i est, li pooirs n'i est mie,' Philippe de Navarre, *op. cit.*, 173, p. 95.

39 M. Laigle, *Le livre de trois vertus de Christine de Pisan et son milieu historique et littéraire* (Paris, 1912), pp. 352–3.

40 Philippe de Navarre, *op. cit.*, 184–5, pp. 100–1.

41 See J. T. Wortley, 'Aging and the Desert Fathers. The Process Reversed', in M. M. Sheehan, ed. *Aging and the Aged in Medieval Europe* (Toronto, 1990), pp. 67–8.

42 P. J. Payer, *The Bridling of Desire. Views of Sex in the Later Middle Ages* (Toronto, 1993), p. 75.

43 Eustache Deschamps, XXXIV, *Autre ballade contre les vieux maris de jeunes femmes* in *Oeuvres complètes*, ed. L. Marquis de Queux de Saint-Hilaire (Paris, 1878), Vol. I, pp. 117–118; CXXXVIII, *Autre ballade sur ceux qui épousent de vieilles femmes*, ibid., pp. 262–3.

44 *Las siete partidas del Rey Don Alfonso el Sabio*, ed. G. Lopez (Salamanca, 1555. Reprint Madrid, 1974), P. II, t. XX, ley 2, p. 69.

45 H. Benveniste, 'Les elèvements: strategies matrimoniales, discours juridique et politique en France à la fin du Moyen-Age', *Revue Historique* 281/1 (1990), p. 27 and note 60; this was also the opinion of Maimonides: 'if she was a child and he was old, or she old and he a child, he is advised to release [his widowed sister-in-law].' Maimonides, *The Repetition of the Law, The Book of Women, Laws of Halitsah and Yibbum* 4(1).

46 *Les XV joies de mariage*, pp. 101–2, D. Herlihy and Ch. Klapisch, *Les Toscans et leurs familles. Étude du catasto florentin de 1427* (Paris, 1978), p. 607; Robert de Blois, *L'enseignement des princes*, in Ch. Langlois, *La vie en France d'après quelques moralistes du temps* (Paris, 1908), pp. 171–172; *Le livre des proverbes français*, ed. M. Le Roux de Lincy (Paris, 1859), Vol. II, p. 374; *The Early English Version of the Gesta Romanorum*, XVII, pp. 60–3; see also *Francisi Petrarchae de Remediis utriusque fortune* (Rotterdam, 1649), L. I, pp. 220–1; *Phisick against Fortune by Francis Petrarch. Englished by Thomas Twyne* (London, 1579), f. 100v.

47 J. Heers, *Le clan familial au moyen age. Étude sur les structures politiques et sociales des milieux urbaines* (Paris, 1974), p. 71; Ch. de la Roncière, 'Tuscan Notables on the Eve of the Renaissance', in *A History of Private Life*, ed. Ph. Ariès and G. Duby, trans. A. Goldhammer (Cambridge, Ma., 1988), Vol. II, p. 294; R. Vaultier, *Le folklore pendant la Guerre de Cent Ans d'après les lettres de rémission du Trésor des Chartes* (Paris, 1965), pp. 141–2.

48 About the charivari (which was not held exclusively when a widow or a widower were about to marry), see *Le charivari*, ed. J. Le Goff and J. C.

Schmitt, *Actes de la Table Ronde organisée à Paris 25–27 Avril 1977* (Paris, 1981).

49 *Les XV joies de mariage*, pp. 102–3.

50 R. E. Marsan, *Itinéraire espagnol du conte médiéval. VIIIe-XVe siècles* (Paris, 1974), pp. 527–35; *The Early English Version of the Gesta Romanorum*, Appendix XXVIII, p. 516; *Les lamentations de Mathieu*, in Ch. Langlois, *La vie en France au Moyen-Age d'après quelques moralistes du temps* (Paris, 1908), p. 250; *Index Exemplorum. A Handbook of Medieval Religious Tales*, ed. F. C. Tubach (F. F. Communications, 204, Helsinki 1981), 1552–3; see also A. K. Nitecki, 'Figures of Old Age in Fourteenth Century English Literature', in *Aging and the Aged in Medieval Europe*, ed. M. M. Sheehan (Toronto, 1990), pp. 107–16.

51 See note 44.

52 'Il porretures en I lit ne sont mie afferable', Philippe de Navarre, *op. cit.*, 173, p. 95.

53 'Il bierres ensambles', J. Ulrich, ed., *La riote du monde, Zeitschrift für Romanische Philologie* 8 (1884), pp. 284–6.

54 Guillaume de Lorris and Jean de Meun, *Le roman de la rose*, ed. F. Lecoy (Paris, 1968), Vol. II, v. 13441–3; *The Romance of the Rose by Guillaume de Lorris and Jean de Meun*, trans. H. W. Robbins (New York, 1962), p. 281.

55 The utopian socialist Charles Fourier was exceptional in assuming that old people, both men and women, needed sexual relations. As part of the revolution in the sexual mores, he even proposed that young people provide sexual services to the aged. These sevices would also be a means and an expression of the elimination of egotism in society. (Thanks to the way of life in the future state, 'Harmony', few old people would be decrepit, so it would be no hardship for the young to have sexual intercourse with them.) Charles Fourier, *Le nouveau monde amoureux* in *Oeuvres complètes*, ed. S. Debout Oleszkiewicz, Vol. 7 (Paris, 1967), pp. LII-LIII, 106–12. My thanks to Dr Stedman Jones for this source. References to the works of Proust and Thomas Mann already appeared in J. A. Burrow, *The Ages of Man* (Oxford, 1986), p. 158.

56 J. P. Delumeau, 'La mémoire des gens d'Arezzo et de Sienne à travers les dépositions de temoins', in *Temps, mémoire, tradition au Moyen Age* (Actes du XIIIe congrès de la Société des historiens médiévistes de l'enseignement supérieur public. Université de Provence, 1983), pp. 45–67.

57 M. W. Labarge, 'Three Medieval Widows and Second Careers' in M. M. Sheehan, ed., *Aging and the Aged in Medieval Europe* (Toronto, 1990), pp. 164–5.

58 G. Duby, 'The Aristocratic Households of Feudal France' in *A History of Private Life*, eds Ph. Ariès and G. Duby, trans. A. Goldhammer (Cambridge, Ma., 1988), Vol. II, p. 71.

59 *The Scrope and Grosvenor Controversy 1385–1390*, ed. N. H. Nicholas (London, 1832), pp. 51–143.

60 G. Minois, *Histoire de la vieillesse. De l'antiquité à la Renaissance* (Paris, 1987), p. 257.

61 *Thirteen Custumals of the Sussex Manors of the Bishop of Chichester*, ed. W. D. Peckham (Sussex Records Society, XXXI, 1925), p. 12; every now and then an 'extent' (evaluation) was held of all the holdings in the estate and of the labour obligations and payments owed by the tenure holders, based on the testimonies of the peasants.

62 F. W. Maitland, ed., *Select Pleas in Manorial and Other Seignorial Courts* (Selden Society, London, 1889), p. 88.

63 The land in question was held from the Archbishop of Canterbury: *Custumals of the Archbishop's Manors in Sussex*, eds B. C. Redwood and A. E. Wilson

(Sussex Records Society, LVII, 1958), p. 26; see also, in reference to the obligatory payments of the peasants who held very small plots and who were known as *cotarii: ibid.*, p. 40.

64 For example, 'Jurati proborum manerii; Willelmus prepositus; Simon Thomas clericus' G. T. Clark, ed., 'Customary of the Manor and Soke of Rothley in the County of Leicester', *Archaeologia* 47 (1882), pp. 99, 111, 115, 126.

65 *English Historical Documents 1189–1327*, Vol. III, ed. trans. H. Rothwell (London, 1975), p. 826.

66 E. Fügedi, 'Verba Volant... Oral Culture and Literacy among the Medieval Hungarian Nobility' in *Kings, Bishops, Nobles and Burghers in Medieval Hungary*, ed. J. M. Back (Variorum, London, 1986), pp. 1–25; another example of the testimonies of old men and women: R. Fossier, *La terre et les hommes en Picardie jusqu'à la fin du XIIIe siècle* (Paris-Louvain, 1968), Vol. 1, p. 280 and note 96; in Germany: G. Elgazi, 'Lords Ask, Peasants Answer: Making Traditions Late Medieval Village Assemblies' in G. Sider and G. Smith, eds, in *History and Histories* (forthcoming).

67 See note 95 to Chapter 1.

68 *Las siete Partidas del Rey Don Alfonso el Sabio*, P. 3, t. 16, ley 2, p. 74.

69 Ch. Klapisch-Zuber, 'L'invention du passé familial à Florence (XIVe-XVe s.)' in *Temps, mémoire, tradition au Moyen-Age* (Actes du XIIIe congrès de la Société des Historiens médiévistes de l'enseignement supérieur public. Université de Provence, 1983), pp. 95–118.

70 See M. T. Clanchy, *From Memory to Written Record. England 1066–1307* (London, 1979); in England the process may have begun earlier than in other countries, except for Italy, where literacy was more widespread than in the others.

71 So it was phrased in the charter of the city of Pas-en-Artois, dating from the last quarter of the twelfth century: G. Espinas, ed., *Documents relatifs à l'histoire du droit municipal en France des origines à la Revolution* (Paris, 1943), Vol. III, p. 220.

72 Concerning the same role in early modern times: K. Thomas, *Age and Authority in Early Modern England* (London, 1976), pp. 31–2.

73 Jean Sire de Joinville, *Histoire de Saint Louis, credo et lettre à Louis X*, ed. M. Natalis de Wailly (Paris, 1874), 760, p. 409.

74 S. E. Garrone, ed. trans., *J'ai connu madame Sainte Claire. Le procès de canonisation de Sainte Claire* (Toulouse, 1961), p. 107 f.

75 R. Pernoud, *Vie et mort de Jeanne d'Arc* (Paris, 1953), pp. 64–90 and annexe IV, p. 283.

76 S. Shahar, 'The Regulation and Presentation of Women in Economic Life (13th-18th centuries)', in *La Donna nell'economia secc. XIII-XVIII*, ed. S. Cavaciocchi (Istituto Internazionale di Storia Economica, 'F. Datini', Prato, 1990), p. 510 and note 27.

77 *Le ménagier de Paris*, ed. J. Pichon (Paris, 1846); *Le ménagier de Paris*, eds G. E. Brereton and J. M. Ferrier (Oxford, 1981), pp. XXI-XXX; see also E. Power, 'The Ménagier's Wife, a Paris Housewife in the Fourteenth Century' in *Medieval People* (reprint Bristol, 1986), pp. 96–119.

78 *Aucassin et Nicolette. Chantefable du XIIIe siècle*, ed. M. Roques (Paris, 1954), pp. 4, 14.

79 *Las siete partidas del Rey Don Alfonso el Sabio*, Pt. 1, tit. 6, ley 38, p. 62.

80 Philippe de Navarre, *op. cit.*, 182–3, pp. 99–100.

CHAPTER 5 'HONOUR THY FATHER AND THY MOTHER'

1 See, for example, J. P. Sartre, *Les Mots* (Paris, 1964), p. 11.

2 D. Herlihy, *Medieval Households* (Cambridge, 1985), pp. 132–4.

3 See R. Fossier, *La terre et les hommes en Picardie jusqu'à la fin du XIIIe siècle* (Paris-Louvain, 1968), Vol. I, pp. 262–73.

4 *Dives and Pauper*, ed. P. Barnum (E.E.T.S. London, 1976), Vol. I, IV, C. 1, p. 304.

5 R. J. Iannuci, *The Treatment of the Capital Sins and the Decalogue in German Sermons* (New York, 1942), p. 18.

6 Leon Battista Alberti, *I libri della famiglia. The Family in Renaissance Florence*, trans. R. M. Watkins (New York, 1969), pp. 40–1.

7 The writers of the age noted this fact. See, for example: Thomas Chobham, *Summa confessorum*, ed. F. Broomfield (Louvain, 1968), p. 29.

8 Bernardino de Siena, *Sermo de honore parentum in Opera omnia*, eds P. P. Collegii Bonaventurae (Florence, 1956), Vol. III, Sermo 17, pp. 311–18.

9 *C'est de la houce* in *Recueil général des Fabliaux*, eds A, Montaiglon and G. Raynaud (Paris, 1872), p. 3.

10 Philippe de Thaün, *Le bestiaire*, ed. E. Walberg (Genève, 1970), V. 2626, p. 95.

11 Bernardino de Siena, *op. cit.*, pp. 306–10.

12 R. M. Smith, 'Some Issues Concerning Families and their Properties in Rural England, 1250–1800' in *Land, Kinship and Life-Cycle*, ed. R. M. Smith (Cambridge, 1984), p. 74; a clause in the compilation of English laws from the beginning of the twelfth century, known as 'the Laws of Henry I', seems to be an exception to the rule. It did not make it a legal obligation to support aged parents but raised the possibility that a parent, or another relative who needed help and did not get it, could disinherit the person (who was supposed to help) and leave his property to another, and that in certain circumstances the court would uphold his action: *Leges Henrici Primi*, ed. trans. L. J. Downer (Oxford, 1972), pp. 274–5.

13 Ch. de la Roncière, 'Tuscan Notables on the Eve of the Renaissance' in *History of Private Life*, eds Ph. Ariès and G. Duby, Vol. 2, *Revelations of the Medieval World*, trans. A. Goldhammer (Cambridge, Ma., 1988), p. 207.

14 Dante, *Convivio* in *Opere di Dante*, ed. M. Barbi (Florence, 1921), IV, 26.

15 See: D. E. Queller, *The Venetian Patriciate. Reality Versus Myth* (University of Illinois Press, 1986), p. 131.

16 *Summula of Bishop Peter* in *Councils and Synods with other Documents Relating to the English Church*, ed. F. M. Powicke (Oxford, 1964), Vol. II, part II, p. 1063–7; John Myrc, *Instructions for Parish Priests*, ed. E. Peacock (London, 1864); Jean Gerson, *Les Dix commandemens de la loy* in *Oeuvres complètes*, ed. Mgr Glorieux (Paris, 1966), Vol. VII, CCCXXXIX, p. 424.

17 *Audun's Story* in *Hrafnkel's Saga and Other Stories*, trans. H. Palsson (Penguin Books, 1983), pp. 121, 126.

18 Francesco Petrarcha, *De remediis utriusque fortune* (Rotterdam, 1649), L. I., Dialogus 83, p. 232; *Phisicke Against Fortune by Francis Petrarch. Englished by Thomas Twyne* (London, 1579), f. 103r.

19 *The Sermons of Thomas Brinton, Bishop of Rochester 1373–1389*, ed. M. A. Devlin (London, 1954), Vol. I, Sermo 7, p. 21; the same story appears also in *The Early English Version of the Gesta Romanorum*, ed. S. J. Herrtage (London, 1879), CCXV, p. 533.

20 Bartholomaeus Anglicus, *Liber de Proprietatibus Rerum* (Strasbourg, 1505), L. VI, C. 14, de patre; *On the Properties of Things. John Trevisa's Translation of*

Bartholomaeus Anglicus' De Proprietatibus Rerum, ed. M. C. Seymour (Oxford, 1975), p. 310.

21 Philippe de Thaün, *Le bestiaire*, v. 2575–2615, pp. 93–4; Petrus Bertorius, *Dictionarium* in *Opera omnia* (Cologne, 1730), pars. 3, p. 87; *Dives and Pauper*, IV, C. 3, p. 309.

22 *Legends of the Holy Rood*, ed. R. Morris, (E.E.T.S. London, 1871), pp. 172–3.

23 *The Sermons of Thomas Brinton*, Vol. II, Sermo 61, p. 281.

24 In this connection, see: S. Shahar, *Childhood in the Middle Ages* (London, 1990), pp. 169–70; for a discussion on the impossibility, in today's Western society, of basing the expectation of help and care of aged parents on a symmetry of mutual duties (because parental duties, which come with the role of parenting, are voluntarily undertaken, whereas filial duties are not similarly self-imposed), see N. Daniel, *Am I My Parents' Keeper? An Essay on Justice between the Young and the Old* (Oxford, 1988), pp. 28–34.

25 Thomas Aquinas, *Super Epistolas Pauli lectura*, ed. R. Raphaelis (Rome, 1953), Vol. I, 317, p. 296.

26 Philippe de Navarre, *Les quatres ages de l'homme*, ed. M. de Fréville (Paris, 1888), 2–3, pp. 2–3.

27 Francesco Petrarca, *op. cit.*, L. I. dialogus 82, pp. 231–2; *Phisicke Against Fortune*, f. 105v.

28 *The Prose Salernitan Questions*, ed. B. Lawn (Oxford, 1979), q. 101, p. 47.

29 *Dives and Pauper*, Vol. I, IV, C. 5, pp. 314–15.

30 Plato, *Republic*, trans. R. Waterfield (Oxford, 1994), 329–30, pp. 6–7 (the speaker is old Cephalus); Cicero, *De senectute* in *Cicero in 28 Volumes* (The Loeb Classical Library, Harvard, 1971), Vol. 20, III8, p. 16.

31 *Le douze mois figurez*, ed. J. Morawski, *Archivum Romanicum* 10 (1926), p. 362; Philippe de Navarre, *op. cit.*, 120, pp. 56–7.

32 Gille Li Muisis, *Li lamentations*, in *Poésies*, ed. M. Kervyn de Lettenhove (Louvain, 1882), vol. I, p. 23.

33 See note 32 to Introduction.

34 Guillaume de Lorris and Jean de Meun, *Le roman de la rose*, ed. F. Lecoy (Paris, 1968), Vol. II, v. 14429–34, p. 189.

35 D. Herlihy and Ch. Klapisch, *Les Toscans et leurs familles. Étude du catasto florentin de 1427* (Paris, 1978), p. 608.

36 *C'est de la houce*, p. 1–7; *Liber exemplorum ad usum praedicantium*, ed. A. G. Little (British Society of Franciscan Studies. Aberdeen, 1908), p. 86; Robert Mannyng Brunne, *Handlyng Synne*, ed. F. Furnivall (E.E.T.S., London, 1901), pp. 41–2; *Index exemplorum. A Handbook of Medieval Religious Tales*, ed. F. C. Tubach (F.F. Communications, 204, Helsinki, 1981), 3601.

37 Francesco Petrarca, *op. cit.*, L.I. dialogus 77, pp. 22–3; L. II, dialogus 47, p. 472; *Phisicke Against Fortune*, f. 101r- 102v.

38 Bernardino de Sienne, *op. cit.*, pp. 307–8; he also added that the worst of all is when the sons become masters of the house.

39 *Dives and Pauper*, Vol. I, IV, C. 4, pp. 312–13.

40 *The Early English Version of the Gesta Romanorum*, LXXIX, pp. 48–53; another medieval version: Robert Glouster, *The Metrical Chronicle*, ed. W. A. Wright (Rolls Series 86, London, 1887), lines 680–870, pp. 50–64; 'I love your Majesty according to my bond, no more no less' William Shakespeare, *King Lear*, Act I, Scene I.

41 A. Macfarlane, *The Origins of English Individualism* (New York, 1979), pp. 131–64; idem, *Marriage and Love in England 1300–1840* (Oxford, 1986), pp. 321–44.

42 P. Amos and S. Harrell, eds *Other Ways of Growing Old. Anthropological Perspectives* (Stanford University Press, 1981), p. 12.
43 In Austria, see M. Mitterauer and R. Sieder, *The European Family. Patriarchy to Partnership from the Middle Ages to the Present*, trans. K. Oosterveen and M. Hörzinger (Oxford, 1982), pp. 166–7; in Italy and France: see notes 35, 36.
44 K. Thomas, *Age and Authority in Early Modern England (London, 1976)*, p. 36; T. R. Cole, *The Journey of Life. A Cultural History of Aging in America* (Cambridge, 1992), p. 150.
45 In this connection, see J. Keith, 'Age in Anthropological Research', in *Handbook of Aging and Social Sciences*, eds R. H. Binstock and E. Shanas (New York, 1985), pp. 254–5.
46 J. B. Given, *Society and Homicide in Thirteenth-Century England* (Stanford, 1977), pp. 158–60; B. Hanawalt, *Crime and Conflict in English Communities 1300–1348* (Cambridge, Ma., 1979), pp. 458–9.
47 Thomas Chobham, *op. cit.*, C.X, pp. 458–9.
48 See note 43, first item.

CHAPTER 6 CHURCHMEN IN THEIR OLD AGE

1 See J. Keith, 'Age in Anthropological Research' in *A Handbook of Aging and the Social Sciences*, eds R. H. Binstock and E. Shanas (New York, 1985), p. 237.
2 See P. T. Baxter and U. Almagor, eds, *Age, Generation and Time. Some Features of East African Age Organization* (London, 1978), p. 24.
3 *Corpus iuris canonici*, ed. A. Friedberg (Leipzig, 1879), Vol. II, L. III, tit. 31, C. 12, 14, cols. 572–3; see also D. Knowles, *The Monastic Orders in England* (Cambridge, 1963), pp. 418–22.
4 *Statuta capitulorum generalium ordinis Cisterciensis*, ed. J. Canivez (Louvain, 1933), Vol. II, pp. 31, 84.
5 J. Moorman, *The History of the Franciscan Order* (Oxford, 1968), pp. 342–4, 352–3.
6 S. Shahar, *Childhood in the Middle Ages* (London, 1990), pp. 192–3, 196–9.
7 *Ibid.*, pp. 203–5.
8 E. Gilliat-Smith, *St Clare of Assisi* (London, 1914), Appendix, p. 288.
9 D. Herlihy and Ch. Klapisch, *Les Toscans et leurs familles. Étude du Catasto Florentin de 1427* (Paris, 1978), pp. 203–4.
10 J. Hatcher, 'Mortality in the 15th Century: Some New Evidence', *The Economic History Review*, 2nd Ser. 39 (1986), pp. 19–38; B. Harvey, *Living and Dying in England 1100–1540. The Monastic Experience* (Oxford, 1995), Ch. 4.
11 A. Lane Poole, *From Domesday Book to Magna Carta* (Oxford, 1955), pp. 444–5.
12 *The Ecclesiastical History of Orderic Vitalis*, ed. trans. M. Chibnall (Oxford, 1978), Vol. II, pp. 126–8.
13 M. Barber, 'Supplying the Crusader States: The Role of the Templars', in *The Horns of Hattin*, ed. B. Z. Kedar (Jerusalem, 1992), pp. 320–1.
14 A. Vauchez, *La sainteté en Occident aux derniers siècles du Moyen-Age d'après les procès de canonisation et les documents hagiographiques* (Ecole française de Rome, 1988), p. 404.
15 A. M. Kleinberg, *Prophets in their Own Country. Living Saints and the Making of Sainthood in the Later Middle Ages* (Chicago, 1992), pp. 134–6.
16 *The Book of St Gilbert*, eds, trans. R. Foreville and G. Keir (Oxford, 1987), pp. XXIII-XXV.

17 Gilles Li Muisis, *Poésies*, ed. M. Kervyn de Lettenhove (Louvain, 1882), Vol. I, pp. XIII–XIV.

18 E. Brett, *Humbert de Romans, his Life and Views of Thirteenth Century Society* (Toronto, 1984), p. 4.

19 D. M. Farmer, *The Oxford Dictionary of Saints* (Oxford, 1989), p. 367.

20 J. C. Schmitt, *Le saint lévrier. Guinefort guérisseur d'enfants depuis le XIIIe siècle* (Paris, 1979), pp. 10–11, 23–5.

21 This was the monastery of St Augustine and St Olave of Wellow by Grimsby: A. H. Thompson, ed. trans., *Visitations of Religious Houses in the Diocese of Lincoln 1420–1449* (Horncastle, 1914), Vol. I, p. 127.

22 M. Rubin, *Charity and Community in Medieval Cambridge* (Cambridge, 1987), p. 132.

23 *Le règle de St Benoit*, eds, trans. J. Neufville and A. de Vogüé (Paris, 1972), Vol. II, C. 37, p. 572.

24 *Guigonis Carthusiae majoris prioris quinti consuetudines*, P. L., Vol. 153, cols 753–4; *The Life of St Hugh of Lincoln*, eds, trans. D. L. Douie and Dom. H. Farmer (London, 1961), pp. 14–15.

25 F. Beer, *Women and Mystical Experience in the Middle Ages* (Woodbridge, 1992), pp. 79–80, 103–4.

26 See, for example, *The Monastic Constitutions of Lanfranc*, ed, trans. D. Knowles (London, 1951), pp. 53, 68, 76, 79, 89, 90, 98, 118, 120; E. Gilliat-Smith, *St Clare of Assisi*, C. 3, 8; *Calendar of Charters and Documents Relating to Selborne and its Priory*, ed. W. D. Macray (Hampshire Records Society, London, 1891), Vol. I, p. 103; *Councils and Synods with Other Documents Relating to the English Church*, eds F. M. Powicke and R. Chency (Oxford, 1964), vol. II, part 2, 47, p. 787.

27 J. Hatcher, *op. cit.*, p. 35; regarding the infirmary at the Cistercian monastery in Rievaulx: Walter Daniel, *Vita Ailredicum cum epistola ad Marcium*, ed. trans. F. M. Powicke (Edinburgh, 1950), p. 38.

28 J. G. Coad, *Denny Abbey* (London, 1989), p. 5.

29 A. M. Kleinberg, *op. cit.*, pp. 31–2.

30 P. Richards, *The Medieval Leper and his Northern Heirs* (London, 1977), Document 3, p. 129; according to the rule of the order of the Templars, a member who contracted leprosy was asked to leave the order and join the order of St Lazarus (an order of lepers). But if he refused, he would not be compelled to do so, but was isolated and treated within his order: *Le règle du Temple*, ed. H. de Curzon (Paris, 1886), 444, p. 240.

31 *Le règle de St Benoit*, Vol. II, C. 66, p. 658.

32 *Visitations of Religious Houses in the Diocese of Lincoln 1420–1449*, Vol. I, pp. 9–10.

33 *The Life of St Anselm Archbishop of Canterbury by Eadmer*, ed. trans. R. W. Southern (London, 1962), pp. 23–4.

34 See, for example, the text which was ascribed, probably by mistake, to Bernard of Clairvaux, and was apparently written by a Benedictine monk: *Tractatus de ordine vitae et morum institutione*, P.L., Vol. 184, C. 3 cols 566–8, C. 6, col. 574.

35 E. Power, *Medieval English Nunneries c. 1275–1535* (Cambridge, 1922), p. 155; J. H. Tillotson, 'Pensions, Corrodies and Religious Houses: An Aspect of the Relations of Crown and Church in Early Fourteenth Century England', *Journal of Religious History*, 8 (1974), pp. 127–43; R. Harper, 'A Note on Corrodies in the Fourteenth Century', *Albion* 15 (1983), pp. 95–101; B. Harvey, *op. cit.*, p. 184.

36 M. G. Fagniez, *Documents relatifs à l'histoire de l'industrie et du commerce en France* (Paris, 1898), Vol. I, p. 68.

37 *Ibid.*, pp. 195–7; in both cases what they were given was defined as a 'fief of office' that could not be inherited.

38 J. T. Rosenthal, 'Retirement and the Life Cycle in Fifteenth Century England' in M. M. Sheehan, ed., *Aging and the Aged in Medieval Europe* (Toronto, 1990), pp. 173–88.

39 Pope Innocent III was elected when he was 37 years old, which was undoubtedly exceptional. Gregory XI was elected at about 42; Clement V at about 45; Nicholas II at about 48, and Boniface IX when he was 49: J. N. D. Kelly, *The Oxford Dictionary of Popes* (Oxford, 1988).

40 It should be noted that the circumstances of the election, abdication and perhaps even the death of Celestine V were exceptional. Even during the Renaissance, the popes were older than all the rulers of Europe, with the exception of the Venetian Doges, though perhaps a little less so than in the Middle Ages. Robert Finley has calculated that the average age of the popes at election was 54, and 64 when they died. Only three of them reached the age of 70: R. Finlay, 'The Venetian Republic as a Gerontocracy: Age and Politics in the Renaissance', *The Journal of Medieval and Renaissance Studies* 8 (1978), pp. 157–8.

41 *The Letters of Peter the Venerable*, ed. G. Constable (Cambridge, Ma., 1967), Vol. I, L. 85, p. 222, L. 121, pp. 314–5; Vol. II, p. 97.

42 G. Minois, *Histoire de la vieillesse. De l'antiquité à la Renaissance* (Paris, 1987), p. 234.

43 Jean Froissart, *Le joli buisson de jonece*, ed. A. Fourrier (Genève, 1975), V. 170–4, p. 53; it was the parish of Estinnes-au-Mont, Hainault, *ibid.*, pp. 29–30.

44 J. T. Rosenthal, *op. cit.*, pp. 180–3; N. Orme, 'The Medieval Almshouse for the Clergy: Clyst Gabriel Hospital near Exeter', *The Journal of Ecclesiastical History* 39 (1988), pp. 1–15; N. Orme, 'Suffering of the Clergy: Illness and Old Age in Exeter Diocese 1300–1540', in *Life, Death and the Elderly. Historical Perspectives*, eds M. Pelling and R. M. Smith (London, 1991), pp. 62–73.

45 Giraldus Cambrensis, *Speculum duorum*, eds, trans. Y. Lefèvre, R. B. C. Huygens and B. Dawson (Cardiff, 1974), pp. XXVI-XXX, 74.

46 *MG.H. Concilia*, Vol. II, pars I (Hanover, 1906), Concilium Aquisgranense, C. 142, p. 417.

47 J. Mansi, *Sacrorum conciliorum nova et amplissima collectio* (Florence and Venice, 1759–98, reprint Graz, 1960), Vol. XXIII, col. 1105.

48 *Select Pleas in Manorial and other Seignorial Courts*, ed. F. W. Maitland (Seldon Society, London, 1889), Vol. I, pp. 126–7.

49 M. Rubin, *op. cit.*, pp. 161, 165–6, 171–3.

50 L. Lallemand, *Histoire de la charité* (Paris, 1906), Vol. III, pp. 132–3; D. Knowles and R. N. Hadock, *Medieval Religious Houses. England and Wales* (London, 1953), pp. 253–4, 250, 302–3, 310.

51 N. Orme, *op. cit.* Only the chaplains of the institution who could no longer serve, and joined the other old clergymen who resided there, were allowed to bequeath half of their property to their relatives. The rest had to be left to the almshouse and its residents.

52 *Testamenta eboracensia, or Wills registered at York*, ed. J. Rain (Publications of the Surtees Society IV/2, London, 1830), pp. 11–25.

53 *Ibid.*, pp. 15, 25, 29, 39, 69.

54 M. Th. Lorcin, *Vivre et mourir en Lyonnais à la fin du Moyen Age* (Paris, 1981), pp. 108–9.

55 *Ibid.*, pp. 109–10; *North Country Wills, being Abstracts of Wills relating to the*

counties of York, Nottingham, Northumberland and Cumberland, 1383–1558, ed. J. W. Clay (Publications of the Surtees Society, CXV, London, 1908), p. 18.

56 R. Harper, op. cit.

57 North Country Wills, p. 30.

58 M. Chibnall, The World of Orderic Vitalis (Oxford, 1984), pp. 37–41.

59 It was: De concordia praescientiae et praedestinationis et gratia Dei cum libero arbitrio. The Life of St Anselm Archbishop of Canterbury by Eadmer, ed. trans. R. W. Southern (London, 1962), pp. 141–2.

60 Abélard, Historia calamitatum, ed. J. Monfrin (Paris, 1967), pp. 67–8.

CHAPTER 7 OLD AGE IN THE RANKS OF THE RULERS AND SOLDIERS

1 The Life of King Edward, ed. trans. F. Barlow (London, 1962), pp. 76–7, 79–80.

2 Brunetto Latini, Li livres dou Trésor, ed. F. J. Carmody (Berkeley, 1948), L. III, C. 73, 4–6, p. 392, C. 75, 1–2, p. 393.

3 Ibid., L. I, C. 101, 3, p. 84.

4 See note 57 to Chapter 1.

5 Leges Genuenses XII. Regulae communis Iannuae anno 1363 in Historiae patriae monumenta XVIII, eds C. Desimondi, A. L. Belgrano and V. Poggi (Torino, 1901), pp. 259, 261, 275; G. Minois, Histoire de la vieillesse de l'antiquité à la Renaissance (Paris, 1987), p. 320.

6 These remarks appear in note made in the margin of manuscript N of the 'Annals of Genoa', attributed to the annalist Jacope d'Oria. Gli annali Genovesi di Caffaro e de suoi continuatori, Vol. 4, ed. Cesare Imperiale (Rome, 1926), p. 34, notes 2(b) (c) (q). My thanks to Mr Emmanuel Vardi for this reference.

7 R. Finlay, 'The Venetian Republic as a Gerontocracy: Age and Politics in the Renaissance', The Journal of Medieval and Renaissance Studies 8 (1978), pp. 157–8.

8 Geoffroi de Villehardouin, La conquête de Constantinople, ed. E. E. Faral (Les classiques de l'histoire de France au Moyen Age, Paris, 1961), Vol. I, pp. 66–70; Villehardouin's Chronicle of the Fourth Crusade and the Conquest of Constantinople in Memoirs of the Crusades. Villehardouin and Joinville, trans. Sir Frank Marzialis (London, 1951), pp. 16–17.

9 R. Finlay, op. cit., note 5; D. E. Queller, The Venetian Patriciate. Reality versus Myth (University of Illinois Press, 1986).

10 K. Lorenz, 'La place des anciens chez les animaux sociaux', Communications 37 (1983), p. 13.

11 R. B. Dobson, ed. trans., The Peasant Revolt of 1381 (London, 1970), p. 372.

12 J. d'Avout, Le meurtre d'Etienne Marcel (Paris, 1960).

13 Byron, Marino Faliero, Doge of Venice. An Historical Tragedy in Five Acts; for the historical Faliero, as opposed to Byron's, and various interpretations of the affair: H. F. Brown, Studies in the History of Venice (London, 1907), Vol. I, pp. 79–106; V. Lazzarini, Marino Faliero (Florence, 1963); Ph. Longworth, The Rise and Fall of Venice (London, 1974), pp. 108–10.

14 Lex Baiwariorum, 2, 9, ed. E. M. von Schwind, M.G.H. Leges nationum germanicarum 5.2 (Hanover, 1926), pp. 302–3.

15 See note 119 to Chapter 1.

16 G. Duby, Guillaume le maréchal ou le meilleur chevalier du monde (Paris, 1984); regarding the witnesses in the dispute between the Grosvenors and the Scropes, see note 59 to Chapter 4.

17 In this connection, see N. B. Lewis, 'The Last Medieval Summons of the English Feudal Levy, 13 June 1385', *English Historical Review* 73 (1958), pp. 1–26.

18 *Tractatus de legibus et consuetudinibus regni anglie qui Glanvilla vocatur*, ed. trans. G. D. G. Hall (London, 1965), L. VII, C. 3, p. 78.

19 See notes 103, 104 to Chapter 1.

20 Norbert Elias, *State Formation and Civilization*, trans. E. Jephcott (Oxford, 1982).

21 *The Early English Version of the Gesta Romanorum*, ed. S. J. H. Herrtage (London, 1879), XIV Adrianus the Emperoure, pp. 45–8.

22 An interesting case of a man who withdrew to a monastery was that of the troubadour Bertran de Born. He had taken part in several battles and introduced the sounds of war into the poetry of the troubadours. He ended his life in a monastery. See *Anthologie des troubadours*, ed. trans. J. Anglade (Paris, 1927), p. 59. It is not known if he actually became a monk, or only lived in the monastery. For an example of a nobleman who retired and took vows, see J. T. Rosenthal, *Nobles and the Noble Life 1295–1500* (London, 1970), Document 68, pp. 183–4.

23 D. Barthélemy, 'Kinship' in *A History of Private Life*, eds Ph. Ariès and G. Duby, Vol. II, *Revelations of the Medieval World*, trans. A. Goldhammer (Cambridge, Ma., 1988), p. 85–116.

24 See note 28 to Chapter 3.

25 Bertran de Born, *Définitions de la jeunesse et de la vieillesse* in *Anthologie des Troubadours*, Line 1, p. 60.

26 G. Duby, 'The Aristocratic Households of Feudal France', in *A History of Private Life*, Vol. II, pp. 70–3.

27 J. Hatcher, 'Mortality in the 15th Century: Some New Evidence', *The Economic History Review*, 2nd Ser. 39 (1986), p. 27.

28 Jean Sire de Joinville, *Histoire de Saint Louis, credo et lettre à Louis X*, ed. trans. M. Natalis de Wailly (Paris, 1874), pp. 503–9.

29 N. B. Lewis, op. cit.; B. D. Lyon, *From Fief to Indenture. The Transition from Feudal to Non-Feudal Contract in Western Europe* (Cambridge, Ma., 1957), particularly pp. 250–70.

30 J. Rosenthal, *Nobles and the Noble Life*, pp. 154–6.

31 R. E. Archer, 'Rich Old Ladies: The Problem of Late Medieval Dowagers', in T. Pollard, ed., *Property and Politics: Essays in Later Medieval English History* (Gloucester, 1984), p. 19 and note 9.

32 See note 35 to Chapter 6, also E. Power, *Medieval English Nunneries c. 1250–1535* (Cambridge, 1922), pp. 197–8.

33 D. Knowles and R. N. Hadcock, *Medieval Religious Houses, England and Wales* (London, 1953), p. 308.

34 Thomas More, *Utopia*, ed. trans. R. N. Adams (New York, 1975), Vol. I, p. 12.

35 M. Mallet, *Mercenaries and their Masters* (London, 1974), pp. 64, 90–1, 121–2, 125–7; J. R. Hale and M. Mallet, *The Military Organization of a Renaissance State: Venice 1400–1617* (Cambridge, 1984), pp. 189–96.

36 See note 68 to Chapter 1.

37 *Memorials of London and London Life*, ed. H. T. Riley (London, 1868), p. 203.

38 *Ibid.*, p. 141.

39 E. Power, *op. cit.*, pp. 151, 155, 190, 196, 206–7; M. Rubin, *Charity and Community in Medieval Cambridge* (Cambridge, 1987), pp. 161, 165–6, 172; note 35 to Chapter 6.

40 John Russell, *The Boke of Nurture*, ed. F. J. Furnivall (London, 1987), line 1216, p. 81.

41 C. Gilbert, 'When Did a Man in the Renaissance Grow Old?' *Studies in the Renaissance* 14 (1967), pp. 27–8.

42 John Fortescue, *The Governance of England*, ed. Ch. Plummer (Oxford, 1885), pp. 153–4; examples of pensions in monasteries granted to royal clerks, the king's household staff and his physician: *ibid.*, p. 338.

43 See R. Harper, 'A Note on Corrodies in the Fourteenth Century', *Albion* 15 (1983), pp. 95–101; B. Harvey, *Living and Dying in England 1100–1540. The Monastic Experience* (Oxford, 1995), Ch. 6.

44 J. T. Rosenthal, 'Retirement and the Life Cycle in Fifteenth Century England' in M. M. Sheehan, ed., *Aging and the Aged in Medieval Europe* (Toronto, 1990), pp. 175–6.

45 On the purchase of pensions by Austrian noblemen in the Late Middle Ages: M. Mitterauer and R. Sieder, *The European Family. Patriarchy to Partnership from the Middle Ages to the Present*, trans. K. Oosterveen and M. Hörzinger (Oxford, 1982), pp. 161–2.

46 D. Hughes, 'From Bride Price to Dowry in Mediterranean Europe', *Journal of Family History* 3 (1978), pp. 262–91.

47 Ch. Klapisch, 'La mère cruelle. Maternité, veuvage et dot dans la Florence des XIVe-XVe siècles', *Annales E.S.C.* 38 (1983), pp. 1097–109.

48 S. Shahar, 'Family Prerogatives and the Limitations of Patriarchy: A Medieval Case', *Tel Aviver Jahrbuch für Deutsche Geschichte*, 22 (1993), pp. 105–15.

49 N. Duff, *Matilda of Tuscany* (London, 1909); P. Ori and P. Giovanni, *Matilde di Canossa* (Milan, 1980).

50 H. Pirenne, *Histoire de Belgique* (Bruxelles, 1902), particularly Vol. I, pp. 248, 251, 321, 334; F. L. Ganshof, 'La Flandre', in F. Lot and R. Fawtier, eds, *Histoire des institutions françaises au Moyen Age*, Vol. I, *Institutions seigneuriales* (Paris, 1957), pp. 367–8, 382, 287, 394.

51 J. Duvernoy, ed., *Registre de l'inquisition de Jacques Fournier évêque de Pamiers, 1318–1325* (Toulouse, 1965), Vol. 3, p. 328.

52 J. T. Rosenthal, 'Aristocratic Widows in Fifteenth Century England', in *Women and the Structure of Society: Selected Research from the Fifth Berkshire Conference on the History of Women*, eds B. J. Harris and J. K. McNamara (Durham, 1984), pp. 36–47.

53 S. Shahar, *op. cit.*; S. Shahar, *The Fourth Estate. A History of Women in the Middle Ages* (reprint, London, 1991), pp. 95–6, 128–31; R. E. Archer, 'Rich Old Ladies: The Problem of Late Medieval Dowagers', pp. 15–35.

54 S. Shahar, *Childhood in the Middle Ages* (London, 1990), pp. 218–19, 254–8.

55 R. E. Archer, *op. cit.*; J. Senderowitz Loengard, 'On the Gift of her Husband: English Dower and its Consequences in the year 1200' in J. Kirschner and S. F. Wemple, eds, *Women of the Medieval World. Essays in Honour of John Mundy* (Oxford, 1985), pp. 215–55. The political implications of the dower (or the jointure), which are also dealt with in these essays, lie outside the subject of the present discussion.

56 E. Cohen and E. Horowitz, 'In Search of the Sacred: Jews, Christians and Rituals of Marriage in the Later Middle Ages', *The Journal of Medieval and Renaissance Studies* 30 (1990), pp. 244–6.

57 J. T. Rosenthal, 'Aristocratic Widows', p. 47.

58 M. Th. Lorcin, *Vivre et mourir en Lyonnais à la fin du Moyen Age* (Paris, 1981), pp. 70–1.

59 See notes 52–57 to Chapter 6.

60 *Testamenta Eboracensia or Wills Registered at York*, ed. J. Rain (Publications of the Surtees Society IV/2, London, 1836), pp. 48, 52, 67, 393, 396; *The Fifty*

Earliest English Wills in the Court Probate of London, ed. F. J. Furnivall (E.E.T.S. London, 1882), pp. 6, 19. (A sum of 20 shillings left to one of the maidservants was stated to be for her dowry); *North Country Wills, Being Abstracts of Wills Relating to the Counties of York, Nottingham, Northumberland, Cumberland 1383–1558*, ed. J. W. Clay (Publications of the Surtees Society CXVI, London, 1908), p. 28; M. Th. Lorcin, *op. cit.*, pp. 109–11.

61 *Testamenta Eboracensia*, p. 39.

62 *North Country Wills*, p. 32; *The Fifty Earliest English Wills*, p. 53.

63 *The Fifty Earliest English Wills*, p. 8.

64 M. Th. Lorcin, *op. cit.*, p. 111.

65 *The Fifty Earliest English Wills*, p. 20.

66 Ch. de la Roncière, 'Tuscan Notables on the Eve of the Renaissance' in *A History of Private Life*, eds Ph. Ariès and G. Duby, Vol. 2, *Revelations of the Medieval World*, trans. A. Goldhammer (Cambridge, Ma., 1988), p. 231.

67 M. Rubin, *Charity and Community in Medieval Cambridge* (Cambridge, 1987), pp. 268–9.

CHAPTER 8 OLD AGE IN URBAN SOCIETY

1 See note 28 to Chapter 4.

2 See notes 75–77, 79–80, 82–83 to Chapter 1.

3 As opposed to the coroners. See note 44 to Chapter 7.

4 S. Thrupp, *The Merchant Class of Medieval London* (Ann Arbor, 1976), p. 194.

5 J. Brucker, ed., *Two Memoirs of Renaissance Florence. The Diaries of Buonaccorso Pitti and Gregorio Dati*, trans. J. Martines (London, 1967).

6 J. Heers, *Le clan familial au Moyen Age. Étude sur les structures politiques et sociales des mileux urbains* (Paris, 1974), p. 71; see also note 19 to Chapter 2, note 14 to Chapter 4, and also *Comptes du sel (libro di ragione e conto di salle de Francesco di Marco Datini pour sa compagnie d'Avignon)*, ed. Ch. Villain-Gandossi (Collection de Documents inédits sur l'Histoire de France, Sr. 8, Vol. 7, Paris, 1969), Ch. 1.

7 J. Heers, *op. cit.*, pp. 219–39.

8 Ch. de la Roncière, 'Tuscan Notables on the Eve of the Renaissance' in *A History of Private Life*, eds Ph. Ariès and G. Duby, Vol. 2, *Revelations of the Medieval World*, trans. A. Goldhammer (Cambridge, Ma., 1988), pp. 205–7.

9 An extreme case of a tyrannical father who appropriated his son's entire property, inherited from his mother and obtained as his wife's dowry, is cited in D. Herlihy and Ch. Klapisch, *Les Toscans et leurs familles. Étude du Catasto florentin du 1427* (Paris, 1978), pp. 608–9.

10 D. Herlihy, 'Age, Property and Career in Medieval Society', in M. M. Sheehan, ed., *Aging and the Aged in Medieval Europe* (Toronto, 1990), pp. 143–58.

11 *Calendar of Letter-Books of the City of London. Letter-Book A. c. 1275–1298*, ed. R. R. Sharpe (London, 1899), pp. 98, 126.

12 *Ibid.*, p. 98. In some cases the lenders or borrowers were brothers: *ibid.*, pp. 101, 110, 114.

13 *Calendar of Plea and Memoranda Rolls Preserved Among the Archives of the Corporation of the City of London at the Guildhall 1364–1381*, ed. A. Thomas (Cambridge, 1929), p. 294; S. Thrupp, *op. cit.*, pp. 151 and note 150, 224, 227, 103–5, 199, 229, 312.

14 Konrad von Megenberg, *Ökonomik*, ed. S. Krüger (*M.G.H. 500–1500, Staatsschriften des Späteren Mittelalters*, Band III, Stuttgart, 1973), L. I/3, C. 12,

pp. 144–5; the author compared the effectiveness of the older physcans to that of older bees, according to Aristotle.

15 M. Le Roux de Lincy, ed., *Le livre des proverbes français* (Paris, 1859), Vol. 2, p. 435.

16 M. Green, 'Women's Medical Practice and Health Care in Medieval Europe', *Signs* 14 (1989), p. 445 and note 36.

17 On these problems in modern industry: P. M. Thane, 'The Debate on the Declining Birth-Rate in Britain: the 'Menace' of an Aging Population 1920–1950s', *Continuity and Change* 5/2 (1990), p. 300.

18 Jean Sire de Joinville, *Histoire de Saint Louis, credo et lettre à Louis X*, ed. trans. M. Natalis de Wailly (Paris, 1874), C. CXLII, 722, p. 392.

19 In England the religious fraternities were also called guilds. An examination of the rules of 471 such guilds, mostly of the fourteenth century, revealed that only about a third included clauses concerning assistance to members. See H. F. Westlake, *The Parish Guilds of Medieval England* (London, 1919), p. 14; in Venice the occupational union, namely, the guild, was called *arte*, and the religious fraternity *scuola*. The latter were not necessarily based on a common occupation. Beginning in the latter half of the fourteenth century, they underwent a distinctive development – a marked separation between the well-off and the impoverished fraternity members. The assistance given by the former to the latter turned the fraternity from a religious institution into a religious-philanthropic one. See B. Pullan, *Rich and Poor in Renaissance Venice* (Oxford, 1971), pp. 66–78.

20 P. Adam. *La vie paroissiale en France au XIVe siècle* (Paris, 1964), pp. 16–17.

21 L. T. Smith, ed., *English Gilds* (London, 1870), p. 5; H. F. Westlake, *op. cit.*, p. 181.

22 *Règlements sur les arts et métiers de Paris rédigés au XIIIe siècle et connus sous le nom du Livre des métiers de Etienne Boileau*, ed. G. B. Depping (Paris, 1837), LXIX, p. 177.

23 Examples of references to the aged: G. Espinas, ed., *Documents relatifs à la draperie de Valenciennes au Moyen Age* (Lille, 1931), 28, p. 57; *Statua gilde*, in *The Acts of the Parliaments of Scotland*, Vol. 1, eds T. Thomson and C. Innes (Edinburgh, 1844), XII, p. 433 (91); L. T. Smith, *op. cit.*, pp. 5–7, 157, 278; H. F. Westlake, *op. cit.*, p. 149, 170, 172.

24 F. J. Furnivall, ed., *The Gild of St Mary Lichfield* (E.E.T.S. London, 1920), p. 8; *Recueil général des anciennes lois françaises depuis l'an 420 jusqu'à la revolution de 1789*, eds A. J. L. Jourdan, Decrusy, F. A. Isambert (Paris, 1822–33), Vol. 4, 111, p. 471.

25 Ch. de la Roncière, 'Pauvres et pauvreté à Florence au XIVe siècle' in M. Mollat, ed., *Études sur l'histoire de la pauvreté. Moyen-Age – XVIe siècle.* (Paris, 1974), Vol. 2, p. 711.

26 L. T. Smith, *op. cit.*, p. 169; H. F. Westlake, *op. cit.*, p. 150.

27 The following are a few examples of weekly payments: 4 pence: G. Espinas, ed., *op. cit.*, 28, p. 57; 6 pence: M. Bateson, ed., *Cambridge Gild Records* (Cambridge, 1903), p. 72; P. Adam, *op. cit.*, pp. 51–2; 7 pence: L. T. Smith, ed., *op. cit.*, pp. 157, 267; 8 pence: *ibid.*, p. 8; 12 pence: *ibid.*, pp. 22, 26; 14 pence: *ibid.*, pp. 5, 31.

28 W. O. Ault, *Open-Field Husbandry and the Village Community* (Transactions of the American Philosophical Society. New Series, 55, part 7, Philadelphia, 1965), pp. 13–14; B. Harvey, ed., *Custumals and Bye-Laws (1386–1526) of the Manor of Islip* (Oxfordshire Records Society Ser. XL, 1959), p. 105.

29 Ch. Dyer, *Standards of Living in the Later Middle Ages. Social Change in England c. 1200–1520* (Cambridge, 1989), p. 253.

30 B. Pullan, *op. cit.*, pp. 63–5.

31 G. Espinas, ed., *op. cit.*, 6, p. 23; *Ordonnance des rois de France*, ed. M. Secousse, Vol. 9 (Paris, 1755), p. 167.

32 L. Lallemand, *Histoire de la charité* (Paris, 1906), Vol. 3, p. 335.

33 H. F. Westlake, *op. cit.*, pp. 149, 236.

34 *Ibid.*, p. 208; L. T. Smith, ed., *op. cit.*, p. 267.

35 M. Bateson, *op. cit.*, p. 93: 'terminum vite sue'; on assistance in the Austrian fraternities, see M. Mitterauer and R. Sieder, *The European Family. Patriarchy to Partnership from the Middle Ages to the Present*, trans. K. Oosterveen and M. Hörzinger (Oxford, 1982), p. 162.

36 See notes 46, 53 to Chapter 7.

37 Ch. Klapisch, 'Demographic Decline and Household Structure: The Example of Prato, Late 14th to Late 15th Century' in *Women, Family and Ritual in Renaissance Italy* (Chicago, 1985), pp. 23–35; Z. Razi, *Life, Marriage and Death in a Medieval Parish. Economy, Society and Demography in Halesowen 1270–1400* (Cambridge, 1980), pp. 138–9.

38 See note 77 to Chapter 4.

39 M. Th. Lorcin, *Vivre et mourir en Lyonnais à la fin du moyen-age* (Paris, 1981), p. 66; D. Herlihy and Ch. Klapisch, *op. cit.*, p. 611; S. Epstein, *Wills and Wealth in Medieval Genoa 1150–1250* (Cambridge, Ma., 1984), p. 108.

40 *Ibid.*, pp. 494–5, 611; on the smaller means available today to women over 65 than to men of the same age, and their causes: S. Reinharz, 'Friends or Foes: Gerontological and Feminist Theory' in R. D. Klein and D. L. Steinberg, eds, *Radical Voices* (Pergamon Press, 1989), pp. 234, 237–8; D. Groves, 'Women and Financial Provision for Old Age', in *Women's Issues in Social Policy*, eds M. Maclean and C. Groves (London, 1991).

41 M. Bateson, ed., *Records of the Borough of Leicester* (London, 1899), p. 389.

42 O. Redon, 'Aspects économiques de la discrimination et la "marginalisation" des femmes, XIIIe-XVIIIe siècles' in *La donna nell economia secc. XII-XVIII*, ed. S. Cavaciocchi (Istituto Internazionale di Storia Economica 'F. Datini', Serie II, 21, Prato, 1990), pp. 441–60.

43 S. Shahar, 'The Regulation and Presentation of Women in Economic Life (13th-18th Centuries)', in *La donna nell economia secc. XIII-XVIII*, ed. S. Cavacioc-chi (Istituto Internazionale di Storia Economia 'F. Datini', Serie II, 21, Prato, 1990), pp. 501–22.

44 L. T. Smith, ed., *op. cit.*, p. 267; M. Bateson, ed., *Cambridge Gild Records*, p. 116.

45 D. Herlihy and Ch. Klapisch, *op. cit.*, pp. 509–11; Ch. Klapisch, ' "A uno pane e uno vino": The Rural Tuscan Family at the Beginning of the 15th Century' in *Women, Family and Ritual in Renaissance Italy* (Chicago, 1985), pp. 36–7.

46 Ch. Klapisch, 'Household and Family in Tuscany in 1427', in *Household and Family in Past Times*, eds P. Laslett and R. Wall (Cambridge, 1972), p. 280.

47 See note 110–111 to Chapter 1.

48 I. Origo, *The Merchant of Prato. Francesco di Marco Datini* (Penguin, 1963), pp. 344, 217–18.

49 R. Trexler, 'A Widows' Asylum of the Renaissance: The Orbatello of Florence' in P. N. Stearns, ed., *Old Age in Preindustrial Society* (London, 1982), pp. 119–49.

50 *Le livre Roisin. Coutumier lillois de la fin du XIIIe siècle*, ed. R. Monier (Lille, 1932), pp. 16–17.

51 M. Rubin, *Charity and Community in Medieval Cambridge* (Cambridge, 1987), p. 172; B. Harvey, *Living and Dying in England 1100–1540. The Monastic Experience* (Oxford, 1995), pp. 200–9.

52 M. Mitterauer and R. Sieder, *op. cit.*, pp. 161–2; on retirement to a Renaissance institution, see: R. Trexler, 'Une table florentin d'espérance de vie', *Annales E.S.C.* 26 (1971), pp. 137–9.

53 H. M. Jewell, 'The Bringing Up of Children in Good Learning and Manners: A Survey of Educational Provisions in the North of England', *Northern History* 18 (1982), p. 11.

54 M. Bateson, ed., *Cambridge Gild Records*, p. 9.

55 Ph. Longworth, *The Rise and Fall of Venice* (London, 1974), p. 127; *Calendar of Letter-Books of the City of London. Letter-Book H. c. 1375–1399*, ed. R. R. Sharpe (London, 1907), p. 202.

56 B. Geremek, *Les marginaux parisiens aux XIVe et XVe siècles* (Paris, 1976), p. 57.

57 V. Groebner, 'Black Money and Language of Things: Observations on the Economy of the Labouring Poor in Late Fifteenth Century Nuremberg' in *Tel-Aviver Jahrbuch für Deutsche Geschichte*, 22 (1993), pp. 275–91.

58 *North Country Wills being Abstracts of Wills, relating to the Counties of York, Nottingham, Northumberland, Cumberland 1383–1558*, ed. J. W. Clay (Publications of the Surtees Society, Vol. CXXVI, London, 1908), p. 2; *The Fifty Earliest English Wills in the Court Probate of London*, ed. F. J. Furnivall (E.E.T.S. London, 1882), pp. 45–6; *Testamenta Eboracensia, or Wills registered at York*, ed. J. Rain (Publications of the Surtees Society, Vol. IV/2, London, 1856), pp. 4, 20, 23, 71, 396; M. Th. Lorcin, *op. cit.*, p. 110; S. Epstein, *op. cit.*, pp. 127–31.

59 V. Groebner, *op. cit.*, p. 290, note 43.

60 *The Fifty Earliest English Wills*, p. 20; *Calendar of the Wills Proved and Enrolled in the Court of Husting, London, 1258–1688*, ed. R. R. Sharpe (London, 1889), Vol. I, pp. 12–13, 37, 66, 70, 114, 122, 144, 131, 175, 180.

61 I. Origo, *op. cit.*, pp. 195, 345; S. Epstein, *op. cit.*, p. 130.

CHAPTER 9 OLD AGE IN THE PEASANTRY

1 Ch. Klapisch, 'Fiscalité et démographie en Toscane (1427–1430)', *Annales E.S.C.* 224 (1969), pp. 1313–37; D. Herlihy and Ch. Klapisch, *Les Toscans et leurs familles. Étude du Catasto florentin de 1427* (Paris, 1978), pp. 370–371, 374–379, 491–497; Ch. Klapisch, ' "A uno pane e uno vino": The Rural Tuscan Family at the Beginning of the 15th Century' in *Women, Family and Ritual in Renaissance Italy* (Chicago, 1985), pp. 36–67; D. Herlihy, 'Age, Property and Career in Medieval Society', in *Aging and the Aged in Medieval Europe*, ed. M. M. Sheehan (Toronto, 1990), pp. 143–58.

2 E. Le Roy Ladurie, *Les paysans de Languedoc* (Paris, 1966), pp. 160–8.

3 G. Minois, *Histoire de la vieillesse. De l'antiquité à Renaissance* (Paris, 1987), pp. 298–300; P. Desportes, 'La population de Reims au XVe siècle d'après un denombrement de 1422', *Le Moyen Age* 72, (1966), p. 485; M. Zerner, 'Une crise de mortalité au XVe siècle à travers les testaments et les rôles d'imposition', *Annales E.S.C.* 34 (1979), pp. 568–689.

4 On retirement agreements in Austria: M. Mitterauer and R. Sieder, *The European Family. Patriarchy to Partnership from the Middle Ages to the Present*, trans. K. Oosterveen and M. Hörzinger (Oxford, 1982), pp. 162–8; examples of retirement and transfer of property to a son in the Lyonnais in France: M. Th.

Lorcin, *Vivre et mourir en Lyonnais à la fin du Moyen Age* (Paris, 1981), pp. 68–73, 90.

5 *Registre de l'inquisition de Jacques Fournier 1318–1325*, ed. J. Duvernoy (Toulouse, 1965), Vol. I, p. 321.

6 J. Keith, 'Age in Anthropological Research', in *Handbook of Aging and Social Sciences*, eds R. H. Binstock and E. Shanas (New York, 1985), pp. 235–7.

7 See note 26 to Chapter 2.

8 On Montaillou: E. Le Roy Ladurie, *Montaillou. Village occitan de 1294–1324* (Paris, 1975), pp. 64–6, 288–91, 294–5, 317, 321–3; *Egil's Saga*, trans. G. Jones (New York, 1960), p. 236.

9 *Montaillou*, pp. 363–5; on the role of the aged as preservers of tradition and the belief in their special knowledge among the Australian Aborigines today: B. Chatwin, *The Songlines* (London, 1987).

10 Widows owned land by dowry or inheritance from their family of origin, by dower, or by inheritance from their husbands in addition to the dower. In England their rights varied from region to region. In some places (e.g. Islip), a widow could retain the entire holding. In others (Launton), she could keep it for a year and a day, and if by then she had not remarried, she had to render it to the lord of the manor and would only retain possession of her dower. See R. M. Smith, 'The Manorial Court and the Elderly Tenant in Late Medieval England' in *Life, Death and The Elderly. Historical Perspectives*, eds, M. Pelling and R. Smith (London, 1991), p. 47.

11 Z. Razi, *Life, Marriage and Death in a Medieval Parish. Economy, Society and Demography in Halesowen 1270–1400* (Cambridge, 1980), pp. 119–20.

12 See note 37 to Chapter 8.

13 See note 41 to Chapter 5.

14 R. M. Smith, *op. cit.*, pp. 39–61.

15 Z. Razi, 'The Myth of the Immutable English Family', *Past and Present* 140 (1993), pp. 26–7; on assistance to offspring in the period before the Black Death and their disinclination to migrate: *ibid.*, pp. 8, 11–12, 15.

16 An example of a transfer agreement with non-kin, which is plainly limited to the stranger's lifetime: 'Rolls of the Manor of Wiston', ed. P. S. Godman, *Sussex Archaeological Collections* 54 (1911), p. 176.

17 E. Clark, 'The Quest for Security in Medieval England', in *Aging and the Aged in Medieval Europe*, ed. M. M. Sheehan (Toronto, 1990), pp. 189–200.

18 F. M. Page, 'The Customary Poor-Law of Three Cambridgeshire Manors', *Cambridge Historical Journal* 3/2 (1930), pp. 130–1.

19 *Documents Relating to Cambridgeshire Villages*, eds W. M. Palmer and H. W. Saunders (Cambridge, 1926), no. 5, p. 90.

20 See note 41 to Chapter 5.

21 In the words of a 1296 agreement: *Durham Halmost Rolls. Halmota prioratus Dunelmensis 1296–1384*, eds W. H. D. Longstaffe and J. Booth (Surtees Society, 1886), p. 9; see also Z. Razi, 'Family, Land and the Village Community in Later Medieval England', *Past and Present* 93 (1981), pp. 7–8.

22 See, for example, G. C. Homans, *English Villagers of the 13th Century* (New York, 1975, first published 1941), pp. 152–3 and note 14 to Chapter 11.

23 E. Clark, *op. cit.*; an example of agreement between mother and son which itemizes the latter's obligations in detail: *Court Rolls of the Manor of Hales 1272–1307*, ed. J. A. Amphlett (Worcester Historical Society, Oxford, 1910), pp. 166–8.

24 Ch. Dyer, *Standards of Living in the Later Middle Ages. Social Change in England c. 1200–1520* (Cambridge, 1989) pp. 151–4, 175.

25 Z. Razi, 'The Myth of the Immutable English Family', p. 8.

26 *Dives and Pauper*, ed. P. Barnum (E.E.T.S., Oxford, 1980), Vol. 1, p. 310.

27 An example of such an agreement from 1294: the parents were to live with the son and at his expense but, if they were dissatisfied, the son was to provide alternative accommodation for them as well as a detailed list of provisions. J. A. Raftis, *Tenure and Mobility. Studies in the Social History of the Medieval Village* (Toronto, 1964), pp. 44–5.

28 M. Th. Lorcin, *op. cit.*, pp. 70–3; M. Gonon, *Les institutions et la société en Forez au XIVe siècle d'après les testaments* (Paris, 1960), p. 66.

29 The size of the holding determined the labour obligations. Though it did not necessarily take the form of personal service, the person heading the holding was responsible for the execution of the labour obligation, and in some cases had to provide additional labourers. An elderly peasant or a widow, who no longer had dependent sons at home, could find it difficult to meet this obligation, from which they were not exempted by old age. Only the sick were exempted, and for not more than one month. *Thirteen Custumals of the Sussex Manors of the Bishop of Chichester*, ed. W. D. Peckham (Sussex Rec. Society 31, 1925), pp. 17, 33–4, 108; *Custumals of the Sussex Manors of the Archbishop of Canterbury*, eds B. C. Redwood and A. E. Wilson (Sussex Rec. Society 57, 1958), pp. 86, 90, 109; see also E. Clark, 'Social Welfare and Mutual Aid in the Medieval Countryside', *Journal of British Studies* 33, (1994), p. 393.

30 Examples of punishments meted to violators: *The Court Baron together with Select Pleas from the Bishop of Ely's Court of Littleport*, eds F. W. Maitland and W. P. Baildon (Selden Society, London, 1891), p. 114; J. F. Raftis, *op. cit.*, Appendix V4, pp. 43–4; G. C. Homans, *op. cit.*, pp. 146–7.

31 E. Clark, 'The Quest for Security in Medieval England', pp. 189–200; *idem.*, 'Social Welfare and Mutual Aid in the Medieval Countryside', pp. 381–400; R. Smith, *op cit.*, pp. 54–7; according to a Danish legal compilation dating from the early thirteenth century (known as the Scania Law), if an old man failed to reach an agreement with his heirs (presumably his offspring) or some other kinsman to support him in his old age in return for the promised bequest of his property, he was free to make such an agreement with a stranger. If the stranger did not fulfil his obligations, the old man could bring it up before the local assembly (*thing*), which would appoint a committee of 'prude men' to examine the complaint. Later compilations, which reflected the growing strength of the monarch, whose officers began to intervene in the activities and, above all, the judicial work of the local assemblies, stipulated that such an offence against an old man was a matter for the royal functionaries, since the king was the defender of the powerless. If the complaint was found to be justified, the man could leave the stranger's house with all his possessions. If it was unjustified, he could still leave, but without his possessions. Similar customary laws existed in other Scandinavian countries. *Andres Sunesons Latinske Parafrase af Skanske Lov*, ed. J. Olrik, in *Danmarks Gamle Landskabslove med Kirkelovene*, eds Brondum-Nielsen and P. J. Jorgensen (Copenhagen, 1945), Vol. I, pp. 484–6; Y. Waldman, *The Danish Royal Charter of 1282* (unpublished doctoral thesis, Tel Aviv University, 1989), p. 233. I thank Dr Yael Waldman for this reference.

32 Examples: F. M. Page, *op. cit.*, p. 126; Z. Razi, *Life, Marriage and Death in a Medieval Parish*, pp. 68–9.

33 B. A. Hanawalt, *The Ties that Bound. Peasant Families in Medieval England* (Oxford, 1986), p. 237.

34 *Documents Relating to Cambridgeshire Villages*, eds W. M. Palmer and H. W.

Saunders (Cambridge, 1926), no. 5, p. 82; the donation of an article belonging to a person who died unshriven was called *Deo dandum, deodand*. Sometimes it was the object which caused the sudden death.

35 Francesco Petrarca, *De remediis utriusque fortune* (Rotterdam, 1649) p. 562; *Phisick against Fortune by Francis Petrarch. Englished by Thomas Twyne* (London, 1579), f. 266r.

36 Fossier's study has shown that in the thirteenth century, the holdings of about a quarter of the peasants of Picardie were too small to sustain them: R. Fossier, *La terre et les hommes en Picardie jusqu'à la fin du XIIIe siècle* (Paris-Louvain, 1968), Vol. 2, pp. 726–8.

37 F. W. Maitland and W. P. Baildon, eds, *op. cit.*, p. 128.

38 *Recueil général des anciennes lois françaises depuis l'an 420 jusqu'à la Révolution de 1789*, eds A. J. L. Jourdan, Decrusy, Isambert (Paris, 1822–33), Vol. I, no. 299, p. 357.

39 W. O. Ault, *Open-Field Husbandry and the Village Community* (Transactions of the American Philosophical Society. New Ser. Vol. 55, part 7, Philadelphia, 1965), pp. 13–15, Appendix 8, p. 56; *Custumals (1391) and Bye-Laws (1386–1526) of the Manor of Islip*, ed. B. Harvey (Oxfordshire Rec. Soc. Ser. 40, 1959), p. 105.

40 W. O. Ault, *op. cit.*, Appendix 8, p. 56; B. Harvey, *op. cit.*, p. 109.

41 W. O. Ault, *op. cit.*, p. 29; Ch. Dyer, *op. cit.*, pp. 253–7.

42 Ch. Dyer, *op. cit.*, p. 257; M. Bourin and R. Durand, *Vivre au village au Moyen-Age* (Paris, 1984), pp. 88–90; Ch. M. de la Roncière, 'Pauvre et pauvreté à Florence au XIVe siècle' in M. Mollat, ed., *Études sur l'histoire de la pauvreté (Moyen Age – XVIe siècle)* (Paris, 1974), Vol. 2, pp. 710–13.

43 D. Herlihy, *Medieval and Renaissance Pistoia. The Social History of an Italian Town 1200–1430* (New Haven, 1967), pp. 92–3; Ch. Dyer, *op. cit.*, p. 253; Ch. M. de la Roncière, *op. cit.*, p. 670.

44 E. Clark, 'Charitable Bequests, Death-Bed Land Sales and the Manor Court in Later Medieval England' in *Village and Small Town Society: Views from Manorial and Other Seigneurial Courts*, eds Z. Razi and R. M. Smith (Oxford, 1996).

45 *Testamenta Eboracensia or Wills Registered at York*, ed. J. Rain (Publications of the Surtees Society IV/2, (London, 1836), p. 313; *The Fifty Earliest English Wills in the Court Probate of London*, ed. F. J. Furnivall (E.E.T.S., London, 1982), pp. 6, 19, 27, 50, 52–3; Ch. Dyer, *op. cit.*, p. 249; Ch. M. de la Roncière, *op. cit.*, pp. 696–7.

46 *The Rolls of the Manor of Hales 1272–1307*, ed. J. A. Amphlett (Worcester Historical Society, Oxford, 1910), p. 336.

47 B. Harvey, *Living and Dying in England 1100–1540. The Monastic Experience* (Oxford, 1995), pp. 192–3. I did not go into the question of the benefits or disadvantages that these purchased pensions had for the monasteries nor into other factors which might have moved people to prefer these arrangements, other than providing for their old age, since these aspects fall outside the present discussion. On this subject, see *ibid.*, Chapter 6.

48 M. Mitterauer and R. Sieder, *op. cit.*, p. 168.

49 Z. Razi, 'The Myth of the Immutable English Family', *Past and Present* 140 (1993), pp. 3–44. Historians of the English peasant society disagree about the chronological and geographical extent of the 'functional extended family'. The article deals with the conflicting views on this subject.

50 R. M. Smith, 'Some Issues Concerning Families and their Properties in Rural

England 1250–1800' in *Land, Kinship and the Life Cycle*, ed. R. M. Smith (Cambridge, 1984), pp. 71–8.

51 J. A. Raftis, 'Social Structures in Five East Midland Villages', *The Economic History Review* 2nd Ser., 18 (1965), pp. 83–99; E. Clark, 'Social Welfare and Mutual Aid in the Medieval Countryside', pp. 397–8.

52 Z. Razi, 'The Myth of the Immutable English Family', pp. 13–14.

53 *Select Cases from the Coroner's Rolls 1265–1413*, ed. Ch. Gross (Selden Society, London, 1896), p. 5.

CHAPTER 10 THE OLD AND THE CHARITABLE ORGANIZATIONS

1 See notes 82, 83 to Chapter 1.

2 Any person could turn to the ecclesiastical court if, having exhausted all the secular legal avenues, he still felt that justice had not been done. The 'technical' unfortunates, however, could do so after a single setback in a secular court. See B. Tierney, *Medieval Poor Law. A Sketch of Canonical Theory and its Application in England* (Berkeley, 1959), pp. 18–19.

3 See note 10 to Introduction.

4 R. Keickhefer, *Unquiet Souls. Fourteenth-Century Saints and their Religious Milieu* (Chicago, 1984), p. 46.

5 M. Rubin, *Charity and Community in Medieval Cambridge* (Cambridge, 1987), pp. 268–9 and note 183.

6 *The Fifty Earliest English Wills in the Court Probate of London*, ed. F. J. Furnivall (E.E.T.S., London, 1882), pp. 23–31; *Calendar of Wills Proved and Enrolled in the Court of Husting, London 1258–1688*, ed. R. R. Sharpe (London, 1889), Vol. 1, p. 115; L. Lallemand, *Histoire de la charité* (Paris, 1906), Vol. 3, p. 329; J. A. Thomson, 'Piety and Charity in Late Medieval London', *Journal of Ecclesiastical History* 16 (1965), p. 180 and note 4.

7 D. W. Witters, 'Pauvres et pauvreté dans les coutumiers monastiques du Moyen Age', in *Étude sur l'histoire de la pauvreté (Moyen Age – XVI siècle)*, ed. M. Mollat (Paris, 1974), Vol. 1, p. 207; B. Harvey, *Living and Dying in England 1100–1540. The Monastic Experience* (Oxford, 1995), p. 19.

8 M. Peaudecerf, 'La pauvreté à l'Abbaye de Cluny d'après son cartulaire', *ibid.*, p. 224.

9 D. Knowles and R. N. Hadcock, *Medieval Religious Houses. England and Wales* (London, 1953), pp. 252, 257–8 and more; on old people in the great hospital of Paris, the Hôtel Dieu: B. Geremek, *Les Marginaux parisiens aux XIVe et XVe siècles* (Paris, 1976), pp. 196–7.

10 On this kind of external charity: B. Pullan, *Rich and Poor in Renaissance Venice* (Oxford, 1971), pp. 63–5; P. Adam, *La vie paroissiale en France au XIVe siècles* (Paris, 1964), p. 66.

11 Roger Bacon, *Opus majus*, ed. J. Bridges (Frankfurt/Main, 1964), Vol. 2, pp. 2, 251.

12 Reference in Ch. Dyer, *Standards of Living in the Later Middle Ages. Social Change in England c. 1200–1520* (Cambridge, 1989), p. 237.

13 See notes 69 and 84 to Chapter 1 and *Recueil général des anciennes lois françaises depuis l'an 420 jusqu'à la Révolution de 1789*, eds A. J. L. Jourdan, Decrusy, F. A. Isambert (Paris, 1822–1833), Vol. 4, no. 211, pp. 700–3.

14 *Ibid.*, no. 161, pp. 576–7.

15 R. Lespinasse, *Les métiers et corporations de la ville de Paris* (Paris, 1886), p. 2.

16 In this connection, see J. Misraki, 'Criminalité et pauvreté en France á l'époque

de la Guerre de Cent Ans', in *Études sur l'histoire de la pauvreté (Moyen Age – XVIe siècle)*, ed. M. Mollat (Paris, 1974), Vol. 2, pp. 535–46.

17 Ch. de la Roncière, 'Pauvres et pauvreté en Florence au XIVe siècle', *ibid.*, pp. 661–745, chiefly pp. 691–5, 719–20.

18 B. Pullan, *op. cit.*, pp. 197–201; see also M. Rubin, *op. cit.*, pp. 68–74.

19 B. Harvey, *op. cit.*, Chapter 1.

20 Ch. Dyer, *op. cit.*, pp. 252–3.

21 On the decline in bequests to the poor in the region of Lyonnais: M. Th. Lorcin, *Vivre et mourir en Lyonnais à la fin du Moyen-Age* (Paris, 1981), Chapter 5.

22 For example: R. Vaultier, *Le folklore pendant la Guerre de Cent Ans d'après les lettres de rémission du trésor des chartes* (Paris, 1965), p. 42; B. Geremek, *op. cit.*, p. 197.

23 In this connection, see N. Daniel, *Am I My Parents' Keeper? An Essay on Justice Between the Young and the Old* (Oxford, 1988).

BIBLIOGRAPHY

PRIMARY SOURCES

Abelard, Peter. *Historia calamitatum*, ed. J. Monfrin. Paris, 1962.

Acta sanctorum. eds the Bollandist Fathers. Paris, 1863–.

Acts of the Parliament of Scotland. Vol. 1, eds T. Thomson and C. Innes. Edinburgh, 1844.

Adam of Eynsham. *The Life of St Hugh of Lincoln*, 2 vols, eds, trans. D. L. Douie and H. Farmer. London, 1961.

Aegidius Romanus [Giles of Rome]. *De regimine principum*. Rome, 1607.

Aelred of Rievaulx. *Sermones inediti*, ed. C. H. Talbot. Rome, 1952.

—— *Speculum caritatis* in *Opera omnia*, eds A. Hoste and C. H. Talbot in *CCCM* 1. Turnhout, 1971.

Alanus de Insulis [Alan of Lille]. *Summa de arte praedicatoria PL* 210: 111–98.

Alberti, Leon Battista. *I libri della famiglia: The Family in Renaissance Florence*, trans. R. M. Watkins. Columbia, SC, 1969.

Albertus Magnus [Albert the Great]. *De morte et vita* in *Parva naturalia* in *Opera omnia* 9, ed. A. Borgent. Paris, 1890.

—— *De aetate sive de juventute et senectute* in *Parva naturalia* in *Opera omnia* 9, ed. A. Borgent. Paris, 1890.

—— *De resurrectione* in *Opera omnia* 26, ed. W. Kubel. Aschendorff, 1958.

—— *Quaestiones super de animalibus* in *Opera omnia* 12, ed. E. Filthaut. Cologne, 1955.

Aldebrandinus de Sienne. *Le régime du corps*, eds L. Landouzy and R. Pépin. Paris, 1911.

Alfonso el Sabio. *Las siete partidas*, ed. G. Lopez. Salamanca, 1555; reprint Madrid, 1974.

Andreas Capellanus. *On Love*, ed. trans. P. G. Walsh. London, 1982.

Anders Sunesøns. *Latinske parafrase af Skanske Lov*, ed. J. Olrik, vol. 1 in *Danmarks Gamle Landskablove med Kirkelovene*. Copenhagen, 1945.

Angela of Foligno. *Le Livre de l'expérience de vrais fidèles*, eds J. Ferré and L. Baudry. Paris, 1927.

Annales S. Iustinae Patavini, ed. G. H. Pertz in *M.G.H. Script* 19. Hanover, 1886; reprint Stuttgart, 1963, pp. 149–93.

Gli annali Genovesi di Caffaro e di suoi continuatori 4, ed. C. Imperiale. Rome, 1926.

Anthologie poétique française: Moyen Age, ed. A. Mary. Paris, 1967.

Aristotle. *Parva naturalia*, trans. W. S. Hett. The Loeb Classical Library 8. Cambridge Ma., 1986.

—— *Ethica nicomachea* in *The Basic Works of Aristotle*, ed. R. Mckeon. New York, 1968.

—— *Rhetorica* in *The Basic Works of Aristotle*, ed. R. Mckeon. New York, 1968.

Arnaldus de Villanova. *De regimine sanitatis* in *Opera omnia*. Basel, 1585.

—— *The Earliest Printed Book on Wine*, trans. H. E. Sigerist. New York, 1943.

Assises de la haute cour in *Recueil des historiens des Croisades*, vol. 1 ('Lois'), ed. Beugnot. Paris, 1841.

Aucassin et Nicolette: Chantefable du XIIIe siècle, ed. M. Roques. Paris, 1954. English trans. A. Lang. London, 1905.

Audun in *Hrafnukel's Saga and Other Stories*, trans. H. Palson. Harmondsworth, 1983.

Augustine. *Sermo 216 ad competentes, PL* 38: 1076–82.

—— *De diversis quaestionibus 83*, ed. A. Mutzenbecher, *CCSL* 44. Turnhout, 1975.

—— *De civitate dei*, eds B. Dombart and A. Kalb, *CCSL* 48. Turnhout, 1955.

—— *Retractationes*, ed. A. Mutzenbecher, *CCSL* 57. Turnhout, 1984.

Bacon, Roger. *The opus majus*, ed. J. H. Bridges. Frankfurt, 1964.

—— *Opus majus*, trans. R. B. Burke. Philadelphia, 1928.

—— *De retardatione accidentium senectutis cum aliis opusculis de rebus medicinalibus*, eds A. G. Little and E. Withington. Oxford, 1928.

—— *The Cure of Old Age and the Preservation of Youth* (English trans. R. Browne of *De retardatione*). London, 1683.

Bartholomew of Exeter, Bishop and Canonist, ed. Dom A. Morey. Cambridge, 1937.

Bartholomaeus Anglicus. *Liber de proprietatibus rerum*. Strasbourg, 1505.

—— *On the Properties of Things: John Trevisa's Translation of Bartholomaeus Anglicus' De proprietatibus rerum*, ed. M. C. Seymour. Oxford, 1975.

Bellemere, Gilles. *Les XV joies de mariage*, ed. J. Rychner. Paris, 1963.

Bernard of Clairvaux. *De diligendo deo, PL* 182: 973–99.

—— *De ordine vitae et morum institutione, PL* 184: 561–83.

—— *De modo bene vivendi, PL* 184: 1199–306.

—— *Ad abbatem Guarinum alpensem*, Epist. 254, *PL* 182: 459–62.

—— *De moribus et officio episcoporum*. Epist. 42, *PL* 182: 810–34.

—— *Ad Arnaldum carnotensem abbatem*. Epist. 310, *PL* 182: 514.

Bernard de Gordon. *De conservatione vitae humanae seu de regimine sanitatis*. Leipzig, 1570.

Bernardino de Sienne. *De calamitatibus et miseriis vitae humanae et maxime senectutis*. Ser. 16 in *Opera omnia* 7: 243–62, eds the Fathers of the Collegium S. Bonaventurae. Florence, 1959.

—— *De honore parentum*. Ser. 17 in *Opera omnia* 3: 306–18, eds the Fathers of the Collegium S. Bonaventurae. Florence, 1956.

Berthold of Regensburg [Ratisbon] *Vollständige Ausgabe seiner Predigten*, 2 vols, ed. F. Pfeiffer. Vienna, 1880.

Berthorius, Petrus [Pierre Bersuire]. *Dictionarium* in *Opera omnia* 3. Cologne, 1730.

Bertran de Born. *Définition de la jeunesse et de la vieillesse* in *Anthologie des troubadours*, ed. trans. J. Anglade. Paris, 1927, pp. 60–2.

Boehmer, H. ed. *Analekten zur Geschichte des Franciscus von Assisi*. Tübingen, 1904.

The Book of Saint Gilbert, eds, trans. R. Foreville and G. Keir. Oxford, 1987.

The Book of Vices and Virtues: A Fourteenth-Century Translation of the 'Somme de roi' of Lorens d'Orleans, ed. W. Francis. London, 1942.

Brinton, Thomas. *The Sermons of Thomas Brinton Bishop of Rochester 1373–1389*, 2 vols, ed. M. A. Devlin, London, 1954.

Bromyard, John. *Summa praedicantium*, 2 vols. Antwerpen, 1614.

Calendar of Charters and Documents Relating to Selborne and Its Priory, ed. D. Macray. Hampshire Records Society 1, 1891.

Calendar of Coroners Rolls of the City of London 1300–1378, ed. R. R. Sharpe. London, 1913.

Calendar of Letter-Books of the City of London, book H (c. AD 1375–1399), ed. R. R. Sharpe. London, 1907.

Calendar of Letter-Books of the City of London, book I (c. AD 1400–1422), ed. R. R. Sharpe. London, 1909.

Calendar of Letter-Books of the City of London, book K, ed. R. R. Sharpe. London, 1911.

Calendar of Pleas and Memoranda Rolls Preserved among the Archives of the City of London at the Guildhall 1364–1381, ed. A. Thomas. Cambridge, 1929.

Calendar of Wills Proved and Enrolled in the Court of Husting London 1258–1688, 2 vols, ed. R. R. Sharpe. London, 1889.

Cambridge Guild Records, ed. M. Bateson. Cambridge, 1903.

Carmen ad Robertum regem, ed. trans. C. Carozzi. Paris, 1979.

La chanson de Guillaume, ed. D. McMillan. Paris, 1949.

Chaucer, Geoffrey. *The Canterbury Tales*, ed. W. W. Skeat. London, 1947.

Chobham, Thomas. *Summa confessorum*, ed. F. Broomfield. Louvain, 1968.

Cicero, Marcus Tulius. *De senectute*, trans. W. A. Falconer. The Loeb Classical Library 20. Cambridge Ma., 1971.

Les constitutions de la France depuis 1789, ed. J. Godechot. Paris, 1970.

Cornaro, Alvise. *Discorsi intorno alla vita sobria*, ed. P. Pancrazzi. Florence, 1946.

Corpus iuris canonici, 2 vols, ed. Ae. Friedberg. Leipzig, 1879.

Councils and Synods with Other Documents relating to the English Church, eds F. M. Powicke and C. R. Cheney. Oxford, 1964.

The Court Baron together with Select Pleas from the Bishop of Ely's Court of Littleport, eds F. W. Maitland and W. P. Baildon. London, 1891.

Court Rolls of the Manor of Hales 1272–1307, ed. J. A. Amphlett. Oxford, 1910.

Coutumiers de Normandie, 2 vols, ed. E. J. Tardif. Rouen, 1881; reprint Geneva, 1977.

Custumals and Bye-Laws (1386–1526) of the Manor of Islip, ed. B. F. Harvey. Oxford, 1959.

Custumals of the Sussex Manors of the Archbishop of Canterbury, eds B. C. Redwood and A. E. Wilson. Sussex Records Society 57. 1958.

Daniel, Walter. *Vita Ailredi cum epistula ad Mauricium*, ed. trans. F. M. Powicke. Edinburgh, 1950.

Dante Alighieri. *Convivio* in *Le opere di Dante*, ed. M. Barbi. Florence, 1921.

—— *Divina Commedia*, ed. trans. Ch. S. Singleton. Princeton, 1982.

Datini, Francesco. *Comptes du sel (Libro di ragione et conto di salle de Francesco di Marco Datini) pour sa compagnie d'Avignon*, ed. Ch. Villain-Gandossi. Collection de Documents inédites sur l'histoire de France 7, Ser. 8. Paris, 1969.

Dechamps, Eustache. *Oeuvres complètes*, 11 vols, ed. le Marquis de Queux de Saint-Hiliare. Paris, 1878–1903.

Deguileville, Guillaume de. *Le pèlerinage de la vie humaine*, ed. J. J. Stürzinger. London, 1893.

Dives and Pauper, 2 vols, ed. P. Barnum. Oxford, 1980.

Dobson, R. B., ed. trans. *The Peasant Revolt of 1381*. London, 1970.

Documents relatifs à la draperie de Valenciennes au Moyen Age, ed. G. Espinas. Lille, 1931.

Documents relatifs à l'histoire de l'industrie et du commerce en France, 2 vols, ed. M. G. Fagniez. Paris, 1898.

Documents Relating to Cambridgeshire Villages, eds W. M. Palmer and H. W. Saunders. Cambridge, 1926.

Les douze mois figurez, ed. J. Morawski. *Archivum Romanicum* 10 (1926), 351–62.

Le droit coutoumier de Cambrai, ed. E. M. Meijers. Haarlem, 1952.

Durham Halmote Rolls: Halmota prioratus dunelmensis 1296–1384, eds W. H. D. Longstaffe and J. Booth. Durham, 1886.

Eadmer. *The Life of St Anselm Archbishop of Canterbury*, ed. trans. R. W. Southern. London, 1962.

Eckermann, J. P. *Conversations with Goethe*, trans. J. Oxenford. London, 1930; reprint 1971.

Eckhart, Meister. *Sermones in Die deutschen und lateinischen Werke* 4, eds E. Benz, B. Decker and J. Koch. Stuttgart, 1956.

Egil's Saga, trans. G. Jones. New York, 1960.

Engelbert of Admont. *Liber de causis longevitatis hominum ante diluvium* in *Thesaurus anecdotarum novissimus*, ed. J. Pertz. Augsburg, 1721, 1: 439–502.

English Gilds, ed. T. Smith. London, 1870.

English Historical Documents 3 (1189–1327), ed. trans. H. Rothwell. London, 1975.

Euripides. *Alcestis* in *Euripides: Verse Translations*, trans. A. S. Way. The Loeb Classical Library 4. Cambridge Ma., 1964.

Frederick II. *Die Konstitutionen Friedrichs II von Hohenstaufen für sein Konigreich Sizilien*, eds T. von der Lieck-Buyken and W. Wagner. Vienna, 1973.

The Fifty Earliest English Wills in the Court Probate of London, ed. F. J. Furnivall. London, 1882.

Fortescue, John. *The Governance of England*, ed. Ch. Plummer. Oxford, 1885.

Fourier, Ch. *Le nouveau monde amoureux* in *Oeuvres complètes* 7, ed. S. Debout Oleszkiewicz. Paris, 1967.

Froissart, Jean. *Le joli buisson de jonece*, ed. A. Fourrier. Geneva, 1975.

Gerson, Jean. *A un vieillard* in *Oeuvres complètes* 2, ed. Mgr Glorieux. Paris, 1960.

—— *Les dix commandemens de la loy* in *Oeuvres complètes* 7, ed. Mgr Glorieux. Paris, 1966.

Gertrude, St. *Le Héraut de l'amour divin: Revelations de sainte Gertrude*, trans. The Benedictine Fathers of Solesmes. Paris, 1898.

The Early English Versions of the Gesta romanorum, ed. S. J. Herrtage. London, 1879.

The Gild of St Mary Lichfield, ed. F. J. Furnivall. London, 1920.

Gilles Li Muisis. *Poèsies*, 2 vols, ed. M. Kervyn de Lettenhove. Louvain, 1882.

Giraldus Cambrensis [Gerald of Wales]. *Gemma ecclesiastica*, ed. by J. Brewer. Rolls Series 21. London, 1862.

—— *Speculum duorum*, eds Y. Lefèvre and R. B. C. Huygens, trans. B. Dawson. Cardiff, 1974.

Glanville. *Tractatus de legibus et consuetudinibus regni Angliae qui Glanvilla vocatur*, ed. trans. G. D. G. Hall. London, 1965.

Godman, P. S. ed. 'Rolls of the Manor of Wiston', *Sussex Archeological Collections* 54 (1911), 130–82.

Guigues de Châtel. *Consuetudines, PL* 153: 631–759.

—— *Epistula seu tractatus ad patres Monte Dei, PL*. 184: 307–64.

Guillaume de Lorris and Jean de Meun. *Le Roman de la Rose*, ed. F. Lecoy. Paris, 1968.

—— *The Romance of the Rose*. trans. H. W. Robbins. New York, 1962.

Henryson, Robert. *The Poems*, ed. D. Fox. Oxford, 1981.

Hildegard of Bingen. *Scivias sive visionum ac revelationum*, PL 197: 383–738.

—— *Liber divinorum operum simplicis hominis*, PL 197: 742–1038.

—— *Causae et curae*, ed. P. Kaiser. Leipzig, 1903.

The History of King Boccus and Sydracke, trans. H. Caumpeden. London, 1530.

Honorius Augustodunensis [Honorius of Autun]. *Gemma animae*, PL 172: 542–738.

—— (falsely attributed; written by William of Conches). *De philosophia mundi libri quattuor*, PL 172: 39–102.

Hrafnkel's Saga and Other Stories, trans. H. Palsson. Harmondsworth, 1983.

Hrosvit. *Abraham* in *Hrosvitae opera*, ed. K. Strecker. Leipzig, 1906, pp. 162–78.

Humbert de Romans. *Sermones*. Venice, 1603.

Innocent III. *Lotharii cardinalis (Innocenti III) De miseria humanae conditionis*, ed. M. Maccarrone. Lugano, 1955.

Jacobus de Voragine. *The Golden Legend*, trans. G. Ryan and H. Ripperger. New York, 1948.

Jocelin of Brakelond. *The Chronicle of Jocelin of Brakelond*, ed. trans. H. E. Butler. London, 1949.

John of Salisbury. *Policraticus*, 2 vols, ed. C. C. J. Webb. Oxford, 1909; reprint Frankfurt, 1965.

Joinville, Jeab Sire de. *Histoire de S. Louis. Credo et lettre à Louis X*, ed. trans. M. Natalis de Wailly. Paris, 1874.

Kempe, Margery. *The Book of Margery Kempe*, eds S. B. Meech and H. E. Allen. London, 1940.

Kitchin, W. G. ed. *The Manor of Manydown*. Hampshire Records Society, 1895.

Konrad von Megenberg. *Ökonomik*, ed. S. Krüger in *Staatsschriften des späteren Mittelalters* 3 MGH, Stuttgart, 1973.

Lanfranc. *The Monastic Constitutions of Lanfranc*, ed. trans. D. Knowles. London, 1951.

Langland, William. *Piers Plowman*, ed. A. V. C. Schmidt. London, 1978.

Latini, Brunetto. *Li livres dou tresor*, ed. F. J. Carmody. Berkeley, 1948.

Laws of Early Iceland: Gragas 1, eds P. Foote and R. Perkins. Winnipeg, 1980.

Leges Henrici primi, ed. trans. L. J. Downer. Oxford, 1972.

Leges Visigothorum. MGH Leges. 1.1, ed. K. Zeumer. Hanover, 1902.

Les Baiuwariorum. MGH Leges 5.2, ed. E. M. von Schwind. Hanover, 1926.

Liber exemplorum ad usum praedicantium, ed. A. G. Little. Aberdeen, 1908.

The Life of King Edward Who Rests at Westminster Attributed to a Monk of St Bertin, ed. trans. F. Barlow. London, 1962.

Le livre des proverbes français, 2 vols, ed. M. Le Roux de Lincy. Paris, 1859.

Le livre Roisin: Coutumier lillois de la fin du XIIIe siècle, ed. R. Monier. Lille, 1932.

Li livres de jostice et de plet, ed L. N. Rapetti. Paris, 1850.

Lollard Sermons, ed. G. Cigman. London, 1989.

Maimonides, Moses. *Mishne Torah* [Hebrew].

—— *Pirke Moshe bi-refuah* [Hebrew], trans. R. Nathan Hameati. Jerusalem, 1970.

Mandeville's Travels, ed. P. Hamelius. London, 1911.

Mannyng Brunne, Robert. *Handlyng Synne*, ed F. J. Furnivall. London, 1901.

Mansi, J. D. *Sacrorum conciliorum nova et amplissima collectio*. Florence and Venice, 1759–1798; reprint Graz, 1960.

Marsan, R. E. ed. *Itinéraire espagnol du conte médiéval VIIIe-XVe siècles*. Paris, 1974.

Memorials of London and London Life, ed. H. T. Riley. London, 1868.

Le ménagier de Paris, 2 vols, ed. J. Pichon. Paris, 1846.

Michelangelo Buonarotti. *The Letters of Michelangelo*, 2 vols, ed. trans. E. H. Ramsden. Stanford, 1963.

More, Thomas. *Utopia*, ed. trans. R. M. Adams. New York, 1975.

Morris, R., ed. *Legends of the Holy Rood*. London, 1871.

Myrc, John. *Instructions for Parish Priests*, ed. E. Peacock. London, 1868.

Njal Saga, trans. M. Magnusson. Harmondsworth, 1960.

North Country Wills being Abstracts of Wills Relating to the Counties of York, Nottingham, Northumberland and Cumberland 1383–1558, ed. J. W. Clay. Surtees Society 115. London, 1908.

Orderic Vitalis. *The Ecclesiastical History of Orderic Vitalis*, 6 vols, ed. trans. M. Chinball. Oxford, 1978.

Ordonnances des rois de France 9, ed. M. Secousse. Paris, 1755.

Paris, Matthew. *Chronica majora*, ed. H. R. Luard. Rolls Series 25 (57). London, 1877.

Peter the Venerable. *The Letters of Peter the Venerable*, 2 vols, ed. G. Constable. Cambridge Ma., 1967.

Petrarca, Francesco. *Canzoniere, Trionfi, rime varie, e una scelta di versi latini*, eds C. Muscetta and D. Ponchiroli. Turin, 1958.

—— *The Triumphs of Petrarch*, trans. E. H. Wilkins. Chicago, 1962.

—— *De remediis utriusque fortune*. Rotterdam, 1649.

—— *Phisick against Fortune*, trans. Thomas Twyne. London, 1579.

—— *Secretum* in *Prose*, ed. G. Martelloti. Milan, 1955.

Petrus Lombardus [Peter Lombard]. *Sententiae in IV libris distinctae*, eds the Fathers of Collegium S. Bonaventurae ad Claras Aquas. Rome, 1981.

Philippe de Beaumanoir. *Coutumes de Clermont en Beauvaisis*, 2 vols, ed. A. Salmon. Paris, 1970.

Philippe de Commynes. *Mémoires*, 2 vols, ed. J. Calmette. Paris, 1965.

Philippe de Navarre. *Les quatre ages de l'homme*, ed. M. de Fréville. Paris, 1888.

Philippe de Thaün. *Le bestiaire*, ed. E. Walberg. Geneva, 1970.

Plato. *The Republic*, trans. R. Waterfield. Oxford, 1994.

Le procès de canonisation de S. Claire (j'ai connu madame S. Claire), ed. trans. S. E. Garrone. Toulouse, 1961.

The Prose Salernitan Questions, ed. B. Lawn. Oxford, 1979.

Proverbes français antérieurs au XVe siècle, ed. J. Morawski. Paris, 1925.

La queste del Saint Graal, ed. A. Pauphilet. Paris, 1923.

Records of the Borough of Leicester, ed. M. Bateson. London, 1899.

Recueil de documents relatif à l'histoire du droit municipal en France des origines a la révolution, 3 vols, ed. G. Espinas. Paris, 1943.

Recueil général des anciennes lois françaises depuis l'an 420 jusqu' a la révolution de 1789, eds A. J. L. Jourdan, Decrusy, and F. A. Isambert. Paris, 1822–33.

Recueil général et complet des fabliaux des XIIe et XIVe siècles, eds A. Montaiglon and G. Raynaud. Paris, 1872.

Registre de l'inquisition de Jacques Fournier évêque de Palmiers 1318–1325, 3 vols, ed. J. Duvernoy. Toulouse, 1965.

La règle de Saint Benoit, 6 vols, eds, trans. J. Neufville and A. Vogüé. Paris, 1972.

Le règle du Temple, ed. H. de Curzon. Paris, 1886.

Règlements sur les arts et métiers de Paris rédiges au XIIIe siècle et connus sous le nom du Livre des métiers d'Etienne Boileau, ed. G. B. Depping. Paris, 1837.

Regulae communis Ianuae anno 1363 in *Historia patriae monumenta*, eds C. Desimondi, A. L. Belgrano and V. Poggi. Turin, 1901.

Reliquiae antiquae, 2 vols, eds T. Wright and J. O. Halliwell. London, 1841.

Robert of Gloucester. *The Metrical Chronical*, ed. W. A. Wright. Rolls Series 86.1 London, 1887.

Rufinus, *Summa decretorum de Magister Rufinus*, ed. H. Singer. Aalen, 1963.

Russell, John. *The Boke of Nurture*, ed. F. J. Furnivall. London, 1867.

The Scrope and Grosvenor Controversy 1385–1390, ed. N. Harris Nicolas. London, 1832.

Secreta seretorum: Three Prose Versions of the Secreta secretorum, ed. R. Steele. London, 1899.

Select Cases from the Coroners' Rolls 1265–1413, ed. Ch. Gross. London, 1896.

Select Pleas in Manorial and Other Seignorial Courts, ed. F. W. Maitland. London, 1889.

Statuta capitulorum generalium ordinis cisterciensis, ed. J. Canivez. Louvain, 1933.

The Statutes of the Realm, eds A. Luders, T. E. Tomlins and J. Raithby. London, 1810–28; repint 1963.

Les statuts synodaux français du XIIIe siècle, 2 vols, ed. O. Pontal. Paris, 1971.

Les statuts synodaux de Jean de Flandre évêque de Liège, ed. E. Schoolmasters. Liège, 1938.

Testamenta eboracensia or Wills Registered at York, ed J. Rain. Surtees Society 4.2. London, 1836.

Thirteen Custumals of the Sussex Manors of the Bishop of Chichester, ed. W. D. Packham. Sussex Records Society 31. Sussex, 1925.

Thomas Aquinas. *Summa theologiae*, trans. The Fathers of Blackfriars. London, 1974.

—— *Super epistolas Pauli lectura*, ed. R. Raphaelis. Rome, 1953.

Thomas of Cantimpré. *Liber de natura rerum*, ed. H. Boese. Berlin, 1973.

La très ancienne coutume de Bretagne, ed. M. Planiol. Rennes, 1896.

Tubach, F. C. ed. *Index exemplorum: A Handbook of Medieval Religious Tales*. Helsinki, 1981.

Two Memoires of Renaissance Florence: The Diaries of Buonaccorso Pitti and Gregoria Dati, ed. J. Brucker, trans. J. Martinez. London, 1967.

Ulrich, J. ed. *'La riote du monde'*, Zeitschrift für romanische Philologie 8 (1884), 283–87.

Usatges de Barcelona el codi a mitjan segle XII, ed. J. Bastardas. Barcelona, 1984.

Villani, Giovanni. *Chronica*, ed. F. G. Dragomanni. Florence, 1845; reprint Frankfurt, 1969.

Villehardouin, Geoffroi. *La conquête de Constantinopole*, ed. E. Faral. Paris, 1961.

Vincent de Beauvais. *Bibliotheca mundi seu speculum quadruplex: naturale, doctrinale, morale, historiale*. Douai, 1624.

Visitations of Religious Houses in the Diocese of Lincoln 1420–1449, 3 vols, ed. A. Hamilton Thompson. Horncastle, 1914–1929.

Walafrid Strabo. *Golssa ordinaria*, PL 113.

William of St Thierry et al. *Sancta Bernardi vita et gesta*, PL 185: 226–368.

Zerbi, Gabriele. *Gerontocomia* in *On the Care of the Aged and Maximianus' Elegies on Old Age and Love*, trans. L. R. Lind. Philadelphia, 1988.

SECONDARY SOURCES

Adam, P. *La vie paroissiale en France au XIVe siècle*. Paris, 1964.

Almagor, M. 'Charisma Fatigue in an East-African Generation Set System', *American Ethnologist* 10.4 (1983), 635–49.

Améry, J. *Du vieillissement. Révolte et résignation*, trans. A. Yaiche. Paris, 1991.

Amos, P. and S. Harrel (eds) *Other Ways of Growing Old: Anthropological Perspectives*. Stanford, 1981.

Amundsen, D. W. and C. J. Diers, 'The Age of Menarche in Medieval Europe', *Human Biology* 45 (1973), 363–9.

Arbel, B. and G. Veinstein. 'La fiscalité vénéto-chypriote au miroir de la législation ottomane: Le qānûnnâme de 1572', *Turcica* 18 (1986), 7–51.

Archer, R. E. 'Rich Old Ladies: The Problem of Late Medieval Dowagers' in *Property and Politics: Essays in Later Medieval English History*, ed. T. Polard. Gloucester, 1984, 15–35.

Ariès, Ph. *L'homme devant la mort*. Paris, 1977.

——'Une histoire de la vieillesse?' an interview, *Communications* 37 (1983), 47–54.

Assoun, P. L. 'Le vieillissement saisi par la psychoanalyse', *Communications* 37 (1983), 167–79.

Ault, W. O. *Open-Field Husbandry and the Village Community*. Transactions of the American Philosophical Society, NS. 55.7. Philadelphia, 1965.

d'Avout, J. *Le Meurtre d'Étienne Marcel*. Paris, 1960.

Barber, M. 'Supplying the Crusader States: The Role of the Templars' in *The Horns of Hattin*, ed. B. Z. Kedar. Jerusalem, 1992, pp. 314–26.

Barkai, R. *Les infortunes de Dinah ou la gynécologie juive au Moyen Age*. Paris, 1991.

Barnett, R. and G. Baruch. 'Women in the Middle Years: Conceptions and Misconceptions' in *Psychology of Women: Selected Readings*, ed. J. H. Williams. New York, 1979, pp. 479–87.

Barthélemy, D. 'Kinship' in *Revelations of the Medieval World*, vol. 2 of *History of Private Life*, eds Ph. Ariès and G. Duby, trans. A. Goldhammer. Cambridge Ma., 1988, pp. 85–155.

Bartlett, R. *Trial by Fire and Water: The Medieval Judicial Ordeal*. Oxford, 1988.

Baxter, T. W. and M. Almagor, eds *Age, Generation, and Time: Some Features of East-African Organisations*. London, 1978.

Beauvoir de, S. *La vieillesse*. 2 vols. Paris, 1979.

Beer, F. *Women and Mystical Experience in the Middle Ages*. Woodbridge, 1992.

Beitscher, J. K. 'The Aged in Medieval Limousin' in *Proceedings of the Fourth Annual Meeting of the Western Society for French History, 11–13 November*, ed. J. D. Falk. Santa Barbara Ca., 1977, pp. 45–52.

—— 'As the Twig Bent . . . Children and Their Parents in an Aristocratic Society', *Journal of Medieval History* 2 (1976), 181–91.

Benoit-Lapierre, N. 'Guérir de vieillesse', *Communications* 37 (1983), 149–65.

Benveniste, H. 'Les enlèvements: stratégies matrimoniales, discours juridique, et discours politique en France à la fin du Moyen Age', *Revue Historique* 283 (1990), 13–35.

Bever, E. 'Old Age and Witchcraft in Early Modern Europe' in *Old Age in Preindustrial Society*, ed. P. N. Stearns. London, 1982, pp. 150–90.

Biraben, J. N. *Les hommes et la peste en France et dans le pays européens et méditerranéens*, 2 vols. Paris, 1975–76.

Boureau, A. *Le simple corps du roi*. Paris, 1988.

Bourin, M. and R. Durand. *Vivre au village au Moyen Age*. Paris, 1984.

Boutrouche, R. J. *Seigneurie et féodalité*, 2 vols. Paris, 1970.

Brett, E. *Humbert de Romans: His Life and Views of Thirteenth-Century Society*. Toronto, 1984.

Brown, H. F. *Studies in the History of Venice*. London, 1907.

Bullough, V. and C. Campbell. 'Female Longevity and Diet in the Middle Ages', *Speculum* 55 (1980), 317–25.

Burrow, J. A. *The Ages of Man*. Oxford, 1986.

Bynum, C. Walker. *Holy Fast and Holy Feast: The Religious Significance of Food to Medieval Women*. Berkeley, 1987.

——'The Female Body and Religious Practice in the Later Middle Ages' in *Fragmentation and Redemption: Essays on Gender and the Human Body in Medieval Religion*. New York, 1991, pp. 181–238.

——'Material Continuity, Personal Survival, and the Resurrection of the Body: A Scholastic Discussion in Its Modern Contexts' in *Fragmentation and Redemption: Essays on Gender and the Human Body in Medieval Religion*. New York, 1991, pp. 239–97.

——'The Body of Christ in the Later Middle Ages: A Reply to Leo Steinberg' in *Fragmentation and Redemption: Essays on Gender and the Human Body in Medieval Religion*. New York, 1991, pp. 79–117.

Cam, H. M. 'An East Anglian Shire-Moot of Stephen's Reign 1148–1153', *English Historical Review* 39 (1924), 569–71.

Campbell, B. M. 'Population Pressure, Inheritance and Land Market in a Fourteenth-Century Peasant Community' in *Land, Kinship, and Life-Cycle*, ed. R. M. Smith. Cambridge, 1984, pp. 87–134.

Carlin, M. L. 'Quelques aspects de la vie religieuse à Nice d'après les testaments (XIVe-XVe siècles)' in *Recueil de mémoires et de travaux d'histoire du droit et des institutions des anciens pays de droit écrit: Mélanges Roger Aubenas* 9 (1974), 121–42.

Carmichael, A. G. *Plague and the Poor in Renaissance Florence*. Cambridge, 1986.

Carruthers, M. *The Books of Memory: A Study of Memory in Medieval Culture*. Cambridge, 1993.

Cecchini, G. 'Raniero Fasani et les Flagellants', *Mélanges de l'École française de Rome. Moyen Age-Temps Modern* 87 (1975), 339–52.

Chinball, M. *The World of Orderic Vitalis*. Oxford, 1984.

Clanchy, M. T. *From Memory to Written Record: England 1066–1307*. London, 1979.

Clark, E. 'The Quest for Security in Medieval England' in *Aging and the Aged in Medieval Europe*, ed. M. M. Sheehan. Toronto, 1990, pp. 189–200.

——'Social Welfare and Mutual Aid in the Medieval Countryside', *Journal of British Studies* 33 (1994), 381–406.

——'Charitable Bequests, Death-bed Land Sales, and the Manor Court in Later Medieval England' in *Medieval Village and Small Town Society: Views from Manorial and Other Seigneurial Courts*, ed. Z. Razi and R. M. Smith. Oxford, 1995.

Clark, J. M. *The Dance of Death in the Middle Ages and the Renaissance*. Glasgow, 1950.

Coad, J. G. *Denny Abbey*. London, 1989.

Coffman, G. R. 'Old Age from Horace to Chaucer: Some Literary Affinities and Adventures of an Idea', *Speculum* 9 (1934), 249–77.

Cohen, E. and E. Horowitz. 'In Search of the Sacred: Jews, Christians, and Rituals of Marriage in the Later Middle Ages', *The Journal of Medieval and Renaissance Studies* 20 (1990), 225–49.

Cohn, S. K., Jr. *Death and Property in Siena 1205–1800: Strategies for the Afterlife*. Baltimore, 1988.

Cole, T. R. *The Journey of Life: A Cultural History of Aging in America*. Cambridge, 1992.

Coleman, J. C. and W. E. Broen. *Abnormal Psychology and Modern Life*. Glenview Ill., 1972.

Contamine, Ph. *Guerre, état et société à la fin du Moyen Age: Études sur les armées des rois de France 1337–1494.* Paris, 1972.

Curtius, E. R. *European Literature and the Latin Middle Ages*, trans. W. R. Trask. New York, 1963.

Daniel, N. *Am I My Parents' Keeper?: An Essay on Justice between the Young and the Old.* Oxford, 1988.

Delumeau, J. P. *La peur en Occident XIVe–XVIIIe siècles.* Paris, 1978.

——'La mémoire des gens d'Arezzo et de Sienne à travers des dépositions de temoins' in *Temps, mémoire, tradition au Moyen Age.* Actes du XIIIe Congrès de la Société des Historiens Médiévistes de l'Enseignement Superieur Public. Université de Provence. Aix-en-Provence, 1983. pp. 45–67.

——*Rassurer et protéger: Le sentiment de securité dans l'Occident d'autrefois.* Paris, 1989.

Demaitre, L. 'The Care and Extension of Old Age in Medieval Medicine' in *Aging and the Aged in Medieval Europe*, ed. M. M. Sheehan. Toronto, 1990. pp. 3–22.

——*Doctor Bernard de Gordon, Professor and Practitioner.* Toronto, 1980.

Desportes, P. 'La population de Reims au XVe siècle d'après un dénombrement de 1422', *Le Moyen Age* 72 (1966), 463–509.

Douie, D. L. *Archbishop Geoffrey Plantagenet and the Chapter of York.* York, 1960.

Dove, M. *The Perfect Age of Man's Life.* Cambridge, 1986.

Duby, G. *Guillaume le Maréchal ou le meilleur chevalier du monde.* Paris, 1984.

——'The Aristocratic Households of Feudal France' in *Revelations of the Medieval World*, vol. 2 of *History of Private Life*, eds Ph. Ariès and G. Duby, trans. A. Goldhammer. Cambridge Ma., 1988. pp. 35–85.

Duff, N. *Matilda of Tuscany.* London, 1909.

Dyer, Ch. *Standards of Living in the Later Middle Ages: Social Change in England c. 1200–1520.* Cambridge, 1989.

Elgazi, G. 'Lords Ask, Peasants Answer: Making Traditions in Late Medieval Village Assemblies' in *History and Histories*, eds G. Sider and G. Smith. Forthcoming.

Eliav-Feldon, M. *Realistic Utopias: The Ideal Imaginary Societies of the Renaissance.* Oxford, 1982.

Epstein, S. *Wills and Wealth in Medieval Genova 1150–1250.* Cambridge Ma., 1984.

Erikson, E. 'Eight Stages of Man' in *Childhood and Society.* New York, 1963, pp. 247–73.

Evans, R. I. *Dialogues with Erik Erikson.* New York, 1967.

Farmer, D. H. *The Oxford Dictionary of Saints.* Oxford, 1987.

Finlay, R. 'The Venetian Republic as a Gerontocracy: Age and Politics in the Renaissance', *The Journal of Medieval and Renaissance Studies* 8 (1978), 157–78.

Finley, M. I. 'Les personnes âgées dans l'antiquité classique', *Communications* 37 (1983), 31–45.

Folts, J. D. 'Senescence and Renascence: Petrarch's Thought on Growing Old', *The Journal of Medieval and Renaissance Studies* (1980) 207–37.

Fontes, J. T. 'El ordenamiento de precios y salarios de Pedro I al reino de Murcia', *Annuario de historia del derecho espanol* 31 (1961), 281–92.

Forbes, T. R. 'A Jury of Matrons', *Medical History* 32 (1988), 23–33.

Fossier, R. *La terre et les hommes en Picardie jusqu'à la fin du XIIIe siècle*, 2 vols. Paris, 1968.

Frugoni, Ch. 'L'iconographie de la femme au cours des XIe–XIIe siècles', *Cahiers de civilization médiévale Xe–XIIe siècles* 20 (1977), 177–88.

Fügedi, E. 'Verba Volant: Oral Culture and Literacy among the Medieval Hungarian

Nobility' in *Kings, Bishops, Nobles, and Burghers in Medieval Hungary*, ed. J. Bak. London, 1986, 1–25.

Ganshof, F. L. 'La Flandre' in *Histoire des institutions françaises au Moyen Age*, 5 vols, eds F. Lot and R. Fawtier. Paris, 1957, 1: 343–426.

Gavazzi, M. 'The Tradition of Killing Old People: Prolegomena to a Revised Methodological Treatment of the Subject' in *Folklore Today: A Festschrift for Richard M. Dorson*, ed. L. Degh. Bloomington, Ind., 1976, 175–80.

Geremek, B. *Les marginaux parisiens au XIVe et XVe siècles*. Paris, 1976.

Ghellinck de, J. 'Juventus, gravitas, senectus' in *Studia medievalia in hon. R. J. Martin*. Bruge, 1948, pp. 39–59.

Gilbert, C. 'When Did a Man in the Renaissance Grow Old?', *Studies in the Renaissance* 14 (1967), 7–32.

Gilliat-Smith, E. *St Clare of Assisi*. London, 1914.

Girard, A. and L. Henry. 'Les attitudes et la conjoncture démographique: Natalité, structure familiale, et limites de la vie active', *Population* 11 (1956), 137–41.

Given, J. B. *Society and Homicide in Thirteenth-Century England*. Stanford, 1977.

Gonon, M. *Les institutions et la société en France au XIVe siècle d'après les testaments*. Paris, 1960.

Graebner, W. *A History of Retirement: The Meaning and Function of an American Institution*. London, 1980.

Green, M. 'Women's Medical Practice and Health-Care in Medieval Europe', *Signs* 14 (1989), 434–73.

Griffin, J. 'A Cross-Cultural Investigation of Behavioral Changes at Menopause' in *Psychology of Women: Selected Readings*, ed. J. H. Williams. New York, 1979, pp. 488–95.

Groebner, V. 'Black Money and the Language of Things: Observations on the Economy of the Labouring Poor in Fifteenth-Century Nuremberg' in *Tel Aviver Jahrbuch für deutsche Geschichte* 22 (1993), 275–91.

Groves, D. 'Women and Financial Provision for Old Age' in *Women's Issues in Social Policy*, ed. M. McLean and D. Groves. London, 1991.

Gruman, G. J. *A History of Ideas about the Prolongation of Life*. Transactions of the American Philosophical Society, ns. 56.9. Philadelphia, 1966.

Gruner, O. C. *A Treatise on the Canon of Medicine of Avicenna incorporating a Translation of the First Book*. London 1930.

Guyon, G. D. 'La Procédure du duel judiciare dans l'ancien droit coutumiers bordelais', *Recueil de mémoires et de travaux d'histoire du droit et des institutions des anciens pays de droit écrit. Mélanges Roger Aubenas* 9 (1974), 385–409.

Hajnal, J. 'Two Kinds of Preindustrial Household Formation System', *Population and Development Review* 8 (1982), 449–94.

Hale, J. R. and M. Mallet. *The Military Organization of a Renaissance State: Venice 1400–1617*. Cambridge, 1984.

Hamilton, G. V. 'Changes in Personality and Psychosexual Phenomena with Age' in *Problems of Aging*, ed. E. V. Cowdry. Baltimore, 1942, 810–31.

Hanawalt, B. *Crime and Conflict in English Communities 1300–1348*. Cambridge Ma., 1979.

——*The Ties that Bound: Peasant Families in Medieval England*. Oxford, 1986.

——'Seeking the Flesh and Blood of Manorial Families', *Journal of Medieval History* 14 (1988), 33–45.

Harper, R. I. 'A Note on Corrodies in the Fourteenth Century', *Albion* 15 (1983), 95–101.

Harvey, B. *Living and Dying in England 110–1540: The Monastic Experience*. Oxford, 1995.

Hatcher, J. 'Mortality in the Fifteenth Century: Some New Evidence', *The Economic History Review*, 2nd Series 39 (1986), 19–38.

Heers, J. *Le Clan familial au Moyen Age: Étude sur les structures politiques et sociales des milieux urbains*. Paris, 1974.

——*Esclaves et domestiques au Moyen Age dans le monde méditerranéen*. Paris, 1981.

Hélin, E. 'Size of Households before the Industrial Revolution: The Case of Liège in 1801' in *Households and Family in Past Time*, eds P. Laslett and R. Wall. Cambridge, 1972, pp. 319–34.

Henry, L. 'La mortalité d'après les inscriptions funéraires', *Population* 12 (1957), 149–52.

——'L'âge du décès d'après les inscriptions funéraires', *Population* 14 (1959), 327–9.

Héritier-Augé, F. 'Older Women, Stout-Hearted Women, Women of Substance' in *Fragments for a History of the Body*, 3 vols, ed. M. F. Feher. New York, 1989, 3: 281–99.

Herlihy, D. *Medieval and Renaissance Pistoia: The Social History of an Italian Town 1200–1430*. New Haven, 1967.

——'Vieillir à Florence au Quattrocento', *Annales E. S. C.* 24 (1969), 1350–51.

——'The Generation in Medieval History', *Viator* 5 (1974), 347–64.

——'Life Expectations for Women in Medieval Society' in *The Role of Women in the Middle Ages* ed. R. T. Morewedge. London, 1975, pp. 1–22.

——*Medieval Households*. Cambridge Ma., 1985.

——'Age, Property and Career in Medieval Society' in *Aging and the Aged in Medieval Europe*, ed. M. M. Sheehan. Toronto, 143–58.

Herlihy, D. and Ch. Klapisch. *Les Toscans et leurs familles: Étude du Castato florentin de 1427*. Paris, 1978.

Hollingsworth, T. H. *Historical Demography*. London, 1976.

Homans, G. C. *English Villagers of the Thirteenth Century*. New York, 1975 [1941].

Hughes, D. 'From Bride Price to Dowry in Mediterranean Europe', *Journal of Family History* 3 (1978), 262–91.

Imhaus, B. 'Un Document démographique et fiscal vénitien concernant le casal du Marethasse (1549).' Μελεταιχαι υπμ-υηνατα 1 (1984), 375–520.

Iannuci, R. J. *The Treatment of the Capital Sins and the Decalogue in German Sermons*. New York, 1942.

Jacquart, D. 'La maladie et le remède d'amour dans quelques écrits medicaux du Moyen Age' in *Actes du colloque: 'Amour, marriage, et transgression au Moyen Age'*. Göppingen, 1984, pp. 93–101.

Jacquart, D. and C. Thomasset. *Sexuality and Medicine in the Middle Ages*, trans. M. Adamson. Oxford, 1988.

Jewell, H. M. 'The Bringing up of Children in Good Learning and Manners: A Survey of Secular Educational Provisions in the North of England', *Northern History* 18 (1982), 1–25.

Jones, G. F. 'The Signs of Old Age in Oswald von Wolkenstein's "Ich Sich und Hor"', *Modern Language Notes* 89 (1974), 767–87.

Kantorowicz, E. H. *The King's Two Bodies: A Study in Medieval Political Theology*. Princeton, 1957.

Kaufman, Sh. R. *The Ageless Self: Sources of Meaning in Late Life*. Madison Wis., 1986.

Keith, J. 'Age in Anthropological Research' in *Handbook of Aging and the Social Sciences*, eds R. H. Binstock and E. Shanas. New York, 1985, pp. 231–63.

Kelly, J. N. *The Oxford Dictionary of Popes*. Oxford, 1986.

Kieckhefer, R. *Unquiet Souls: Fourteenth-Century Saints and Their Religious Milieu*. Chicago, 1984.

Kirshner, J. and A. Molho. 'The Dowry Funds and the Marriage Market in Early Quattrocento Florence', *Journal of Modern History* 50 (1978), 403–38.

Klapisch, Ch. 'Fiscalité et démographie en Toscane (1427–1430)', *Annales E. S. C.* 24 (1969), 1313–37.

——'Household and Family in Tuscany in 1427' in *Households and Family in Past Time*, eds P. Laslett and R. Wall. Cambridge, 1972, pp. 267–81.

——'La mère cruelle: Maternité, veuvage, et dot dans la Florence des XIVe-XVe siècles', *Annales E. S. C.* 38 (1983), 1097–109.

Klapisch-Zuber, Ch. ' "A uno pane e uno vino": The Rural Tuscan Family at the Beginning of the Fifteenth Century' in *Women, Family and Ritual in Renaissance Italy*. Chicago, 1985, pp. 36–67.

——'Demographic Decline and Household Structure: The Example of Prato, Late Fourteenth to Late Fifteenth Century' in *Women, Family and Ritual in Renaissance Italy*. Chicago, 1985, pp. 23–35.

——'Le dernier enfant: Fécondité et vieillissement chez les Florentines XIVe-XVe siècles' in *Mélanges offerts a Jacques Dupaquier*. Paris, 1993, pp. 277–90.

——'L'invention du passé familial a Florence (XIVe-XVe s.)' in *Temps, mémoire, tradition au Moyen Age*. Actes du XIIIe congrès de la Société des Historiens Médiévistes de l'Enseignement Superieur Public, Université de Provence. Aix-en-Provence, 1983, pp. 95–118.

Kleinberg, A. M. *Prophets in Their Own Country: Living Saints and the Making of Sainthood in the Later Middle Ages*. Chicago, 1992.

Knowles, D. *The Monastic Orders in England*. Cambridge, 1963.

Knowles, D. and R. N. Hadcock, *Medieval Religious Houses: England and Wales*. London, 1953.

Kondratowitz von, H. J. 'The Medicalization of Old Age: Community and Change in Germany from the Late Eighteenth to the Early Twentieth Century' in *Life, Death, and the Elderly: Historical Perspectives* eds M. Pelling and R. M. Smith. London, 1991, pp. 134–64.

Kutal, A. *Gothic Art in Bohemia and Moravia*. London, 1971.

Labarge, M. W. 'Three Medieval Widows and Second Careers' in *Aging and the Aged in Medieval Europe*, ed. M. M. Sheehan. Toronto, 1990, pp. 159–72.

Laigle, M. *Le livre des trois vertus de Christine de Pisan et son milieu historique et littéraire*. Paris, 1912.

Lallemand, L. *Histoire de la charité*, 3 vols. Paris, 1906.

Lamausky, V. *Secrets d'état de Venise: Documents, extraits, notices, et études*, 2 vols. St Petersburg, 1884.

Langlois, Ch. V. *La vie en France au Moyen Age d'après quelques moralistes du temps*. Paris, 1908.

——*La connaissance de la nature au Moyen Age d'après quelques écrits français à l'usage des laics*. Paris, 1911.

——*La vie spirituelle: Enseignements, méditations, et controverses*. Paris, 1928.

Laslett, P. 'Mean Houschold Size in England since the Sixteenth Century' in *Household and Family in Past Time*, eds P. Laslett and R. Wall. Cambridge, 1972, pp. 125–58.

——'History of Aging and the Aged' in *Family Life and Illicit Love in Earlier Generations*. Cambridge, 1977, pp. 174–213.

Lauwers, M. 'La mort et le corps des saints: La scène de la mort dans les *vitae* du Moyen Age', *Le Moyen Age* 94 (1988), 21–50.

Lazzarini, V. *Marino Faliero*. Florence, 1963.

LeGoff, J. 'Corps et idéologie dans l'Occident médiéval' in *L'imaginaire médiéval*. Paris, 1985, pp. 124–48.

LeGoff, J. and J. C. Schmitt, eds *Le charivari*. Paris, 1981.

Le Roy Ladurie, E. *Les paysans de Languedoc*, 2 vols. Paris, 1966.

——*Montaillou, village Occitan de 1294–1324*. Paris, 1975.

Lespinasse, R. de. *Les métiers et corporations de la ville de Paris*. Paris, 1886.

Lévi-Strauss, C. *Tristes tropique*, trans. J. and D. Weightman. London, 1989.

Levine, R. A. 'Comparative Notes on the Life Course' in *Transitions: The Family and the Life-Course in Historical Perspectives*, ed. T. K. Hareven. New York, 1978.

Levinson, D. J. *The Seasons of Man's Life*. New York, 1979.

Lewis, N. B. 'The Last Medieval Summons of the English Feudal Levy, 13 June 1385', *English Historical Review* 73 (1958), 1–26.

Liebert, R. S. *Michelangelo*. New Haven, 1983.

Livi-Bacci, M. 'Social and Biological Aging: Contradictions of Development', *Population and Development Review* 8 (1982), 771–81.

Loë, P. de. 'De vita et scriptis B. Alberti Magni', *Analecta Bollandiana* 20 (1901), 274–310.

Longworth, F. *The Rise and Fall of Venice*. London, 1974.

Lorcin, M. Th. *Vivre et mourir en Lyonnais à la fin du Moyen Age*. Paris, 1981.

——'Le corps a ses raisons dans les Fabliaux', *Le Moyen Age* 90 (1984), 443–53.

Lorenz, K. 'La place des anciens chez les animaux sociaux', *Communications* 37 (1983), 7–15.

Lyon, B. D. *From Fief to Indenture: The Transition from Feudal to Non-Feudal Contract in Western Europe*. Cambridge Ma., 1957.

Macfarlane, A. *The Origins of English Individualism*. New York, 1979.

——*Marriage and Love in England 1300–1840*. Oxford, 1986.

McLeod, E. *The Order of the Rose: The Life and Ideas of Christine de Pizan*. London, 1975.

Maddox, G. L. and R. T. Campbell. 'Scope, Concepts, and Methods in the Study of Aging' in *Handbook of Aging and Social Sciences*, eds R. H. Binstock and E. Shanas. New York, 1985, pp. 3–31.

Mallet, M. *Mercenaries and Their Masters*. London, 1974.

Minois, G. *Histoire de la vieillesse. De l'Antiquité à la Renaissance*. Paris, 1987.

Misraki, J. 'Criminalité et pauverté en France à l'époque de la guerre de Cent Ans' in *Étude sur l'histoire de la pauvreté: Moyen Age – XVIe siècle*, 2 vols, ed. M. Mollat. Paris, 1974, 2: 535–46.

Mitterauer, M. and R. Sieder. *The European Family: Patriarchy to Partnership, from the Middle Ages to the Present*, trans. K. Oosterveen and M. Hörzinger. Oxford, 1982.

Moorman, J. *The History of the Franciscan Order*. Oxford, 1968.

Mora, George. 'Mind-Body Concepts in the Middle Ages: The Classical Background and Its Merging with the Judeo-Christian Tradition in the Early Middle Ages', *Journal of History of the Behavioral Sciences* 14 (1978), 344–61.

——'Mind-Body Concepts in the Middle Ages: The Moslem Influence, the Great Theological Systems and Cultural Attitudes towards the Mentally Ill in the Middle Ages', *Journal of the History of the Behavioral Sciences* 16 (1980), 58–72.

Newman Brown, W. 'The Receipt of Poor Relief and Family Situation: Aldenham, Hertfordshire 1630–1690' in *Land, Kinship and Life-Cycle*, ed. R. Smith. Cambridge, 1984, pp. 405–22.

Niebyl, P. H. 'Old Age, Fever and the Lamp Metaphor', *Journal of the History of Medicine and Allied Sciences* 26 (1971), 351–68.

Nitecki, A. K. 'The Convention of the Old Man's Lament in the Pardoner's Tale', *Chaucer Review* 16 (1981–2), 76–84.

——'Figures of Old Age in Fourteenth-Century English Literature' in *Aging and the Aged in Medieval Europe*, ed. M. M. Sheehan. Toronto, 1990. pp. 107–16.

Ori, P. and P. Giovanni. *Matilde di Canossa*. Milan, 1980.

Origo, I. *The Merchant of Prato: Francesco di Marco Datini*. Harmondsworth, 1963.

Orme, N. 'Children and the Church in Medieval England', *The Journal of Ecclesiastical History* 45.4 (1994), 563–87.

——'The Medieval Almshouse for the Clergy: Clyst Gabriel Hospital near Exeter', *The Journal of Ecclesiastical History* 39 (1988), 1–15.

——'Suffering of the Clergy: Illness and Old Age in Exeter Diocese 1300–1540' in *Life, Death, and the Elderly: Historical Perspectives*, eds M. Pelling and R. M. Smith. London, 1991, pp. 62–73.

Owst, G. R. *Preaching in Medieval England*. Cambridge, 1926.

Page, F. M. 'The Customary Poor-Law of Three Cambridgeshire Manors', *Cambridge Historical Journal* 3.2 (1930), 125–33.

Payer, P. J. *The Bridling of Desire: Views of Sex in the Later Middle Ages*. Toronto, 1993.

Payne, R. 'Some Theoretical Approaches to the Sociology of Aging', *Social Forces* 38 (1960), 359–62.

Peaudecerf, M. 'La pauvreté à l'abbaye de Cluny d'après son cartulaire' in *Étude sur l'histoire de la pauvreté: Moyen Age – XVIe siècle*, 2 vols, ed. M. Mollat. Paris, 1927, 1: 217–27.

Pernoud, R. *Vie et mort de Jeanne d'Arc*. Paris, 1953.

Pertile, A. *Storia del diritto italiano della caduca dell' Impero romano alla codificazione*. Turin, 1892–1902.

Pirenne, H. *Histoire de Belgique*. Brussels, 1902.

Planche, A. 'Le corps en vieillesse: Regards sur la poèsie du Moyen Age tardif', *Razo* 4 (1984), 39–57.

Pollock, F. and F. W. Maitland. *A History of English Law*, 2 vols. Cambridge, 1968.

Post, J. B. 'Age of Menarche and Menopause: Some Medieval Authorities', *Population Studies* 25 (1971), 83–7.

Poole, A. L. *From Domesday Book to Magna Carta 1087–1216*. Oxford, 1955.

Pouchelle, M.-Ch. *The Body and Surgery in the Middle Ages*, trans. R. Morris. Oxford, 1990.

Poumarède, J. 'Puissance paternelle et esprit communautaire dans les coutumes du sud-ouest de la France au Moyen Age' in *Recueil de mémoires et de travaux d'histoire du droit et des institutions des anciens pays de droit écrit. Mélanges Roger Aubenas* 9 (1974), 651–63.

Power, E. *Medieval English Nunneries 1275–1535*. Cambridge, 1922.

——*Medieval People*. London, 1986.

Pullan, B. *Rich and Poor in Renaissance Venice*. Oxford, 1971.

Queller, D. E. 'The Civic Irresponsibility of the Venetian Nobility' in *Economy, Society, and Government in Medieval Italy: Essays in Memory of R. L. Reynolds*, eds D. Herlihy, R. S. Lopez and S. Slessarev. Kent, Oh., 1969, pp. 223–35.

——*The Venetian Patriciate: Reality versus Myth*. Chicago, 1986.

Rabinowitz, M. *A Man's Age* [Hebrew]. Tel Aviv, 1985.

Raftis, A. J. *Tenure and Mobility: Studies in the Social History of the Medieval Village*. Toronto, 1964.

——'Social Structures in Five East-Midland Villages', *The Economic History Review* 2nd Ser. 18 (1965), 83–99.

Razi, Z. *Life, Marriage and Death in a Medieval Parish: Economy, Society, and Demography in Halesowen 1270–1400.* Cambridge, 1980.

——'Family, Land, and the Village Community in Later Medieval England', *Past and Present* 93 (1981), 3–36.

——'The Myth of the Immutable English Family', *Past and Present* 140 (1993), 3–44.

Redon, O. 'Aspects économiques de la discriminisation et la "marginalisation" des femmes XIIIe-XVIIIe siècles' in *La donna nell' economica sec. XIII-XVIII*, ed. S. Cavaciocchi. Prato, 1990, pp. 441–60.

Reinharz, Sh. 'Friends or Foes: Gerontological and Feminist Theory' in *Radical Voices*, eds R. D. Klein and D. Lynn Steinberg. 1989, pp. 222–39.

Richards, P. *The Medieval Leper and His Northern Heirs.* London, 1977.

Riegel, K. F. 'Personality Theory and Aging' in *Handbook of Aging and the Individual*, ed. J. Birren. Chicago, 1959, pp. 797–851.

Ring, G. *A Century of French Painting 1400–1500.* London, 1949.

Roncière, Ch. M. de. 'Pauvres et pauvreté à Florence au XIVe siècle' in *Étude sur l'histoire de la pauvreté: Moyen Age – XVIe siècle*, 2 vols, ed. M. Mollat. Paris, 1974, 2: 661–745.

——'Tuscan Notables on the Eve of the Renaissance' in *Revelations of the Medieval World*, vol. 2 of *History of Private Life*, eds Ph. Ariès and G. Duby, trans. A. Goldhammer. Cambridge Ma., 1988, pp. 157–312.

Rosenfeld, H. *Der mittelalterliche Totentanz.* Münster, 1954.

Rosenthal, J. T. 'Medieval Longevity and the Secular Peerage 1350–1500', *Population Studies* 27 (1973), 287–93.

——*Nobles and the Noble Life 1295–1500.* London, 1976.

——'Aristocratic Widows in Fifteenth-Century England' in *Women and the Structure of Society: Selected Research from the Fifth Berkshire Conference on the History of Women*, eds B. J. Harris and J. A. McNamara. Durham, 1984, pp. 36–47.

——'Retirement and the Life Cycle in Fifteenth-century England' in *Aging and the Aged in Medieval Europe*, ed. M. M. Sheehan. Toronto, 1990, pp. 173–88.

Rubin, M. *Charity and Community in Medieval Cambridge.* Cambridge, 1987.

Russell, J. C. 'Length of Life in England, 1250–1348', *Human Biology* 9 (1937), 528–41.

——'Effects of Pestilence and Plague 1315–1385', *Comparative Studies in Society and History* 8.4 (1966), 464–73.

——'How Many of the Population Were Aged?' in *Aging and the Aged in Medieval Europe*, ed. M. M. Sheehan. Toronto, 1990, pp. 119–27.

Sauerlander, W. *Le siècle de cathedrales 1140–1260.* Paris, 1989.

Sears, E. *The Ages of Man: Medieval Interpretations of the Life-Cycle.* Princeton, 1986.

Senderowitz Loengard, J. 'On the Gift of her Husband: English Dower and its Consequences in the Year 1200' in *Women of the Medieval World: Essays in Memory of John Mundy*, eds J. Kirshner and S. F. Wemple. Oxford, 1985, pp. 215–55.

Shahar, S. *Childhood in the Middle Ages.* London, 1990.

——*The Fourth Estate: A History of Women in the Middle Ages.* London, 1983.

——'Family Prerogatives and the Limitations of Patriarchy: A Medieval Case' in *Tel Aviver Jahrbuch für deutsche Geschichte* 22 (1993), 105–15.

——'The Regulation and Presentation of Women in Economic Life (Thirteenth to Eighteenth Centuries)' in *La donna nell' economica sec. XIII-XVIII*, ed. S. Cavaciocchi. Prato, 1990, pp. 501–22.

——'Who were Old in the Middle Ages?' *Social History of Medicine* 6 (1993), 313–41.

Shatzmiller, J. and R. Lavoie. 'Médicine et gynécologie au Moyen Age: Un exemple provençal', *Razo* 4 (1984), 133–43.

Sheehy, G. *Passages: Predictable Crises of Adult Life*. New York, 1977.

Signer, M. A. 'Honour the Hoary Head: The Aged in Medieval European Jewish Community' in *Aging and the Aged in Medieval Europe*, ed. M. M. Sheehan. Toronto, 1990, pp. 39–48.

Smith, R. M. 'Some Issues concerning Families and Their Property in Rural England 1250–1800' in *Land, Kinship and Life-Cycle*, ed. R. M. Smith. Cambridge, 1984, pp. 1–86.

——'The Manorial Court and the Elderly Tenant in Late Medieval England' in *Life, Death, and the Elderly: Historical Perspectives*, eds M. Pelling and R. M. Smith. London, 1991, pp. 39–61.

Sontag, S. 'The Double Standard of Aging' in *Psychology of Women: Selected Readings*, ed. J. H. Williams. New York, 1979, pp. 462–78.

Southern, R. W. *St Anselm and His Biographer: A Study of Monastic Life and Thought 1059–1130*. Cambridge, 1966.

Sprandel, R. 'Alter und Todesfürcht nach der spätmittelalterlichen Biblexegese' in *Death in the Middle Ages*, eds H. Braet and W. Verbeke. Louvain, 1983.

Steadman, J. M. 'Old Age and Contemptus Mundi in the Pardoner's Tale', *Medium Aevum* 33 (1964), 121–30.

Stearns, P. M. 'Introduction' in *Old Age in Preindustrial Society*, ed. P. M. Stearns. London, 1982, pp. 1–18.

Steinberg, Leo. *The Sexuality of Christ in Renaissance Art and Modern Oblivion*. New York, 1983.

Tanner, N. P. *The Church in Late Medieval Norwich 1370–1532*. Toronto, 1984.

Tatham, E. H. R. *Francesco Petrarca: His Life and Correspondence*. London, 1925.

Thane, P. M. 'The Debate on the Declining Birth-Rate in Britain: The "Menace" of an Aging Population 1920–1950', *Continuity and Change* 5.2 (1990), 283–305.

——'Old Age in English History' in *Zur Kulturgeschichte des Alters (Toward a Cultural History of Aging)*, eds C. Conrad and H. J. von Kondratowitz. Berlin, 1993, pp. 17–35.

Tenenti, A. *La vie et la mort à travers l'art du XVe siècle*. Paris, 1952.

Thomas, K. *Age and Authority in Early Modern England*. London, 1976.

Thomasset, C. 'The Nature of Women' in *A History of Women in the West*, ed. Ch. Klapisch-Zuber. London, 1992, pp. 43–69.

Thompson, P., C. Itzin and M. Abendstern. *I Don't Feel Old*. Oxford, 1991.

Thomson, J. A. 'Piety and Charity in Late Medieval London', *Journal of Ecclesiastical History* 16 (1965), 175–95.

Thrupp, S. *The Merchant Class of Medieval London 1300–1500*. Ann Arbor Mi., 1976.

Tierney, B. *Medieval Poor Law: A Sketch of Canonical Theory and Its Application in England*. Berkeley, 1959.

Tillotson, J. H. 'Pensions, Corrodies, and Religious Houses: An Aspect of the Relations of Crown and Church in Early Fourteenth-Century England', *Journal of Religious History* 8 (1974), 127–43.

Trexler, R. 'Une table florentine d'espérance de vie', *Annales E. S. C.* 26 (1971), 137–9.

——*Public Life in Renaissance Florence*. New York, 1980.

——'A Widows' Asylum of the Renaissance: The Orbatello of Florence' in *Old Age in Preindustrial Society*, ed. P. M. Stearns. London, 1982, pp. 119–49.

Varagnac, A. *Civilisation traditionelle et genres de vie*. Paris, 1948.

Vauchez, A. *La sainteté en Occident aux derniers siècles du Moyen Age d'après les procès de canonisation et les documents hagiographiques*. Rome, 1988.

Vaultier, R. *Le Folklore pendant la Guerre de Cent Ans d'après les lettres de rémission du trésor des chartes*. Paris, 1965.

Vigarello, G. *Concepts of Cleanliness: Changing Attitudes in France since the Middle Ages*, trans. J. Birrel. Cambridge, 1988.

Vischer, A. L. *Old Age: Its Compensations and Rewards*. London, 1947.

Waldman, Y. 'The Danish Royal Charter of 1282' PhD Diss. Tel Aviv University, 1989.

Wales, T. 'Poverty, Poor Relief and the Life Cycle: Some Evidence from Seventeenth Century Norfolk' in *Land, Kinship and Life-Cycle*, ed. R. Smith. Cambridge, 1984, pp. 351–420.

Wall, R. 'Mean Household Size in England from Printed Sources' in *Household and Family in Past Time*, eds P. Laslett and R. Wall. Cambridge, 1972, pp. 159–203.

Warner, M. *Joan of Arc: The Image of Female Heroism*. Harmondsworth, 1983.

Westlake, H. F. *The Parish Gilds of Medieval England*. London, 1919.

Windt, E. B. de. *Land and People in Holywell-cum-Medingworth: Structures of Tenure and Patterns of Social Organization in an East Anglian Midlands Village*. Toronto, 1972.

Witters, D. W. 'Pauvres et pauvreté dans les coutumiers monastiques du Moyen Age' in *Étude sur l'histoire de la pauvreté: Moyen Age – XVIe siècle*, 2 vols, ed. M. Mollat. Paris, 1974, 1: 177–215.

Wortley, J. T. 'Aging and the Desert Fathers: The Process Reversed' in *Aging and the Aged in Medieval Europe*, ed. M. M. Sheehan. Toronto, 1990, pp. 63–73.

Wrigley, E. A. and R. Schofield. 'Infant and Child Mortality in the Later Tudor and Early Stuart Period' in *Health, Medicine, and Mortality in the Sixteenth Century*. Cambridge, 1979.

Zarnecki, G. *The Art of the Medieval World*. New York, 1975.

Zerner, M. 'Une crise de mortalité au XVe siècle à travers les testaments et les rôles d'imposition', *Annals E. S. C.* 34 (1979), 566–89.

INDEX

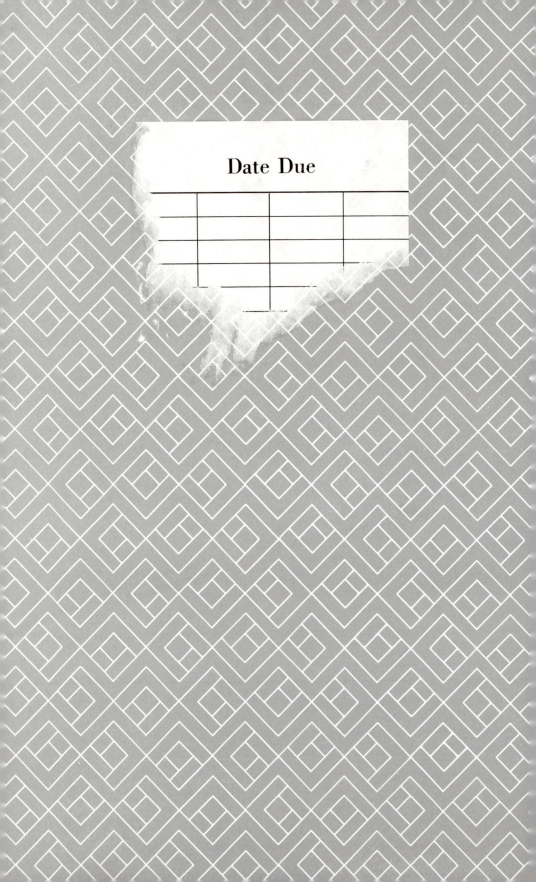

Date Due
